# Alun, Gweno & Freda

*To Lorraine, Eliot, Zelda and Anna, who lived through it all*

# Alun, Gweno & Freda

### JOHN PIKOULIS

Seren is the book imprint of
Poetry Wales Press Ltd.
57 Nolton Street, Bridgend, Wales, CF31 3AE

www.serenbooks.com
facebook.com/SerenBooks
Twitter: @SerenBooks

ISBN 978-1-78172-283-1
Mobi 978-1-78172-303-6
Ebook 978-1-78172-304-3

A CIP record for this title is available from the British Library.

The publisher acknowledges the financial assistance of the Welsh Books
Council.

Printed in Times New Roman by The CPI Group (UK) Ltd, Croydon

# CONTENTS

# LIST OF ILLUSTRATIONS

'After the book, what about 'The Making of a Biography' – our correspondence – mildly expurgated!'

'Isn't it fascinating to see how it has all, from this truthful & perceptive beginning, worked out absolutely that way, & more, so much more? And the goal: the better & fuller to know Alun Lewis.'

*Freda Aykroyd to the author, 4th September 1978*

# Introduction

This book tells two stories simultaneously: how I came to research Alun Lewis and what I discovered about him. The two run together, from his birth in Cwmaman, south Wales, in 1915 to his death in Burma 28 years later, and beyond.

Two issues were left unresolved. The first was the manner of his death. An Army Board of Inquiry in 1944 concluded it was an accident, but it remained a subject of speculation. Then there is the question of what happened to him in India, including a romantic involvement. Both issues hung in suspense during the decades that followed, only occasionally ruffling the silence that had fallen on him.

I began to research Lewis in 1970. By that time, matters had altered somewhat. His wife, Gweno, his family (including his mother, Gwladys; Tom Lewis had died in 1967) and friends of his like Freda Aykroyd and Dick Mills readily responded to my enquiries as part of an attempt to stimulate attention for him at a time when his reputation was beginning to fade. A drama that had lain dormant for 30 years was coming to life. As I was later to discover, this was a development anticipated by Lewis himself.

I had particular help from the two women whose names I have joined to his in my title. The fresh information they gave me revived painful memories. Gweno had met Alun in 1939 (they were at university together but no friendship developed between them at the time) and was with him when he enlisted in the Royal Engineers in 1940 and joined the 6th Battalion, South Wales Borderers in November 1942. He and Freda met in India in July 1943 while he was staying with her and her husband on a period of leave.

*Alun, Gweno and Freda* recounts my discoveries about Lewis in the order in which they occurred since this inevitably affects the way they will be received. It is a hybrid work, a biography of a biography as well as a biography proper. My search for Lewis, and the way it came about, forms the book's central spine but woven around it, and frequently disturbing the chronology, comes a considered account of his life and work drawing on material first aired in my *Alun Lewis, A Life* (1884, second edition, 1991), though I wrote there more circumspectly out of consideration for the sensitivities of those involved.

This twin-track structure of the book will not, I hope, prove confusing. The 'search' narrative begins in 1970 and is complemented by the analytical one, which goes back to his youth, sometimes further back, to provide the necessary context. This appeared to me to be the most revealing way of telling a story that proved testing to all who were involved in it.

My own part in it is more prominent than I either expected or wished. I saw myself as a Jamesian 'ficelle', someone who enables others to reveal themselves, but in time my involvement grew. However, that was the price I had to pay for being admitted into the drama, now as messenger, sometimes confused with his message, now as one others could project their conflicting emotions onto.

*Alun Lewis, A Life* left a gap between what I could assert and what adduce by way of evidence. *Alun, Gweno and Freda* fills that gap. Remarkably, it offers the first comprehensive account of Lewis 70 years after his death and 100 after his birth.

John Pikoulis, May 2015

# Part One
## *Alun the soldier*

Two poets in particular are associated with World War II: Alun Lewis and Keith Douglas. Their achievement has been widely recognised though inevitably overshadowed by the poets of the First World War, the first to explore the impact of mechanised warfare on conscript armies. It was they who altered our concept of war and the notion of martial honour that flourished at the apogee of Empire. The war Lewis and Douglas were involved in was very different, being waged by civilians as well as soldiers over a wider area. No longer was there any innocence to be lost, only an experience to be shared no 'front lines', no 'home fires burning', only different stories told by different people, combatants and non-combatants alike. Unsurprisingly, their impression was more mixed.

In his blurb for his first volume of poems, *Raiders' Dawn and other poems* (1942), Lewis wrote:

> The continuity between his poems and those of the last war is most clearly expressed in his Lines to Edward Thomas, for like Thomas the war has become an integral part of his life experience, not a violent thought-slaying wound as it was to Owen.

Where Owen wrote about war, Thomas, like Lewis after him, wrote about a 'life experience' that included war:

> Whereas men like Owen and Sassoon were severed from home by the continuous horror of the trench massacres he has been with the civilians in the bombed cities as well as with the soldiers in their isolated camps.

Being a soldier was evidently only half the story.

In 1940, Lewis enlisted as railway clerk in the Royal Engineers

at the No 1 Railway Training Centre, Longmoor, Hampshire. From
there, he could see the balloon barrage above Portsmouth 20 miles
away and the fires raging there after air raids. He wanted the sappers
to be allowed to join in the rescue work, pleading his case in the
Battalion newspaper, *The Sandpiper*:

> Teach us demolition, first aid, fire-fighting and give us a
> chance to show our mettle and succour our fellow human
> beings. Or let us start knitting classes and send 'comforts' to
> the evacuees, the poor, the homeless.
>       Let's do *something*, for God's sake!

Even as a joke, the notion of recruits knitting for the poor is
strange, though it accurately reflects his frustration. While bombs
rained down on Portsmouth and Southampton, he was obliged to
judge hop, skip and jump races as P.T. Instructor.

Longmoor threw Lewis into a round of fatigue parties, guard duty
and digging trenches, the men grumbling like 'so many grains of
underdone rice'. Packed eight to a tent, feet against the tentpole, kit
piled high beside them, they cut their toenails or sewed on buttons.
Meals of tinned herring and the South African delicacy called snoek
left them stinking of fish. Then there were endless hours of 'technical
training' (or 'tremendous trifles', as he called them): squad drill,
camouflaging parapets with new turf, polishing bayonets, section-
leading, field works, map-reading, studying forms for the loading,
unloading and despatching of cargoes or goods, filling railway
wagons with timber, lagging latrine pipes and cisterns and the odd
lecture ('imagine three lessons a week in school!', he told his teacher-
parents).

Albert Harden, editor of *The Sandpiper*, recalls:

> … I found myself in a Railway Company then forming and
> joined Alun in that most boring of tasks – Platelaying –
> which consisted of dashing down the rail track, breaking the
> line somewhere, sometimes blowing it up and then at risk to
> life and limb rebuild and relay the track before the train was
> due. All very hectic stuff and interesting for the first dozen
> times but thereafter very boring. When this palled we would
> be given large hammers and sent down the lines to bang in
> the 'dogs', huge nails which held the lines in place. This was
> unbearably boring and something neither Alun nor I could
> stomach.

Alun told his parents:

> I'm sitting under a clump of pines on the hill above camp –
> the boles are as straight and finely spaced as the Acropolis
> and there's a blue mist over the burnt heather and the distant
> green fields. It's the dinner hour – I was on duty from 12.30
> to 1.30 watching over the anti-waste bin, to catch any fifth
> columnists throwing gristle away. Now I've got ten minutes
> before the bell rings for afternoon school – is it still 1939?

And is there honey still for tea?

In March 1941, he devised a series of Saturday morning lectures on 'International Affairs and Historical Trends' intended to throw light on the war by examining the Napoleonic and Franco-Prussian wars, the foreign policy of Italy and Russia and the operations of the League of Nations. In his first lecture, he ran into trouble when he said 'Japanese imports were restricted into British colonies by the Ottawa agreement'. At this suggestion that the enemy might have a grievance, the Regimental Colonel rose to his feet: 'That's a lie,' he called out. 'Tell the truth or I'll stop the lecture', to which Lewis replied: 'Stop the lecture if you wish, sir. I've told no lie'. The Colonel then addressed the men: 'You've been listening to lies. I call the meeting closed'. Eventually, he had to apologise and the lectures resumed. So much for 'Alun in Blunderland'.

Within a year, so bored was he that he applied for an officers' training course, 'like the intelligent moth, attracted & revolted by the fire'.

> I *couldn't possibly* stay in the comfortable security of
> Longmoor for the duration – I wouldn't write another poem
> if I were that sort of bloke and looked at life with the attitude
> of 'Let someone else do the dirty work, I'll just bang the
> drum or supply the effects'.

Albert Harden recalls:

> Though he was sure of himself in respect of his abilities he
> lacked the confidence in himself to lead others and shunned
> promotion in his early days in the Army until he realised that
> advancement was his only means to achieve his aims in
> respect to others i.e. restructuring of society.

He said Lewis 'held left-wing views far more profound than I ever could have' though he was no stranger to adversity himself, being the youngest of six whose father had died when he was 11 and who joined the building trade at 18:

> Though his arguments were convincing, he never managed to convert many to this philosophy due in part to one's knowledge that he had never experienced poverty at first hand, so how could he presume to talk to the masses of their lack of understanding the importance of socialism when survival was paramount in everyone's thoughts. He was a great stimulator of argument having the knack of choosing subjects dear to the hearts of those in his company at that time. I liked and respected him, trusted him to support the underdog whilst knowing without doubt that soon he would be joining the officer ranks.

Lewis wrote to his fiancée, Gweno Ellis: 'I'm as restless as a terrier. Longmoor is my chain'. To his parents, he explained

> how much more perilous and mouvementee is the civilians' life than the soldiers'. We just keep up appearances, week after week. It beats me – it's quite unlike my expectations. I'd be much more *useful* doing civilian work – evacuee or work like Cheney's.

The fact that civilians were having a harder time of it than those who were being trained to protect them came back to haunt him when he returned to Wales at Whitsun 1941 to find that his longed-for reunion with Gweno had been ruined by a German air raid that had killed two and blasted out the doors and windows of her house. Everyone was caught up in this war and it was waged everywhere.

Lewis's attitude to war reflects his training as an historian. At Aberystwyth (1932-5), he studied mediaeval English political and constitutional history; at Manchester in the next two years, his M.A. thesis concerned the activities of Cardinal Ottobono, who helped resolve the Barons' Revolt. (It has since become a standard work). R.F. Treharne, his Aberystwyth Professor, wrote: 'his history was always conceived in terms of human personality and character'. For him, the war was the latest in a long line of conflicts that presented men with a more than physical challenge. In 'Autumn 1939', it appears as a quasi-Tennysonian drama: red leaves float down a flooded meadow as, 'half in dream/ Seen in a mirror cracked by broken vows', knights 'jog listlessly to town/ To fight for love in some unreal war'. A knight lies mouldering on a 'rotting bier' as the casements are drawn shut tight. Apparently, the deaths to follow will be as futile as those that preceded it.

In 'From a Play' (the play being Aeschylus's *The Eumenides*), Chorus speaks:

> We are the little men grown huge with death.
> Stolid in squads or grumbling on fatigues,
> We held the honour of the regiment
> And stifled our antipathies.
> Stiff-backed and parrot-wise with pamphlet learning,
> We officiated at the slaughter of the riverine peoples
> In butcheries beyond the scope of our pamphlets.
> We had certain authority for this;
> Not ours, but Another's;
> Our innocence remained with us.

Lewis ponders whether the war will cause men to develop a carapace of brutality even though they remain goodhearts, caricatures of themselves who yearn for the world they have left behind. Their 'lonely destiny' is divined in the 'stony glitter' of the eyes of 'The blond great-breasted goddess of pre-history' – '*And no returning*'.

Another Longmoor poem, 'The Odyssey', tells of the men who returned to Ithaca after 'shamefully' putting Troy to the torch. They lapse into a 'strange indifference', hungering for 'the simpler things' they enjoyed before war lust maddened them, 'the common satisfaction/ Forfeited when we answered wrong with wrong':

> And what blind man, singing of ruined Troy,
> Will understand and pity her destroyers?
>
> And what old mangy dog will know us when we come
> To Ithaca, and shiver with delight?

None, apparently.

In 'On Embarkation', the men loading cargo into the ship that is about to carry them to India are 'good-natured agents of a groping purpose' tempted to forget 'Such villages as linger in the mind,/ Lidice on the road from Bethlehem'. Lewis ponders

> ... whether kindness will persist in hearts
> Plagued by the snags and rapids of a curse,
> And whether the fortunate few will
> ...feel their failures broaden into manhood,
> Or take the Bren's straightforward road
> And grow voluptuous at the sight of blood?

Each man carries 'a shrunken inkling of the Good', but will it be enough to save him?

When Dick Mills, his friend from university days, enlisted, Lewis told him he wanted to follow his example

> because I want to experience life in as many phases as I'm capable of – i.e. I'm more a writer than a moralist, I suppose. But I don't know – I'm not going to kill. Be killed, perhaps, instead.

– which makes it sound as if war was as much an artistic as a political imperative for him:

> Plunge in? Into what? Socialism through bloodshed? Or fall in – into line?'…. It's making a mess of life *when we have it* that I hate. But death is something I have more than once, in the climax of past agonies, imagined completely. And so it may come when it may. Meanwhile I live…. There is a worse battle than war or peace to fight – the heart is my battle-ground, a bloody place. But that also is untellable.

Keith Douglas viewed war very differently. His poems treat death with a cool detachment masking an element of romance. There is a photograph of him in uniform which he himself decorated with pillars, laurel wreaths, hearts and a halo with the motto: 'Dulce et decorum est' – the very same Wilfred Owen used to illustrate 'the pity of war'. It was as provocative a gesture as possible. Douglas believed war brought glory; it was a reduction (or intensification) to essence and in his poems he regularly aestheticises violence to considerable effect. Par excellence, he was the dandy in uniform.

With which compare Julian MacLaren-Ross's account of meeting Lewis in April 1942:

> In a few moments a young officer came running down [the stairs]. He wore one pip and service dress, but without his Sam Browne belt, as though he were awaiting trial by

court-martial. He had a Welsh face, dark, with eyes set deep. I came smartly to attention and saluted. '6027033 Private Ross J. reporting for duty, sir.'

To my surprise the face of Mr Lewis flushed even darker at this. He turned his head away and muttered something in a voice so low that I couldn't catch the words: I said 'I beg your pardon, sir?'

He muttered, but more audibly this time: 'I'm Alun Lewis.' He held out his hand. In a second we were shaking hands heartily.

I said: 'I'd no idea. They just said Mr Lewis and I was to report to you straight away.'

'The fools,' he said. 'My god, isn't that typical. When you saluted I thought you were making fun of me.' He smiled, a quick boyish grin. He spoke very quickly, too, and with a strong Welsh intonation which I found difficult at first to understand. Later this wore off and I discovered it was a mark of embarrassment. He was extraordinarily shy.

The Lewis he describes cannot quite believe he is a soldier, being modest, sincere, fallible.

When we got outside Lewis had to rush back in his for his Sam Browne: 'I'm always forgetting the damn thing.' He walked along the street beside me buckling on the belt. My R.S.M. [Regimental Sergeant Major] was passing on the other side of the parade. He gave Lewis an eyes-right and his stiff jerky salute, imitated behind his back through the battalion. Lewis attempted to return the salute and the belt fell to the ground. He stopped to retrieve it while the R.S.M. passed on stiffly disapproving in his rubber-soled shoes.

'I made a mess of that,' Lewis said ruefully, getting the Sam Browne round him at last. 'An R.S.M., too.'

'That's my R.S.M.,' I said. 'Used to be a milkman.'

'Nothing against him,' Lewis said, 'that's class distinction.'

The following day, MacLaren-Ross sent him some of his work via an orderly:

He returned with an odd story. He had accosted a fatigue party who were coal-heaving outside – why, at that time of year, I can't imagine. He asked where Mr Lewis could be found. One of the fatigue party, in shirt sleeves and covered

with coal dust, had turned and said: 'Here I am.' This had
so shaken the orderly that he'd delivered the packet of
MSS. without remembering to salute. I don't suppose that
Lewis minded.

# Part Two
## *Rumours*

### I

I first began reading Lewis in 1969 after being appointed lecturer in what is now called Cardiff University. It seemed natural to me to want to explore the literature of the university's immediate hinterland, especially one with a history so rich and turbulent. I was impressed by his humane temper and sensitivity. True, he was given to overstatement ('Love cries and cries in me// And summer blossoms break above my head/ With all the beauty of the dead.' ('"Odi et Amo"')) but since this was a characteristic of a good deal of writing from the time it possessed a documentary flavour. Some instinct of seriousness led men to want to confess themselves, as if in a last statement. The results might jar but they accurately reflected the 'phoney war'.

'After Dunkirk' opens in superheated style but quickly modulates into a more considered account of 'the rough immediate life of camp':

> The subterfuges of democracy, the stench
> Of breath in crowded tents, the grousing queues,
> And bawdy songs incessantly resung
> And dull relaxing in the dirty bar;
> The difficult tolerance of all that is
> Mere rigid brute routine; the odd
> Sardonic scorn of desolate self-pity,
> The pathetic contempt of the lonely for the crowd....

Here was the authentic voice of the ranks, though with a finickiness that suggests Lewis became a warrior *malgre lui*. He wanted his first collection of verse to be called *The Soldier & Other Poems*.

From the start, I encountered two rumours about him: first, that he had committed suicide, and second, that he had fallen in love with a woman in India. His life was wrapped in mystery. Occasionally, the two rumours ran together, as when it was suggested that he killed himself because he felt guilty at betraying his wife. Others pointed the finger at his deteriorating relations with his Commanding Officer, Colonel Robin Cresswell – a remarkable suggestion. It is easy to understand why arguments between officers should flare up, especially in times of tension and especially when one of them is sufficiently domineering and the other sufficiently vulnerable. Even so, it strains credulity to believe they caused Lewis's death. One officer told me Cresswell 'nagged [Lewis] to death', another (with no very high estimate of his intelligence) that he had 'hounded' him, passing off some of his insecurity onto him. Another thought Lewis 'carried the can' for Cresswell: the more the one pressed, the more self-conscious the other grew. One squaddie told me Cresswell had driven him into a corner. This bully/victim thesis might carry conviction were it not that Lewis was subject to tensions of his own. He might very well have found Cresswell's company uncongenial  but the most that can be said about him is that he might have tipped the balance.

The two men met in Martlesham, Suffolk, when Lewis joined the South Wales Borderers as a Second Lieutenant in November 1941. At that time, the Borderers were training night and day in mock battles, endurance tests, signal exercises, field firing and the like. In July 1942, they were designated a mechanised corps but reconverted to infantry in India in April 1943 to prepare for an amphibious assault on Burma from the Andaman Islands in the autumn. The monsoon was at its height: it grew so hot and sticky that the men's skin became waterlogged and could rip easily. Continuous blue sheet lightning heralded rain that washed away tents and sent palm trees crashing.

Cresswell succeeded V.J.F. ('Pop') Popham as Colonel of the Sixth Battalion, the South Wales Borderers, in June that year. Vivian Popham was a thick-set man of the old school, a disciplinarian but fair with it. In some ways, Cresswell was the ideal regular – blunt, straightforward, professional, perhaps more thorough than sensible. He gave orders better than he led and liked ticking off the men for the least offence. The battalion carried him rather than he the battalion, some thought. Unusually tall and with a querulous voice, he became the Umbrella Man in Burma on account of his habit of carrying an umbrella with him. Lewis called him 'a shouting and petulant C.O.', 'my long bamboo shoot of a colonel', and protested against his tendency to see for himself rather than rely on his officers, especially when they were commissioned officers.

> He has a weak hankering to see things. Unless his eyes see, his mind cannot grasp. So he must be up in the front, & see the puff where the machine gun is located. If companies have to attack he always chooses the approach which allows him to see them, rather than a covered approach giving them concealment. I decided I had better bend my brains, and the influence I have over him, to guide him to safer counsels.

Even so, Cresswell leaned on him from time to time:

> When I'm 'in the field' I find it incredibly easy to take a decision or make a judgment swiftly. I don't shilly shally about the implications and alternatives. I see them, weigh them & discard them in one movement of the brain & then I'm ready to carry out my decision. It's a greater accession of self reliance than I possess at normal times, because normally I am continually widening the horizon & multiplying the possibilities & breaking down the apparent simplicities into their components.

Such confidence did not last long. He felt tested by Cresswell, who went through five I.O.s in the war, an unusually large number, so there was nothing personal about his treatment of him. As battle approached, raised voices could be heard coming from the C.O.'s tent when his Intelligence Officer was with him. Lewis protested that Cresswell treated him like a lap dog and wanted to play cards. He also resented having to submit his literary work to him before it was forwarded to the Director of Press Relations at Headquarters and had to plead with Cresswell to be allowed spare petrol to record his poems for All-India Radio in Bombay.

In 1979, Robin Cresswell was living in Llangorse, near Brecon. I wrote to him asking for an interview and he said he would do his best to answer my questions. However, since only so much can be gained through correspondence, I restated my preference for an interview. He did not reply, so I wrote again. He responded:

> I did not reply to your letter of 5 Oct. as I had already told you that I would be prepared to endeavour to answer questions which you would like to put to me. This still stands

& if I consider the questions suitable I will answer them; but
I do not wish to give an interview.

Accordingly, I sent him a list of questions. He told me he was
surprised by some of them:

> In order to help me in my replies please let me know
> 1. If you have been in the Forces – T.A. – University Training
> Unit etc.
> 2. What part did you take in the war
> 3. (a) Have you contacted Lewis' family & are they aware
> you are writing his autobiography?
>    (b) Do they approve & have they given you assistance
> 4. Please let me have the address of Lewis's next-of-kin.
> 5. What other officers of my Regiment have you contacted.

He said it was 'obvious' I had no idea how a Regimental Unit worked
or what the relations between officers and men were:

> I would suggest you contact your nearest T.A. Unit and if
> possible join it.... You will be doing yourself a good turn and
> possibly your country as well.

When I asked him why he had chosen Lewis as his Intelligence
Officer, he wrote:

> ...he had an extremely accurate and agile brain and was very
> capable of making deductions; he was also a good organiser.
> The I.O. worked directly under the C.O.. His job and the job
> of his section was briefly, to collect & disburse information
> about the enemy & surrounding troops. Keep up to date the
> battle map. Keep in touch with superior formation & keep
> everybody informed with regards to the general situation.
> This involved giving lectures.

He called him 'a popular & cheerful officer who carried out his
duties adequately' and rated his performance as 'good'. Since the
Intelligence Officer is one of four who comprise the battalion's nerve
centre (the others being the Colonel, the 2nd i/c and the Adjutant),
his note of reservation is worth observing.

Alun Chalfont, who was the battalion's Adjutant, echoed Cresswell when he wrote that Lewis did his work 'adequately well'. In his
autobiography, *The Shadow of my Hand*, he says Lewis

.... seemed to do nothing but talk about the problems of writing poetry and the awful agony that the act of creation was, which always seemed to me to be slightly exaggerated.

Yet he could be courageous to the point of foolhardiness. On the battalion's first night in India, a storm converted a river into a torrent; rather than wait for it to subside, Lewis swam across, anxious to prove that nothing frightened him. Such impulsiveness was the obverse of his introspection.

When I asked Cresswell what he thought of Lewis's work, he told me: 'I have, in the distant past, read some of Lewis's poems. I was not particularly impressed'. A similar view, though more kindly expressed, came from a member of Lewis's platoon:

> There is not much I can say about Mr Alun Lewis that would be helpful towards your book, but I would like to say this, and I am sure the rest of my army mates would agree. He was a real gentleman.
>
> On one occasion when we were at Poona, he gave a lecture about Poetry which I attended. He also lent me a book of Poetry which he had written, but I am afraid I am not very interested in Poetry. I will end by saying that his death was a great blow to me, and the battalion in general.

In south Walian argot, 'gentleman' refers to one who is above the rough and tumble of life, though it contains an element of respect for the difference. Another squaddie recalled that Lewis had read a lesson on a Sunday morning church parade down a Suffolk country lane. He had never heard anything so beautiful.

It was never likely that Lewis would take to obeying orders or training in the arts of violence in a theatre where force remained the ultimate arbiter, yet, before accepting Cresswell's (and his own) estimate, it is worth noting the opinion of his C.O. at Heysham Towers, Lancashire, where he completed his Officers' Training Course in 1941. His Cadet Record Sheet reads:

> First month
> A quiet but definite personality who works very seriously. His map-reading is progressing quite well, though he has little previous experience of it. His weapon training is satisfactory. His written work is very fair.

Second month
Has worked very well indeed. His section training has been
very good. He has good control and has grasped the princi-
ples of tactics. His general theoretical work in all subjects
has been quite outstanding. A valuable cadet.

Third month
He has taken a keen interest in all tactical problems, he thinks
clearly and his orders and plans are good. He has good
powers of leadership, an unusual but attractive personality,
and plenty of intelligence. His drill has been quite fair and
his mapreading sound. He has a good word of command.

This of a man who could scarcely make himself heard in a classroom.

He has worked hard and has shown ability to lead.

The question is: did he want to?

# II

In the summer of 1972, I published an essay on Lewis in *The Critical
Quarterly*. In my mind, this focussed on a single poem, 'The Way
Back' but, on re-reading it, I discover it was more wide-ranging, not
always to its benefit. Lewis published two books of poems, *Raiders'
Dawn* (1942) and *Ha! Ha! Among the Trumpets* (1945). I found them
interesting though not necessarily impressive, but there was a
whisper of seriousness about them that registered without cohering
into a fixed impression.

It was about two-thirds through the second volume – rather late
in the day – that I stopped and found I could not go on. The poem
that arrested me was 'The Way Back'. It was that rare thing in Lewis,
an expression of joyful emotion. It was then I decided I wanted to
write about him, as much to explain the poem's impact on me as
anything else. In a real sense, my involvement with Lewis began with
'The Way Back'. For me, it was the way in.

> Six days and two thousand miles
> I have watched the shafted rain
> Feminise the burning land,
> Cloaking with a green distress

The cerulean and the ochre
Of the season's ruthlessness.
Six days and two thousand miles
I have gone alone
With a green mind and you
Burning in the stubborn bone.

Soldiers quickened by your breath
Feel the sudden spur and rush
Of the life they put away
Lest the war should break and crush
Beauties more profound than death.

I swam within your naked lake
And breasted with exquisite ease
The foaming arabesques of joy
And in the sarabande of trees
Of guava and papaya
And crimson blown poinsettia,
The millrace of my blood
Beat against my smile,
And were you answering my smile
Or the millrace of my blood?

But now the iron beasts deploy
And all my effort is my fate
With gladiators and levies
All laconic disciplined men
I pass beyond your golden gate.

And in the hardness of this world
And in the brilliance of this pain
I exult with such a passion
To be squandered, to be hurled,
To be joined to you again.

The mood is ebullient, the language exotic: 'arabesques', 'sarabande', 'cerulean', 'ochre', 'golden gate'. Something had happened. In a review for The Observer, A. Alvarez once remarked that in India Lewis had 'had some kind of crisis, or revelation, which answered all his restlessness'. 'The Way Back' belongs to that crisis.

Anxious to discover more about the circumstances of the poem, I approached Lewis's widow, Gweno, who taught German, Music and Physical Education at Mountain Ash Grammar School. Looking back, I marvel at my temerity. She replied:

> Of course I am interested to hear that you are working on a
> study of my husband's work & I shall be pleased to help you
> if I can.

I sent her a list of questions and she explained:

> 'The Way Back' I would place about the end of July & the
> beginning of August [1943]. Alun had spent his leave at the
> home of a very hospitable & cultured English family in the
> Nilgiri Hills in Southern India at the end of July. He loved
> the atmosphere of a civilized home & of civilized talk again
> & he loved swimming in an icy mountain lake nearby. He
> left here for Karachi where he had to attend at the Intelli-
> gence School for several weeks of intensive study & training.
> Hence the 'six days & two thousand miles'. It's a love poem
> – in a letter of Aug 26th he writes – 'Wherever I am Love
> relates itself softly to the physical influences of the land &
> when the mood & the place are fully integrated I write…'.

'The Way Back' was a love poem – but to whom? According to
Gweno, it was more an ode to the spirit of place.

The 'cultured English family' were Wallace and Freda Aykroyd,
who lived in Coonoor with their daughter, Gilly. (Their eldest child,
Peter, had been evacuated to Canada with his school at the outbreak
of war.) Wallace, a nutritional scientist, was director of the Nutrition
Research Laboratories while Freda, eleven years his junior, wrote,
painted, did some radio work and fished and hunted a little. The
couple kept open house for any army officers on leave. One such was
Dick Mills, who recommended the place to Lewis. He arrived there
on July 24 1943, just as Freda was recovering from an appendix
operation in Nagercoil and Wallace was in Hot Springs, in the United
States, attending a conference that led to the formation of the United
Nations Food and Agriculture Organisation in 1946.

Such was the immediate context of the poem, though it did not
explain its charge of emotion.

The annual monsoons arrived late in May 1943 following months
of sterility and searing heat. Lewis told Brenda Chamberlain the rain
'turned the burning cruel hills into green glades & the scorched
withered valleys & plains into green lush pastures'. In 'The Way
Back', the 'shafted rain' feminises the burning land and cloaks it with

a 'green distress'. The poem addresses a 'you' who is 'Burning in the stubborn bone'. The rapturous tone suggests the fertilising flood is human as well as natural. Thanks to 'you', soldiers are quickened by 'the sudden spur and rush' of the life they thought they had left behind. ('Soldiers', at the beginning of the poem, becomes one soldier at the end, a trick repeated in 'All day it has rained…'.)

> I swam within your naked lake
> And breasted with exquisite ease
> The foaming arabesques of joy….

For Lewis, swimming brought him 'nearest to complete being with the universe' and it is this sense of liberation that stirs 'the millrace of my blood'.

When Gweno first read the poem (Lewis posted all his poems to her for typing and distribution), she took fright. Lewis sought to allay her fears:

> I was delighted with your vituperations against the sexual preoccupations of my typewriter – breasts, breasts, breasts you roar in a splendid Presbyterian Wesleyan rage. Well, unfortunately, the world is full of breasts. I can't help it any more than you can. And where there are human beings there's sex. And I just write how I see things – and I see a lot more sex than I ever write.

The romantic idyll of 'The Way Back' is complicated, however, by a sense of an ending. In its closing lines, the soldier passes through the beloved's 'golden gate' and rejoins the 'gladiators and levies/ All laconic disciplined men'. Lewis broadens the perspective to evoke Roman and Biblical times:

> But now the iron beasts deploy
> And all my effort is my fate
> With gladiators and levies
> All laconic disciplined men
> I pass beyond your golden gate.

The iambic tramp of the closing line resembles a march to the gallows. Lewis embraces his destiny with a burnished eloquence but the effect is anything but triumphal. 'Iron beasts' suggests the tanks the battalion had been training in until April 1943 and conjures an image of fate, a

Hardyesque Spirit of the Years who presides over human life indifferently and presently demands the separation of the lovers. Lewis considers his fate with mounting urgency:

> And in the hardness of this world
> And in the brilliance of this pain
> I exult with such a passion
> To be squandered, to be hurled,
> To be joined to you again.

The lovers will meet again, but only after some cataclysm ('squandered'). Theirs will be a reunion of mortal remains. Two hammering stresses in each line save the last add to the mounting rhetoric: 'And' – 'And', then 'To be' (or not to be?) thrice in two lines. The running metre comes to a climax with the lovers' embrace, the emphases falling on 'joined', 'you', 'again', exhilaration vying with despair.

In my essay, I suggested the poem's drama went beyond the personal to create a 'poemagogic' image of the act of writing involving the breakdown of the poet and his restoration, his fragments shored against his ruin. A parched being discovers his essence through a Muse-like 'you' in a watery world that 'quenches', that is to say, destroys and restores. It is both benign and malign, lethal yet transcendent.

The poem shows Lewis to be passionately seeking but there is something inhuman about its exultation that renders it oppressive. The death anticipated, I wrote, is a 'release from constraint and suffering into a consummating joy which is not easy to distinguish from a final despair'. The sexual implications of 'golden gate' and 'consummating' emphasise the poem's character as a liebestod, a love song in the presence of death. Even so, there is something uncomplicatedly magnificent about it, the magnificence of achieved utterance. In 'The Way Back', Lewis enters his golden realm: through initiation to sacrifice, through sacrifice to fulfilment. His is a fertile destruction. Writing to Freda Aykroyd, he once remarked:

> When I think of it, the poems are an act of daring, always daring, to plunge and tear and enter....

# III

I wrote another essay in 1975, 'Alun Lewis and the Imagination', as part of a special number of *Poetry Wales* with contributions by (amongst others) Gweno Lewis, Gwladys Lewis (his mother), and Mair (Fenn), his sister. Again, it concentrated on a single work, 'Attitude', published in the Aberystwyth university magazine, *The Dragon*, in 1938. It tells of two historians, Peter and Frieda; like Lewis, Frieda is a poet who is reluctantly engaged in research on the Papal legates of the thirteenth century. She believes 'only what the heart feels is real' and that 'intellectual perceptions are remote things', but these are supreme for Peter. Frieda represents the Muse, he the ailing ego suffering from an 'impotence to change'.

At the start, Peter lies ill in bed in their holiday cottage while Frieda goes for a walk, glad to escape his 'distant, disembodied realm'. Dissatisfied by the poems she has written, she regrets that none has appeared since her marriage. By allying herself with Peter, she has jeopardised her gift. The scholarly is the enemy of the imaginative.

Out walking, Freda reflects:

> … the flowers and trees and birds and animals were enough and more than enough. They had been terribly wrong to neglect these things and to concentrate instead on their own selves…. They must turn again to these essential, beautiful things. For they are the realities, the makers of love, the quickeners.

Standing on a wooden bridge, she tears at the rails with her polished nails. 'Everything, Peter, if only you can feel it'.

When she returns to the cottage, Peter is dead. It as if her wish were father to the deed. I wrote:

> Entering the kitchen garden, she [Frieda] plucks the last 'drooping red flower… Love lies bleeding' as a token of her regard for Peter and the news she brings him. It is not difficult for the reader to mark the ambiguity of her behaviour. Once more, she cuts with her nails, once more, we measure the intensity of her feeling for life against the destructive tendency it harbours so that we infer that, whatever his failings, Peter is as much her victim as one who separates her from the poetic realm. Love indeed lies bleeding – and

Peter may well have had to steel himself against the ravages of Frieda's passion in order to protect himself from that which he had guessed would disintegrate him had he come too close to it. Sure enough, on re-entering his room with the flower in her bosom, she tastes his lips only to find them 'cold as death'. The human compact, never finally despaired of, has nevertheless escaped Frieda. She has helped kill it even as she tried to nurture it and all because of her pursuit of the imagination.... If intellectuality is a kind of death, as she and Peter have experienced, then so is poetry; it grants one the certainty of 'Truth' – only at the expense of part of oneself.

As it happens, Lewis was a gifted scholar and had won several scholarships, including the Harry Pickles Studentship, open to all graduates of British universities, which funded his M.A. studies at Manchester University in 1935-7. Only gratitude for his parents' sacrifices and the lack of any ready alternative prevented him from throwing it up. It was at Manchester that he suffered his first depressive crisis, one so severe he contemplated suicide. Having studied for two decades, he had had enough.

Gwladys Lewis wrote to tell me she had read my essay 'with much pleasure and thoughtfulness' and invited me to lunch at her home in Sarnau, near Penbryn, on the Cardigan coast.

Gweno thinks your article on 'Attitude' is brilliant. As I hadn't a copy & didn't know the story she sent me the original script and asked for my comments, a copy of which I enclose for your perusal.

This is part of what she had written:

I have read and re-read Mr Pikoulis's article on Alun's story 'Attitude' and the story itself and I have pondered long and deeply. I think it is a sensitively probing exploration into a state of 'being' expounded in detail with all its complications.

Each time two questions remain unanswered and almost unanswerable in my mind. Firstly: *must* 'the Muse' exact such total submission to her tenets? And secondly – allow the destruction of the human body if obeying his direction necessitates it? Mr Pikoulis allows that Alun was drawn more and more forcibly to this 'inner-world' to find refuge from the brutalising effect of the daily routine of army life and its subjugation of the soul. Also the arid nature of the Indian landscape, in spite of its vast vistas, gave him no uplift of the spirit, while the poverty and degraded state of the lower castes of India distressed and perplexed him; and seeing no way of improving his condition, he was again tempted to seek sanctuary in this 'inner-world', the imagination if you like.

As to this leading to the destruction of the physical body, it was a dangerous field of exploration for such a sensitive mind.

In the case of Peter and Frieda I can see no other solution for their lives had reached an impasse; but it need not always be the answer; far from it....

I have a feeling that this 'otherness' was a passing phase brought to extremes by the universal conditions under which he was living and had the Fates brought him back to his family who loved him so dearly, especially to Gweno, and to normal civilised living, he would gradually have changed his perspective on life, though he would never have been the same again: probably wiser and more mature.

Because 'the Muse' is a state of 'being' his new environment would have persuaded him that all mental exercises, like research, are not of necessity dead and dull but result in discoveries that make exciting possibilities for a fuller and better way of life. Our physical activities, maybe, need processing by a method like Marie Curie's purification by fire: eliminating the dross until only the healing glowing crystal is left in the crucible.

So a new Blessed Trinity emerges; the harmonious blending of the physical, the mental and the 'inner-world' which cannot fail to be ennobling.

She dated the paper 'Pengarreg 26/8/75'.

Gwladys's comments reflect the widely-held belief in the 1930s in education as a means of self-improvement and resolving international conflict. Her reference to Alun's 'inner-world' recalls a remark made by Mair in her *Poetry Wales* article about his 'Within-World'.

...for each the way is different and each must find it for himself, integrity being the compass that will guide the seeker to his goal. For Alun, the jungle through whose dark tangles he had to find his way yard by yard on reconnaissance patrol, was the perfect outward expression of this inward search.

# IV

Before meeting Gwladys, I received a letter from another Freda – Freda Aykroyd. (Freda, christened 'Frieda', had her name changed to 'Freda' during the First World War in order to make it seem less Germanic. Lewis, however, always called her 'Frieda'.)

> I have read with great interest your article on Alun Lewis in Poetry Wales. It seems to me that you have defined very subtly the conflict between the imagination and the confining elements of the scientific mind....
>
> I have heard from Richard Mills (who introduced me to Alun Lewis) that you have written an appreciation of the poem The Way Back and have long wanted to read it but have not known how to procure a copy of it. I will be most grateful indeed if you can tell me how to do so.
>
> I am in the process of editing a collection of letters from Alun to myself and writing a memoir of him drawn, as far as possible, from the brief time we were together. He stayed in my house in the Nilgiri Hills above Madras on his leave in 1943.

I sent Freda a copy of the article and asked her for an interview. She said she would be pleased to see me after she and Wallace returned from overseeing a barn restoration on a property of theirs in the Lot and Garonne. Before leaving, however, she read the article and responded promptly:

> Where do I begin in discussing The Way Back? I say nothing in saying I found it a profoundly moving experience to read your acutely sensitive and perceptive analysis of a poem which means so much to me, has meant for more than thirty years.
>
> There is nothing in your article which, in my knowledge of Alun Lewis, and judging by what is evident in his letters to me, is not absolutely true. You have filled out what I apprehended from the beginning and what I have gradually come more fully to realise since his death. You have done so by applying your professional skill and learning to what I knew by instinct and a sensitivity heightened by love.
>
> Your analysis shattered me. For many reasons. I had always wondered why this poem, so obviously a love poem and so easily placed chronologically, had ever come to be

included in Ha! Ha! Among the Trumpets. When I tell you
that Alun once wrote to me thus: '...my one fear is *for*
Gweno. I would rather lie or die or never be born than hurt
her like that,' you will understand why I felt this. And
Gweno's observation that it is a love poem and her quotation
from his explanation of the necessary mood and physical
influences essential to the stirring of poetry in him breaks
my heart – for her. This must have been the protective covering he threw about her when he sent her the poem for
inclusion in the collection. That he should have done this,
risking her comprehension, is an indication of the importance
he gave to the poem....He sent it to me on the back of a letter
written in a railway train at Delhi Junction. If I quote it or
anything else from his letters please do not think I do so
lightly: I have thought about copying them out for you a long
time before deciding to do so. I feel somehow that you should
know what I can, within reason, tell you. This is how he
wrote the first draft:

The Return.

Six days and two thousand miles
I have watched the shafted rain
Feminise the burning land
Cloaking with a green distress
The cerulean and ochre
Of the season's ruthlessness.

Six days and two thousand miles
I have gone alone
With a green mind and with you
Blazing in the stubborn bone.

Soldiers quickened by your breath
Feel the sudden spur and rush
Of the life they put away
Lest the war should break and crush
Beauties more profound than death.

And swimming in the naked lake
I breasted with exquisite ease
The foaming arabesques of joy
And in the sarabande of trees,
Of guava and papaya
And crimson blown poinsettia,

Like a lark within its nest
Laid my hand upon your breast,

But the iron beasts deploy
And all my effort is my fate,
With gladiators and levies,
All laconic disciplined men,
I pass beyond your golden gate
To murder and destroy.

And in the hardness of the world
And in the brilliance of this pain
I exult with such a passion
To be squandered, to be hurled
To be joined to you again.

Here lay the reference to 'your breast' which had so disturbed Gweno
when she first read it and which he altered to the millrace of the
blood, implying physical arousal while avoiding the explicitly sexual.
Here, too, lay a definition of war ('To murder and destroy') which
shows how far he had drifted from the idealistic motives that had
made him enlist.

'The Return' plays on two meanings of the word: Lewis's return
to the army and his reunion with Freda. She told me the poem was

> written on the back of a letter which ran: '…I think perpetu-
> ally of you, darling, and through you I am enamoured of this
> no-world of the railway train where thought is free and has
> its own time. That's why I really don't want the journey to
> end.' A page later: '…The lights are failing now (as Sir
> Edward Grey once muttered) and I'd better retire gracefully,
> after saying I had a bath and a meal in the evening [passen-
> gers could at that time take a bath on Indian trains] and wrote
> a poem in the morning and loved you and loved you and
> loved you all the day. The lights are a bit better, and I'll write
> the poem on the last page. All today I've been thinking of
> the lake. What did it all mean? How did it do so much? The
> only answer is in your eyes and in your lips'.

The circumstances of 'The Way Back''s composition were now clear.
The letter ended:

> How truly you speak when you say there is something

magnificent about those last lines! I have always thought this.
I have, indeed, always thought it one of his major poems,
The Jungle being another. But those last lines have a sort of
defiant joy and freedom about them. I was moved to read:
'…the one poem which marks Alun Lewis's final maturing
into his poetic self and thus defines the nature of his achievement'. This is a tremendous fact.

I wonder how you sensitively understood his 'vision of
some tremendous disturbance whereby the essential self,
caught up in a physical cataclysm, at last achieves the object
of its desires'. He wrote to me saying he had day-dreamed
of being killed and coming back under a new name and living
and writing (with me) more fully than he ever could before
that death. Then 'fool! escapist!' he cried to himself.

The joy you describe which illumines the poem was truly
there. I have tried to tell in my memories of him of his
ecstatic return from Ooty where I had sent him for a few
days, holding in his hands as he climbed up through the
woods, scorning the drive up to the house, the poems he had
written there, his face alight with achievement. He must have
held them in his hands all the way down the 11 miles of the
hill in the rickety bus. They were Peasant Song, Wood Song,
Hands, It had been easier not loving, Beloved Beware. He
led me into the drawing-room and immediately read them to
me. I am sure his joy in achieving poetic utterance was as
great as the joy of his return.

…Actually there had been no sexual experience in the
accepted sense then. We met again in Bombay later.

I knew, of course, of the fascination death held for him –
as anyone close to him must have known. I had been ill, as
so often in India, had some sort of operation and I do not
know exactly what I said in a letter to him but doubtless
something to the effect that if I had to die I would have
accepted it. (This is true.)

… I knew very early of his longing for 'aloneness'. He
spoke of it often – ambiguously. It so happens that I too have
always loved to escape into a solitary world and especially
to withdraw from love in order to love more intensely. Before
I realised this longing for emotional freedom and just after
he left the Nilgiris I wrote what can hardly be called a poem
but what came of an irresistible impulse to put into words
the secret joy within the pain of parting, knowing that love
would be intensified by separation:

It matters little that you are away from me

I do not seek to measure time nor yet to see
Eternity lying between this little soul of mine
And that great coldly flashing star.
I do not seek to hold its light within my hand
That it shines and you are in the world
Is all I understand.

This moved him very much. He spoke of it from time to
time in his letters and referred to it in his last letter to me –
one which I knew to be a farewell.

He composed an allegory of two tawny beasts 'about
their own Ways' in the jungle, meeting sometimes and
thereby becoming sublime. We thought of ourselves thus.

…I have been looking through the letters in order to find
a reference to Malmund lake which would interest you, but
in doing so I have come upon so many paragraphs which are
relevant to your reasoning that I found myself copying them
out. Now I just don't know whether to send them to you or
not. Oh, I am so torn in all directions! I keep thinking, since
reading The Way Back, that you should take charge of these
letters. But I have not even met you!

In a postscript, she added: 'I was older than he – by five years'.

Lewis's reference to the 'two tawny beasts' recalls 'Post-Script:
for Gweno', which contrasts her to 'Death the wild beast', a symbol
of war via Twrch Trwyth, the wild boar that ravaged Ireland and
Wales in Culhwch ac Olwen, one of the Mabinogion tales. It also
recalls Siegfried Sassoon's 'the wild beast of battle on the ridge' in
'Prelude: The Troops', which Wilfred Owen thought 'the most
exquisitely painful war poem of any language or time'. Lewis used
the image again in 'War Wedding', an account of his marriage to
Gweno in July 1941, where he is 'the wounded beast'. In 'Midnight
in India', the last poem in *Ha! Ha! Among the Trumpets*, he is 'the
wild beast' who lies dying 'In unknown worlds' in her hands.

Freda's letter moved me deeply. Has any researcher received so
heartfelt a response to something he has written, one so freighted
with joy and pain? It is remarkable that she felt able to write as she
did to a stranger. It is as if a dam had burst in her, releasing emotions
pent up for thirty years, emotions all the more intense for their
suppression. During that time, memories of Lewis continued to
revolve in her mind without resolution – a species of grieving without
end. Now, however, the moment of release had arrived and she could

write to me as she did because I had understood before I needed to be told. Years later, she informed me:

> It was this so long shut away knowledge of him and his destiny which burst forth when I read your article and which, once I knew I could trust you, made me tell you with a great fullness of heart about what was the most momentous period of his life – and mine.

In one respect, however, her letter proved me wrong. 'The Way Back' does not reflect sexual experience. That was to come later, though its prospect was thrilling. The poem sublimates sex, as do all Lewis's other poems to her, burdened as they are with sadness at the thought of the pain they are causing others and their impending separation. The beautiful possibility so recently disclosed to them is overshadowed by anxiety. 'The Way Back', though, describes a time when passion held sway. Its pain and longing are those proper to the emotion of love, desire held at bay until it detonates.

In my reply to Freda, I kept my academic's hat on firmly:

> Any reading of 'The Way Back' must make more than I did of the transparent subject of the poem, a declaration of love by a man to a woman he is separated from. I made less of this than I should simply because of the circumstances you have since clarified. You will notice that I refer throughout to the woman in the poem as 'the beloved', a euphemism hinting at what I sensed but could not prove. Everything, of course, turns on the 'you' of the poem and I do not think I was wrong to detect a threefold definition of the pronoun: a woman, the Indian land and the poetic muse. The inspiration of the poem is linked to the loved one who is its subject, as is the feminisation of the land with the outpouring of feeling for her....
>
> I am glad you have a regard for 'The Jungle', an even more magnificent rhetorical performance of taxing complexity. I knew when I first read it that this was so, but 'The Way Back' moved me more mysteriously and inwardly. It teased and puzzled me, gradually delivering Alun Lewis's work to me and leaving me anxious to know it better.

Freda confirmed that the picnic in the poem had taken place at Malmund lake, adding she was conscious of the privilege of 'the overwhelming gift of his love and concern' and that it had supported her through times of darkness. She went on:

> I was enchanted to read of the feelings that the first
> reading of The Way Back invoked in you. Also to know that
> it was this poem which brought you to him, so to speak. I
> would like to tell you of my first reading of it. I had not
> thought of him during his visit to Coonoor and immediately
> after it as a poet. To tell the truth I had never heard of him.
> We were isolated on the top of the Nilgiri hills, remote at any
> time and culturally cut off, and new poets or writers came
> our way usually by accident, by the finding of a new period-
> ical, the occasional arrival of a literary review. When Richard
> Mills came up to the Nilgiris and talked about his friend Alun
> Lewis and showed me Raiders' Dawn I'm afraid I was not
> over-impressed by it. I liked certain things in it – the dream
> quality of All Day it has Rained, (a similar trance-like
> feeling, do you not think?, in The Jungle) and To Edward
> Thomas and Postscript for Gweno ('you remain, a singing
> rib within my dreaming side') and others. But I think I did
> not give much concentrated thought to the reading of the
> little collection. I felt his tremendous strength of feeling
> most, and wondered what this intense young soldier was
> really like. But I thought Raiders' Dawn, on the whole, young
> and much of it naïve. I felt he did not compare very impres-
> sively with Sidney Keyes whom I admired. After I met him,
> as I told you, we were too close, too enchanted for me to
> think of the *quality* of his poetry though all the time aware
> of the poet in him. The poems he wrote to me up in the hills
> and read to me on his return to Coonoor made me much more
> aware of his talent. But it was The Way Back which brought
> the shock of recognition of his being a fine poet indeed. I
> used to wait in the garden for the postman each morning.
> When the letter arrived I read it in the sharp morning
> sunlight, then the poem on the back of the last page of it and
> I remember vividly the *breathlessness* I felt as I put it back
> in the envelope and into my shirt front as I walked about the
> garden thinking about it. I knew then that he was remarkable.

As was the woman who wrote like this.

Freda and I met at the Randolph Hotel, Oxford, on July 19th
1975. We talked long into the afternoon, after the other guests had
drifted away and waiters hovered by to clear the tables as the evening
shadows lengthened. With much emotion, she described how Alun
and she had fallen in love at first sight and had spent five enchanted

days together in Coonoor before Wallace's return from America. As the day for this approached, she sent him to Ratantata, the officers' rest home in Ooty, from where he returned with a sheaf of poems he read to her with heightened emotion. They met only once more – in Bombay, at the end of September, again for five days. It was there that their love was consummated.

Freda then surprised me by saying Lewis was impotent. She wept as she spoke. She had become aware of this on his last day at Coonoor, when they took a walk in the woods round Highfield; at one point, they sat down and fell into an embrace. He placed her hand on his phallus, which then wilted. Ashen-faced, he rose, proudly threw back his head and said: 'Well, I can take it if it has to be like that. I would never have written a line if it were not so.' Previously, his attentions had been affectionate rather than physical, which she welcomed; it so different from the way men usually approached her. After their lovemaking in Bombay, he told her he felt like a prince. Evidently, his difficulties were intermittent; 'erectile dysfunction' might be a more accurate way of defining them.

In an unpublished notebook of 1941, Lewis offers this allegory of his condition:

> Things constantly change in size like balloons in & de flated – the sex act is pre excellently this. It has become so beautiful now, so holy flesh, & yet I am afraid before it & my power goes out in fear not humility before it: & at the portals as the gates will open to any touch I am afraid to touch & my hands will not raise themselves & go out & push. Then I push the gate & it sways open and my hands pall in weariness at the contact with the gate & I do not enter [.] But in my mind are the holy gardens intact, beautiful with lawns & grey walls and fluted pillars rising to broken arches of sky....

The loved one may say: 'The flesh is ready' but he is trammelled in difficulties when attempting sexual penetration because the flesh that attracts also daunts by virtue of its holiness and beauty, which deflate his passion. 'Hands' that are willing to touch and push 'pall in weariness'.

Writing to Gweno of May 26th 1943, Lewis declared:

> Gweno, death doesn't fascinate me half as powerfully as life: you half hinted so when you mentioned that article on Hillary [by Arthur Koestler in *Horizon* in 1943 describing

the injuries sustained by Richard Hillary in an air crash, his
return to active service and his death in a flying accident at
the age of 23]: but you know really, darling, how I turn
insatiably to more and more life, don't you? Death is the
great mystery, who can ignore him? But I don't seek him. Oh
no – only I would like to 'place' him. I think he is another
instance of the contrary twist we always meet sooner or later
in our fascinations – like the atrophy that time we walked up
the hill in the dark and that you with your Life spirit battled
so hugely to dispel, astounding yourself, I know, and you
were big enough to take me as a stranger and 'make' me
again....

When I asked Gweno to explain what this 'atrophy' might be, she
replied: 'I'm sorry, I cannot recall this situation'. This was odd, since
her memory never failed her. Freda had provided me with my answer.

The text of the above letter is reproduced as it appears in *In the
Green Tree* (1949). Forty years later, Gweno printed an improved
version in *Letters to my Wife*:

... like the atrophy at Llangranog when we walked up the
hill in the dark and that you with your Life spirit battled so
hugely to dispel, astounding yourself I know. And again at
Aber, on the hillside that Easter before we went to Borth y
Gest. When again you were big enough to take me as a
stranger and 'make' me again....

Evidently, the 'atrophy' at Llangranog recurred in Aberystwyth.
Lewis occasionally used the word to describe his depressions, which
Gweno likened to his disappearing behind a pane of glass. She attributed this to the frustrations of the age and the chemical
malfunctioning of his brain. (His mother believed it was an aspect of
his sensitivity.) In May 1937, while attending a student international
conference in Pontigny, in Burgundy, he verged on 'complete
atrophy', feeling numb and dumb, hopeless, chewed up with introspection. However, it wasn't lack of energy that characterised
episodes like this as a sense of waste, a failure to fulfil his promise.
At such times, he was consumed with apathy and inertia, like a sick
animal, an awful lack of spiritual power and compression of the brain.

Several instances of 'atrophy' in the more specific sense occur in
Lewis's work. In 'In Hospital: Poona (1)', he lies awake at midnight
in the Junior Officers' Ward of the hospital and spans the distance

between himself and Gweno, who rides 'like a legend' in her red yacht in Cardigan Bay:

> And the great mountains, Dafydd and Llewelyn,
> Plynlimmon, Cader Idris and Eryri
> Threshing the darkness back from head and fin,
> And also the small nameless mining valley
>
> Whose slopes are scratched with streets and sprawling graves
> Dark in the lap of firwoods and great boulders
> Where you lay waiting, listening to the waves –
> My hot hands touched your white despondent shoulders....

The two of them had holidayed in north Wales at Easter 1940, carrying their sandwiches in a string and eating them on a grassy knoll above Beddgelert. Writing to his artist friends, Brenda Chamberlain and John Petts, Lewis explained:

> We were walking up by the Llyn there, & then had to go back
> – to the war & all the unknown; so we stood a few minutes
> to watch our other selves go on, on, into the darkening, stony
> screes at the head of the valley.

In the poem, Gweno is 'despondent' when Alun places his 'hot' hands on her shoulders not because she regrets his doing so nor because she doubts her response nor yet because of the shadow of war that hangs over them but because he has tried and failed to make love to her. Eventually, she manages to 'dispel' his 'atrophy' and passion is expressed.

In an unpublished notebook, Lewis describes a similar springtime meeting by the sea:

> The kiss on the bare shoulder, the white breast,
> The weeping under the sycamore, the broken
> girl and the silent tormented boy,
> The passionate struggle of the
> adolescent soul....

Writing to Gweno shortly before embarking for India in October 1942, he referred again to the incident:

> You have often been a pillar of great strength and beauty to
> me. No one has ever spoken with such authentic faith to me

or so convinced me by simplicity as you did, you know when.

She had become his mainstay.

> You saved me twice in the deepest and loneliest pitch of night. And brought me back and sustained me – and this is the most wonderful of all perhaps, you made me return that way again and so destroyed the failure that had so nearly destroyed us.

In the autumn of 1942, she visited him at Southend. He recalled

> … that little spiritual crisis on Sunday was so exhausting and deeprooted that perhaps I have never been so quietly triumphant as when I lay on that twin green bed and tried and tried and tried to cast off the hollowness and frozen misery the Army had bound in me as I marched – and you came towards me along the road we couldn't see, and the distance slowly got less, and then at last, oh what a relief! I could *feel* your love and your care tingling in my exhaustion, and I felt myself surge back and be no longer isolated and effaced. And you have the power, if you will not be hurt by my coldness, and if you love me enough to use it. It's the most necessary thing I can ask of you, and darling I will have to ask it of you sometimes. It's in the nature of the beast.

Previously, he had said he would make love to her only out of doors – a remarkable condition implying the need to escape home. In 'Lines on a Young Girl' (the girl is Mair), he refers to 'her restless body/ Chafing within this chaste much-mothered home'. In the great outdoors, 'mother' vanishes.

In his last poem, 'The Jungle', Lewis writes a retrospect of childhood modelled on Yeats's 'A Dialogue of Self and Soul'. Here is Yeats:

> What matter if I live it all once more?
> Endure the toil of growing up;
> The ignominy of boyhood; the distress
> Of boyhood changing into man;
> The unfinished man and his pain
> Brought face to face with his own clumsiness;

Then Lewis:

> The vagueness of the child, the lover's deep
> And inarticulate bewilderment,
> The willingness to please that made a wound,
> The kneeling darkness and the hungry prayer;
> Cargoes of anguish in the holds of joy,
> The smooth deceitful stranger in the heart,
> The tangled wrack of motives drifting down
> An oceanic tide of Wrong.
> And though the state has enemies we know
> The greater enmity within ourselves.

Where Yeats looks back at his younger self from a period of later fulfilment, Lewis's agony continues unabated. The passage may refer to youth's difficulties in general but its intensity carries sexual overtones (as 'the willingness to please' suggests). The pleasure principle so regularly confounded in him 'made a wound' in himself and others. Where there should have been joy, there was pain, or joy mixed with pain. That was at the root of his discord, the 'stranger in the heart' that grew until it assumed universal proportions – 'An oceanic tide of Wrong' (a Freudian-sounding phrase). Thus turned in on himself, he was beyond healing.

## V

At the time of our meeting, Freda was in her sixties, a silver-haired woman about five and a half feet tall, with full lips and dark, watery eyes. Standing by the door to greet me, she leaned back on her heels, her head cocked to one side. The expression on her face promised quickness of response and generous feeling. Her clothes were finely-tailored and in subdued colours, her chunky jewellery accentuating her snub fingers and compact body.

In manner and speech, she might have been a Home Counties hostess: she knew everyone and was an expert raconteuse, cook, bridge player, gardener, traveller and collector. She liked buying and restoring houses and filling them with *objets* – painted chairs, peeling mirrors in ornate gilded frames, faded fabrics – juxtaposing these with more contemporary items. The style might be bohemian country house or palazzo crossed with pied a terre, the grand sitting beside the intimate, the theatrical with the more modest. She might have been a professional designer or antiques dealer had her interest in possessions and sense of social privilege been more developed. Her intelligence was both natural and acquired; her favourite authors were Graham Greene, Isaac Rosenberg, Keats, Rupert Brooke, David Jones and Edward Thomas. At that time, she was planning to write a play on Ruskin. Of all those I met during my research, she was the only one who was able to discuss Lewis's work with me in any depth.

For some time, she had been trying to write a memoir but feared Gweno would refuse permission for her to quote from his letters and lived in dread of the refusal. This grew more acute when I informed her Gweno had complained about her use of them in an article of hers in *Modern Reading* in 1952, a copy of which I had posted her. Nonetheless, she worked at it conscious she would never be able to tell the true story.

Over the years, Freda had read and re-read these letters until she could quote stretches of them from memory. She pored over them like some devoted exegete, every time drawing comfort and inspiration from them. They were what filled the silence and made it tolerable. She was able to draw fresh nuances from them at every reading. At such moments, Alun was near to her, his voice blowing through her mind like a fresh wind, present emptiness echoing to past joy.

In conversation, Freda reaped discoveries as she went along; in her letters to me, however, the tone deepened. Lewis once told Dick Mills: 'Freda's letters are a tempest of wonder'. That is what those to me were, too, both voluminous and numerous, some 20 pages long, recto and verso, with marginalia and revisions. Some early ones were even preceded by drafts and carbon copied – all without losing their freshness. Truly, they were a labour of love, testament to a vanished reality and drawing on wells of deep emotion, memory vying with analysis and emotion with conscience as she relived what had been left out to dry for too long.

Freda was, I think, conscious of her lack of formal education. For example, she was disconcerted to read Roland Mathias's objection to Brenda Chamberlain's tampering with the text of his letters to her. But when the subject was Lewis, she rose to the challenge. After Wallace's health began to deteriorate, they became a rare source of solace.

> You *can't* know with what pleasure & anticipation I open
> [your letters] …. it is the one *fact* which warms me, holds
> some sort of pleasurable excitement for the future.

With her help, I constructed a detailed history of their meeting.

# Part Three
## *Alun and Freda*

### I

Two months before arriving in Coonoor, Lewis was involved in gruelling training exercises in the sand dunes and forests of the coastal strip above Bombay. After that, he was granted a ten day period of leave and ordered to report to the newly-formed Military Intelligence School in Karachi. Previously, the School had concentrated on the German and Italian forces but was now turning its attention to the Japanese. At first, Lewis thought of visiting his mother's sister, Connie, and her husband, Ernie Phelps, in Darjeeling (Ernie had been a surveyor in Cwmaman and was manager of the East India Coal Company). When that proved to be too far away, he accepted Dick Mills's suggestion and travelled to the Nilgiri Hills in southern India.

In a draft of her memoir, Freda set the scene thus:

> We did not then know Alun Lewis but I had been asked by a mutual friend, Richard Mills, if he and Alun might come to stay for ten days. Richard was eager that Alun should, as he himself was to do, enjoy a relief from the heat of the plains and the strains and exertions of military life. Richard loved our house in its tree-encircled garden set in the hills where the downlands have suggested to many generations of homesick exiles the rolling downs of England. Wide and wild they were, with 'cholas' (patches of woodland) where orchids grew lying in their valleys and trout streams, clear as glass, veining their uplands. The blue mountains – which is the meaning of their name [the Nilgiris] – rose to eleven thousand feet, a misty lavender in the bright, sharp sunlight of the Indian mornings. Coarse grass through which jackals loped and, from time to time, a panther trod greenly mantled their lower slopes. They were inhabited here and there by a

sparse and dying race of curious people, the Todas. The grass
huts of these people appeared, infrequently, in the sheltered
pockets of the downs; the Todas, clad in white druid-like
garments, the men long-bearded, would stare at the lone
fisherman who might come upon them, disappearing
nervously if approached.

A short taxi ride from the station carried him to Highfield, the
Aykroyds' two-storey house with double veranda set in lawns and
bluegums. As he went, a strange sense of elation grew in him,

> a tremendous vivid premonition, like a birth of the spirit; all
> the time I drew nearer this exultation grew and when at last
> the taxi took me from the station to Highfield I was incan-
> descent it was marvellous. And yet it had no physical point,
> no physical purpose, no foresight or expectation. It wasn't
> conscious thought.

A servant showed him up to the first floor, where Freda was
helping her daughter, Gilly, erect a toy theatre she had made for her.
Since the date of his arrival had been fixed for the following day, she
was not expecting anyone so she was curious who the caller might
be. She rose and consciously assumed the role of hostess again. As
he approached from an inner landing through a tall blue door, there
was a peculiar look of recognition in his eyes. With the sunlight
picking out the tawny-blond hair on her shoulders, her eyes large and
set apart, her eyelids lazy, a small nose rising above full lips, she
appeared to him 'more beautiful than fate'.

> Beloved when we stood
> And saw each other standing there
> I did not know that all
> The ordinary days
> Had fallen from the earth….
> And did you know then
> How I had been closed
> By the steady expectation of death?
> How did you hope
> That hardness to break
> Of the man who no longer asks
> For love and its ache?

The lines are notable for the intimacy assumed between a man who has recently closed himself to 'the steady expectation of death' and become one of 'the morose, the taciturnly dead' and the woman who comes to revive him: 'you were the flash of a sword and I was bewildered and very tranquil'. As a draft of 'Ways' (see Appendix Two) has it: 'The rock you touched became a stream/ and all reality an ugly dream'.

Here was an extraordinary turn of events. As he wrote later: 'The greater part of "Fate" is attraction, isn't it, the machination of a force like a subterranean river. Attraction. Fate. Fate. Attraction.'

Life was too elemental to dissemble.
Being among soldiers and peasants
I learnt the endurance of their lives
And ordinary suffering,
A shelter of leaves for sleeping,
And the sharpening of knives.

How could I help but tremble
Entering your gate
And discovering you there
Standing by the tall blue window
With the sunlight on your hair,
Oh more beautiful than fate.

The 'gate' is the one he passes through in 'The Way Back'.

Freda Kathleen Buttery was born in Shropshire in 1910, the youngest of four sisters. Part of her childhood was spent in South Africa, where her father, Harry, raised sheep. After her mother's death and his subsequent remarriage, she was sent, aged 8, to live with an aunt in London, feeling she had been rejected by her family. On the 18th October 1930, she married Wallace, eleven years her senior, at once father-figure, lover and companion. After a period with the health section of the League of Nations in Geneva, he became Director of the Nutrition Research Laboratories in Coonoor in 1935. The town was dominated by the army, the Indian Civil Service and the tea-planters; it shared a club with Wellington. Ootacamund ('Ooty') lay eleven miles away.

By nature, Freda was restless. Though she got on well with the army wives, she found their company restricting. She hunted, fished, rode, painted, sculpted, wrote and, for a year, read the news and announced on All-India Radio as well as acting with the film star, Andre Morrell. (Years later, she was an extra in *The Nun's Story*, starring Audrey Hepburn, but her scene was cut.) Lewis called her 'the hostess with the strange & fascinating confidence and élan that sets you a little apart'.

On their first night, he pirouetted her on the dance floor. Afterwards, at Highfield, he spoke to her of the feeling he knew to exist between them. Standing on the porch in a quiet embrace, she felt faint.

> God, what *repose* I found in you, Frieda, that Saturday night when they all went and I knew your silky hair on my cheek at last, at first. From the moment I put my left arm around your neck and touched your shoulder and drew your lovely head down to me and my lips lay in your hair I loved you, darling, and love you love love you.

Freda wrote:

> His gentleness and undemanding love, while he was at Coonoor, was so different from anything I had ever experienced; it seemed very beautiful and comforting that he didn't, as other men always did, make some unwanted, usually hated, attempt to physically approach me. I loved him very much for it.
>
> I, certainly, for my part, felt no-one except Wallace had ever or could ever be so close, so understanding of every aspect of me, my life as it was and had been and what I was and wanted and needed. His gentleness and undemanding love, while he was in Coonoor, was so different from anything I had ever experienced.

Their mornings were full of breathless pleasure,

> that particular love too fragile and exquisite for either of us to put into words while we were together - a curious and significant withholding, surely?, for two young creatures suddenly and blindingly in love? – and also the hollow fear and pain of knowing it would end, a knowledge we never admitted, even to ourselves.

In the afternoon, Muniswamee (in *A Cypress Walk*, he is 'Mari') carried the gramophone onto the lawn, where they read poetry and discussed books. In 'Some Letters of Alun Lewis', she wrote:

One day when some soldiers had come to tea Alun listened to what they had to say, answered and questioned them seriously – for they had been in the African campaign and had much to tell him. They were talking among themselves when glancing in Alun's direction, I was surprised, almost disconcerted, at the tranced look in his face. His eyes, strange blind-seeming eyes, gazed out into the garden with so still and hypnotised an expression that the soldiers who noticed it ceased their talk. He came back, as it were, slowly into our midst and I had the impression that he had not been brooding upon the African campaign but had been in some far remoter world.

She recalled:

There was a frailty about him, a look of not belonging in all the horror and mess of war, that gave his white face and high forehead, his strange, blind-seeming eyes and soft voice a particular pathos.

Even so, he expressed his opinions vigorously and his lithe body promised action.

Walking in the woods one day, they gazed into a stream that ran between the eucalyptus trees; because of its purple iridescence, that was where he said the moles lay, 'dappled moles of warm blue sunlight', 'rose moles all in stipple in your little stream', an echo of his story, 'Duration', in which a 'flat broad stream' carries 'dimples of ripeness and little moles of calm lying in oily streaks along the filmy surface'.

If we were both here or both where you are I'd write – given time I'd write purely – I'd have a mind like stones in a clear pool, smooth & clean & rough-smooth & coloured.... I dream of this other time, of deep freedom.

As he prepared to go to Ratantata, Freda wept; in this brief separation, she sensed the larger one to come. In 'Parting', she wrote:

Last night you wept and your bowed head
Was touching and defenceless as a child's.
Your quiet weeping was my strength –
I stood between you and the world.
But today in the cold and cruel dawn,

> Today, uncompromising day, the grey light
> Awakened you to your own strength
> And left me to my helplessness.
> As your fingers fastened buckles deftly,
> Efficient and tidy – oh for what? –
> Your lips were firm, I could not see your eyes.
> Your khaki jacket rustled stiffly
> As you jerked it down behind,
> Efficient and clean and ready,
> A straw in the wind, a leaf upon the flood.
> As you turned to go I saw your eyes
> And knew my strength was but despair
> And that your own could not prevail.

Later, he wrote of 'that bitter day in the empty room in Ratan Tata' and the 'black' night he spent wrestling with poems he wanted to write for her. Next morning, he hired a bicycle and rode into the hills through the mists.

On his return to Highfield – again unannounced – he read her the poems he had completed, an episode recalling one from his childhood when he came back from a walk on the Graig (or mountain) and read the poem he had written to his mother, flushed with triumph.

Lewis's poems speak of love but are freighted by a sense of betrayal:

> Only love me if you can
> Give what no-one else can claim,
> For both the woman and the man
> Wither at the touch of shame.
>                                   ('Beloved Beware')

He feared there had been a huge destruction but insisted monogamy was not the only virtue:

> my whole being has other loyalties or at least other ways of attaining the consummation that Rilke calls harmony between the individual & the universal cycle of beauty.

Yet he could not forget the hurt he was causing Gweno:

> … all words, all explanations are hard & doubtful. I shrink from such words or the labour of making them audible and cogent.

He knew he owed her a great deal:

> ... she was always strong enough to make the terrible journey herself. Sometimes it was a real journey, by train; sometimes it was in bed, whether before we married or after. It would be impossible for me not to love her.

'Hands' (subtitled 'NOT to Frieda, but to TIME') opens:

> Unbearable ecstasy, how can I answer,
> Possessed with your splendour, having no choice,
> That other bitter agony
> That other broken voice?
> Am I not cruel as you are
> So to rejoice?

He said his 'deepest longing' was for aloneness; like Keats, he was trying to act within the situation:

> ... I've always refused to submit to a rule – Jesuit, Anglican, Nonconformist, military – out of fear: and I've clung as long as possible to the freedom that does not decide and scarcely has an opinion, that suddenly acts from an overpowering conviction that appears to be simple intuition, and acts always in the situation, and not according to rules that one applies to the situation.

He could attain his 'true self' only by following the law of love.

Of the 29 poems in the 'India' section of *Ha! Ha! Among the Trumpets*, five are to Freda. The first is 'The Way Back', the second 'Ways':

> It had been easier, not loving.
>
> I knew I had grown harder than the trees
> In which I held you all the afternoon,
> The tall blue slender saplings leaning
> Each on each, their strength outgrowing.
> And suddenly we two were swaying
> Each upon the other leaning.
>
> It had been easier, not loving.

From the start, Lewis counted the cost of his new love. The 'broken rhythm' of the woods has sexual connotations that are amplified by 'harder', 'swaying', 'their strength outgrowing'.

> It was much easier, all alone.
>
> The tall slim saplings were exhausted so
> With tallness and with slenderness they bowed
> At the touch of wind or bird.
> And the lightness of your hands
> Bowed me also with their guerdon,
> Love being gravel in the wound
> When the silent lovers know
> Swaying in the misty rain
> The old oppression of the burden
> Growing in them as they go,
> Though trees are felled and grow again,
> Far and farther each from each.
> Longing hardens like a stone.
>
> Lovers go but hardly, all alone.

It would have been simpler had they not fallen in love; in a different sense, however, remaining alone would have added to their anguish. They will part yet they remain inseparable ('hardly' suggesting 'barely' as well as 'with difficulty'). The swaying lines convey sorrow with tender delicacy, joy fused with sadness. It is this combination that best expresses their love.

'Guerdon' (line 7), signifying a 'reward' or 'recompense' (in the sense of 'just desserts'), is a Keatsian word ('The guerdon of their murder they had got' ('Isabella')). It adds dignity to the occasion. Humbled by Freda's gift of love, he falters in expressing it. But then nothing could adequately express it.

A third verse originally followed (see Appendix Two) :

> Living was a simpler task by day.
> I loved the friendliness of light
> The quick resilience of a boy
> Taking hardness lightly and with joy
> And yet I chose the fastness of the night
> And bore the hardness of its crags
> Until a stream broke from the rocks [deleted line]
> Until the rock gave forth a stream
> When you kissed me in my sleep.

And always, waking or in dream,
You bend above the blinded head,
And stroke away the hardness of the night
And break the iron trance of war
With the graver thrill of peace.
But [originally 'yet'] I will always dread the night
Till its carnal slaughters cease.
Yet in the grey [originally 'soft'] reprisals of the dawn
Can [originally 'You'] such a thing as love be born?
When you kissed me in my sleep
Why, beloved, did you weep? 87

This refers to the tears Freda shed before he went to Ratantata,
though she forgot he was asleep when she entered his room and that
she had woken him with a kiss.

'Wood Song' opens:

The pine trees cast their needles softly
Darling for your gipsy bed
And the tall blue saplings swaying
Whisper more than can be said.

The plaintive tone contrasts with the ebullience of 'The Way Back'.
Were there ever such sad love poems?

Piteously the world is happening
Beyond this cool stockade of trees
Enduring passions penetrate
These quiet rides with agonies
That love can never consummate.

The 'enduring passions' are those that reach the lovers from the
battlefield and those that bind them to others. Such are the 'agonies'
love cannot heal.

And we must go because we love
Beyond ourselves, beyond these trees
That sway above your golden head
Till wind and war and sky and dove
Become again the murmur of your breath
And your body the white shew-bread.

(The sacramental 'shew-bread' refers to the loaves left on the altar on the Sabbath for the priests, implying the completion of the self.) Formally yet lyrically, Lewis accepts that he and Freda cannot be. Time pushes each in a different direction – he to the war passed 'your golden head' (c.f. 'your golden gate' in 'The Way Back'), she to the 'stockade' of Coonoor.

The day before he left for Karachi, the two strolled in the woods round Highfield; again, both wept. What followed I described in my biography thus: 'He tried to express his love for her but failed'. I felt confident readers would assume this referred to a verbal failure. Twenty years later, Freda came nearer the truth:

> Alun stopped beneath a tree and slowly drew me down beside him. He then lay back, his dark hair among the leaves, and very gently took my hand and laid it upon his body so that I felt him move and strengthen beneath my hand. He sighed breathlessly. Then came the bitter failure when his strength left him, his passion faded. He got up, and threw back his head in a proud agony. His face was white. 'Well if that's the way it must be…' his voice trembled.

I took the precaution of asking her to describe the event for me. She replied:

> On the day before he left he took my hand and led me into the woods where he drew me down beside him on the ground….
>
> He did it very gently with a sort of hesitancy, as though he must, as though this had to be. I remember very clearly my sense of his doing this in obedience to the law of love, with no urgency in him but this tangible sense of inevitability, almost of sadness.

(Megan Lloyd-Jones, Lewis's girlfriend in 1935-7, said his lovemaking was more willed than spontaneous.)

> Nor was he thinking that I desired this – he knew I did not. He was gentle, trusting me to understand. His manhood stirred and strengthened where he had laid my hand upon him, and then, while strong within my hand, slowly, with the inexorability of any other death, failed and died….. He got up, his face white, and putting back his head in a heart-breaking proud gesture, he said, as much to himself as to me: 'Well, I can take it if it has to be like that: I would never have

written a line' (did he say of poetry? Memory cheats me) 'if it were not like that'. I was distraught at sight of the suffering in his face and begged him not to despair, not to believe it would always be so. I had no reason at all to believe that this was some passing failure of sexual power, but because he was in such anguish, I felt I *had* to say something, anything to lessen his pain. 'I *know*, I *know* it will be alright,' I told him. 'Please, please believe me; I am so sure it will be alright.' I did not know and was not sure. What I did know was that he was very fully a man, that the power of attraction to me in him was the essence of manhood – 'attraction like the force of a subterranean river'.

In his Karachi journal, Lewis refers to the scene again (see Appendix Two).

> And when you lay within my arms
> The human passion in me cried
> With the voice of every man
> Who had that wound within his side
> And I knew the beauty of this world
> And hated that by which he died.

Later, he told Freda:

> I should be used to my unsuccessful self by now. It's good for me too, humbling me so completely. I don't show it to anyone: I've learnt that much savoir faire. I showed it to you because you will understand it and be willing to take it, as you did the last day I was in Coonoor, in the narrow ride in the wood among the dead leaves.... I want you to know of this poverty... it's in poverty that you must find me if you love me.

Lewis associated the 'broken rhythm of the wood' with Yeats's 'Solomon and the Witch', a favourite poem of his:

> The night has fallen; not a sound
> In the forbidden sacred grove
> Unless a petal hit the ground,
> Nor any human sight within it
> But the crushed grass where we have lain;
> And the moon is wilder every minute.
> O! Solomon! Let us try again.

Another letter refers to 'the dark lane in the wood when I felt the barren rock cry out with its terrible invincible hardness in the open heart I had'. Freda picked up the phrase 'the barren rock' years later in 'The Wood':

> The wood enfolds me yet
> In city square and cavernous avenue,
> Thin arms reach up and delicate fingers touch
> As branch and dappled leaf arch in sweet protection
>             o'er your head,
> There where you wept. Your grief ran from you, blood
> Of your hidden wound.
> The wood re-echoes yet
> 'Neath high leaning walls and steel-engraved street,
> The green tunnel where the beat
> Of your steadying heart yet sounds
> As you rose at last and, shaking back your head,
> Proud and white, you found
> A word of comfort for your hurt,
> As though a barren rock had been washed by a gentle rain.
> The wood enfolds me yet
> And soft the feel of moulded leaves beneath my feet
> Down hot side-walks before the blinded gaze
> Of window panes where city sunsets glow.
> The wood is all about me, but 'tis I who weep, and oh
> The rock is barren once again.

## II

Lewis left Coonoor early in the morning of August 3rd 1943. As Manswamee (another version of the butler's name) carried his luggage to the car, he entered the drawing room at Highfield in his newly-laundered khaki tunic and left the gramophone open, knowing Freda would find the half-played records there on her return from the station. As the train drew up, she kissed him and he climbed aboard, his eyes full of pain. She had to restrain the urge to run after him. To the tea-sellers' cries of 'Cha, cha' and 'Orangee', the train pulled out.

On her return to Highfield, she wrote 'The Exquisite Moment'.

> This is the moment of happiness,

> Now when the heart knows surely
> This new love given purely,
> Love in its loveliness.
>
> When only the heart stirs, not brain
> Nor blood nor any sensual need....

Lewis's first letter to her is from Arkonam and is headed 'The first day'.

> ...this morning the day is lovely & a bell is ringing in the town & the day has come very softly and unobtrusively on us and I can see & feel & hear you and speak to you, but not here, nor these words: but instead in your own woods, where the moles lie in the sunny water and you smile and, for all the world you know of, yet you are shy and very young, and innocent in a way you cannot hide....
>
> Freda beloved, things were queerly reversed and in a way it was a pity for yesterday which hurts in me more than the finger with the blue nail coming off. [He had caught it in an electric fan.] But it was bitter, perhaps, for now there is no pretence in any sort, but only a beginning from the beginning, darling, and not from where I left off in life with certain achievements.

Evidently, the failure in the woods preyed on his mind.

In his next letter, he said he was

> examining ruthlessly the basis of the tranquillity which you filled me with, examining its implications, assessing its enormous costs.... That tranquillity was so deep, I can't fathom it...

His mind was now 'working in the lowest coal seams', a mining image suggestive of the profound effect she had had on him.

> I know I am involved utterly & entirely in what is happening, and I know that more depends upon it than just life; yet I am somehow as impartial as a battleground, and I wait as best I can. Another part of me actively seeks you, plans to meet you, fixes a time & a place which I couldn't ask you when we were together nor can I ask you with my pen now.

She had suggested 'an unbearable greatness' in him:

I…write always *against* the tug of the war & the horror &
tedium of it: and all I'm trying to write is love. And you made
peace. And I wrote those poems of peace because you
abolished the war for me…. Christ, don't I *loathe* the bloody
war? I hate it with my guts, because it's just plain rottenness
and it has no satisfaction at all, either to the living or the
being killed. But my tapeworm, my writing bug, he's alright.
He's alive and obdurate, no matter how many other ways I
fail. And I've got his courage to discard all death forms that
these times seek to impose.

(Lewis was fond of the tapeworm image; in 'After Dunkirk', he
writes that, though silent a lifetime, he has wept inwardly: 'And only
the little worm,/ The small white tapeworm of the soul,/ Lived on
unknown within my blood'.)

I've always wanted and longed for another illumination, to
encounter and know and merge with the same living stream
in whoever it flows. In you, and you, and you. In childhood,
boyhood, manhood, in time and out of time. Why should that
hurt? Because somehow it is hurting others: it hurts the
possessive in others, wounds them, distresses & confounds
them.

As how could it not?
    To an extent, he hoped the situation would resolve itself and
Gweno would grow less dependent on him:

…there's an exquisite symphonic rhythm in being separate
– in being able to decide within oneself on this stroke, this
risk, this refusal, this acceptance – but the real [twice under-
lined] music is in being thrillingly & sensitively aware of the
separateness of the other one with whom you share love &
who is in your arms or in bed with you or five thousand miles
away from you. But always you are aware that the beloved
is complete, herself, a life that, just by being itself strikes
incessant music out of the silences. And when you do come
together then God! What music is audible, drowns you, yet
is only just audible, beautiful. That's the way I want to love,
not this begging & this leaning, but a calm, independent love
that endures absence & rejoices in meeting, & doesn't
destroy or crimp or cripple. I know I'm talking about ideal
things, but it's the only thing for which I can strive. You've
got it in you, I know. I knew long ago that – never to follow,

but always to meet in freedom, the freedom of the will. Oh
come and meet me, Frieda.

He said there were two kinds of loving, two kinds of lovers:

There are situations, obligations, yes, yes, yes – but not now:
nor when we meet again.

Out of the 'uncanny understanding' between them, '– so close
that it becomes invisible, immanent, unnecessary', came 'The Way
Back'. Like 'The Orange Grove', it represented

a spiritual Parnassus in the centre of a physical hurly burly.
I love it when it's like that – it's a thrilling synthesis of living
& writing, thought & deed, wrong & right. It's like being in
love.

He couldn't believe he had written it – his hand had, poetry being 'a
spontaneous action in the world of thought' and the poet its medium:

All today I've been thinking of the lake. What did it all
mean? How did it do so much? The only answer is in your
eyes and in your lips.... perhaps you were sixteen when you
hid your face smiling & hiding your face by the lakeside.
And I thought no more than a peasant does, life being one
thing & knowing the centre of it there.

On the imaginative level, the violence in 'The Way Back' parallels
the act of writing ('daring, always daring, to plunge & tear & enter'),
both recalling the vigour of the erotic act that precedes the sowing
of seed: the creative and procreative are one and the same. At
Coonoor, he had said *Raiders' Dawn* was 'not a *bad* book' but a 'very
young one. Full of seed, every page is seed; no harvest, only seed,
seed, seed'. That seed bore fruit in 'The Way Back'.

When Freda expressed her admiration for the poem, he replied:

I hadn't read it since I wrote it – I read it this afternoon and
it seemed strange that it should be there, clear and hard as a
lump of coal.... I imagine a mother looks at her child in some
moods and is incredulous that she has borne it.

Again, the colliery and maternal images reflect on their formative
influence in his life.

Oh Frieda, do you know how deeply you have pierced in me? How everywhere you have restated, revived, broken down & compelled in me, so that, as I gradually encounter the beliefs I had, I find one after another is changed, maybe replaced, maybe just lost & nothing yet in its place? And now I am hunger & thirst & effort & this strange intense joy that really is pain as well as joy, not because it is complex but because it is commensurate with life, & with all that the imagination has ever explored & identified & known.

A virtual gloss on 'The Way Back', with its play on the disruptive and creative effects of passion.

Difficulties remained:

Even in the unnatural lucidity of late July, when I never needed any food and wrote my last poems I knew that these unmanageable colonies were forming in myself and I saw by Malmund lake that love would not be easy and joyous or a continuous sharing of happiness for either of us.

Freda echoed him when she wrote:

[A]s I write I read the letters and cannot drag my attention from them, so often shaken by tears at the sweet love and concern he gave me, knowing me as no-else ever did, and at the bitter realisation that the wonder we shared could not be ours for longer than that brief intense eight months because both life and death prevented it.

Lewis told her:

Darling Frieda, I'm very old in my familiarity with hurt & hardness: I pray that you are also. We will love most best through a bravery shared and not spoken of again by me, ever, ever. Joy is manifestly a thing that comes & goes. We need it and love it, but I will never try & hold it: it hurts too badly to hold it against its will, and perhaps what you & I will need most is bravery. I can't explain; I only know we'll have to hang on to nothing for long tracts of time, Frieda, and that it is imperishable – this.

He said he was

just an instinct when it becomes real and there are no embell-ishments. It is that instinct I want to give to you…

From Karachi, he pressed her to meet him in Bombay while reminding her he loved Gweno 'very deeply':

> The trouble is in the conflict of two tides of loving. I hoped devoutly there need be no conflict; perhaps later there won't be, perhaps my being will grow enough to understand the coexistence of things: but now its trouble in me, trouble in the mind & in the body, and I don't know, I just don't know, darling.....
>
> And I can write this to you, yet I couldn't write it to Gweno.... I couldn't tell her that I love you, though I can tell you much more easily than I thought I could.
>
> Frieda, I'm not asking you for advice or to do anything. I only want you to know. If you know it will be infinitely happier for me. I can love you if you know how I am made. Perhaps there is nothing new in this to you. I think of you saying Yes, you knew it all. Does it alter anything? Will you still come, and will you know that the love I give you is true love?

Freda did come:

> though infidelity seemed unthinkable, I yet could not accept that I would never see him again. In me it was longing, in him a need.

For many years, she and Wallace had been trying for a third child and she had recently undergone an exploratory laparotomy during which she suffered a near-death experience.

> You say something of yourself – Tod und die Mädchen – that moves me massively & makes me deny it wildly & possessively for you against Death & take you to Kashmir or Vezelay where HE can't come. But darling, are you also within the charmed circle? And isn't it in some ways very beautiful? To accept just whatever it will be. But we will not accept, Frieda.

Tod und die Mädchen – Death and the Maiden.

The lovers met in Bombay on September 21st 1943. En route, she broke her journey off to see Dick Mills in Poona. As she made her way from hotel bedroom to dining room, she felt suddenly sick at the smell of bacon. She realised at once she was pregnant – that explained why she had felt faint on the porch at Coonoor on his first night there. At the very moment she was travelling to see him, she discovered she was with child. This added to her nervousness, since women did not travel alone far from home at that time. Nevertheless, she longed to join him, to solace him and receive the sympathy only he could give her.

At Victoria Terminus, Bombay, he felt his life 'swing into a single orbit'. For her part, she was moved by his youthfulness and by his shouldering the responsibility for their situation. He had taken a small guest house by the sea and it was there she told him about her pregnancy. He wrote that it was like 'a kind of forest fire in my body'. Nevertheless, his hurt quickly gave way to understanding and, later that night, they consummated their love. 'I feel like a prince. Do I look like a prince?', he cried.

The next five days were spent in the manner descibed in 'The Transmigration of Love'. Every morning, they would stroll along the curving seawalk and enter the pleasure parks. He told Dick Mills:

> When Frieda & I were in Bombay a little boy brought us lotus flowers, blue spiked firm flowers, every morning, and I had that feeling then, of being water in the river, fruit on the tree, anything natural & gentle & self-sufficient.

What had happened was astonishing to them both, he trapped in the army, she in colonial life, both yearning for a fuller existence:

> ...I had been virginal and continent for a long long time and something in me was surprised and exhausted by that much greater wave that overflowed in me; and it was always not enough, and this other little virgin thing murmuring 'But you two lovers need months, years, time, time, not to be exhausted but to attain a calmer fruition.' And I don't know whether the little sigh & murmur is right, and all I know is that it was a vain and impossible murmur that we must, we simply had to overwhelm.

In the following months, he frequently recalled the image of the open bedroom window above cool Colaba bay, people strolling along the esplanade below in the deep night, 'holy, body unto body & the peace of that', followed by the innocent boundlessness of the fore-dawn, the seawind laving their bodies 'and a nearness that made the world a heaven'. In 'In Fear of My Love', Freda wrote:

When in night's gentle darkness
I feel him beside me so quietly sleeping,
I know that my spirit is free of all else but love
And in fear for my love I lie weeping.
And when the true darkness thins
(An invisible blanket is swiftly withdrawn
Though the darkness remains) I know that the finding and loss
Was for this and for this was I born.

And when the soft dawn wind blows
Touching our nakedness with little unborn hands,
Fear drowns me and I let my lover hear my weeping
Nor care if he understands.

Lewis told her:

I love your poems, Frieda, I do honestly. You can write
poetry as well as being a poet – the writing is just something
very difficult that one is able or unable to do....

In late 1943, he suggested they collaborate on a play exploring the
reaction of the British in India to the presence of the Japanese on the
border.

When the time for leaving came, they both sensed they had met
for a last time. Once again, Lewis wept:

there was no desperation in my simple wish to leave fresh
flowers where we'd been so happy, but just a sense of right-
ness and order.

Together, they travelled to Poona, where they finally parted. Freda
told me:

Love had been such an enchantment – yet more: so tender,
close, fraternal almost, winged with such joy, such
undreamed of fulfilment. But we moved on, myself into
another, different love, domestic and demanding, he further
and further into the other extreme: that of life ending, love
and living joy, all living things for him ending and he entering into it while I remained, joy gone out like the sun at
evening.

To an extent, she was protected from her pain by her pregnancy but a deeper pain awaited her:

> I had felt that implacable drawing towards the void in him
> for so long, but I didn't understand what the voice that called
> him was. I think understanding of something frightening,
> some haunting in which I was not involved, touched me as I
> stood in the departing train at Poona and he, unable to look
> up, stood with his head lowered, despair shaping his hunched
> shoulders. Something more than bereavement at parting –
> for the last time, as I knew – possessed him while my heart
> broke.

Evidently, he had given up hope he might ever be free. As she leaned
out of her carriage window, she expected to see him looking after
her, perhaps waving; instead, she saw the 'most extraordinary picture
of absolute misery', his head hanging as if poleaxed.

> .... I did write, of course, but not often enough. He should
> never have had to write: 'Frieda, make a great effort and
> write to me. I need your letters.' I loved him always, always.
> Never for a second, ever, did I not love him – nor all these
> years. But I drifted away in the practical world I lived in, as
> he had to through the war involvement and all he had to do.
> Love remained in both of us, but ailing, sad, though hope
> always remained, however faint, until just before the end.

Lewis wrote:

> The problem is so utterly simple, darling, and so utterly insol-
> uble. I would come to you through all evil elements and
> death-surges; and yet I cannot come to you except when I am
> with you. (This isn't true.) When I am with you the problem
> has ceased to exist. We are. That is complete. At all other
> times this love is a cruelty to the other love I receive and have
> given, which so powerfully shaped and directed me that its
> compulsions & recollections are as normal and real as my
> daily answers to the daily tasks & situations in which I live
> in the army. You know all this.... And I would not have
> imagined that this also could happen which happened to us,
> nor that we could enter of ourselves into such liberty and
> such untrammelled ways. It was bound to be restricted in
> many ways. The most obvious is the impediment of time....
> And the other obstructions lie inside us and sometimes they
> choke me. I've fought very hard you know, darling, since I

met you, very very hard. Really fought and fought. And when
it's been very hard I've made myself endure the hardness &
not try to end it in some false way. And I know we need a
long time for ourselves to be understood... I am not afraid
of you or me. There is only one fear in me at all. That is *for*
Gweno. I love her and can hurt her too much. I would prefer
to lie or die or not be born than hurt her like that. Oh Frieda
darling, I don't know what all this is going to become. Do
you, beloved?....Don't call me conscience-ridden. There's
never been guilt in us, thank God, never from the beginning
of time have we – you to me & I to you – had guilt.

But there was guilt, of course.

The fluency of Lewis's letters is remarkable. Their passionate
anguish, one heart beating to another, captivates. Though they are
written in the press of emotion, he remains unemotional, blending
warmth with discrimination even when most involved. No sooner is
feeling expressed than it is shaded with thought.

I am just an instinct when it becomes real and there are no
embellishments. It is that instinct I want to give to you.

In his letters to Christopher Cheney, Lewis plays the arch graduate,
to his parents he is the optimistic son, to Gweno the devoted husband,
to Dick Mills the ever-loyal friend. Only those to Freda reveal the
full range of his emotions. She tried to convey this in her *Modern
Reading* article:

There was about Alun Lewis, the remarkable and ardent
young poet who was killed in Burma in 1944, a rare spiritual
quality. To those who knew him personally it was this quality
in him which was most immediately arresting.

Citing Max Beerbohm's remark that voices in wartime are
'inevitably, rightly' loud, she said Lewis's was not:

... on the morning of his visit to us he apologised for having
arrived without warning, in a voice so quiet I had difficulty
in hearing him. He spoke always in this quiet voice, wore
always this look of being apart.

Only a portion of Lewis's letters have been published, mostly in
edited form. In them, he is disclosed in all his pain and confusion,

longing and determination. As William Carlos Williams said of
Robert Lowell's *Life Studies*, there is no lying permitted a man who
writes like that.

# III

On returning to Highfield, Freda embraced Gilly and

> a great wave of love swept over me for her, for the baby, for
> Wallace, for Alun; love in all its gentleness, its compassion,
> its reassurance suddenly supplanted all else. Loss, anxiety,
> guilt, bewilderment were swept away by this sudden, all-
> enveloping love. It seemed so simple: love could not be
> measured – there was no longer a question of whom or how
> much one loved, love in itself was enough. It has many faces,
> I thought, each beautiful, and to accept love unquestioningly
> was to accept life in all its aspects.

She here repeats Lewis's view that the 'huge destruction' he feared
had occurred had, in fact, been averted.

Back at Lake Kharakvasla, he told Dick Mills:

> I don't know what will happen to Frieda & me. It's a univer-
> sal sensation in us just now, of joy and distress, but they are
> only cloud showers over the essential act of recognition, of
> having known each other since we were born. I don't know
> what will happen & I feel overborne.

To Freda, he confessed:

> When I had to stand once and wait for about 30 minutes in
> the darkness at the corner of a paddy field I was so tormented
> in my hollow tired mind by the realisation of your absence
> that I prayed that I should stop thinking. Today, marching
> back to camp, I have been feeling a sense of loss, and anger
> against the smooth counsel of resignation and a fierce unwill-
> ingness to be satisfied with this life of camp and physical
> labour and war training. I still feel this loss and it aches and
> I am a bit flat and sad. There is also something imprisoned.
> It was locked away when you left me at Poona and I hated it
> being locked away then. I wanted it terribly much on Poona
> station those last few minutes but perhaps it was wiser than

us. I'm sure it is wiser than me. And I am nothing without it.
I am waiting for it to speak. Perhaps I'm wrong in thinking
it's imprisoned in you; perhaps you're free. Though you are
so uncannily close to me in the moods and times of feeling
that I feel you are so, too.

They had come to each other out of 'some brittle nowhere where
nothing mattered', leaving the 'old negative world' for 'the simple
and supreme syllable of love'. Earlier, he had told her he could not
write her 'the real real poems yet':

A very big thing happens & after it, under its impact, one is
for a long time apparently smaller. Like concussion.... And
yet it is true that I cannot write you the poetry that is yours
until long after this is over and it is part of me & I have made
myself see the world again with my new eyes that you said
were blind, as of course they are, as a newborn animal's are.

He continued:

Writing poetry does not satisfy, it exhausts. I don't know
when one experiences pleasure: there is no place for pleasure
in the process of writing poetry as far as I can see: yet one
would rather write poetry than do anything else on earth.
Strange, isn't it?

Poetry-writing was, for him, a long wrestle with words and rhythms.
Nothing might come of it but he was not vexed by failure, only
exhausted:

The only things I respect in myself are the poems and stories
I haven't yet written. These I work for with all the power I
can gather, fiercely as any mother.

Now suffering from writer's block, he turned to letter-writing as
a substitute, as Freda noted in her *Modern Reading* article:

While he was prevented from writing poetry or stories I think
he must have regarded the writing of the letters he poured
out to his relatives and friends as a faith-keeping act.

Reading them, she gained 'some comprehension of what lies hidden
in the dark of the imagination – glimpses of an inescapable beauty,

undefined and inexpressible'. He told her:

> We hanker after one-ness, it's the dominant urge – monothe-
> ism, monogamy, the uniquely beloved whose face and body
> is always immanent in distance and danger & despondency
> and the homeward dream – and I only slowly admit to myself
> that my whole being has other loyalties or at least other ways
> of attaining the consummation that Rilke calls a harmony
> between the individual & the universal cycle of beauty.

Whenever he saw a beautiful lake or river or bay, he became one
with it:

> In the activity of living I know now that I've always wanted
> and longed for another illumination, to encounter and know
> and merge with the same living stream in whoever it flows.
> In you, and you, and you. In childhood, boyhood, manhood,
> in time and out of time.

Yet he could not forget the hurt they were causing others:

> I've growingly had the sensation this last year of the
> separateness of each one, of the *necessity* for each one to be
> separate and not try to be identified with someone else. This
> I mean in terms of personal relations, not political – in
> politics we must join. But individually, let us be separate, I
> say….

At this point in the published text, Freda omitted a passage in which
Alun confesses Gweno's fears for him set him on edge. He wished
she could

> be *herself* – not crudely that, but to become indestructible as
> I am becoming slowly. And not having anything to lose, but
> make everything alright in herself.

By way of contrast, Freda offered 'a calm independent love'.

> I had two disquieting letters from Gweno today: she's
> living in a sort of hourly anxiety, it's such a deadly strain on
> her spirit, & she must somehow push those black fears back
> into the sub sub sub conscious & lock them up, like a funeral
> dress. To wear them daily isn't right at all: and to so empty
> herself of everything but love: it disturbs me very deeply.

And yet I know that I can't help her & that it is her own task entirely. It is in fact her *self*.

Not the least remarkable aspect of this letter is the freedom with which he discusses Gweno with Freda.

As the months wore on, the tone darkened.

He wrote me a long, beautiful letter, explaining his love, his hurt to Gweno, his hope for he and me. Everything he felt. Already his letters had begun to be inhibited, though, beginning 'Frieda' or 'Frieda dear' and ending 'Goodnight Frieda darling, my mark' and a curious shakey kiss then 'Ever love and love and poverty, Alun'. Or 'My love to Gilly, And to you myself. Do you want it?' Or 'Frieda, Frieda – All my love and longing, Alun'. The beginning, as I say, of inhibition, sickness, fear to speak more, a determination to shut out the 'burning image' and get on with the war – or to be wholly loyal to Gweno? Who knows? Both, perhaps. Anyway, there came this long, full letter. I was at this time terribly preoccupied with the thought of this baby. Thinking of it now it seems incomprehensible. All I know is that I *was*. It wasn't all happy either. I worried. There were worries. Awful medical arrangements in India, a Caesarean-like scar recently performed – I won't bore you with it. And a sort of unbelieving joy after ten years of waiting. I didn't answer his letter for ten days. (Is that very long?) He received it in hospital and wrote back thus: 'Dear Frieda, After twelve days of nothing I received your letter. I think it is the 30th (Oct) today – Saturday anyway. I've been in bed for three days shaking off a temp and catarrh and typing out some poems which I'm enclosing. I'm sorry my long letter had to be how it was and you had to dig so deep and hard in replying to it. I'm sorry, because perhaps I've pestered you: and been fussy and foolishly impatient and too eager to find words and give hospitality to intuitions. I knew I was weary of the perpetual illuminations that kept everything awake and forbade any sleep. And these poems are perpetuating them to your discomfiture perhaps.... Don't read them unless you feel sturdy enough....It's so much better to be simple and not involved. I covet your patience'.

She was grief-stricken to think she had neglected him:

He talks – throughout all these letters indeed – of our 'being

far away'. 'I don't know how it can be right unless we are
alone and far away somewhere', 'Frieda, to be away from all
this and alone by an open window...' [as in Bombay], 'I
could be *so* happy there' (a beach with huts) '*we* could be,
alone there'. His longing as he grows more lost is appalling
to read. He actually says in one of his last letters 'I want you
to know that I shall strive to be nearer to you the further I go'.

He felt like a dolt:

> ...whatever it was that happened, now seems to have been
> so swift & so beyond me & greater than me that I sit like a
> lump in my chair.... If it had happened slower, so that I
> needn't have closed up like this & excluded my bewildered
> self like this.Did it happen too quickly for *you*? I know it did.
> And it now seems incomprehensible that we were in a
> window, high & unassailable and perfected & you spoke of
> goodness & god; and I knew only the charm and not the
> hardness that succeeds it. Yet I *did* know of the hardness
> because it is always my ancient enemy, and has an old claim
> on me. But you'd so spirited it away that I couldn't  I get
> no nearer by talking, Frieda darling: it's the old childish
> hankering that I haven't outgrown, the hankering for a
> continuous happiness. Happiness brings its own nemesis;
> feeling its own atrophy.

It was a familiar sensation: 'One way or another I make a lot of
shadows where I go. Everywhere I go, inevitably'.
Freda felt helpless to combat his despair, but he reassured her:

> ...I know now that you have much more love to waken in
> my body than has yet stirred. And in me there has never been
> such ease as you made. Ease on earth is nothing. But ease in
> those unapproachable heavens is scarcely to be spoken of
> afterwards.... I shall always say somewhere, deeply &
> secretly, 'It was she'.

He realised now there was 'no time left for the beginnings to become'
and longed for 'the veil to fall off, the reality to come':

> ...your letters were in my pocket all night & I've been
> quietly reading them & my heart saying Yes & No & Yes &
> No to you all the time. I had a swift dream as I read – one
> second perhaps – of being posted as missing believed killed

> & coming back & fetching you and being with you after-
> wards all the time and writing under a new name & living
> under a new name & being more intensely & completely
> ourselves than we could ever be before that death and then
> swift as the dream came the   Johnsonian NO. ABSURD.
> ESCAPIST. IDIOT. BAS. It was a sweet dream...

'The Way Back' anticipates just such an ending.

By late October 1943, he was back in Poona hospital for a fortnight with suspected malaria and 'congested lungs' and had a brief vision of their meeting again:

> Away from you I can never find the utter almost childish
> peace which you unfailingly give when I'm with you. When
> we are separated the sadness grows and we seem to be
> spinning one of those bitter webs of Greek legend, like
> traumatic subjects of a broad and indifferent destiny whose
> mind has long been made up.

She who has left him is also with him forever. In signing off, he enclosed his signature in a maze of wavy lines.

> I've been wandering in tedious unrhythmic circles and spirals
> in the wilderness of the last few weeks. Oh Christ, I want to
> be with you in Tuticorin. Oh how much! I have been leaning
> on you, evidently. You had to reassure me, hadn't you? I'm
> sorry darling. I love to lie just before going to sleep out on
> an exercise, consider the stars amply and equally, and some
> free voice in me says in equipoise: 'Frieda'. It says it so
> tranquilly, freely, easily – neither passionless nor muted by
> passion, but as if something has been inherited and is being
> used according to its true nature. When it is like that it
> doesn't matter that we have no idea what will happen: it is
> the simple existence of us that speaks - it doesn't even make
> a sentence – no verb or object in it. It isn't often like that,
> nor could it be, me being such dross. But as long as it's
> sometimes I'll be alright.

He now asked her to send him a gold ring: 'I've never been so cast off, so worthless, purposeless, unresponsive'. Only the memory of Bombay sustained him:

> ...I saw you with an amazingly natural immediacy in your
> yellow frock and your heaped bushels of fair hair at Victoria

Terminus Bombay and I felt exactly the same sensitive
communication of a trouble I knew instinctively I could
soothe and a birdlike wildness I knew at once would furl its
wings and nest with me. And you then and I then were free
of all complexities; and everything to which we belonged
and which shaped us, and to which we owed ourselves fell
away, ceasing to perturb us with the strained phantasies of
uncertainty.

The image of 'furling' implies comfort but there is an element of
ambiguity in it (see 'Burma Casualty', where the angel of death
caresses the wounded).

By now thoroughly depressed, Lewis went to swim in Lake
Kharakvasla only to discover the expected happiness failed to materialise. Lying by the water's edge, he let the heat smooth his body and
genitals:

My body was thinking of you and me. But my mind said very
remotely, like an arbiter 'Body is captivated, but the mind is
not at one with the body.' And at that antilogy the body
withdrew its thoughts & its desire as if rebuked and I went
& swam my body and came back wet & fishlike & insentient.
You were *not* there; and my mind said it so implacably: the
world has harsh and final demands which I must fulfil.

'Swam my body' suggests some dislocation of mind and body. For
the first time, Freda is absent. Plagued by a sense worthlessness,
waste and incompetence, he longed to cry out in sorrow and hurt:

At other times in these long inadequacies I suffer I think I
want it to go a little further, that I might explore the fields of
insanity. That is a temptation that attracts & repels with like
force & I don't act towards it: it's just a thought in me, not
an impulse. I know it's danger: but it's very closely
connected with the bit of poetry there is in me, the writing &
creating mystery that wants to break down the last barriers
and explore the deep involutions of trouble and complexity
& relationship of things. But I don't really know whether the
great poems were really written in madness. I think they were
written in intervals of sanity. Madness I fear is chaos, a
greater bewilderment, a worse darkness. Has any apprehension of the mystery of everything and the mystic varieties &
interconnections of the universe ever come to anybody

except in a moment of exalted lucidity? I don't know.

I don't know my family antecedents: I don't know whether my great great grandfather or my maternal great uncle had moods of darkness. They say the Welsh are more prone to depression, but I see it as more in the writers of all countries than anywhere else & I think it's a disease that poets are prone to: I don't think it's a matter of race or blood.

Even now, he manages to stay lucid.

Freda believed his state was related to their frustrated love. Yet he told her: 'I don't need many letters from you, Frieda. One can last me a long time'. Again: 'I am doing nothing except read, write letters, sit & think, worry, do odd jobs, wait for the pistol'.

> ...I get this chilly premonition of distance; I want to break out of it like a clown through a paper hoop. Break out of this into that – will it be the same each side like the clown's hoop, or amazingly different like the chrysalid & the butterfly?

Evidently, a time of great change was nearing. Echoing Edward Thomas (who, in 'The Glory', wrote: 'I cannot bite the day to its core'), he wrote:

> I want to mark each day with my nails or my lips, but I have to let them go as they came, these days.

Try as he might, they drifted away.

By now, he was his own scapegoat:

> I'm getting fatalistic: indeed impatient to have a showdown with fate: I've lived a queer unnatural life these last three years.

At Christmas time, he wrote:

> ...there are so many imponderable antagonistic forces and so many weaknesses in me that prevent & prevent. I wish I hadn't this capacity for pain. It so wearies me. I wish I was strong like oak. And less aware of the waste & the going wrong of things and mea culpa in it all. But not in us.

Freda interpreted this as proof of the tides of feeling in him, joy contending with pain and longing with loss. 'Have I lost at least for a long time the virtue of the poet?', he mused. Neither he nor Freda believed they could start a new life together. What had happened was miraculous – 'two great wonders uniting in a third which is not me but infinitely more than me' – but nothing could grow from it.

> To be alone with you, overlooking a cool bay, at an open window, in a deep night, holy, body unto body & the peace of that.

Yet even that memory now failed him:

> I couldn't look from the window onto Colaba bay & the people on the esplanade.

It was all quite literally beyond him.

Freda believed the difficulty lay in his inability to free himself from his childhood:

> ...breaking with the past meant also breaking with the first early influences – Gweno being very much part of them – which moved him to write his first stories and poems; the first realisation of himself as a writer. And that being sentimental breaking with, or disturbing the close family affections and associations, also contributed to his reluctance to begin life again with me – for all he dreamed, a waking dream, that he had died and come back again with a new name to a life of fulfilment with me. The past, as he wrote to me, had 'made him' in the part of him which mattered most: the writer and poet.

By the same token, the present and the all-too-conceivable future were unmaking him.

Lewis's last poems to Freda are 'Peasant Song' and 'A Fragment' and they are different  from the earlier conscious-stricken poems. The former (originally called 'The Field') was posted to her a fortnight after Coonoor and ends with her weeping. The first eight lines of 'The Field' and 'Peasant Song' are identical but then the former continues:

> While you are sleeping
> And lie beside you till you wake
> And we will go reaping.

> If the sun and rain are kind
> The fields will be abundant as my heart
> And plenteous as my mind.
>
> Oh why are you weeping?

In 'Peasant Song', the poem carries the disguise of a peasant tilling the soil:

> The seed is costly
> Sow it carefully
> I have only this small plough
> To turn the mighty earth.

His difficulty in sewing crops echoes the poet's difficulty in sewing his seed.

> And will you kiss me now
>
> And with mysterious birth
> Bless this hut of rod and reed
> And I will turn the mighty earth
> And you will hold the seed.

'You' is both the land and the loved one. Lewis pleads with Freda to keep faith: he will love her, they *will* share in the processes of creation.

> But if I should go
> And you be left behind
> Among the tall red ant hills and the maize
> Would you hear my plough still singing
> And, bearing endless days,
> Somehow give praise?

Note the near-identical opening of 'Post-Script: for Gweno': 'If I should go away...'. As it happens, there are no red anthills in Coonoor, though some existed further up country. Lewis here recalls Freda's childhood in South Africa (in one of his letters he refers to her as 'Frieda Mealie-frock', 'mealie' being South African for sweet-corn).

The question 'Peasant Song' poses is one that had long preoccu-pied him: what survives? Before the war, when he was trying to decide whether or not to enlist, he asked himself:

> Why then this sadness in your heart of hearts? Are you so
> selfless that you still grieve that your death won't mend the
> world & the old miseries, by plaguing those who survive,
> plague your dead spirit also? Are you really as selfless as
> that, Alun? I would like to think you are, but I do not believe
> it.

'Peasant Song' ponders what will happen after he has 'gone', leaving
the loved one behind. In the seemingly-endless years after his death,
will Freda rejoice in the promise of his 'plough', his seed-like potential as lover and poet? The poet's afterlife is bequeathed to the loved
one – *that* much of him will survive.

Lewis's last Freda poem, 'A Fragment', was posted to her on
November 22nd 1943:

> Where aloneness fiercely
> Trumpets the unsounded night
> And the silence surges higher
> Than hands or seas or mountains' height
> I the deep shaft sinking
> Through the quivering Unknown
> Feel your anguish beat its answer
> As you grow round me, flesh and bone.
>
> The wild beast in the cave
> Is all our pride; and will not be
>
> Again until the world's blind travail
> Breaks in crimson flower from the tree
>
> I am, in Thee. 161

The 'deep shaft sinking'(c.f. 'The Rhondda', where the colliers sink
into the 'pitch-black shaft') recalls his mining roots while implying
sexual fulfilment. Though parted, he and Freda are members of a
whole rather than separate entities. In 'To Rilke', he refers to the 'IS'
he and Gweno achieved 'but in Oh a distant land'. As 'Post-Script:
for Gweno' has it:

> For you abide,
> A singing rib within my dreaming side.

Now again, two become one.

A week later, Lewis described the composition of 'A Fragment' to Gweno:

> In the nights I get restless about midnight and I can't read or
> write and night after night I've written a poem that I scorn
> in the morning, it's like cleaning my teeth – something I've
> got to do before going to sleep. Do you like this one? It's one
> I don't scorn because it is itself. Tell me if you like it, Gwen.

At that moment, a man entered his tent to play a record, thus delaying the poem's posting. It was eventually sent on December 3rd together with photographs of him Freda had taken in Coonoor. It was as near as he came to confessing what had happened:

> You can see I am not wasting away nor do I look as gloomy
> as I often sound – and feel – which is just as well, for I'd
> frighten young girls and children if I had a black visage as a
> mood!

Naturally, Gweno assumed that, since the poem was sent to her, it was written for her, though both the text and photographs imply otherwise. *Suggestio falsi, suppressio veri.*

'A Fragment' is the penultimate poem in *Ha! Ha! Among the Trumpets*, followed by 'Midnight in India', written six months earlier and addressed to Gweno. It recalls how, as a boy, he 'set the earth aflame/ And brought the high dominions down,/ And soiled each simple act with shame/ And had no feelings of my own'. Though full of yearning, he has experienced disappointment

> Until you woke me with a sigh
> And eased the dark compression in my head
> And sang and did not cease when I
> Broke your heart like holy bread.

(That image again!)

> We cast away the bitter death
> That holds the fine circumference of life
> And gathered in a single breath
> All that begins and ends in man and wife....

Though racked with suffering, her 'calm white face' restores him.

She is the goddess in kindly guise:

> Mysterious tremors stir the beast,
> In unknown worlds he dies;
> I lie within your hands, within your peace,
> And watch this last effulgent world arise.

In 'Post-Script: For Gweno', the lovers withstood the terror of the wild beast; now, as dawn rises for a last time, Lewis commits his body to his wife. *That* much of him survives. He gives his mortal remains to Gweno, his living self to Freda.

Lewis's peripenultimate letter to Freda is dated 24th January 1944:

> ... I can't look at the future. I can't see any distance at all... Will you give my dearest love to Gillian, very specially please. And for yourself know I am conscious all the time that a whole life is being thrown away all the time we are denying and denied each other. That other life haunts me inescapably and I desire it ineluctably. It makes the rest of living sad.

Freda took this to be his 'real farewell letter':

> For one thing, he never, ever called Gilly Gillian, in speaking or writing. And the 'very specially please' is an unusual emphasis. And his declaration to me, when he found it so difficult (and increasingly) to write about his love, seems a testament to what had happened to us, one which had to be said at the end.

The last letter of all was dated 30th January 1944:

> Frieda, I can't write to you. You know the aloneness and the seemingly impotent and closed-in love that is outside the perimeter of the aloneness. It's almost more than I can get my pen to write to say that I think all the time of you – and baby – and will strive to be near you the farther away I go. And of you and Gilly and some gentle impulse is always smoothing your hair and her hair with a hand softer than mine but me. And other things I can't say at all.

At the end, he drew a heart pierced with an arrow and inscribed it:

'TRUE LOVE'. Two months earlier, he had written:

> You were afraid of something that might turn into resentment in me: and of something in me that in cowardice and for peace of mind would shut away this love, this burning image and deep reflection of you in me and in the world. But it would only happen like that if I died also within myself: and I need to be as terrified of that as you, oh more than you. But I don't believe it at all. Many things might happen to us, but nothing that can trap and destroy the – the what? – the freedom of heaven and earth and time. Isn't that what we apprehended?

Their 'IS' was safe - as his and Gweno's had once been.

# Part Four
## *Gweno Lewis and Gwladys Lewis*

### I

Shortly before lunching with Gwladys Lewis, I was rung by Gweno Lewis, who asked if she could accompany me on my visit. She said Gwladys was frail and she wanted to ease the burden on her by preparing our meal. Immediately, I suspected her true motive was to discover what I had learned about Freda; accordingly, I asked Freda whether I could tell her the truth should the subject arise. She agreed. Neither of us could see any advantage in prevaricating on a subject of such importance to her.

Earlier that year (1975), Freda and her daughter, Gilly, and Gilly's husband, Peter Somerville-Large, had visited Mair Fenn (*nee* Lewis) in Schull, in Ireland, where she ran a centre for Transcendental Meditation. Freda was struck by the physical resemblance between brother and sister. She was invited back the following day, when Mair told her she had always 'somehow known' about what had happened in Coonoor.

> She was very interesting about Gweno – and myself very surprised. 'If only you could both meet I am sure you'd get on so well together and she'd understand perhaps.' This, no doubt, out of her TM influenced faith in the good-heartedness of people. I told her it was not possible and she sighed: 'If only Gweno was not so – well, somehow *virgin*; not only about Alun but about everything.' I felt I understood what she meant and the significance of her saying: 'If only she'd allowed his journals and letters to be published…'.

Mair believed Gweno had never 'come out' of herself. She had invited her to stay many times but she had always found a reason to cry off.

> Then she told me something which astounded me. She said
> Gweno had got over Alun's death 'quite quickly'. She had
> suffered very much 'from day to day, just taking the next
> step' then 'she suddenly got over the hump' describing it with
> her hands 'and she was alright'.

Even so, she did not believe Gweno could face the truth. Shortly after
the war, the two of them had visited London, where Gweno met
Freda and the battalion Adjutant, Alun Gwynne Jones (later Lord
Chalfont):

> On the return journey Gweno was terribly distressed in the
> train, vomiting and weeping. 'He must have told her
> something terribly cruel,' Mair said. Gweno would not tell
> her the cause of her distress. Was it, I wondered, that Gwynne
> Jones told her Alun had taken his life? To tell the truth I am
> sure that *none* of them have any idea of what was happening
> to him.... I do not think he wrote to anyone as he wrote to
> me – I mean in any way suggesting the depths of his bewil-
> derment and despair.... What is amazing is that they all
> refuse to believe (or *face* the fact) that he took his own life.
> 'It wasn't like him,' says Mair with absolute conviction –
> which shows how little she understood him.

At the time, I did not share Freda's view – the evidence seemed to
me inconclusive – though it weighed heavily on me.

On Saturday October 4th 1975, I picked Gweno up in Mountain
Ash and drove west with her. In his letters, Lewis remarked the
resemblance between her and the film actress, Bette Davies, and they
were indeed alike; Gweno was as self-possessed though taller and
more graceful. I found her easy to talk to, though the fact that she
was sitting beside me on the passenger seat, thus restricting eye-
contact, helped. She welcomed the recent quickening of interest in
her husband's work (Ian Hamilton's *Alun Lewis Selected Poetry and
Prose* had appeared in 1966 and two M.A. theses had recently been
completed). I said how impressed I had been by the extracts from his
letters she had published in the *Poetry Wales* special number and
asked if she would consider a wider programme of publication now
that the war-time editions of his work were going out of print. (Three
years before, Richard Burton was complaining: 'I wish someone
would reprint that slim volume of Alun Lewis which contains the
poem 'All day it has rained' and 'For Gweno' etc., a companion of

my teens, when I was more poet than most, indeed the time when I read and acquired by familiarity the vast store of memorized and memorable verse that still lies here in my head.') She agreed this was desirable but pleaded pressure of work. Everything would have to wait until her retirement.

Gweno then turned to rumours about his suicide and a possible love affair and said she was open-minded about both. No reliable proof of either existed, but people would talk. Alun had been prey to depression and had reached a particularly low point in the autumn of 1943 but had recovered by the time the Borderers set sail for Burma in February 1944, as he always did. The Court of Enquiry into his death concluded that it was an accident and there matters rested. I told her I thought her caution was justified.

After Lewis's death, she had told Christopher Cheney:

> I have a little snap too taken just before they left for the front: he is in his bathing trunks & looks so brown & fit, so vital. It makes his death seem all the more incredible. For the last months he had one of his bad old moods but it vanished & he wrote out of a clear spirit before he went.
>
> The colonel wrote describing the absurdly simple details of the accident. They were in the Arakan & Alun's lot had gone up on detachment. They were carrying their loaded revolvers & Alun just fell on a narrow path! He was unconscious when they picked him up & remained so till he died – 8 a.m. our time on March 5th. He is buried in a front line graveyard along with other soldiers.
>
> His death was swift & unexpected & sometimes I think it is better he died like that. You see he was 'intelligence' & ran a greater risk of being taken prisoner & questioned.

His death was both accidental and providential.

Gweno was less sceptical about a possible romantic attachment and, at one point, mentioned Freda. The anticipated moment had arrived. I replied to her as matter-of-factly as I could, saying their love was both a source of joy and anguish to them. She listened silently before moving on to other subjects. Everything passed off more peacefully than I could have imagined. Not once did she lose her composure. There is a silence that is full of tension and one that reassures – Gweno's was of the latter variety, which is why I was able to speak to her without embarrassment. I could only guess at the reserves of character that permitted such stoicism.

Even so, I suspected that nothing I told her was news. I had only confirmed what she already knew (or suspected). As I have noted, Lewis posted all his poems to her for typing and distribution. When she read 'The Way Back', she took fright. Though he managed to reassure her, a seed of doubt had been sewn. His reassurances, of course, were self-serving and contradictory, first, saying he was only reporting what he saw, then that his love poems referred to an imaginary voyage, 'a sifting of imagined lives and other people's experiences as much as my own'. However, the opening line of 'The Way Back' is extraordinarily precise: 'Six days and two thousand miles', measurements which point not to the land of faery but a location far from Wales (c.f. 'ten thousand miles of daylight grew/ Between us', 'In Hospital: Poona (1)'.) Strangely enough, the details had escaped detection, but then Lewis's poems have a tendency to the secretive even at their most transparent.

Gweno had also read 'The Transmigration of Love', with its detailed account of the lovers' rendezvous in Bombay, 'Wood Song' and 'Ways', which refers to the lovers embracing, 'Each on each their strength outgrowing/...Each one on the other leaning'. These may not have registered consciously but help account for the fact that she listened to me so quietly and why she was chary about committing herself to further editorial work on his behalf, a task that must have struck her as a looming burden rather than a pleasure deferred.

After the war, she had told Christopher Cheney:

> I'll take a header into the enormous draw where I keep everything precious & bring them out into the light once more. I intended doing this years ago but the publishers have been nagging me about a large edition of his letters, but I've decided against that for the nonce.

If his writing were precious, however, why the delay? The answer appears to be: because memories were still raw. Gweno was a private person and shied from exposure to comment by pleading pressure of work.

After Lewis's death, she had edited *In the Green Tree* (1949), a collection of his letters and stories. *Letters from India*, a dry run for it, appeared three years earlier with the following note: 'Gleanings from his other letters and journals can be left to help a biographer'. 174 While *In the Green Tree* was in the press, she told Lewis's publisher, Philip Unwin, that she was

turning over and over in my mind the problem as to whether
I should enlarge the letters and add the journals or not. Poets'
wives have a name for being overzealous and I should prefer
to keep the material in the hope it might be of help to
someone interested enough to write a biography one day.

However, none had appeared. After the success of *In the Green Tree* –
two-thirds of the edition sold out in two months – Unwin pressed her
for more material, in vain.

Forty years later, in a note to her edition of Lewis's letters, she
wrote:

> The letters contained in this volume represent most of the
> letters Alun Lewis wrote to me after joining up in May 1940.
> Some have gone inexplicably astray. Perhaps they are still
> between the pages of *Iphigenie auf Tauris, Prinz von
> Homburg* or *Tonio Kroger*, my German texts, left there after
> another greedy read between lessons. The more grievous,
> however, was the accidental burning of the letters written in
> the last months of 1943. During the upheaval of leaving
> Mountain Ash for Aberystwyth I had to get rid of the detritus
> left for nearly forty years in the classroom – notes, old
> copybooks etc., and hidden in a pile of papers in went the
> copybook containing the precious letters.

There are several mislayings here. Just as retirement and the long-
promised editorial project approach, some letters go missing. It is
strange how 'precious' and 'detritus' are juxtaposed in her account.
While no doubt sincerely wishing to promote Alun's work,
something stayed her hand, some unresolved aspect of her attitude
towards him that led her to mislay what she was ostensibly committed to preserve. She may not have been left resentful but neither was
she eager.

# II

Gwladys Lewis's cottage in Pengarreg, near Sarnau, on the Cardi-
gan-Aberystwyth coastal road, lay in a field. Thick walls enclosed
small rooms, a living area to one side, a kitchen to the other, two
bedrooms above. They were surrounded by drystone walls and
yellow gorse while spindly trees bent low against the prevailing

westerlies. I was surprised she should live alone in so remote a location but the answer lay in its proximity to Penbryn, the family's summer holiday home. Her youngest son, Huw, lived a few miles away at Aberporth and Glyn a little farther off in Rhydargaeau, near Carmarthen.

Gwladys was a tiny, bird-like woman barely five feet tall. She had shiny pink skin and grey-blue eyes that darted about as she spoke. Her manner was girlish and her face wore an eager expression, though it could go blank on you sometimes. She drew her whispy grey hair back into a bun, adding a touch of severity to her appearance. She spoke softly and crisply and if, at any time, she was tired by our conversation she did not show it.

Gweno joined us before lunch and at one point raised the possibility of a biography. Mutti (as she referred to her) agreed, clapping her hands together. Gweno then bobbed her head in my direction, indicating I might be a suitable candidate for writing one. Considering what had gone before, I had escaped lightly.

After Gweno had withdrawn, Gwladys spoke to me about life in the valleys during the Depression. She sat in an armchair, a floor lamp beside her. The warm October sun flooded the room, adding to the heat from a coal burner and helping create an intimate atmosphere. There was a pile of rugs on the stone floor and the previous Sunday's newspapers were strewn on a sofa nearby. In her light, quick way, she told me how she would encourage Cwmaman parents to stop taking *The News of the World* and read *The Observer* or *The Sunday Times* if they wanted to improve their children's chances in life. She said she had met her husband at a suffragettes' meeting in Aberdare – in the nick of time, for she was not cut out to be a teacher. Her pastor father thought Tom was beneath her, but they married in 1914. Shortly afterwards, he was called up, though his period of service was brought to an end by a wound he received to the thigh in March 1918. When the War Office telegram arrived, she cried: 'Hurrah! Tom's been wounded!'

Alun, their first child, was born in 1915. As she explained in her privately-printed memoir, *Alun Lewis My Son* in 1968, he was conceived during her and Tom's first consummation. He was followed by Glyn (1917), Huw (1919) and Mair (1921). Gwladys believed an extraordinary affinity existed between herself and Alun, one 'akin to the awareness that lovers have to each other's presence in a room, even when separated by a distance'. Years later, Alun described her to Freda as one 'whose life & quality deserve great gifts. And she asks only the gifts of bread & beauty & closeness'. In his draft 'Author's Note' to *Raiders' Dawn,* he wrote: 'I have two acknowledgements to make; one to my mother and one to my wife'; on publication, 'mother' had been changed to 'parents'. With obvious pride, Gwladys remembered how he had returned from a walk on the Graig above Cwmaman carrying a poem in his hand which he said was for her and which he read excitedly to her. (Gweno believed the poem, 'The Poet', first printed in *Time and Tide* in 1938 and collected in *Raiders' Dawn*, was too mature for a teenager to have written.)

Gwladys then moved on to Wallace and Freda Aykroyd. She assured me nothing had happened between Alun and Mrs Aykroyd. Then she stopped. This in itself was unusual; it was as if there were something in what she had just said that stuck in her throat. Her cold grey eyes fixed on me, creating an air of mild tension. I felt she had challenged me to contradict her, not deliberately but distinctly, and was slightly irritated. Gweno already knew the truth (though Gwladys could not have known as much) yet here she was denying it.

Evidently, Freda had been a subject of discussion for some time; like Gweno, Gwladys seized the occasion to clarify matters once and for all. Yet the way she did so – denying the rumours and inviting me to disagree – caught her off-guard. Did she suspect (or fear) that what she had just said was an untruth?

Time seemed to stream between us before I found my throat unsticking, allowing me to say that something had indeed happened. She took a sharp breath, bit her lower lip, closed her eyes and, raising her hands to her face, bowed her head into it. That image of mortifi-cation remains with me to this day. She had been wounded – there was no doubt of that – though whether the wound were to her moral sense or her pride I could not say. Perhaps the latter, for I felt oddly unmoved. *Her* Alun had done something unaccountable. Signifi-cantly, she made no attempt to persuade me I was mistaken.

A few weeks later, I received the following reply to my letter of thanks:

Dear John,

Thank you for your letter. I hope you gathered at least atmos-phere, if little information, on Saturday and that you feel you understand Alun slightly better for your visit.

I was glad to meet you and hope you will call again

whenever you come within hailing distance of my cottage...

Now I want to introduce a delicate subject which I hope you will accept in the spirit I mean it to be taken. It is the relationship that existed between Alun and Freda Aykroyd during the few days he was her guest.

It wasn't until your pamphlet on 'The Way Back' that I became aware of what might be made of it if irresponsible gossips in the literary world saw the possibilities. Even Mair described the poem as a 'true love poem', to which I took objection. I would be shattered if Gweno were cruelly hurt and publicly humiliated as would be the case if tongues began to wag. She is too nice to suffer such treatment.

I would hate Alun to be involved in such sordid revelations as the exposures of the love-life of Virginia Woolf, the Nicholsons, Lloyd George and so on that have lately defiled some of our most respectable newspapers.

I have tried to examine the facts as objectively and unemotionally as I can and the verdict is bound to be 'non-proven' or 'open'.

Only Alun and Freda know the facts. Alun isn't here to tell his story and both you and I know that by Freda's very nature, her evidence is bound to be unreliable and 'heightened'. So we had better leave the stones unturned and firmly pressed in.

I have discussed the possibility of this kind of trouble, when I am no longer here, with my family and they would unite to fight as fiercely as an unwarrantable intrusion into someone's private life.

If I understood you aright, Freda has already betrayed her trust by speaking frankly to you. It couldn't help to assess Alun's work better, except perhaps 'The Way Back', for a few days in 28 years is such a fraction of time spent.

So let us close the file for good, to the infinite relief of his mother and his family. I hope no whiff of this has reached Gweno. My love to you & yours & you are welcome any time.

G.E.L.

Once again, I was left unmoved. Her assumption that Gweno was safe from 'wagging tongues' or that she required protection from them puzzled me, as did the distance she implied existed between them. At our meeting, they treated each other with elaborate respect of a formal rather than affectionate kind. When Gwladys writes about 'family', she evidently does not include Gweno in it: this is the 'family''s trouble and the family will have to save her from it. It is also odd she should want to question Freda's veracity. The two had met after the war and Freda had recently copied out for her all Alun's references to her in his letters.

Gwladys's contention that 'The Way Back' is the only poem that could benefit from knowledge of her was another of her untruths, as was her contention that he would have returned to 'normal civilised living' after the war. As 'From a Play' makes clear, his destiny was determined not by Gweno's 'calm white face' but the 'stony glitter' of the eyes of the 'blond great-breasted goddess of pre-history', the goddess in her malign guise, who pronounces his fate thus:

> *And no returning.*

True, in his letters he sometimes held out the prospect of returning from India: 'When I come home I shall always tackle my writing through Welsh life and ways of thoughts' or: 'I regret my lack of Welsh very deeply: I really will learn it when I come home again'. These remarks, however, were designed for his parents' consumption. It appears that he knew there would be '*no returning*', and so, I think, did Gwladys, for the one subject she avoided mentioning at our meeting was his death. She described it thus in her memoir:

> The intelligence corps to which Alun belonged was sent out on detachment to probe in all directions. Alun and his batman, Tudor, made a very efficient working unit and they were given a lonely and dangerous assignment for the next day's duty. Tudor has told me that he was apprehensive, but Alun was excited and elated at the prospect. They were up before dawn and, while Tudor was preparing breakfast, Alun – with revolver at the ready because of the imminence of the enemy – walked towards a near-by nullah [or gully]. In the half-light he must have stepped over the edge and fallen into the depth below, his revolver going off as he fell. Tudor heard the shot and, sensing danger, ran in that direction. Alun was lying on a ledge down the side of the nullah and, as Tudor reached him, murmured 'Gweno' and sank into unconsciousness. Tudor ran for help, and Alun was taken to a field-station nearby: but the wound was mortal. The faithful Tudor stayed beside him till, with his last departing breath, Alun 'snatched at the apple-bough' and joined the Immortals.

The last image in this romantic account was borrowed from Robert Graves, who, in his reply to her letter of thanks for his introduction to *Ha! Ha! Among the Trumpets*, wrote:

> About Alun: he is now among the Immortals. Do you ever feel that Shakespeare is *dead* in the sense that George V (say) is? Like the Welsh poet of the 15th century, when The Prince of the Air carried him off, he snatched at the apple-bough – i.e. poetic immortality – and so escaped.

Seven months after his death, Gwladys wrote 'Such Aching':

> When you cried in your cot,
> Afraid of the dark loneliness,
> I took your tiny hand in mine
> And blessed sleep returned.
>
> This was your Talisman
> Through all your early years.
> Your hand in mine
> Resolved your childish fears.
>
> And then you grew
> So gently kind,
> So understanding and informed
> That I had learned
> To lean on you
> Not questioning your word.
>
> What fun we had!
> How much we laughed
> Those days!
> For what pleased one
> Pleased both,
> Being alike in ways.
>
> And when with prescience
> You felt
> The shiver of impending doom,
> Its passing tremor
> Rarely touched
> Our happiness with gloom.
>
> I am now the small child

> Crying in the dark.
> If only you might take
> My groping hand,
> I should not ache
> Nor feel so desolate.

She posted this to Gwyn Jones, who was then just re-starting *The Welsh Review* after the war. (In 1940, she had sent him another poem revised by Alun using only one rhyme.) She said her son's death was 'in very truth a limb torn from the living':

> I can't bear to think of your first issue coming out without a contribution from Alun. So just to keep the family flag flying I am offering this if it comes anywhere near your standard.

In the poem, she speaks not only *for* Alun but *as* Alun (something repeated by Gweno in *Letters to My Wife*).

'To My Sons (Overseas)' reads:

> Freed by the joyous pain of birth
> From your soft vigil in my womb,
> You, to whom I owe so much,
> Have taught me all I know of worth.
>
> And by the love that you owe me,
> I beg you, come to me again,
> Here, on this living breath Earth,
> I dare not say 'Thy Will be done'.

The 'sons' addressed might be forgiven for understanding it refers to one of them in particular.

In 1948, Gwladys told John Petts (then busy preparing his illustrations for *In the Green Tree*) that Alun's death had left her 'numb and wooden':

> Although I do all that is required of me as far as this life is concerned, and satisfactorily, I think, it is rather as an observer than a participant in life – as though a glass screen had come down between me and it. It's the protective tissue which shields my mortal wound.

Lewis himself employed this image to describe his depressions. She urged Petts to capture 'the gay nonchalance' that had made them all 'love him to the point of adoration':

> I know he had his dark moments but they were slight
> shadows compared with the bright happy patches.

In her reply to Leslie Sykes's letter of condolence, however, she
struck a different note:

> a terrible thing has happened to our family and we shall never
> cease to mourn for Alun. He was exceptional as a son and
> with me he had a very special and close relationship that had
> always existed from his earliest days. I feel as though a limb
> had been torn from my living soul. Huw says 'Alun was
> more than a brother to me, he was a way of life.' And I'm
> sure that is how we all feel about him. Our memories of him
> are unclouded and I think now that it had to be so, for we
> were to enjoy his company for such a short while. I don't
> know but sometimes I feel sure Alun knew he wasn't coming
> back and I think I felt it too. Ever since he went abroad, there
> always seems to have been the pointing finger and then the
> inevitable accident.

She struck the same note of foreboding in a letter to Freda in 1944:

> I am so perplexed about so many things that seem to have
> stirred you too, that I wish I could talk to you. Sometimes I
> think that both he and I had some foreknowledge. I don't
> know and I am very troubled.

Gwladys appears to hint at more than she can say here, and Graves's
'torn limb' image suggests why, for no-one survives dismemberment.
She had done what she could to suppress her fears for the sake of her
daughter-in-law, who, as she told Freda, was 'the most precious thing
he has left us', but they had never gone away.

## III

Gwladys was the oldest of seven children. Her father, Melchizedec
Evans, was a preacher. (The Biblical Melchizedec was the priest or
king who blessed Abraham and offered him bread and wine). After
his mother's death, he was rescued from the furnaces of the copper

works at Cwmavon (Port Talbot), where he worked with his father, and raised by relatives in the Rhondda. Having gone down the pit for a short time, he then enrolled in Theological College in Carmarthen and was ordained in the Congregational faith in 1879. Though Welsh-speaking, his entire ministry was spent in English-speaking churches.

In 1894, Melchizedec and his wife, Bridget, left Wales for Bradford. She died there of pneumonia during her eighth pregnancy in the very week Gwladys was to sit her matriculation exams. She was left to raise her younger brothers and sisters (including a baby and a difficult child) and to manage a large household on a minister's salary. The shepherding instinct was forced on her early.

In 1903, Melchizedec returned to Wales after he decided to become a Unitarian. In her *Poetry Wales* article, Mair Fenn recalled how he,

> always imperturbable, would sit in his study reading occult books and doing yogi exercises. As might be expected, Yoga and Calvin were not easily reconcilable and, despite his seven children, Melchizedec resigned his living. For a time he travelled from door to door with education books – until finally he found a home with the Unitarians where his inner and outer Gods were reconciled.

Melchizedek himself left the following account of the 'fights and sleepless nights' he endured before he could sever the connection with the denomination of his youth:

> It was a painful work, but the freedom one has gained in the pulpit and elsewhere is a valuable compensation for the loss of old associations and old friends. The way from 'ortho-doxy' to the broader field, where you are able to seek what is true and not what is 'safe' is a very painful one, but the freedom of soul that comes when the battle is won is very refreshing, and one is glad there is one body of Christians which is willing to accept men who seek truth and not doctri-nal 'safety'.

In 1911, he left the Highland Place Church, Aberdare, for the Bradford area and died in 1924 in New Mill.

Gwladys shared her father's interest in spiritual matters. As a girl, she liked raiding the top shelves of his library for books which, unknown to his parishioners, he studied – books by Annie Besant, Madame Blavatsky and the like. For a while, she thought of becoming a Quaker before deciding she was agnostic. Her spiritual bent was passed to Mair, with her Transcendental Meditation, and Alun, who viewed life as a quest. Travelling to India, he said, represented

> a journey I have long wished to make, but never had the time
> or money or understanding either to envisage or plan. A
> journey through lands whose existence I did not know but
> whose location I had been ignorant of till then. The map of
> the spirit's geography.

Even before India, he believed that life was 'a perpetual search for new experience and wider circles of consciousness'. In early 1943, he was 'deliberately exploring the spirit world', a 'soul world, space, life, eternity' where 'there are no landmarks, signposts, familiar faces or ideas, nothing solid'.

Tom Lewis was made of solider stuff. His father, Job Lewis, left Efail Wen, in the parish of Cilymaenllwyd, Pembrokeshire, in 1880 for Shepherd's Colliery in Cwmaman. According to Mair, he was

> a Bible-black, God-fearing man who never kissed his
> children, whose house on Sundays was a morgue and who
> persuaded mother, against her judgment but to save family
> irritation, to have us all sign the pledge when we were four
> years old....

Alun remembered him as a patriarch, a collier and deacon who wrote poems, a fact revealed only on his deathbed. One such, 'The girl that I once met', was an elegy in Welsh to his wife, Mari, who died, aged 75, in 1920.

Tom, the youngest of six children, graduated from Bangor Technical College and taught at the Glynhafod Council School, Cwmaman. A tall, stern-looking man, he was quiet and gentle. In a B.B.C. interview, Mair recalled:

> Mother was a revolutionary and Daddy was a sort of village
> lad, but they complemented one another perfectly.

Years before, Alun told Freda:

> ... it isn't that she ever wanted to know or direct or interrupt

but perhaps somehow she herself is a little de trop, she extends too much in the family for there not to be a little friction when we're all together over years… Daddy is the rock of love, she's the wind about it. He would grieve but not break. She would be desperate. He's been very good to us always, always, but sometimes he was too stolid for mother. I knew all that since very early, long before I knew anything about sex.

He told Gweno he was descended from 'the trace-kicking Lewis or Evans' families but there was evidently more trace-kicking in the one than in the other.

'Thoughts on the Eve of a Great Battle' (revised as 'Prelude and Fugue') opens:

> My grandfather ploughed his master's land;
> My father had the ancestral peace of mind,
> My mother had the dance in her,
> The deep despair and the unbounded hope;
> Passionate loyalty betrayed her ways
> And such complexity tied down her tongue
> That she kept silent long, yet not too long.
> Yet when at last she spoke we sat and listened
> And wisdom flowed on us within the quiet that followed.
> Both she and I have had the dream of darkness,
> Of darkness beating and beating implacably into the brain
> Where we cowered and sweated in weakness, knowing the
>             poor
> And the poverty of others that made us weak and rage….

In the revised version, the last two lines read:

> … the brain
> Of the preacher unheeded and pitiful on the hillside,
> And the poor no different for all his anguish.

The 'preacher' is Melchizedec, whose fine words do so little for the poor. Tom Lewis is placid, in the manner of rural folk, while Gwladys experiences despair and joy. Her 'silence' suggests that she keeps such knowledge from all but her eldest son who, like her, suffers the 'darkness beating and beating implacably into the brain'.

> My brother wanted to play Rugger for Wales.

> He took nothing seriously, and least himself
> He twisted to his own ways, both women and bad luck.
> My sister had always desired to be herself
> As a young foal or a lonely seagull
> When the wind is wild on the sea pastures –
> And she also dreamed of the darkness.

Evidently, Alun felt closest to Mair. Huw, full of fun, was always ready for a dare (as he himself had been as a schoolboy), 'the little dashing quicksilver bugger that he is'. Glyn is notable by his absence.

Tom wanted the children to attend the family chapel, Moriahaman Congregational, if only to learn some Welsh, but Gwladys would have none of it. In those days, chapel could be repressive and she wanted them to be free to roam the mountains on a Sunday morning rather than sit in stuffy vestries. As for Welsh, that was unlikely to advance their careers and, in any case, counted less than the plight of the miners, whose cause she supported with her Women's Social Club. In *Alun Lewis My Son*, she wrote:

> The school-children needed boots and shoes and free meals for which my husband was responsible, while in the Women's Club we ran 'make-do and mend' groups, dress-making classes, singing groups, gymnastic meetings and folk-dancing: anything that would help constructively and any form of diversion that would keep up morale and help to revive drooping spirits. Alun was deeply concerned when he saw how his old school-mates were frustrated and wasted, and he burned with indignation as he saw a sturdy village community gradually disintegrate under the pressure of unemployment. Many of the husbands of my club-members were out of work for ten years – and some even longer. The young and enterprising sought refuge in the workshops of the Midlands, Slough and London, and the village was the poorer for their going.

Years later, I was surprised by the force of exception Rhiannon Davies, one of her nieces, took to Gwladys. A woman of strong convictions, she did not count the cost of isolating her family thus. Like the other mining villages, Cwmaman's monoculture was based on a single industry and the ties it bred were exceptionally strong, particularly in times of crisis – and when was it not crisis time in the valleys? Dai Smith has written of Lewis:

... he lived in a place, and at a time, when identification and
involvement with others were seen as vital to art, politics,
personal morality, even psychological health. He was denied
those things in any straightforward way; to his credit he
sought them out.

It is easy to appreciate Rhiannon's objections when one considers
her parents – her mother, Gwen, was a midwife, her father, Edward,
a collier (from the age of 9, as a fireman rather than a hewer of coal).
Alun called him 'my Orphean uncle'; in 'Bequest', he recalls him
'trudging coal-black from the pit/ With such transcendent music in
his head/ I heard the stars all singing/ The night that he lay dead'.
Edward (or 'Ned'), the second son of Job and Mari, wanted to be a
musician but his father thought this was beneath any man, so he went
down the pit instead though he studied music theory in the family's
front room. Later, he attended lessons in Ferndale and Swansea. The
Lewises' nursery maid, Sarah Jane Evans, told me how disappointed
he had been to discover that his wife's fingers were too small to play
the violin, so he tied iron weights to them and hung them out of the
window in a vain attempt to lengthen them.

From 1908, Ned conducted the Cwmaman Choral Society in
Elgar, Bach, Rossini and Handel; in 1932, it was Brahms's *A German
Requiem* and Ralph Vaughan Williams's *Toward the Unknown
Region*, with the composer present in Cwmaman Hall as guest
conductor. In 1935, at the age of 58, he was appointed full-time
music tutor for the National Council for Social Service and in the
same year organised the first Male Voice Festival for the
unemployed. He was also responsible for creating 'listening groups'
in Hirwaun, Trecynon, Gadlys, Aberdare, Cwmbach, Aberaman,
Cwmaman and Abercwmboi.

Ned was, *par excellence*, the cultured collier and his benevolence
started at home. He helped his older brother, Timothy (later Reader
in Philology and Palaeography at University College, Aberystwyth),
with his studies, as he did Daniel and Tom. (Daniel, a minister, died
young). According to Rhiannon, he bought Tom's house at 61
Brynhyfryd, it being his ambition to buy a house for each of his five
daughters, though some believe it unlikely he could do so on a
miner's salary. When Tom became director of education for Aberdare
in February 1938, it was Edward who bought 7 Elm Grove for him.

Compared to Ned, Gwladys must have appeared odd. Dressed in
her white ankle socks and with a fillet band in her hair, she could

chat as easily as a schoolgirl. Still, the Lewises were the nobility of the valley. In a place where doors remained open, you did not just drop in to see her. Years later, she told John Lehmann she would have liked to become a writer and had won several prizes for her reviews. In 1932, her one-act play, *Pleasant Place* (an ironic reference to the south Wales mining villages) won first prize in a competition sponsored by the South Wales Council of Social Service. It is written in the vernacular, though as by an author who does not use it herself. Gwladys remained punctilious in speech and was called 'Mother' by the children, not 'Mam', while Tom was 'Daddy', even to her.

The heroine of *Pleasant Place*, Mari, understands why poor rates of pay, unemployment and sickness should have driven people to Red Revolution but she has faith in the younger generation – men like her son, Alun. 'Alun?' a visitor asks. 'What a pretty name! You have such musical names in Welsh. How do you spell it?' Mari replies:

> A – l – u – n, but 'u' in Welsh is like 'I' in English. [Gwladys pronounced the name nearer 'Aleen' than 'Alin', never 'Aluhn'.] I always said that if we had a boy, he should be Alun, and he is our eldest son.

One of Lewis's girlfriends, Megan Lloyd-Jones, believed the play was embarrassing to him though he admired its author.

> His relationship with women must have been affected by his mother who, in my opinion, was a silly, sentimental woman. She had an unfortunate influence upon him.

She believed Gwladys fed his morbidity and encouraged the element of hyperbole in his work, which she mistook for fine writing.

The clash between Gwladys and Tom's temperaments was no less important.

> Mother seems very busy and happy – all this evacuee work is like wine to her – helping people, fitting them up, doing something human, useful - she gets much more delight out of it than Daddy, for she's much more of a social reformer than he. He's naturally inclined to the domestic and the quiet, the farm gate and the fireside; and don't bother others. I've got a bit of both in me...

Tom was diffident, though with a touch of dourness about him; you did not cross him easily. Alun felt he treated him like 'an unbalanced little enthusiast' and wanted him to settle down; writing seemed an odd way of doing it. Years later, he wrote:

> mother's quiet support was everything I needed, & daddy's inarticulateness was like a shadow all over me so that I avoided him.

To Dick Mills, he referred to Tom as 'my very pragmatic and tanta-lisingly sober father'.

In 1938, Tom was honoured for 18 years' service as local secre-tary of the National Union of Teachers; later that year, he became Director of Education for Aberdare and President of the Glamorgan County Teachers' Association. Alun told Christopher Cheney:

> Mother's full of ideas for getting shoes and milk and things for the slum schools and Daddy says he's not going to have any Assistant Directors; but she's insuppressible.

At the time, he himself was mired in a mass of poems, stories and novels that just would not come right. Despite his first-class degree, he failed to get a teaching post but, at the end of 1939, a temporary position became vacant at the Lewis School, Pengam, which later became permanent. Tom said he had begun to live at last, his mother that he was earning a living.

## IV

The present-day visitor to Cwmaman will find rows of red-brick houses crammed into a narrow valley towered over by rough-hewn mountains. The streets are named after the English poets – Spenser, Milton, Byron and so on. In Lewis's time, five collieries worked there day and night. The tips burned with slag and there was always a risk of spontaneous combustion in the air. All the pits have since vanished.

Shortly after the war the Lewises rented an end-of-terrace property at 61 Brynhyfryd, Glynhafod, at the western edge of the village, where the valley broadens out. There were whinberries in profusion on the Graig, from where one could enjoy panoramic views over to the Bristol Channel. Opposite the house lay Brown's colliery.

The mechanical screens grading coal into the waiting trucks sent up a tremendous rattle while dust clouds filled the air. Beside ran the Nant Aman Fach down from Weekes' farm, the local dairy, following a hidden spur of the valley. The children tickled trout on the slimy bellies of the stones and swam in that part of the river that had been converted into a concrete bathing pool (the Cwmaman Lido). When the mines fell idle, they slid down the steel hawsers that used to tip coal into waiting trucks. The scene is evoked memorably in 'The Housekeeper':

> The back garden was about four yards wide, and as the house was built against the side of the hill, the garden sloped up steeply to the shed at the top. It was fenced off from the gardens of the next door houses by a hotch-potch barrier of old zinc sheeting, rusted iron bedsteads, and tin advertisements of Colman's Mustard and Brooke Bond's Tea. There was no door to the shed, and the tarred felting which covered the thin wooden front hung over in flapping folds, like the crippled wing of a black vulture. The garden itself was a patch of rubble and ash, holding nothing but a few rows of rotting beansticks, a line of seed cabbage with knobbly whitening stems, a couple of purple pickling cabbage, and three currant bushes. Next door up had a line of washing out – long workman's pants where the darning had given way, a pair of patched sheets, three tiny frayed vests – flapping and beating in the gusty weather.

The passage makes poetry out of arithmetic: the garden is four yards wide, there is one line of cabbage seed, two purple cabbages, a pair of sheets, three currant bushes and three vests. Myfanwy, the housekeeper, is a partial portrait of Gwladys. She makes do with her unemployed miner husband, his quarrelsome mother and two boys (the younger of whom, Jackie, she calls her 'little husband'). She despairs of their prospects and longs to escape the valleys herself.

By the mid-Thirties, most of Cwmaman was out of work. The men stood before empty shops in the deserted streets wearing their worn-out navy suits and collarless shirts. In 'The Miner's Son', written at the end of August 1937, Meirion Edwards rails against the Employment Exchange for obliging his sister to work as a cinema usherette from 3 p.m. until 11 p.m. for 15 shillings a week, twelve deducted from her father's unemployment allowance. He thinks of the

rickety kids shivering on their way home from school, and
their fathers scratching like rats for coal among the slag
heaps. It might improve things if a few Cabinet ministers had
to find their own warmth like that.... I'd rather have blood
and war and revolt rather than this callous indifference. And
then his savageness went out, for violence revolted his body
and reason.

Life for the Lewises was less pressing. Glyn estimated his father's
earnings (including night classes) at £200 a year, which was four
times a miner's wage. They enjoyed annual holidays – an unheard-
of luxury save for railway employees – and hired a nursery maid,
though the maid in question, Sarah Jane Evans, told me this was not
unusual. From 1925, they rented a small mill cottage in Penbryn, on
the Cardiganshire coast, a stone's throw from the sandy beach
following a steep wooded cwm, great cliffs towering over the dunes.
A mile south lay Tresaith, with its small waterfall and sand-and-
shingle beach, to the north Llangranog with its headland. Such was
their refuge from the surplus of the human in Cwmaman and they
had the place virtually to themselves. Gwladys called it their 'lovely
little green hiding place on the west coast of Wales', somewhere
where they

played and laughed, swam, read and lazed to our heart's
content, and when, in looking back, the sun seems always to
have been shining, the sky and sea blue and the land
shimmering gold.... The wild, unspoilt beauty had a lasting
effect on Alun who was so responsive to its call that, for the
rest of his life until war called him, he had to return for
refreshment and inspiration to his beloved Penbryn. The rural
life around them gave the children an insight to a new world.

'Private Jones' breathes its atmosphere. In a letter to his parents in
February 1942, Lewis called it 'my new Penbryn story of a soljer
boy'. Shenkin, a kind-hearted Cardi (Cardigan man) from Penyrheol,
exchanges life as a parish trapper for the army. Everyone conde-
scends to him but he survives with his innocence intact. Lewis liked
playing Shenkin in camp concerts. The story radiates comic warmth
and the atmosphere of long summers in the country at a time when
lovingkindness was at a premium.

This same quality distinguishes 'On Embarkation', which records
his visit to Llangranog with Gweno in 1942. The poem signals the

emergence of a poet of considerable power and sensitivity:

> Just here you leave this Cardiganshire lane,
> Here by these milk churns and this telegraph pole,
> Latch up the gate and cut across the fields.
> Some things you see in detail, those you need;
> Squirting your face across the reaping meadow,
> The strange machine-shaped scarab beetle
> His scalloped legs clung bandy to a stalk,
> The Jews'-harp bee with saddlebags of gold,
> The wheat as thin as hair on flinty slopes,
> The harsh hewn faces of the farming folks,
> Opinion humming like a nest of wasps,
> The dark-clothed brethren at the chapel gates;
> And further on the mortgaged crumbling farm
> Where Shonni Rhys, that rough backsliding man
> Has found the sheep again within the corn
> And fills the evening with his sour oaths;
> The curse of failure's in his shambling gait.

Lewis writes no longer as one of *y gweithfeydd* (i.e. from the southern heartlands) but as a 'Cardi'.

In 1926, success in his 11 Plus exam gained him a scholarship to Cowbridge Grammar School, the nearest thing to a public school in Glamorgan. Founded in 1608-9, the school nestled in a small Georgian town where ladies wore bonnets and farmers rode to market on horse or pony and trap. The coincidence of Lewis's going there and the General Strike is notable. Seventeen years later, Lieutenant Anthony Weston in 'Ward "0" 3 b' reflects:

> I used to watch the wheel of the pit spin round year after year, after school and Saturdays and Sundays; and then from 1926 on I watched it not turning round at all, and I can't ever get that wheel out of my mind. It still spins and idles, and there's money and nystagmus coming into the house or no work and worse than nystagmus. I just missed the wheel sucking me down the shaft. I got a scholarship to the county school. I don't know when I started rebelling. Against that wheel in my head.

The social dislocation mirrors the private one – indeed, may have caused it.

Mair Lewis recalls the preparations made against his departure:

> Mother had to get a new trunk and this, that and the other.
> And it was packed with three pairs of socks and five shirts –
> I mean, the whole family had only five shirts between them,
> you know – and all these wonderful things were going into
> his trunk. And Alun was excited, I mean we were all getting
> excited as we watched it happening and we think he is going
> to heaven or somewhere.

The note of wry resentment in her account suggests why she should have been 'on edge' with her mother until she, too, left for College.

Lewis's time at Cowbridge was unhappy. At one point, he was threatened with expulsion when caught out of bounds with a girl but the crisis blew over. Being at the school induced a sense of social guilt in him, though he was not above sporting the school blazer in Cwmaman in the holidays. It was one thing not having to rise at five in the morning and walk two and a half miles to the coalface for seven hours, six days a week, fifty weeks a year for 19/- to 30/- a week, quite another to attend a lantern lecture explaining how coal is extracted, pit roofs kept up and air circulated.

There was a more personal edge to his suffering:

> At the door of the Headmaster's study mother was torn from
> me. I can remember the hurt of it. Then I was immediately
> led through the dining hall… and with a click of the latch
> thrust into the schoolroom…. I felt utterly, utterly betrayed.

His childhood security had vanished, never to return. Years later, he wrote in whimsical vein to Freda:

> Now you must bundle me off before school, in good time
> you know, woollen muffler, stockings pulled up over pink
> knees if there are hailstones, little Dai-cap down over untidy
> cow's lick hair – that's how mother used to send me off - &
> when I was teaching in Pengam [this when he was 24] she'd
> be just the same, in the kitchen in her dressing gown making
> hot toast and tea & cutting sandwiches for my attaché case
> with all the textbooks or boys' essays marked in blue lead &
> a book of poems for the train, dark winter mornings when
> the dead ashes in the grate are so frozen-looking.

The heroine of *Pleasant Place* recalls how her 'Alun' has won certificates and prizes on Speech Day, like Lewis, when one of his stories was commended:

> And when I saw him on the platform and heard the boys clap,
> it all came over me how poor we were and how we could let
> him go and things like that, and the tears just rolled down
> my cheeks till I couldn't see at all for the mist in my eyes...
> Well then, I said to myself: 'Here Mari Jones, stop being a
> fool. Here's one poor boy been and done it, and why
> shouldn't another?' So I dried my eyes and made up my mind
> that, God helping me, Alun should go on.

That, too, is what Myfanwy wishes for Jackie in 'The Housekeeper',
playing Gertrude Morel to his Paul.

> There must be some way of getting away. An easier way than
> the one facing Jackie – years of study and borrowing and
> doing without, poor kid. If they could tear themselves loose,
> rip the old cloth, get away from the rut of pig sties and idle
> collieries and dreary monotonous days. What sort of life was
> this? House work, gossiping over the garden wall, child-
> bearing, patching and darning, making ends meet, putting a
> little aside to get the children's shoes tapped before the
> winter, looking bleakly ahead, narrowly, timidly. Ever since
> the pit closed down it had gone on changelessly, a gradual
> decline which the people faced with the self-defensive cheer-
> fulness of consumptives.

Gwladys Lewis regretted sending Alun to Cowbridge, however
beneficial she thought it would be:

> 'Obey without reasoning' was the order of the day. This irked
> Alun's independent spirit which we had fostered through the
> years and he was never happy there. He enjoyed the compan-
> ionship of the boys but he loathed the subjugation of the spirit.

When the time came for him to go to Aberystwyth, he read History:

> Why History when English was the obvious choice? I am
> afraid I was largely responsible for that. I had a hunch that
> the edge of Alun's creative gift would be blunted if he
> dragged his precious English through the stresses and strains
> of competitive examination work....the discipline of collect-
> ing, collating, discarding historical facts and putting them
> down in terse, precise terms was good for him temperamen-
> tally, and for his prose which was lacking control and too
> exuberant just then.

That is not an unreasonable consideration though, by an irony that will be appreciated by every parent who has offered advice to their children, the very discipline she wished for him precipitated his first depression.

When Lewis moved to Manchester, his digs lay in a slum area near the University, since demolished. He said they were 'enough to pucker a major prophet's brow', an excellent example of south Walian wit.

> I used to think every day how simple it is to die. A train passing, a lorry rumbling outside, a train on a platform – so easy. Death was a comforting dark thought in me.

He was so crazy with 'death-love' that he deterred even those who wanted to help him: 'I didn't live in any positive way and my brain was all barbed wire'. Better social work or fighting in Spain than academic study.

> I got to loathe it, I got so lost in it and lost to my own age, my own friends. I had no politics, no poems, nothing except a vast impossible mass of research.

From Aberdare, he wrote to Christopher Cheney:

> I do nothing but look at it all. If I could get stuck into it like Mother, and pother about Unemployment Clubs and get little shillings from all sorts of people for the fathering of skinny little child-legs and expectant mothers – but I'm miles away from them all. They wouldn't have me hanging around and I'm afraid I feel no overpowering call to hang around.

Years later, he recalled

> the long novels & plays I've written and thrown away, the blind persistence & humility of hammering at my typewriter in my mother's house [an interesting locution] while she dusted and cooked, & the utter lack of disappointment when I realised that 300 pages of typescript were no good.

In his more hopeful moods, he tried to be what his mother wanted him to be and in his Longmoor journal even interprets his presence in the army as the pursuit of her ideals:

> When I was a little boy I used to run down the village to the grocer's shop after morning school to get mother a tin of corned beef for dinner. Now I am running down into the world to get her those things which she wanted her children to inherit when she brought them first into the world, but which, for a variety of reasons, have been made more difficult to obtain than they need be.

There sounds the loyal son and democrat.

Matters reached crisis point at Easter 1937, as Gwladys recalled:

> I suggested he should count his blessings, and see how far they outnumbered his misfortunes. Then we drifted to a discussion of life in general till the small hours of the morning. He came down to breakfast looking a different boy, and as he left the table he bent over and whispered: 'Thank God you talked to me last night'. He was usually very gay company, and it was such fun living with him; but from time to time these black moods descended upon him when all seemed lost, and he reviled himself.

Later that summer, she had to rock him in her arms till he stopped crying. He said he was worthless, had achieved nothing, felt barren, cut off: 'I'm no good, mother, no good at all'. Alarmed, she rounded on him. Yet how recover when dependency on his mother was part of his condition?

In an unpublished play, 'The Tunnel', the hero is 'dried up'. Only occasionally – as on the previous day – does he experience moments of vision, when nothing stands between him and his ambition:

> I was right up the top of the river – you know – where the valley is nothing more than a gorge in the mountains – and the grass swaying and glancing with the sun, and the river singing, and the silver birch that grows like an angel undressing

Perhaps this was when he wrote 'The Poet', hurrying back through the birches to read it to the woman who had inspired it.

Another unpublished work, 'The Miner's Son', offers this self-portrait:

> Dark like his race, but not sallow, brown wavy hair and pale cheeks hollowing beneath high cheekbones, full-lipped mouth falling in a bitter slant at one corner.

An Aberystwyth friend describes him thus:

> There was about Alun, the student, a certain sensitivity, an
> air of languid gentleness, even when tearing up and down the
> playing fields. Some of us rugby team roughnecks thought
> there was something slightly sissy for men to play the girls'
> game, hockey, even when they were as good and lethal at it
> as Alun proved to be. Alun was no mean all round athlete.
> Before the end of the decade, some of those gentler souls,
> Alun among them, once in uniform out-toughed many of the
> he-men – but who knows at what cost to their inner nature.

Megan Lloyd-Jones recalled:

> One lazy eye, one foot turning in, a slow walk and a drawling
> voice, but very energetic when playing games. A lop-sided
> smile. Very observant – not only heard but always *saw*
> cuckoos, even drab female ones – spotted water rats & did
> not find their bottoms offensive.
> Wore plus-fours.
> Not at all embarrassed as I was in such lordly establishments
> as Brown's of Chester where we had to buy stockings to
> replace the ones I had ruined falling into the Dee. He *never*
> fell, always sure-footed crossing mountain streams or climb-
> ing rocks. He did everything well.

His mother offered this more romantic portrait:

> Alun in the easy artistic, slightly Bohemian, style he
> observed in civilian dress – grey blue worsted slacks: more
> blue than grey; grey blue sports coat, more grey than blue; a
> deep blue soft shirt with turn-down collar and a bright red
> tie. And above all, his radiant laughing face and fine head
> with its wavy hair. Do you remember the Portrait of a Young
> Man by Van Gogh?... it breathed the very spirit of Alun as
> we knew and loved and laughed with him.

When he and Gweno became engaged in 1940, he told her his
mother was

> full of advice about doing the right thing – as soon as my
> wages come I *must* buy you a nice ring, and get it announced
> in the Western Mail; or at least I *must* ask you if you'd like
> it to be announced, in case you do. And several other words

of experience. To which I reply as you did – do I need any
telling about her? The only way I can hurt her no amount of
motherly advice could prevent.

Gweno did not want an engagement ring, not being that 'sort of girl',
so he bought her a piano instead. At Gwladys's insistence, he also
purchased her an emerald ring, which she mislaid a few years later.

# Part Five
## *Alun and Gweno*

### I

After visiting Gwladys Lewis with me in October 1975, Gweno sent me a cache of Alun's letters from just before Coonoor till his death seven months later, 59 in all, i.e. written at the rate of more than one a week. Also included were his Karachi notebook, two unpublished poems ('The Transmigration of Love' and 'Nothing about the Dead'), a letter to Dick Mills and drafts of 'The Orange Grove' and 'the Indian love poems'. She added: 'In a way, it's a pity, some more prose might have been more important'.

'The Transmigration of Love' recounts Alun and Freda's stay in Bombay:

> There was the sea moving against the seawall along a
>     curving league
> And the pleasure parks where time is killed by playboys
>     and the more
> Fresh-air sort of whores,
> And two loving each other, linked in the spying crowd,
> Their bodies radiating and fulfilling each other from a window
> To which a chokra child brought a lotus every day.
>
> When the world entered the minds of these lovers
> It more nearly attained its peaceful potential,
> And ugliness achieved its long-refused transcendence
> Over suffering as authentic as the strata of mountains.
>
> Naked within their love in a bed in a window
> They made the end an image of their love.
> And the end was death,
> Not for them only, but all the time for someone
> In a bomb or bullet, malaria, cholera, sunstroke;

And the end for these two lovers began away back in
    the beginning,
In the perception of life perhaps of a child of seven
Seeing a baby born or a new kind of grasshopper,
And growing through the loneliness of youth,
The uniqueness that is like a virginity in youth,
Into a wilder, deeper, more general prevision –

Envisaging a slim spaced forest, a gladed darkness
Fretted with fireflies and the touch
Of long cool grasses each on each,
And through the scrub the instinctive trails and spoors,
The opaque yielding awareness of animals,
Wild beasts, smooth and evasive, tawny-eyed complete
    creatures –

And in that deep familiar darkness the loving elements
    conjoined
In the endlessly desired mutation of decay and generation.

The poem associates 'decay' with death, ugliness, suffering and disease, and 'generation' with lovers, children and the meeting of beasts in a forest clearing. At key moments, though, the two merge, as when the lovers, having made 'an image of their love' their end, discover their peace is part of a universal process they have only briefly interrupted. Their rendezvous in the 'glade' of a hotel bedroom-window contains destructive as well as creative forces and cannot protect them from suffering that is 'as authentic as the strata of mountains'.

Gweno wrote:

> Now, of course, I can see the connection between Transmigration & Alun's description – in passing – of the small but expensive boarding house which he spent a leave in Bombay after leaving Karachi.
>
> Of course the poems – and then after his death the arrival of the journal & the typescripts amongst his effects made me very uneasy, but I was completely beguiled by his letters.
>
> I feel very sad & depressed by it all, but I am deeply grateful to you, nevertheless.
>
> Yours sincerely,
> Gweno.

Her letter touched – still touches – me. There was something fine about Gweno, a strictness of temper that allowed her to meet her difficulties without complaining, a practicality reinforced by a temperamental inclination towards patience. Even in love, she was chary, hedging emotion with caution and allowing her shrewdness free play. Proof against extremes, she avoided unnecessary heart-break. At the same time, no rapport sprang up between us. We met only infrequently and her letters to me were brief and to the point. After all, I was the messenger who bore ill-tidings. Besides, she was not the confiding sort, being too cautious and self-reliant, too proud and hurt. She kept herself to herself, never happier than when in the company of family and friends.

As Mair Fenn noted, the passage of the years had allowed her to regain her composure so that, when we met, she was prepared against further shock. She knew she could never follow Alun into the realm of poetry and did not try; she would, she said, much rather have washed Brahms's socks than marry a literary man, music being the purer art. The Alun she knew was companion, suitor, democrat, soldier – the poet was what came with the rest of him. He may have puzzled her but brought something fresh to her life. On one occasion, when I had asked her about his reading habits, she replied: 'I have no further material to offer about Alun Lewis's reading enthusiasms or antipathies'. Her reply was honest if incurious. Nor was she any more forthcoming about the poems she had decided to exclude from *Ha! Ha! Among the Trumpets* on the grounds that they were too personal.

Freda once wrote:

> Is it not interesting that other poets have loved first a 'safe', often older, woman before falling romantically and desper-ately in love with their muse-love? Keats had the curious affair with Isabella Jones, older than he, before Fanny Brawn possessed his imagination; Rupert Brooke was anxiously in love with Ka Cox until he suddenly lost it and fell romanti-cally in love with Kathleen Nesbitt. It is as though a poet is compelled towards love though he does not recognise that it is only, to use the meditators' jargon, the 'mantra' around which his creative imagination plays, and a 'safe' love, suggesting a mother still protectively at hand, liberates the poetry in him without, his unknowing self feels, the demands and exactions of a wilder love. Until he finds his true muse-love. Or is this nonsense?

Gweno offered a 'safe' love outside poetry while still encouraging it.

> Gweno nourished him when he was in his dark 'moods' and he needed this – and was grateful to her. When he wrote of her overwhelming love and the feeling of wonder it induced in him he added: 'It also frightens me'. I think this was much to do with his impotence. He describes her thus: 'She's very deep, uncannily natural in all she sees, only she doesn't trust life and won't go far enough because of that caution she has, and that unwillingness. She's got far fewer delusions than me, and fewer dreams. The dreams and loyalties she does have possess her entirely. They're the simplest and most personal ones imaginable. She also has some ultimate reality that dwarfs her'.

Perhaps this 'ultimate reality' urged caution in her from the start. When visiting Alun in Hengoed in 1940, where he had taken digs during the week while teaching at Pengam, he

> … remembered how you refused to believe, and how once on Hengoed station, you said it was all meaningless, and how personally hurt I was, that you wouldn't believe, but seemed to question my sincerity, and the sincerity of love. I wondered why you were so unwilling to believe, and why you never speak of those things, but keep silent, silent: and how little of you I know: and, horrible doubt, whether you thought that the inexplicable deaths of me, when I felt nothing, responded to nothing, valued nothing – whether you thought 'he is inconstant, unreal, deluding himself with false affirmations which he regrets sooner or later and tries, subconsciously perhaps, to disclaim and deny.'… Do you know that I've always felt that mistrust of yours? From the day I first talked to you.

Hengoed is the setting of 'Destruction': 'This is the street I inhabit./ Where my bread is earned my body must stay', which makes it sound as if teaching were his captivity.

> And I in bitterness wonder
> Why love's silk thread should snap,
> Though the hands be never so gentle.

Gweno's mistrust of Alun arose from his 'nervous strain', his 'inexplicable deaths', when he 'felt nothing, responded to nothing, valued nothing'. He would wake in a mad turmoil, agonised by thought, or jump up from the kitchen table with 'You won't be hurt if I go off a while?', grab his rucksack and disappear. Then there was the 'horrible black twisting' of their love-making at Llanthony Abbey and North Wales in the spring of 1940. 'I'm like life –' he told her,

> capable of going terribly wrong, capable of dying; it's in the nature…. So take me as I am, as I take you – birds aren't all song.

She grew used to moments when an 'icy cold compression' settled on his nerves and brain, cutting him off, 'so easily upset, like a wrist watch, by a bad jolt'; 'something falls across my mind all the time so that I can't feel properly'. Then he would return and a newly-insistent note of affection would enter his voice. He wrote:

> … you are fundamental to me: and can endure my eclipses because you are not the body that passes between me and the light. You've made me, Gweno, that's the simple truth. You've just made me. I've realised myself in you – not wholly yet, but you have begun the process and there is only the continuance through you.

This is this fundamental simplicity he describes in 'To Rilke': 'For that which IS I thought you need not seek'. Gweno had rendered them proof against time – 'For IS is everlasting, and happenings go their way'.

But when he lapsed again, her old distrust grew. She had hesitated the first time he asked to kiss her and hesitated again when he proposed. Knowing him hadn't made things any easier:

> You were silent for two whole minutes before you agreed to enter it [the marriage], weren't you? And then you thought 'Well, he'll be worse still without me', so you said yes, rather doubtfully…. Even when you 'didn't know' at Gloucester in that little hotel, I knew.

More surprisingly, her hesitation was to return on their last night together.

# II

Alun and Gweno met in May 1939 at the annual Three Valleys Music Festival in Mountain Ash. There was no 'instant combustion' but she was attracted. Years later, he wrote:

> …you say I was like the breath of life to you in that first summer. It was reciprocal, for you set me afire and yet the fire was cool and delightful as icy water or sea upon sand and wind among crops. And as fundamental and natural and pure.

With his wavy hair and deep-set hazel eyes, he reminded her of his Uncle Tim, the Ellises' near-neighbour in Aberystwyth, while she struck him as 'a tall fair girl, Welsh and sea-faring'. He told Christopher Cheney: 'You can guess her when I say we'll have lots of quarrels over personality – she retains her integrity by freehold'.

At this time, he was struggling with his writing and feeling 'abominably lonely'. Nevertheless, in manner he was easy-going, his hands in his pockets, his head tilted to one side, as if avoiding his own pipe-smoke. Gweno called him 'near', one who got on with all sorts of people. At the end of the summer term, they walked in the Brecon Beacons and went on holiday with a teacher friend of hers to St Dogmael's, near Cardigan. The two were 'humpy' with each other; he called her his 'little highnecked colt', 'a fountain of joy, very lively. We live together tempestuously'.

Gweno and Alun had been at university together and served on the Students' Representative Council with Dick Mills, but no friendship between them sprang up. He was something of a loner while she lived at home, to an extent missing out on the camaraderie of student life (captured by Emyr Humphreys in his Land of the Living sequence). The Ellises lived in the Chateau, a substantial redbrick house they had built at the turn of the century at the top of Constitution Hill. Her subject, German, was taught in a small department, thus further removing her from mainstream student life. She swam, rowed, won athletic colours and joined the German, Music and Gym Clubs while he played hockey, joined the Debating Society and drank at the Black Angel.

Gweno's father, Captain William Ellis, was a merchant sailor and Congregational preacher; Alun called him a 'Viking': '…I just marvel at him, standing against all the elemental powers of tide and snow and dark'. In 'Bequest', he is

> That quick-tempered chapel man
> Who loved the sea and all its gear,
> He had a broken house, and a trim yacht,
> And lived in mysteries and did not fear.

The 'mysteries' were religious while the 'broken' house refers to
repairs that had to be made to it:

> The fashionable architect who built our house had no idea
> how to build a flat roof for these climes. By the twenties the
> damage was revealed in all its horror – wet and dry rot in all
> the joists! My parents calmly reviewed the situation and
> decided their priorities. By this time there were five chicks
> to nurture and to educate according to their various abilities,
> so he beavered away assiduously at the repairs himself.
> Inserting steel girders, mixing cement for rotten sills and
> lintels. Whenever a girder or lintel had to be hoisted into
> place he would make a pulley, marshall us all to the spot,
> sing out a halyard shanty and we hauled away like old
> capehorners. My sweet mother was the anchorman always.
> By the end of the thirties there remained only the youngest
> at college and my father started consulting builders to take
> over the remaining work to be done. Then war was declared
> and an embargo on all building materials put an end to his
> plans and that was that for a long time to come.

Her typically brisk account breathes family pride.
  Gweno took issue with 'Bequest':

> For the sake of poetic licence and economy he makes my
> father sound like someone out of a Caradoc Evans short
> story. Steadfast in the faith, my father was an Elder of our
> English Prebyterian connection here where we, unlike the
> Lewis children, were all brought up. And no harm done, I
> guess!
>   I wouldn't have said that 'quick-tempered' described him
> either. He was active and lively and interested. He was quite
> an astronomer and liked to watch the stars in their courses
> through his big telescope. He would tell us their names and,
> as a little girl, I thought they were so musical, like a spell.

It was Captain Ellis who called her 'Gweno', Welsh for Venus, the evening star. This accounts for Lewis's identification of her with stellar imagery e.g. 'Post-script: For Gweno', 'It's a Long Way to Go' and the first Poona Hospital poem. 'Her' constellation was Cassiopeia. He gave her a reproduction of a detail from Botticelli's 'The Birth of Venus' as a wedding gift.

When Gweno wanted to compare him to other men, it was to her brothers (three of them as well as a sister; one of them, Hywel, was also at College with them). Similarly, when she referred to 'home', it was the Chateau, not Mountain Ash, even after she shared the house with him. Such family loyalty disconcerted him.

> He had, after all, spent most of his life away from home and felt puzzled and impatient at my emotional dependence on my parents and home. Alun would call me 'reactionary' and 'an enemy of the people' because, he would say, all I wanted from life was that he and my three brothers should survive the war and that my parents should grow younger every day! I would retaliate by grumbling about his stock character, that [of] a tedious little student. And then we would burst out laughing.
>
> I was one of five children of devoted parents and brought up in a sleepy University town. The reverberations of distress of the twenties and thirties never penetrated our cosy liberalism. I was a typical product – staid and uncomplicated, not tormented or emotionally deprived. Not 'interesting'. Alun must have found me a frightful bore.

Gweno had visited Germany, had German friends and loved all things German; she feared the war would cost everyone dear. Alun's reservations were expressed in two articles in 1938 for *The Aberdare Leader* under the initials 'A.N.L.S'. In them, he declared he 'could hit a man with his fists, but I do not think I could stick a bayonet into him. Nor could I bomb an open town.'

> ...how many of us are willing to give our lives – our LIVES – for the defence of British capital?.... And has a Government the right to demand the lives of its 'subjects' in order to remedy a situation which is largely of its own making?

He ended: 'I for one object to dying on behalf of a Government with such a record of bungling and error.' The war was as likely to kill as cure.

However, if a cause were worth defending, he was prepared to fight, as when he proposed running the blockade of Spanish ports during the Civil War with his friend, Chris Germanacos, whose family were ships' chandlers in Barry. Gwladys Lewis recalled:

> Alun, my third son Huw, and I were washing up after dinner and, as usual, passionately discussing world affairs with a view to putting the world right. Hitler, after his victory in Austria, was threatening to invade Czechoslovakia. Mr Chamberlain had stated publicly that he wasn't prepared to plunge Britain in war for the sake of a small, unknown country. Alun was very indignant and Huw said that it was either a small war then or a bigger one later on. I replied that I was not prepared to lose a son because Czechoslovakia was in trouble. In a choked voice Alun said: 'Mother, I have never heard you say such a vulgar thing', using vulgar in its precise meaning. I felt abashed. Another time he said to me, as if thinking aloud: 'When your friends are in a spot you don't say 'I told you so'; you do all you can to help them and afterwards you have a show-down'.

Gweno advised him: 'Take your chances with the rest', so he went to his medical in Pontypridd on 4th May 1940, passing in the first grade. He was recorded as being 24 years old, 5 foot 7 inches tall, with light brown eyes and dark brown hair. The Medical Corps was his first choice, followed by the Merchant Navy and Intelligence – anywhere where 'there's less chance of sticking a man in the bowels'. It was the first time he had contemplated enlisting without revulsion.

Despite being in a reserved occupation, he left Hengoed on the 16th May 1940 'on the hop, no one being more astonished than myself':

> I left school suddenly in mid-week, went to London to join Gweno's brother aboard ship (had just docked), found there was a vacancy, tramped the shipping agencies for two days in vain, saw a poster asking for dockers in the RES, took the address, Tower bridge, crossed the lovely sunny dirty Thames, & became a soldier.

By joining the Engineers, he hoped to join the war effort without killing anyone – digging ditches, checking ships' manifests, building bridges and the like. Hywel Ellis believed this paradox of a pacifist who enlists was at the root of his difficulties.

Lewis explained his position to a teacher friend, Andrew Davies:

> I believe that what I am fighting for is worth my death – even
> to me; to mother, to Gweno, to the best in them. And I'm no
> Utopian; simply, I rejoice in doing what I can for the ideals
> I have. Those ideals are simple ones – freedom, social equal-
> ity, opportunity, love. Regimentation I abhor. Army life is
> durable as a present expedient. Hitlerism would be its perpet-
> uation. I would become a saboteur, conspirator – or lose the
> courage of my socialism.

There speaks the valleys boy, eloquent, idealistic, defiant. By enlisting, he joined a movement that was to bear fruit after the war with
the election of a Labour government. As he told his parents: 'I must
know what I'm fighting for'. To Gweno, he wrote:

> I've got few illusions about the people we're supposed to be
> defending. We're defending a lot of profiteers and shirkers
> and cowards, I know; and as for defending our homes, we're
> not; they're being ruined every night the war goes on. But
> there's a lot more at stake than Mr Churchill dreams of; and
> far more to lose than most people can imagine.

## III

Alun and Gweno's relations were marked by the foreshortenings and
confusions of any wartime romance. In the two and a half years
between May 1940 and October 1942, they met about two dozen
times. In November 1940 (eighteen months after their first meeting),
they became engaged. He thought that their enforced separation

> gives us a personality and integrity that wouldn't have shaped
> ourselves so decisively and boldly in 'peace-time'. From the
> lonely heights of slavery I think a lot of a warless civilisation
> where people pair off in couples and cover themselves with
> sheets and ceilings and roofs and books and children and
> salaries and insurance policies and neighbours. Now we are
> uncovered.

Their very lack of togetherness had proved them.

> When I pause for a moment we're still in South Harting on

> the wooded hill where the earth is white and the grass grey
> and the violets half-hidden in leaf mould. It was a sweet
> place, wasn't it? But, oh, how quickly it went, like a little
> finch, whip-snip-off!

Once again, he associates Gweno with a country setting.

Home-leave at Whitsuntide 1941 turned out a disaster. Enemy
bombers flying up the Bristol Channel to Liverpool dropped any
surplus bombs on towns that lay on their return flight path and one
such had damaged Gweno's house. When Gwladys heard the news,
she turned pale; Gweno's sister-in-law cried alarm. Alun remained
unmoved:

> As if this were the first bomb in Genesis, instead of the
> millionth on the poor people of the whole world. Why make
> a fuss over one?

He could only think that his weekend had been ruined. As late as
June 1943, he wrote to Gweno:

> I still have an awful twinge of conscience when I think of
> that Whitsun 1941 when I didn't bother to go down to Bryng-
> wyn [her house] to find out whether you were hurt or not. It
> was part of my whole make-up in those days. A sort of fatal-
> ism, a shrug of the shoulders, and disbelief in danger, 'of
> course she's alright', my mind said, rejecting the innumer-
> able alarms of life as undignified and too exhausting to be
> listened to. I'm sorry darling. I'm sorrier still for the awful
> devil in me the next day. I was so rude to you and behaved
> so badly. I'd wanted to go away on Sunday, and you'd
> dismissed it all in a sentence in the bus and something
> immediately froze in me and I became horrible and dead.
> Gutch! as mother says.

An 'icy cold compression' had descended on his brain and nerves,
leaving him '"closed", not feeling properly'.

> I am a slave of some capricious demon, don't love my
> demon, or *me* alone. Understand us both, and save us both.

In July 1941, he reported to the Infantry Training Centre,
Gloucester, en route to Lancashire for an officer's training course.
On impulse, he rang Gweno at school and asked her to marry him

'this Saturday'. He had proposed to her the previous month and she had promised to speak to her Headmaster (Glamorgan County Council having taken the decision not to employ married women during the war, her job was at stake.) Somewhat reluctantly, she caught a train to Bristol on Friday 4th July and they travelled back to Gloucester together. So exhausted with worry was he that he neither kissed nor spoke to her. At the New Inn, Gloucester, he proposed again; for a full two minutes, she hesitated before agreeing. 'Even when you 'didn't know' at Gloucester in that little hotel,' he wrote, 'I knew'.

The next day, they purchased a brown floral costume with matching straw hat and upturned brim for her and a wedding ring at the first jeweller's shop they came across. As they hurried to the register office, he snatched a spray of roses that hung over a garden wall as her bouquet. Two army friends served as witnesses. After the ceremony, she made a move to leave but the Registrar called her back, placed her hand on Lewis's and asked them to leave together. Neither had told their parents about the wedding.

'War Wedding', is Lewis's celebration of the occasion. It is divided into seven parts, the first four constituting 'the violent half', reflecting his anxiety about her decision:

> She will not touch the blindness from my eyes
> Nor stroke the hair of silence on my loins
> Nor bare her wistful breasts.
> For first I must encounter
> My dreaming German soldier.

She will yield to him only when his body 'falls away', at which point she will be his 'useless saviour'. However, when she changes her mind, the stars 'light the dark bruised seed./ The unborn children are singing/ As we sail softly homing'. In section five, 'a thrust/ Of natural fertility' blesses 'The fragile universe of self'.

In section six, Gweno speaks:

> My lover is a soldier,
> He brought me all his trouble;
> I thought my heart would break
> That bitter joy to slake.
>
> But now he lies like a honeysuckle
> His wounded hands a blessing on my breasts.

> And softly the night still slants in silver
> On the four white towers gliding down-river.

The towers are those Chepstow Castle, which they visited the following morning.

Several of Lewis's stories include descriptions of the sexual difficulties of married couples. 'The Children', for example, relates how a 7-year-old boy and his sweetheart lose themselves in a forest. The second section flashes forward to their adult selves before reverting to their emergence from the forest in the last. In the middle section, they are married but parted by war. Leaning on a trench parapet, the soldier muses on her pregnancy:

> But not like the first ignorant longing when his sex sang unsatisfied in him, and love was a brutal imperative in the blood. And she withheld herself, leaving him sucked-out and vapid, without conversation for daily deeds or spirit for daily routine, imagining nothing and enjoying nothing, animal in food and breath. Saying 'I do not love her. I do not love her. I only want her, to draw her into the darkness, into the destruction in me'.

The woman's resistance implies ambivalence on her part while he is guilty of forcing sex on her. It is part of the destructive element in him.

In 'Duration', a soldier pleads for sex on his last night with his girl: 'Youth and desire surging desperately over her, his passion and his apprehension of death forcing her hard'. She replies: 'It's no good, not now'. There is no time and, besides, they have no contraceptives. Their 'failure' reveals his fear that impulsive sex will lead to 'ignorance' rather than satisfaction, involving as it does 'violence' and 'injury'. Lust – 'internal injury bleeding', 'cruel violence', a loss of control - contrasts with love and he repents 'this bitter bitter desire urging him to vileness', 'the chaotic anguish and vain rebellious defiance that so ached and flustered him'. Thus confounded, he hopes to emerge '[n]either burdened with desire and contempt [a contempt for desire?] nor diseased with corrupt regrets and puffy hates'. *Per eros ad astra*.

This point is repeated in 'The Children':

> She had come to him in the darkness, in the boarding-house bedroom at the week-end village and helped him, begging

him to help her. In the darkness of tossed sheets and heated
bodies, blind with nakedness and desperate with failure he
had lain in her soft voice, believing against himself that her
words were true because she spoke them. Her voice was the
only thing he still knew in his immense unbearable agony.
She quieted his sobbing and held him close in sleep.

Their failure is mutual and breeds compassion in them:

The second night, the third night, and after a month of other
things, the fourth, fifth, sixth nights they were alone together
she guided and loved him out of his hell, and by her faith she
made apparent the miracle of beauty. And on the sixth night
she slept in his arms at last and he became the possessor of
truth. He had been so lonely, so lost and beaten; and the
success had been so violent, so hungry….

The 'truth' revealed is paradoxical: the spirit is greater than the flesh.
Sexual satisfaction is only the prelude to a deeper satisfaction.
    In 'On Embarkation', a soldier

                   sees the 'tween decks turn
        To fields of home, each tree with its rustling shadow
        Slipped like a young girl's dress down to its ankles;
        Where lovers lay in chestnut shadows….

Out of doors sex was always easier but even when it was indoors (as
in 'Compassion' and 'Encirclement') it is attended by natural
imagery (as in the former: 'the meadows of her breath'). In 'The
Soldier', birds

                        lust
        And squabble and die;
        Say their glancing copulation,
        Poised flutter on a twig,
        Ignores the holy mystery
        Of boy and girl together
        Timelessly.

# IV

Gweno visited Alun at Heysham Towers for three weeks in August 1941. Afterwards, he wrote:

> … it was lovely to be with you day after day, with Saturdays and Sundays all to ourselves and you in your dressing gown when I came back from night schemes, with hot soup and your arms warm and your face so sweet and happy and your hair with its golden thread all neat and lovely to touch.

However, she had to cut her visit short to see her father, who was unwell, and attend a nephew's christening. Alun complained:

> …I had no idea I'd be so hurt at you going back after only three weeks of your seven weeks holiday. When people asked me whether you had only three weeks holiday from school I always said yes; and I used to think of your staff room raising its eyebrows next week when you said you'd spent a month at home. And I've tried to stop the silly resentment going on and on inside me, because it is so ugly and painful and it's prevented me from enjoying in retrospect the honeymoon we did have, and I feel thoroughly ashamed of the whole affair. I know it's selfish of me to want you; and I suppose you really didn't want to go; I suppose you were under a conflict between duty and delight. It's silly to nag about it: indeed I'm not nagging: but I must write it out of my system and hear you say something to kill the malicious voices. And, when I get to the bottom of it, what is it that I find? Just the plain belief, as strong as iron and steel, that the membranes of young lovers need, like grafted skin, the close presence of each with each: and now that it's so rare a thing for us to be able to be together, I thought you were tearing the living flesh apart before you need or ought to have done. I know you acted out of love of your parents and brothers and nephew, and I admire you for it: but I think you were wrong: I'm a little surprised that your woman's instinct didn't compel you to stay with your husband as long as you possibly could.

It was difficult being lovers in wartime: he was always pressing her to stay, she chasing trains, buses and hired rooms. Such was 'the ghostly way separated lovers have', meeting 'by the station wall, standing together with suitcase and tin hat in the sun among the railway crowds, kissing kissing solong and running away over the bridge'.

On November 29 1941, he joined the 6th Battalion, the South Wales Borderers in Martlesham, Suffolk. He told John Petts: 'It's my own choice – I'm made like that: a bird that will not nest'. And what an uncomfortable nest it turned out to be! He called it 'this little Dachau', and it plunged him into his deepest depression yet. He found it hard to identify '2/Lt A. Lewis' with 'Alun Lewis'. To Christopher Cheney, he wrote that he had become an officer 'as successfully as I once became a medieval scholard'. He told Brenda Chamberlain and John Petts:

> I find being an officer somehow immoral and ludicrous. I have to make conversation in the Mess, assume anger or dignity to the men; I can't lounge about listening to the natural & earthy talk of barrack room & pub any more. There is a whole world of caste and stiff tradition fencing me off.

That feeling never left him. Two years later, he told Gweno:

> I can be a moderately good soldier but not very good because I have too many scruples and a certain detachment from it all that tends to undermine my physical energy and enthusiasm.

Lord Chalfont called him 'one of the most unlikely characters ever to put on the uniform of an infantry officer':

> He was a young man of brooding and saturnine aspect, non-conformist and iconoclastic by instinct. His appearance in uniform was, to say the least, unconventional. He had a remarkable ability to make everything he wore look as though it had been made for someone else, either much smaller or much bigger than he was. If a piece of equipment could be worn backwards or upside down, that is how he was inclined to wear it. He was, as he frequently declared, much more at home with the soldiers or other ranks than with the officers. His nature was almost unnaturally gentle, his smile disarmingly sweet and his voice, with marked Welsh intonations, soft and insinuating.

He said he was an Englishman's idea of a Welshman, small, dark and intense and with a rare, slow smile, deep, mysterious and endearing. Bernard Gutteridge recalled that he was known as '"our poet" in a thoroughly affectionate way – and that says a lot, I think'.

Even so, his closeness to Other Ranks meant he came to be regarded as a Trojan horse by his fellow-officers, an extension of the barracks into the Mess. Despite his being an all-round athlete (boxing, running, hockey, football), an introspective quality about him left them uneasy. One officer called him 'the complete village idiot with a drawling Welsh accent and stupid grin' (Lewis as Shenkin), a 'crude type of left-wing socialist and alien to the refinements expected of an officer'. His Colonel thought he wasn't much use and Gwynne Jones looked through him. Trapped in a world of snobbery and feeling unsure, he became 'a sick animal'.

He warned Gweno that when she visited him she would find 'only some attenuated spasmodic Alun, a face at a window, coming and going'. He told her he realised he was 'not an officer at heart or head':

> I want to know my job, which I don't: as I want my brain to get better, which it won't – it's as it was in 1937 when I'd been crazy with death-love for two years and didn't live in any positive way and my brain was all barbed wire.

Gweno fretted at her inability to help him but he rounded on her:

> And why do you say you're no help to me? Why do you say such things? You know I'm no good to anybody sometimes, Gwen. Don't blame our relationship, please darling. It's the secret truth in which I exult, and which made me always want to marry you, that you are fundamental to me: and can endure my eclipses because you are not the body that passes between me and the light: in the end you push obstruction away: so again I ask you in such times to be patient and take no hurt into yourself.

Evidently, he was short on happiness but long in explanation.

In the spring of 1942, the battalion was mechanised and moved to Bovington, in Dorset, for tank training. Gweno now saw him more frequently, either at Bradford on Avon, Westbury or Bath, and it is from this time that references to the possibility of their having a child appear. A few months later, Julian MacLaren-Ross reported it as a 'fact' that Gweno was 'expecting' and noted Lewis's 'deep love and respect' for women and his hostility to anything that smacked of 'a sophisticated approach to sex'. Jack Aistrop, a Longmoor friend, remarked that he showed little interest in the liberties the men gained on nightly raids on NAAFI quarters.

From Bovington, Alun told Gweno:

> I think Saturday and Sunday were in their quiet way the happiest days we've had. I realise it now more than I did when it was actually happening – which is characteristic of all true joy, the absence of self-consciousness or the detached part of you that is worried by other thoughts at the same time and will not give itself and you wholly to that joy. I don't think I've been so happy; I've been more ecstatic – but not more happy, quietly, tranquilly happy.... You've made me, Gweno, that's the simple truth. You've just made me. I've realised myself in you....

'Corfe Castle' marks the climacteric of their love.

> Love grows impulsive here: the best forget;
> The failures of the earth will try again.
> She would go back to him if he but asked.
> The tawny thrush is silent; when he sings
> His silence is fulfilled. Who wants to talk
> As trippers do? Yet, love,
> Before we go be simple as this grass.
> Lie rustling for this last time in my arms.
> Quicken the dying island with your breath.

Their consummation ('dying', 'breath') fertilises ('quickens') an island at war for 'this last time'. The play on 'death' to imply orgasm deepens the implications of 'quicken'. 'Impulsive' love opposes 'failure' as failure opposes 'trying again'

In the summer of 1942, they went back to Yr Hendre, the farm near St Dogmael's where they had holidayed in 1939. Back in Mountain Ash, the last day of his leave was spent typing out his poems, for Gweno 'wished it to appear like the middle day in a steady lifetime'. 'On Embarkation' once again raises the possibility of children:

> And on the cliff's green brink where nothing stirs,
> Unless the wind should stir it, I perceive
> A child grow shapely in the loins I love.

It ends:

> … I pray my unborn tiny child
> Has five good senses and an earth as kind
> As the sweet breast of her who gives him milk
> And waves me down this first clandestine mile.

The description of their parting at Cardiff station is the locus classicus of that quintessence of wartime romance, the railway farewell.

> But now each railway station makes and breaks
> The certain hold and drifts us all apart.
> Some women know exactly what's implied.
> Ten Years, they say behind their smiling eyes,
> Thinking of children, pensions, looks that fade,
> The slow forgetfulness that strips the mind
> Of its apparel and wears down the thread;
> Or maybe when he laughs and bends to make
> Her laugh with him she sees that he must die
> Because his eyes declare it plain as day.
> And it is here, if anywhere, that words
> – Debased like money by the same diseases –
> Cast off their habitual clichés of fatigue
> – The women hoping it will soon blow over,
> The fat men saying it depends on Russia –
> And all are poets when they say Goodbye
> And what they say will live and fructify.

The iambic pentameter lends dignity to the occasion.

Another poem, 'Destruction', tells how, with enemy bombers droning overhead, Gweno caught the 8 p.m. from Hengoed:

> For the night was about her, blinding her when she crossed it,
> And the train that took her roaring towards the dayspring
> Is rocking her through the dawn down empty sidings
> Between dark tenements in the neutral city
> To the street she must inhabit.

These poems, I think, influenced Philip Larkin's 'Whitsun Weddings'. (Larkin included Lewis – but not these poems – in his *Oxford Book of English Verse*.)

From Cardiff, he travelled to Southend, from where he wrote to say 'either the child or your relief work must fill your heart'. He prayed 'that life will start a new cycle in you' and that 'our baby will win this little tussle this time'. Gweno visited in October only to find him in another 'little spiritual crisis'

> so exhausting and deep rooted that perhaps I have never been
> so quietly triumphant as when I lay on the green twin bed
> and tried and tried and tried to cast off the hollowness and
> frozen misery the Army had bound in me as I marched – and
> you came towards me along the road we couldn't see, and
> the distance slowly got less, and then at last, oh, what relief!
> I could feel your love and your care tingling in my exhaus-
> tion, and I felt myself surge back and be no longer isolated
> and effaced. And you have that power, if you will not be hurt
> by my coldness, and if you love me enough to use it. It's the
> most necessary thing I can ask of you, and darling I will have
> to ask it of you sometimes. It's in the nature of the beast.

Apparently, there had been another failure and Gweno once again helped him 'surge back'. Shortly after, he travelled to Cardiff, unaware she had cancelled their rendezvous; after touring the city hotels, he arrived in Bryngwyn with the milk van for a snatched two-hour stay.

Their last meeting took place in Liverpool, where he was part of the advance baggage party. He sent her a coded message at school ('How's your liver?') and she came up for one last 'ecstatic' reunion. In the hotel bedroom, he placed a shilling in the gas meter and watched her as she slipped off her dress. She suggested leaving some dry flowers and gas for the next resident and kissed his eyes closed; she gazed at him full of apprehension. At that moment, her old unease resurfaced. It was, he said,

> like meeting an old friend, your doubt, that I used to meet so
> often once upon a time, but who ceased to live in our house
> till he suddenly on the last night poked his nose in at the door
> and grinned all over his face and went away.

Lewis's 'Goodbye' (which Larkin included in his Oxford anthology) opens:

> So we must say Goodbye, my darling,
> And go, as lovers go, for ever;
> Tonight remains, to pack and fix on labels
> And make an end of lying down together.

And closes:

> Yet when all's done you'll keep the emerald
> I placed upon your finger in the street;
> And I will keep the patches that you sewed
> On my old battledress tonight, my sweet.

Tender, truthful lines which articulate a lover's emotion with moving simplicity. No sooner is feeling released than it is restrained, as is suggested by the halting metre. Once more, the lovers are 'Eternity's masters,/ Slaves of Time' ('Raiders' Dawn'), an idea glossed in 'Last Pages of a Long Journal':

> The lovers remembering the nakedness of the first night know now that they do not after all possess mastery over Time. But their mastery may be over Eternity. That is the hope in us, a little germ in us, the seed that is in us we do not know how, and not all the irreparable cruelties and blind malignance and loss of war can kill the germ, the seed of humanity.

Next morning at 5 a.m., Gweno felt like screaming. Reaching out for his handkerchief, she found it covered with blood, the result of a head cold. He embraced her so tightly that his trenchcoat pips hurt. At the door, he turned, saluted and left.

'Goodbye' stands in sharp contrast to 'The Way Back'. The latter is passionate and violent ('shafted', 'burning', 'distress', 'spur and rush', 'crush', 'beat', 'squandered', 'hurled'), in anticipation of a rending consummation, whereas 'Goodbye' is gentle, 'warm and safe'. Alun's letters to Gweno can be mawkish ('you the bow and I the strings, you the music and I the breath') whimsical, citing German and English folk songs and fairy tales, and fanciful. 'I'll teach you [chess] when I come home next and we'll play together when the rain and the frost close the doors and windows of our cottage.

> I'm consumed with eagerness and heartache to hear from you straight away – and to know whether a child is still tucked away in God's crèche or whether our wishes reached a mirac-ulous fulfilment on my last night in England…. [may] the little ones come toddling out of Heaven to share our struggles.

At such times, gratitude guides his pen as much as affection.

> And yet I know, when I think of this question of mutual
> suffering, that it is you who in the crisis of danger are the
> coolest and wisest and alone can save. You saved me twice
> in the deepest and loneliest pitch of night. And brought me
> back and sustained me – and this is the most wonderful of
> all perhaps, you made me return that way again and so
> destroyed us.

As his mother had rescued him in his student days, so Gweno encouraged him to 'return that way again' and save their marriage.

Aboard *The Athlone Castle*, he pleaded with her not to fret 'about
the non-arrival of a child this time':

> I can't talk of that hope we have – because there is the censor,
> you know: but if the dove does bring a green leaf to you this
> time – Oh God, Gwen, how I would rejoice, but if it is to be,
> then you and I are alone, and have we ever asked more than
> that?

Shortly after, he returned to 'the incomplete idea of children':

> How I wish we were together talking about this, and I'd reach
> a gap in thought as I did that sad afternoon when the heavy
> warning of a breathless impending trial made everything so
> dark and confined. And you said just two words that I take
> with me now wherever I go…

Another reference to Bedgellert.

There were never any children. In 'Song' (written aboard *The
Athlone Castle*) 'she' speaks:

> The first month of his absence
> I was numb and sick
> And where he'd left promise
> Life did not turn or kick.
> The seed, the seed of love was sick.

From India, he wrote to say he was 'dying to know', though he had
'a queer sinking feeling, unreasonable though it be, because hope
dies hard'. When it was clear there were to be no children, he wrote:
'Maybe it was better so – and anyway, we didn't deserve a kiddy,

leaving it till the last moment like that. It served us right'. To Dick Mills, he remarked: 'Gweno hoped to have a baby, but it went wrong, and we were very very sad about it, very very very'.

On *The Athlone Castle*, he recorded a 'long brave chain of visions'. These summarise his relations with Gweno:

> The hill above Beddgelert after we'd skimmed stones and talked to the tramp and sat back eating our Bwythyn sandwiches – and Bradford [on Avon] by the canal, by the yellow lilies and me plopping into the stream like an old water rat and floating down to you, and the downs that lovely Sunday when we talked of friends, and the pumping station was pulsing its heavy beats, and we sat on the hillside without shoes and didn't care whether we missed the bus or not. Those weeks were 'safe', somehow, warm and safe. Like little children in a world not warring. I'm glad that came our way.

The 'and'-'and'-'and' structure, a frequent reflex in Lewis, sees him spinning emotion out at the nib of his pen.

# Part Six
## *Freda and Gweno*

### I

The fact that Gweno and I were now in regular communiction led to something of a crisis in Freda, particularly after I told her I could not reveal to her what had passed between us. She reminded me she had always been open with me and wanted me to be open with her – that was the basis of our co-operation. I agreed but even so felt I was treading a fine line. I had told Gweno about her but only with her permission – Gweno had not released me from her confidences. Nonetheless, the fact remains that I regarded Freda as a fellow-researcher with whom I could discuss matters and analyse the poetry. Not that I treated her views differently from Gweno's, or Gwladys's for that matter, nor that we did not disagree. Freda wrote:

> [Y]ou yourself speak of writing openly to me as a fellow-researcher in this curious, painful and so beautiful re-experiencing of Alun Lewis. Your saying that makes me very proud and pleased and I feel that my long hours of thinking and writing to you are not wasted. Of course the only way you could and must communicate with me is the absolutely honest, absolutely truthful and direct way. I would hate it unutterably if you did not do so, and would be very quickly aware of any attempt, out of kindness, to sweeten any pill for my easier swallowing. It is your directness and honesty that has so won me over to the idea of your writing the book which must be written on him.

It is also true that, by this time, Gweno and the Lewises had come to regard me as a go-between. That being the case, I could see no reason why I could not share my information with her and never regretted doing so.

A deeper resentment stirred in her:

> I can't bear any longer to sit beyond the circle of warm
> reassurance made about her, myself as the seductress who,
> while possessing everything Gweno had not, yet solicited the
> love which was by right her own.

She hated the lies she had been forced to tell and the more to come
and, for a while, stopped working on her memoir.

> But since I am suffering because of what I have done to Alun
> and because I cannot without conscience hurt anyone as
> deeply as I knew at once Gweno must be hurt, I myself must
> try to make reparation. I can't remain coldly outside what so
> deeply concerns me.

Freda was a convert to Roman Catholicism but wore her religion
lightly. Notwithstanding that, she was genuine in her wish to make
reparation to Gweno. It become the mainstay of her life.

After Lewis's death, a strange silence had fallen on all who had
known him. Gweno was left to mourn a husband, the Lewises a son
and brother, Freda a lover. Yet all sensed that a day of reckoning
would eventually come. After Gweno's *In the Green Tree* in 1948
and Freda's 'Remembering Alun Lewis' in 1952, the silence held
sway until my essay on 'The Way Back' appeared 20 years later. By
then, Lewis's reputation had begun to fade, trapped as he was in some
Haversham-like suspension of time. The much that needed to be said
was muffling what he himself had written until the silence grew
deafening. Then, cracks began to appear. Freda welcomed them but
shied from the prospect of publicity. Nonetheless, the love so long
suppressed in her could no longer be denied – indeed, was all the
more intense for its suppression. Her buried life stirred.

> It is debasing to have to diminish, for Gweno's sake, the
> rapture, the living joy we held steadily above the involve-
> ments and commitments of our lives and the violence of the
> world we were living in…. 'If only the world really were you
> and me,' he wrote, 'if there were only you and me.'

At the same time, she felt contrite towards Gweno:

> I hate to think of her (it hurts me because of her own suffer-
> ing and, more, because of him) searching through his letters,
> calculating the time of their being written and making her
> anguished conclusions.

'Oh John,' she wrote, 'I'm sorry that I've made your task more difficult. But not sorry for trying to make her less unhappy'.

> I can't help feeling that she should not wish for this kind of comfort though I UNDERSTAND HER NEED AND HER HURT, and both haunt me. But surely she does not see his tender and painstaking attempts to protect her, his longing back to a safety he needed, something approaching a misleading guile and duplicity.

She was thinking of his letters to Gweno, which protest his love for her in ever-warmer terms.

> The thought distresses me. It was all so far beyond our ability to recompose it to something less overwhelming; there was no guile in it. He wrote: 'I've been thinking and feeling a lot today – not more than any other day, but it seems to be resolving itself today into a clearer understanding of life. So that I know that it is not a matter of enchantment but of living and dying, being with and being without, losing and finding, trying and failing, sharing and not sharing. Oh God, it's the real texture of my life, and it will have all my weaknesses and all the ways in which I am disappointing and disconcerting in it. And it will have you as you are and were and will be. And I want to talk to you about all the sadnesses and all the joy and all the hardness and all the gentleness we've begun. I want to be with you where nobody else is, just for long enough for us to understand what it is. You will be there, Frieda, won't you? Otherwise perhaps we will never understand, never attain. It's the hardest thing I have ever tried, Frieda, it is. I love you and want to be with you....' These anguished deliberations are not those of a man who is likely to use guile in an attempt to cover the betrayal of his wife.

She felt neither she nor Gweno should 'feel in any narrow way' about him:

> We were both greatly privileged, as few in this world can be, and if this privilege which brought such overwhelming gifts brought also its own Nemesis – as it did for us both – we should still thank God for it. I feel strongly, deeply for her – but her mind is too closed to herself, to the real truth and she'd be the less tormented if it were not so.

She wanted to protect Gweno from the truth but also wanted her to understand it was greater than either of them.

She recognised how much Gweno had done for him:

> But I think gradually he grew to feel the restricted intensity of her feeling for him. (I felt this in his letters strongly.) A smouldering charge in a restricted, very personal love, one which, he knew, if detonated by any hint of disclaiming by him, would induce, because of its intensity, terrible destruction. That is why he suffered so much; why after I read your letter the second time I felt so desperate about her pain. I want to say something here which may sound very selfish, heartless even. But I know you are able always to sense the deeper causes of what I try to say. John, when Alun killed himself my suffering was very great. He had illuminated my world and (except for the coming baby) it suddenly became very dark. The light he brought into it was not only intense but it revealed how pale was the sunlight of the rest of life. He felt this, too, and said so, passionately. My feeling of guilt all these years, feeling thus and realising Gweno's unrealised hurt but one committed, has forced me to stand apart suppressing, in some sense, my own involvement, feeling it to be invalid. Since I've opened the wound by re-reading the letters and speaking of it to you and since Gweno is now sentiently part of it I have taken another look at this self standing guiltily apart and something has come to life in me, not defensive so much as proud: not proud of myself but using pride as an instrument of justifiable self-respect. You see, a marriage contract, I feel, does not give one an exclusive right to pain or the world's sympathy; any more than the lack of one gives one immunity to both. But it greatly [affects] the world's attitude. Mrs Lewis's open-mouthed horror is evidence of this. I no longer feel any guilt, realising these things, only a terrible remorse at being the cause of betraying Alun's most intense anxiety to protect Gweno. But no guilt.

She, too, had suffered.

Freda knew that my telling Gweno about her had added to her distress but it is a nice question whether not speaking to her would have been less distressing. Lewis's repeated assurances in his letters are overinsistent in a way she could not have failed to register. They may have comforted her then – but not after what she had learned about Freda. The silence had produced its after-echo.

Until now, Freda had shielded her family from the truth (one reason, perhaps, why she could speak to me so candidly). She offered them brief factual explanations embellished with romantic touches, all veiled under a cloak of fraternal sympathy and emotional solace. Now, a very different light was about to be shed on them and she feared the effect on her children. Would they respect her less and draw nearer their father?

> I telephoned Gilly last night, told her you'd set the cat among the pigeons – not in those words, of course! – and she murmured thoughtfully, sighed and finally said: 'Yes, I think he had to do it. But I do think you must write to her [Gweno] yourself.'

To say what, though? Over the years, she had tried writing but failed to post any of her attempts for fear of what the postman might bring by way of reply.

> Not that I like dropping into the hole like a trapdoor spider, closing the trap silently and invisibly and pretending not to be there.

Having equivocated before, she decided to change tack.

> Do not see what I write as anything other than – yes, a self-defence in part, but also what you have shown to me: an attempt to find the truth because I see more and more clearly having lived so painfully in the writing of what is untruth, that it is essential and the only right and acceptable thing to do if one is to be articulate at all about this man, this Alun.

Shortly after visiting Gwladys Lewis with me, Gweno rang to ask about the paternity of Juliet, Wallace and Freda's youngest child, who was born on 16th May, 1944. As Freda had anticipated, she had been going through Lewis's letters calculating the time and reaching her anguished conclusions. She asked if Juliet were Alun's 'bastard', adding that it was doubtful whether much weight could be placed on so brief an affair. 'What is two weeks in 28 years of life?'. Like Freda before, she reminded me the last poem in *Ha! Ha! Among the Trumpets* is dedicated to her.

Now it was Freda's turn to be hurt:

Because I admire your impartiality and because I have an
affection for you may I tell you that Gweno's telephoning
you to ask about the paternal legitimacy of my child angered
me. How could you possibly know? You who was outside
our lives, even more than Dick Mills is, and who could not
even in his own recent implication in our history find literary
use for the truth of such a fact. It is an appalling thing to ask
of a stranger, a grave suspicion to put into his mind, one
affecting many other lives than my own. Perhaps this
question which so torments her is to do, poor Gweno, with
her own unfulfillment though she would not recognise this.
And her reiterated: 'Does Wallace know?' I wonder what she
would feel at knowing what he does. About our being in love,
that is. And I ask myself, in being so clever about other
people, if I am clever at looking into my own heart.

Freda did write to Gweno and received a reply that

moved me very much for it was, if I may use so big a word,
a noble letter. She reveals herself as being what I always
thought a very nice woman. Far more. Strong and straight. I
am so glad I wrote to her. I knew it was essential that I did
but I dreaded doing it. She tells me something which shatters
me – and I wonder if you know it; you must do having read
the journals: that it was not so much the fact of his being in
love with someone else but that he left her totally unprepared
for this revelation which made her so unhappy. I'll quote her:
'No, the problem is far more complex than that. Perhaps it's
the way he handled the situation, and his ignorance of the
female psyche that has left me with a psychological hang up
about him ever since. I know, I know he hadn't enough time
left, so he preferred to remain silent. I really don't think he
gave it another thought – at least there's no evidence of it in
his journals.'

It's true that Lewis did not tell Gweno about Freda in so many
words, but neither was he silent about her. His poems tell all, as her
reaction to them proved ('breasts, breasts, breasts'). When, therefore,
she complains he did not confess to her, she is, by a reverse logic,
admitting he had, though not in the way she would have preferred .
That was her 'psychological hang up'.
Freda told me:

...in my answer to her letter (of which more later) I tried

desperately to think of some reason to comfort her. I had for
years thought that the sending to her of the love poems was
very curious and concluded in a vague sort of way that on
this subject – the most important to his very existence – the
subject of his poetry, he was blind, without insight.

Gweno told Freda:

> I was completely unprepared for the revelations in his
> journals and literary detritus [that word again!] which arrived
> home soon after his death. You can imagine how I felt! I
> found his love for you very well documented. He seemed to
> be living in an ecstatic Now with no past and no future. But
> when I read of the naked lovers happily conjoined on a bed
> in a window of a Bombay hotel with a view of the sea and of
> how these lovers emerged in the cool of the evening to stroll
> with arms entwined through the Malabar Gardens, watching
> the life go by and of the little boy who brought the woman a
> lotus flower every day, I couldn't believe it and recoiled in a
> panic from admitting to myself who the lovers were. All
> these years it has been like a tumour in my brain and a stone
> in the heart. John Pikoulis only confirmed my fears.

She had known from the beginning, after all. What she had wanted
was some direct acknowledgement, from him to her.

Freda believed Gweno's paraphrase of 'The Transmigration of
Love' revealed 'a clarity not evident in the rest of her letter, a vivid-
ness which testifies to the precise realisation of every beautiful and
enchanted moment of our time together', and it made her all the more
determined to make amends. Accordingly, she told Gweno that
Lewis's 'inability to see further than the actual fulfilment of one's
powerful creative motivation' meant that his poems did not reflect
his feelings accurately. Gweno remained sceptical, but she persisted:

> I tried very hard to find some way to comfort her for I really
> feel humbled by the awfulness of what she must have
> suffered when those journals and poems came back to her –
> as well as his death. And now I must tell you what else I said
> and I am reluctant to admit it but must. I've brooded for days
> about it since posting the letter – and indeed kept the letter
> unposted for a week....
>     I had to find something to at least lessen her anxious
> brooding. (After thirty years – it seems incredible.) I

described as best I could how I discovered I was pregnant
the day after I got to Poona where I was to visit Dick. What
led up to it, proving that Juliet is without any shadow of a
doubt Wallace's child. Then I went on, oh so reluctantly, to
tell her that the Bombay poem is romanticised, only half true,
indeed hardly true in all intense love and ecstatic realisation.
I had to do this. I hated doing it and I tell you this because I
must and I would like you to destroy this letter, please. You
know because you have read his letters and because I have
told you that what I wrote her was not true and that when he
later wrote that he saw things on a later visit to Bombay
which he had not seen when we were there 'because enchantment sealed my forehead' – you know that this was true. It
is especially important that you should know the truth
because of the book you will write. I dishonour him by
making light of it all, make meaningless the agony he
suffered. And I tell it to you with some apprehension because
you are honest to a frightening degree and will probably not
like my having done this. But I couldn't let her remaining
years be as bitter as the past thirty years or so, that she should
have a 'hang up' about him is too bitterly sad. What would
he feel? I'm sure – and I've thought so long about it – he
would approve of my lying to her.

With the best of intentions, she now added another difficulty to the
many that already existed. Of course, my opinion mattered not a jot
but, somewhat to my surprise, I find I expressed my reservations,
warning her that she was stoking up trouble. It made me all the more
determined not to mislead Gweno myself.

Freda was nettled and raised the counter-accusation that I had
spoken to Gwladys about her without permission. She was willing
for me to talk to Gweno but not his mother, though she understood
why I had done so. She said Mair Fenn had visited Gwladys shortly
after my visit and found her 'distressed about what she knows –
though refuses to believe'.

> ...if life hadn't mucked me about I'd have waited forsome-
> one like [Alun] to come along or gone out and found him.
> As it was I rushed to safety, to reassurance, to what seemed
> a rock of stability. I couldn't have hurt Wallace by leaving
> him – something as old as I was myself, belonging to the
> heartbreak of early childhood, held me. So I weep sometimes
> when I read his letters, for all the half-truths, half-hopes, half-

realisation. But you are right when you say that my letter to Gweno might (you say 'will') be used to defend a false impression of Alun and of Alun and Freda. It kept me sleepless for nights, considering the letter. But what could I do? I could not let her go on suffering because of me. I felt – and do feel – that because I have told you the truth and because I know that you recognise it by every sign given by him as being the truth that protects him.... I feel now that any help or truth I can give you is far more important than anything I may write myself.

If she could not be an honest remembrancer, I could: 'the real book is what I so dimly saw when I first began to write to you', and of its character she could be in no doubt.

I was certain of two things about Alun Lewis: one was that he had committed suicide – in that my judgment never for a moment wavered – and the other was that the love affair we had was the greatest thing that had ever happened to him.

Yet here she was diminishing it for Gweno's sake. However, she felt she had no alternative: she, too, was trying to act 'within the situation'. She realised that Lewis must have written some false letters to Gweno but thought they had begun to drift apart even before Coonoor. The war that had brought them together was now driving them apart.

I was so blinded by his constant concern and grief for her that I did not see very clearly. Only in one letter when he cannot help blurting out, as it were, '...and she has some ultimate reality which dwarfs her'... did it become clear that there was something he actually recognised and rejected in her. And now this letter from her so powerfully drives home this fact. I was amazed. But saw with the greatest precision what he meant by some ultimate reality dwarfing her.

Freda was always in two minds about Gweno. Though full of a compassionate respect for her, she felt she was unworthy of Alun's love:

But a total lack of the remotest conception of what the imagination, the creative sensitivity is. She understands his gift for it is manifest (I always knew this for she wrote him intelli-

gent letters about his poetry) and she writes with a sure,
experienced appreciation of the use of words, BUT the –
what? – lightness of perception, lack of any deep understanding of what went on in him as a sensitive creature strikes one
like a rock between the eyes. I have quoted the most moving
recitation of what she read in the poem. You'd think that in
such a letter she would continue in just as feeling a manner,
wouldn't you? She might, indeed I half expected her to, write
very bitterly, stingingly – only at the end is there a touch of
this – but no! she writes in a light-hearted, curiously merry
way: she tells me many reasons for his death not being
suicide… 'everyone is firmly convinced that he took his own
life – after all he was a poet and that is what it seems all poets
are supposed to do…'. 'Alun had one characteristic failing
which might have been the cause of his death. He never
looked where he was going. As we rampaged about the
mountains of Snowdonia or scrambled down the cliffs to the
sea, as he landed with a shuddering jerk or a sprawl down
below the air was rent by my constant exhortations to watch
his step.' That he never looked where he was going is so like
a rather over-driven governess speaking that one wonders if
the memory of him as being dreamy, withdrawn, absorbed
in thought is not a bit over-drawn! The letter is all written in
this clear, cheerful way.

Gweno's failure of style represented a failure in perception, too.

The reader will have gone ahead of me in registering unease at
Freda's habit of reporting Gweno's letters to me. However, it was no
more than part of the open exchange we had established and lacked
an ulterior motive. Though I felt it threatened my impartiality as a
biographer, it also had the effect of putting me on my guard against
any appeal to my sympathies. She was not citing Gweno to me in
order to advance her position – rather the reverse. She was telling
me what she had done and why.


# II


During this time, I went through the letters and journal Gweno had
sent me. As Intelligence Officer, Lewis studied maps, but none filled
him with greater dread than that of Burma. It was a Damoclean sword
hanging over him and reminder of all the friends he had lost in

Europe, Africa and Asia. In 'Nothing but the Dead' (previously unpublished), he wrote:

> I cannot think of them for long.
> Dreams and intuitions go.
> Tomorrow in the jungle and the guns
> The heart will harden, Love will grow
> Cold and incredible as snow
> Over a hundred violent acres
> Massive hands will rip the flesh
> Like used-up hoardings from a wall
> And delicate relations flow
> Like blood away, like blood away.
>
> And what can love or friendship say
> One way or the other way?

Nothing, apparently. Lewis wrote this poem after Karachi and sent it to Gweno with 'The Transmigration of Love'. It tells how love and friendship will 'flow away' until he is left alone: first, the hardening of the heart, then the rending of the flesh. Circumstance and instinct alike insist: love goes into death.

'Maps' (or 'The Map'), posted to Freda, reads:

> But loveliness is no man's bride.
> Your name is mixed with battles on the map.
> And I can lie no longer by your side
> Because the world has laid away the map,
> And I can never lay away the world.

Evidently, a great tussle was going on at the time: 'the world' was forcing him to surrender the love that he had only recently found. What he greeted so exultantly in 'The Way Back' 'Maps' forlornly acknowledges.

I sent Gweno my conclusions, as she had requested.

> It is difficult for me to write to you about the letters, as I must, with the disinterest of a student of your husband's work when, for you, they cannot but be of the warmest personal interest. And yet it is only from a detached point of view that their significance can be appreciated and adjusted to all the other material, literary and biographical, that has accumulated. For that their significance is *not* easily apparent is

something you yourself have discovered. Having read them, I believe that they are a sustained attempt to comfort and protect you from any direct knowledge of what was happening to him in India....it is clear from 'The Orange Grove', written, as the letters make clear, some time before the visit to Coonoor, that the process that was to lead Alun to his death was well under way and clearly anticipated. So that, while it was expected that the letters would make no mention of Freda Aykroyd that was not innocuous, it is altogether unexpected that they should be so anxious not to confess the suffering that was steadily overtaking him. And, indeed, it is this reluctance to touch on his unhappiness that alerted me, as an outsider, to the suspicion that the suffering was very real indeed, for the tone of the letters, while constantly endearing, sentimental, reassuring, with now and then more unsettling passages setting it off in relief, is never wholly convincing. It is the tone of a man thinking and feeling himself back to a whole way of life – of which you, naturally, were the lynch-pin – which is nevertheless slipping away from him.

In his penultimate letter to Brenda Chamberlain, I wrote, he confessed: 'I'm becoming very taciturn & secretive about what happens to me in India'. In part, I was referring to Freda but the sensation predated her:

No doubt his falling in love with Freda, coming so unexpectedly and briefly and intensely, followed by the tortured conscience with regard to you, played its own significant part in the process, though I cannot pretend I understand all of it yet.

At Coonoor, he suffered a reverse:

In the last letter to Brenda, he recalls his visit to the Nilgiris as leaving him 'as deeply and innocently in love with life as I've ever been'. Yet the next sentence declares how feeble a hold it had on him. 'Since then I've gone steadily downwards'. He also told Brenda that 'I am grappling & clinging a long way from the safe & fructifying life Gweno made about me & I made about her'.

He was not his own master.
From Karachi, he tried to tell her what had happened at Coonoor:

> I don't know why it was, but up in that brilliant cold mountain country [i.e. the Nilgiris] I was dissociated somehow from anything before or after and I lived in a strange new way – angelically almost. I had no cares; no future; no duties; no past. Everything just flowed and flowed, the hills and Beethoven and Schumann and Handel that I played to myself every morning, and the clear water in the brooks through the woods that had dappled moles of warm blue sunlight in them where the branches and the wind made a way.

Familiar imagery, though Gweno could not have understood as much. In Coonoor, he repeated an experience that had occurred shortly after his arrival in India when, standing before a stone Buddha by a roadside, his consciousness was swallowed up in a transcendent, physical Now.

He urged Gweno: 'Make yourself separate from the necessities and accidents of the war as I am making myself separate'. Where before he had protested whenever he thought she was paying him insufficient attention, now he urged her to think first of herself:

> Thank you, Gweno darling, for so much love and thought; but oh Gweno, PLEASE be easy. Don't fret at it like this, sweetheart, please, please, please.

On August 14th 1943 (i.e. three days after reaching Karachi), he told Dick Mills:

> And now that I am married I feel as if I've entered into a fullness that I'd only longed for emptily before. Yet I'm not a monogamous creature. I know that the guiding force in me sees always the leading vision of love and recognises and desires it whenever it appears and whoever is wearing or bearing it. How such things work out I don't know. But every idea I inherit I find I must either break it or expand it. 'Fidelity' is an expanding not a brittle ideal, I hope.

He was happily married but also happily in love again.

Lewis enjoyed Karachi; for him, it was like being at university again. So impressed were his superiors that they offered him a staff officer's job, which he rejected on the grounds it would be presumptuous of him to accept before he had seen battle. He wrote to Freda:

> I want to be with my own gang when the bad dreams become

a series of reverberant facts. So many of the men are from my own home, were taught by my father or delivered groceries to the house, or worked with my Orphean uncle in Shepperd's pit or Brown's pit. I do belong to them and I always think of the peace in terms of their jobs & their kids. I always feel glad when I'm part of them.... It was a tremendous emotional tug, a crying loyalty to the Welsh soldiers when I was away. I refused that job which meant 900 rupees a month and a real mental and physical challenge, because I wanted to be back with these boys. And now that I'm here, I feel that it was sentiment and selfishness.

To Gweno, he wrote:

When I was leaving Karachi, one of the instructors said to me, 'You're the most selfish man I've ever met, Lewis. You think the war exists for you to write books about it.' I didn't deny it, though it's all wrong. I hadn't the strength to explain what is instinctive and categorical in me, the need to experience. The writing is only a proof of the sincerity of the experience, that's all.

Gweno now believed this was no more than a disguise for his wish to be with Freda in Bombay. However, he told Freda:

I want to run the gamut: and it's quite a mature wish, too: – it isn't for the thrill of it nor for the horror of it, though both these attract. It's for two reasons – to have authority in the long fight of peace, and to share the comradeship of a war, and of death. Sounds very British Legion, to write it: still, it's sound enough.

On August 12th, he told Gweno: 'I feel now that the only place worth going to is the Jungle'. On the 26th August, he told Freda: 'I want to get beyond this poverty of the imagination. I know there is a way – and intuition says the way is through Burma'. Burma was his tryst with destiny and he dreamed of a time of 'deep freedom' for 'this poem, for you, for whatever happens inside me'.

It happened on the evening of August 23rd.

One huge thing happened to me on Monday night when was all alone – I sang it to myself, the thing that happened; the room was empty & I was naked splashing water over myself

& singing this enormous & dreadful joy that came up to me
so casually & said something quite final & terrible to me &
I laughed and sang it back. It was in my sleep, too, & when
I woke, yesterday morning & this morning, and I'm delighted
that I can sing it & not shudder over it.

Struck by this passage, I asked Freda what she made of it. She
replied:

I don't know what the thing that happened when he was
splashing water over himself and singing. He never told me.
I assumed at the time that he had decided to accept our need
of each other and the resulting casting away of the past.
Since, I wonder if he had looked death in the face and,
perhaps, accepted it without shuddering? With some sort of
joy? But this is not likely as he was filled with delight at our
newly awakened knowledge of each other.

A fuller account of this episode appears in Lewis's Karachi
journal:

There are many sadnesses, justified & inevitable & established: why should I make another? I make no sadnesses –
and last night I was singing and there was death quite clear
& familiar at last after all the groping and revulsion and I
sang of it in my tuneless man's voice Did she be close unto
thee, Billy Boy, Billy Boy? Yes she lay close unto me as the
bark is to the tree And me Nancy tickled me fancy oh my
darling Billy Boy: and the places on the map faded away
from me pleasantly & the jungles of Burma came towards
me & flowed round me familiarly & I could count the days
that remained neatly, in a neat pile on a white cloth, and I
knew that this little gesture, this joy of my pen writing this
word, is the good spending of one of my days.
    Though the world be wrong & commit men's
blasphemies and deadly enemies against itself I will not add
to those lecheries in the days that remain, nor hope less or
love less, but more yea more & more love & ever love, & be
less & less the nothing that does not exist & cannot breathe.
    I am glad & I am in love and I don't care.

Once more, water, singing and death form a revelation that is both
dreadful and ecstatic. At last, death stands clear before him and he
vows, in the time left, to love without reservation.

One of Emily Dickinson's poems suggests the tangle of emotions that may come to a man in the presence of a death foretold:

> While we were fearing it, it came –
> But came with less of fear
> Because that fearing it so long
> Had almost made it fair –
>
> There is a Fitting – a Dismay –
> A fitting – a Despair –
> 'Tis harder knowing it is Due
> Than knowing it is Here.
>
> The Trying on the Utmost
> The Morning it is new
> Is Terribler than wearing it
> A whole existence through.

Daunted by the prospect of death, he nonetheless salutes it when it finally arrives.

Freda agreed with my interpretation but felt 'I am glad & I am in love and I don't care' referred specifically to her.

> The first letter, quoting his suicide note. It cannot be other than that. It is quite clear.... I read it with heart-shaking emotion. A new letter, so to speak, from him, his living voice was disturbing. I remembered things I had forgotten....I read your letter several times that day. The next day, sitting down to my typewriter, I read it yet again and was suddenly shaken with such a torrent of weeping that I have seldom experienced in my life. Having got through that I became very sane, almost objective about the whole thing. And I have remained in that mood ever since. A business-like mood, almost. The brooding and speculating, the re-living of the past which I have been doing so obsessionally for the past four years and especially since I was in touch with you seem now unhealthy and restricting.

Where before she interpreted Lewis's dilemma as part of the division between herself and Gweno, now she felt it 'minor' in comparison with his argument about death:

> The men going 'over the top' in the first war to certain death never quite believed they would die – those who survived

testified to this. Wallace says dying people seldom believe in their own death until literally the last breath.

Regarding the showers episode, she wrote:

> Can it be that his writing about being in love with me – and the cry that he doesn't care, that he is happy because he is in love (I could hardly believe this and thought for one idiotic moment that you'd invented it! God and Pikoulis forgive me!) that he should have written it knowing Gweno would read it, could it be that by then (and it was his last journal) the terrifying absorption with death had swept everything, even his desire not to hurt Gweno, from his mind which was why he wrote it?... I think that his long agony was not only a grappling with his maniac but a desperate attempt to piece together the various parts of his fragmented self, to make clear to himself what he was.

There was another consideration that nagged at her:

> I felt I must convince Gweno that her observation that Alun 'never gave it another thought' [i.e. about her] was sheer madness, or that he was living 'in an ecstatic Now'.
> Surely so curious a mixture of joy and anguish never before existed side by side – until the anguish triumphed?

I believed the showers episode proved he was drifting from her, too, but she felt a loving undertone persisted, despite everything.

> In some moods I can read his letters and see them as quite simply those of a man in love, in pain at betraying another love, frustrated by the war and its inhibiting effects on his work, and ill and depressed. In other moods and with you to interpret I see other realisations. We must be very careful not to be absolute in our convictions but to leave some looseness of interpretation, some room for inclusive speculation.

Even so, she was 'amazed' he should say 'I am very far away' and thought it 'extraordinary' the accepted death so 'sanguinely'.

Two months later, Brenda Chamberlain wrote to say she and John Petts had parted. Replying, Alun wished her 'fortitude and independence of spirit & a certain physical immunity from the hurt of things':

> They are what I wish for myself when I'm sane. There's a

> maniac in me that cries out only to be sensitive to hurt. He's
> more concerned with poetry than normal natural happiness
> and he drives me to odd places. I let him, too. I'm dull and
> platitudinous when he's away from me and I welcome his
> return with a secret exultant trepidation, although I know that
> he has no intention of allowing me to retain the deep happi-
> ness of body & mind that Gweno brought with her when at
> last she came to me. I thought life could stand still on that
> foundation. But I was wrong. Life moves and moves and I
> change & change.

Freda was struck by this when I pointed it out to her. Both of us
agreed it gave coded expression to Coonoor: as Brenda and John had
parted, so something significant had occurred to Alun and Gweno's
relation. Divided between the 'maniac' and a 'dull and platitudinous'
self (Siencyn, again), the former drove him to strange places. In the
showers episode, he greets Love and Death – or Love-and-Death –
with exultant trepidation.

Lewis told Brenda that India had made him 'harder & shrewder
& more daring':

> I try to mask the change so that I don't burn my boats, but I
> don't care what happens as long as I am continually myself.

When he cried 'I am in love and I don't care', he became himself.

The phrase 'as the war folds round me out here' recalls images
of folding and furling in Lewis's poems. In 'Burma Casualty', a
wounded soldier lies 'Thinking of all the lads the dark enfolds/ So
secretly' as an 'angel' touches him gently 'round your heart'. In
Karachi, the angel gathered ('folded') him into her arms.

> Well, Brenda, God bless you. I hope we meet again some
> time. I won't write to John [Petts] until he writes to me, but
> I hope I see you both say in 1948 or 9. I don't expect to be
> home earlier, if ever.

One part of him tries to fix a time for their reunion, the other implies
it will never happen. Siencyn holds on, the maniac lets go.

# III

In his Karachi journal, Lewis drafted a versified version of the showers episode.

> Sadnesses manifold, ineluctable and established
> Grow as the rough grass everywhere in India.
> I shall not add another, this is singing
> Counting my days upon my fingers
> Neat piles of days on a white napkin
> Now after all the groping and revulsion
> Come clear at last entertain my death
> With singing. Did she lie close unto thee?
> Yes she lay close unto me
> As the bark is to the tree, my billy boy
> And my nancy tickled my fancy, Billy boy.
>
> The innumerable places on the map
> Fade from me pleasantly the jungles wind
> Their mortal coils about me dulcetly
> And this sweet joy of writing is the right spending
> Of one day that remains me out of ninety.
> Though the world commit countless blasphemies
> I will not add dismay to its treacheries
> Nor love less, but more and more love
> And ever more love, growing less and less
> The nothingness that exists not, cannot breathe
> This I write to you love, to whom the stones
> Are the river's songs....
> India, torn by a century's wilderness,
> Many good men have entered. Now be brave.
> Bear as a child within you the huge error.
> Endure what all must suffer
> Be healed without miracle, without saviour.

('Ninety', in line 5, verse 2, was originally 'seventy', anticipating an amphibious assault on Burma from the Andaman Islands planned for autumn 1943. Six months later, this became a land invasion, hence the revision.) The allusion to Hamlet's 'mortal coils' in line 3, verse 2, suggests death will free him from nothingness as from a world grown huge with error and grief. To carry on living would only add to its error and grief. Lewis enters the wilderness a good man and a child.

This agon in him was resolved by another significant episode in the Karachi journal:

> Fields of golden sesamum, pollen trickling in untidy yellow
> streams down your green overalls & leaden boots, snakes of
> the earth in 50 yards of deep yellow flowers & you kneeling
> away among them listening to the order of a man you hate –
> listening coldly & obeying coldly & exactly because hatred
> takes away warmth. And later your heart is hot with an unfor-
> giveable sorrow kneeling over a man you love who has bled
> away in your hands, hiding swiftly his horrible wounds and
> gently slowly reluctantly his unresponsive face.

With unnerving composure, Lewis anticipates his end. Mind and
body are discrete entities: the latter grows 'insentient' while the
former continues. One self acts against another and, in doing so,
suffers 'unforgiveable sorrow' – 'unforgivable' because culpable,
mourning the death of another he himself is responsible for. He has
killed the man he loves (or realises now he loves), this being the
obverse of the 'Other''s hatred of him for obeying his orders. The
execution is dutifully if reluctantly performed.

Smuggled into this scene is Lewis's long-anticipated encounter
with a Japanese soldier, though the setting is anything but realistic.
The conflict is internal rather than external and conducted with eerie
calm, as of a ritual execution faithfully performed. The atmosphere
is conducive to high deeds, as is suggested by 'fields of golden
sesamum'. ('Sesamum', from The Upanishads, lends dignity to the
occasion.) While snakes slide over the earth, yellow pollen trickles
over the dead man's clothes and boots. 'In Hospital Poona (1)',
Gweno rescued him from 'the venom of the snake'. No longer.

'The Earth is a Syllable' (written earlier that year) also draws on
The Upanishads' notion of the earth as the syllable 'him', signifying
spring, breath, dawn, 'the threefold knowledge'. A mortally-wounded
soldier being transferred from an advanced dressing station to the
main one confesses, in an echo of Hemingway, whom Lewis had
recently been reading, that he

> never liked the idea of Burma. He'd always known he'd die
> if he caught up with it in Burma…. He didn't want to go to
> Burma; he knew it would be a bad place for him.

What the bend in the river was to Nick Adams in 'The Big Two-
Hearted River', Burma is to him.

Shortly before dying, he senses

> a translucent golden influence at the core of his being. He
> could see his wife. She'd wanted a child before he left
> England, but it hadn't turned out that way. And now in a way
> he was glad.

'Golden' influence recalls the 'golden gate' of 'The Way Back' as
well as 'fields of golden sesamum'. Lewis told Freda:

> Frieda darling,...I know there is a way – and intuition says
> the way is through Burma... all the time the malaise has
> grown and I'm sick of it hammering away, hammering,
> hammering. I need your real presence & that is all I need.
> Otherwise I only ache for oblivion, the desert and the laugh-
> ter of a spirit grappling with brutality. All bad things: it's
> ugly, this silken fascination that evil has sometimes.

He hoped writing about it would release him from it and this, in a
way, is what the sesamum field passage does.
    Freda once told me:

> ...Alun must have suffered the appalling experience of griev-
> ing for his own death. It is possible: one grieves for all that
> is lost or unfulfilled in the dead; how much more would one
> grieve at knowing the loss and unfulfilment in one's own
> certain death? No-one quite believes he will ever really die
> except the suicide. He knows he will. Or part of him, the
> suicidal part, knows.

But this is not what Gweno believed. Even so, he wrote to her:

> I've made my peace with life and am willing to go on into
> and through and beyond. The only thing that prevents me is
> my body, which grows tired, and my mind which grows dull,
> and my heart which has a grief and a love that these things,
> these perpetual heres and nows do not permit to exceed them.

Even before Karachi, he sensed that, on the level of 'IS', time
mattered little:

> If I grow healthier and more oxlike and tougher and duller for
> the next year or two, and get nowhere, even lay aside the
> desire to think – does it matter? Even if it were to end like

> that, would time end for me?... I seek no consolation – nor
> am I compelled to imagine some compensating dream
> world....I'm alright myself – I can afford to lose all I am
> losing – you, Gweno, and myself – for an indeterminate time.
> Because I know that there is something indestructible in me...

Melchizedec Evans could not have put it better: the self continues
after consciousness has ceased or, as the Katha Upanishad puts it:

> The knowing self is never born; nor does he die at any
> time. He sprang from nothing and nothing sprang from him.
> He is unborn, eternal, abiding and primeval. He is not slain
> when the body is slain.

Three months later, Lewis told Gweno he was caught up in 'one
of those cyclical expeditions that take place and take me willy-nilly
with them,... these swings from the existing'. Employing an image
whose origin is not far to seek, he remarked:

> I wonder sometimes if there is a yellow-eyed beast in the
> jungle and that is me. I would be happier if I knew there was
> such a beast and it was me.

The quest for selfhood was nearing its end: he was approaching a
dawn when he could be 'particular and exact', free, like Brahma, of
evil, death, grief, hunger, thirst.

Lewis long pondered the question: 'What survives?' The question
was first posed in 'They Came' (1941), which tells of a soldier's
mourning for his wife, killed in an air-raid. Without the consolations
of religion, Lewis wrote: 'Be healed without miracle, without
saviour'. In 'All day it has rained...' and 'To Edward Thomas', his
sorrow for Thomas's death is qualified by the belief that the older
poet lives on in him. Might not his death obey the same principle?

In 'Dusty Hermitage' (1942), written when his love for Gweno
was at its height, Lewis quotes T.E. Lawrence: 'As for fame after
death, it's a thing to spit at; the only minds worth winning are the
warm ones about us', i.e. those we work with, 'the imagination alive
with goodness'. A year later, only the imagination was left. Review-
ing Rilke for *Poetry* (London) (something Lewis would almost
certainly have read), Lawrence Durrell argued that poetry was 'a
man's death coming alive in him': 'The poem is an incubator in which
the spirit can kill itself off in order to gain a kind of eternity in time';

Rilke had 'conquered Death by making it personal': 'Death is our reverted, our unilluminated, side of life'. In this view, affirmation of life and affirmation of death are one and the same; accepting the one without the other constitutes 'a restriction that excludes all infinity'.

Such was the spiritual map Lewis followed in India. Confined to Poona Hospital with a broken jaw in January 1943, he approached 'what Edward Thomas foresaw – the land he must enter and leave alone'. Far from being a conclusion, death was a venture into the 'clearer less bounded incorporeal space of endlessness'. In the showers episode, Lewis greets Eros and Thanatos equally thanks to his conviction that Freda is his continuator, that part of him that will survive.

> I know we are also ourselves, two separate historical beings, but I have this feeling always that I can ask of you anything I can ask of myself: that if there is in me either desire or willingness or, these being absent, pure passive faith in what comes to pass, then it is also in you.

Freda echoed this when she told me:

> We thought the same very often – as he once wrote – without reference to each other. With him, being with him, was like being of him. The sort of closeness one has with one's child. He describes in one letter this feeling the first night he was at Highfield and another man came to fetch me to dinner and Alun and I were so close that the other man seemed a total stranger. Yet he, Alun, had only arrived that afternoon.

In an unpublished poem, she wrote: 'You and I are not separate but are one creature'.

Freda feared what she initiated when she first approached me:

> I wish it were possible to perform some miracle and change the past – but there are no redemptions, no healing, no transfiguring moments in our relations to the past. It is there, wrapped up in the awful sentence of silence imposed on it by the years. As Alun is wrapped up in the awful silence. I wonder sometimes if I have the right to break it. Would he have wanted it or not? And in what manner?

But she was doing what Lewis intended. Was it not part of their compact that, after the silence had fallen and begun to lift, carrying away with it the years of guilt and sorrow, after people's feelings had grown less raw, chafe though they might under the restraints placed on them – after everything, there would come a final valuation and she would be responsible for bringing it about? The silence would, after all, resound to his name. As 'Peasant Song' has it:

> But if I should go
> And you be left behind…
> Would you hear my plough still singing
> And, bearing endless days,
> Somehow give praise?

Freda would 'somehow give praise'.

> …in some unenlightened part of my mind was a vague feeling when I read what he wrote that he was writing for someone who would perceive what he was – all he was. This may sound exaggerated but I really did have the feeling that some ghost stood by him as he wrote. And I began, as I received your letters, to think you were that ghost.

I was, as it were, the essential inessential, the means by which Freda could give praise:

> I must try not to have this absurd feeling that Alun himself has in some way directed all the curious incidents that have led to where we are now! Who is to say it was not…Alun who…led me to you and prompted me to pester you in that bewildered way?

Immediately after the war, sitting in a London park with Juliet in her pram, she wrote 'Speak in Me'. (I cite the original version.)

> Speak in me –
> Oh speak within my listening heart.
> I have waited on your teaching,
> Served so long your gentleness of thought.
> Silent, with love green-growing in my mind,
> I hear your voice, but far – so infinitely far.
> Today the Spring has moved the earth at last
> And alone and longing, I cry out
> Oh speak in me.

He was speaking to her again now and I taking her every word down, though at the time I did not appreciate as much.

# Part Seven
## *Gweno and Alun*

### I

I discussed my interpretation of the showers episode with Gweno:

> The whole passage beginning on page 45 and ending on page
> 46 then constitutes what I believe we may call Alun's suicide
> note. It is then versified on the following pages, particularly
> on page 49, which even adds the number of days left to him.

I said I thought it amounted to a

> premonition of death in the jungle of Burma which appeared
> to him in the guise of a necessary, inevitable consummation
> of himself, of his poetic self, primarily. And it is from all this
> that he felt he had to protect you as he wrote to you three or
> four times a week. Having to say nothing of Freda, even
> though she pressed so greatly on him, must have seemed the
> lesser evasion.

Re-reading this, I am taken aback by its clinical tone. I was telling
her no more than I had told Freda but their situations were different
and I should have allowed for that fact. In my defence, I can only
say that Freda's recent equivocations had made me more  determined
not to mislead Gweno. She had asked me for my opinion and I was
giving it to her, though more artlessly than was either kind or necessary. What I said might modify her views, but these were not at issue.
In love, Gweno was the essence of singlemindedness, so that what I
said could not but have cut her to the quick, particularly since the
subject of suicide exercised her far more than Freda. A man might
fall in love in war – that is what happened – but suicide challenged
her understanding of the man. He had made her uneasy from the start
but she had buried her reservations in his embrace. To question him

now would have been insupportable. Even so, I doubt whether evasion would have made her any less resentful. If offence there were to be, better honesty than prevarication. I had spoken to her frankly about Freda and survived.

Not this time.

Gweno's reply, dated April 1976, was – unusually, for her – typed and ran to more than four pages. She started:

> … may I warn you very earnestly against *over*-interpreting and building up a too solid fabric of evidence pointing to a consistent death-wish since Alun's first depression back in 1935-37.

At their first meeting, she said, Alun had been in good mental health but became depressed when he joined the Borderers two years later. Anxious to prove himself, he doubted whether he were officer material:

> He felt all at sea and lost his confidence. However, apart from a brief reference to it in the work-out of a poem which died on the page anyway, it doesn't show in any of his work of this period.

His depression lifted only to return in October 1943. Back in Poona Hospital again, he wrote:

> I've been aware of the most depressing thoughts and morbid reasonings during the last week, thoroughly depressing. And I've tried to counter them by saying: 'It's this bit of fever makes you think like this!' But really I don't know how long I could stand up to such a morbid neurosis. I suppose I could take it indefinitely: I had to when I was $20 - 21 - 22 - I've$ *almost forgotten the horrible slumps and no man's lands I used to stray into those days* [Gweno's emphasis]. Anyway this last week made the whole world seem chaotic and brutish and pretty grim and hopeless.

He reached his nadir in mid-February 1944, just as the Borderers were entraining for Burma. Gweno's emphasis above implies he was sufficiently healthy after 1938 to ignore his previous 'slumps'. 'His journals all bear testimony to this. There is no sign of morbidity'.

My difficulty in responding to this was that her evidence was drawn from a source Lewis took care would not disturb her – his letters. Yet here she was perfectly understandably quoting them to me as an accurate reflection of his views, despite the evidence of his poems, stories and letters to others. Also ignored was his first hospital stay in January/February 1943, when the depression he suffered was at least as severe as any before, but because it was kept hidden from her, it did not exist. It was not kept hidden from Dick Mills:

> ... I kicked against the pricks a devil of a lot. The world seemed to have been frozen – a vast icecap lay on it – & life was an isolation of the spirit, seeking through impossible lengths of time, attempting to define, & chart & measure. And it got me down, this coldness & inhumanity of mind. I got frightened.

He gave no details but added that he had not told Gweno or his parents out of 'a reluctance to sound happy when I'm not'.

Several months later, he told Brenda Chamberlain he had gone downhill since Coonoor, i.e. from August 1943. Gweno, though, believed he was well until October and characterised this remark as 'one of Alun's broader statements'. In Karachi, he had made a new officer friend and enjoyed the course; besides as she put it, 'he was in a state of elation at the incredible progress of his affair with F.A.' ('I am glad & I am in love and I don't care') .

With regard to the showers and sesamum field passages, Gweno observed:

> At last he has been able, through the help of the kind fates in giving him a new exciting love soon to be consummated, to reconcile himself to his *possible* death – he's not *wishing* it, he's – what he called in an earlier letter – *placing it*. It's what we older people do anyway as time goes on [Gweno had yet to reach retirement age]. With the delirious prospect of a soldier's dream of a week ahead of him, he makes his peace with life and is prepared (in his emotional way) to go on and through and beyond. When he returned to his camp after-wards, he wrote and told me and when I replied, I twitted him about it. By this time the euphoria had gone and he agreed glumly, he had indeed sounded sententious, and he no longer felt that way.

Explanation offered and denied.

   After the climacteric in Bombay and his return to the

battalion, an unhappy emotional situation begins to develop.
It was his first letter to me after their adultery that he writes:
'this is your odd husband darling Gweno – I'm sorry you had
to go and marry me – anyone rather than me – for I'm just
some animation the world has set flowing and compelled to
develop into and out from itself – 'and he continues in this
fanciful way until the old sweat he has to share a tent in starts
making a nuisance of himself. From then on until the following February, nearly five months, he suffers a painful
anti-climax. In addition he develops a bronchial infection.
He is sent to hospital and by Nov. 2nd he is back in the toils
of his ancient foe. Was he paying the piper?....

And so he began cascading downhill. F.A. didn't help
much. She admits she didn't write too often, she didn't cling
to him and anyway by this time she was absorbed in her new
pregnancy.

Freda had done her work well. Gweno wrote of 'his whirlwind affair
with F.A. and its long drawn out aftermath'. Like Lewis's before, she
had been offered a version of events she could accept.

In support of her view that Alun had recovered by the time the
battalion went to Burma, she cited his letter to her of February 23rd
1944 (i.e. a fortnight before his death):

And the long self-torture I've been through is resolving itself
into a discipline of the emotions (freeing himself from his
emotional entanglement with F.A.?) and hopes of you and
me and Shan and the Remington typewriter, and I can feel
my reason taking control and working carefully and methodically.

The bracketed parenthesis offers a tentative interpretation which
promptly hardens into fact: having recovered from his 'entanglement', Alun went off to fight the good fight.

Regarding his death, she wrote:

When Alun insisted on joining a forward company within
25 yards of the Japs, he was impelled by a desire for an
encounter at last and the need to find out for himself what
was going on. He was very aware of his importance to the
men in his sector for their safety and for their success. All
his special training was towards this end. Did his strange
enemy overtake him, or did he really lose his footing in the

dark as he went to relieve himself in a ditch? To infer categorically that this was the final escape of a young death-wishing poet is wrong. I do hope I've explained why.

Equally categorically, she infers it was not.

When Alun made the long journey with his driver and wrote the Orange Grove and when he went in the autumn on exercise into the jungle, it gave him such a sense of release from army pressures and the bloody war. It wasn't the desire for death. He had often wished before he joined up to live in a remote cottage. On our long rambles in Snowdonia and in the Black Mountains we often searched for such a place. We found two, one near Beddgelert and one high above Llanthony Abbey. He used to refer to them with longing in India. Somewhere where he could be at peace. He often warned me not to feel hurt if the rucksack vanished from behind the scullery door sometimes. I think he liked to model himself on Ed Thomas. If he was sometimes pre-occupied, desiring solitude and the 'deep brooding silences that are necessary for this trade of poetry', if he was a selfish and wilful lover, if he allowed himself to be carried by the cross currents and tides of chance, wanting more and more experience – all this belonged to the creative side of him, the dark side – what he called his alter ego. But it is of the greatest importance not to relate this to a state of depression. The early stories you read which reveal a crushing introspection all belong to the period of his first illness. But there was another side of Alun, too, the creature with an outsize social conscience which could just as well have hurled him into political journalism after the war. When Alun wrote gloomily of his chances of surviving the war, Robert Graves told him not to mind overmuch about those feelings. That's how most women feel about their first confinement, he said.

Gweno mixes shrewdness with impatience here, placing her trust in the man she loved rather than the unsatisfactory poet and lover he could be.

As for the sesamum field passage:

Don't you think it's possible that while lying on the ground amongst the flowers during a lull in an exercise, he should suddenly imagine vividly the real situation of having to kill an enemy at close quarters – a man he didn't even hate?

Yet the episode is anything but realistic. It is brightly lit, ceremonious, the atmosphere rapt, as at the end of a tragedy, not the Burma of
leeches, malaria, dengue fever, dysentery, typhus, three-days' rations
on one's back, grenades, spare clothes, weapons, ammunition,
sudden storms and stumbling over uneven ground through dense
thickets in pursuit of an invisible enemy.

Gweno ended her letter with a reference to the editorial work that
awaited her:

> Having commenced the task of reading and extracting
> from his journals and letters I can see it's going to take a long
> time. Running a home, having to shop, cook, see one's
> friends etc. etc. are serious interruptions to a task I want to
> finish and have done with. When I've put together every-
> thing, may I send it to you for your suggestions and
> comments?

A surprisingly friendly end to a letter marked by such significant
disagreement.

As it happens, Lewis's company was not 'within 25 yards' of the
enemy. Perhaps this is what Gweno was told by someone wishing to
dramatise the situation for her. Or maybe she had confused 'yards'
with 'miles'. The furthest the Japanese Ha-Go offensive of February
1944 reached was Taung Bazar and Biasco Bridge, some five miles
from Goppe Pass, the scene of Lewis's death. After that, they fell
back to their main line, which was some way beyond the British main
line, itself fifteen miles from Goppe Pass.

Writing about Alun, Gweno repeats Tom Lewis's view of him as
'an unbalanced little enthusiast' and places her emphasis on his
'fanciful way' of writing, his tendency to 'broad statements', his
unaccountable behaviour and his desire to model himself on 'Ed'
Thomas. He could be a 'selfish and wilful lover', but all these
belonged to the 'creative side of him', the 'dark side' which every
now and then clouded his cheerful self, which was his truest self.
Her point of view is tolerant and commonsensical ('It's what we
older people do anyway as time goes on'). On one subject, however,
she was firm: Alun had recovered from his 'whirlwind affair' and its
'emotional entanglement'.

I was not sure how – or whether – to reply. It was tempting (and
certainly more tactful) to set aside our disagreements and work on
the biography. Yet I felt this would only postpone the evil day; better

confront them now, even at the risk of entrenching Gweno in her views. Accordingly, I wrote, offering to clarify any 'misunderstandings' that might have arisen. I said I agreed with much of what she had said but stressed that it was 'of the greatest importance not to relate [the creative side of him] to a state of depression'. I also noted that the evidence for suicide was 'of the poetic kind, obeying somewhat different rules of proof from the ones applied to normal occurrences of human suffering'. His fascination for death, I said, was not restricted to periods of depression – indeed, at Karachi, it induced in him a strange sense of elation. The difference between us lay rather in her inclination to identify 'the dark side' of him with the mind that creates rather than the man who suffers. 'My understanding goes the other way: that, imaginative as they were, they were not reserved for the page'.

Turning to the sesamum field passage, I suggested the conflict it describes was internal. The 'you' 'kneeling away' in the sesamum flowers listening to 'the man you hate' is also the man who bends over 'a man you love who has bled away in your hands'.

> The most important clue to the meaning of the episode lies in that division and in the use of the word 'unforgiveable' to describe the sorrow of the survivor as he bends over the dead man. It is 'unforgiveable' because it is not merited, cannot be forgiven by the man who died. And with that goes the feeling that the latter tried to prevent his death but was in the end unable to do so, may even have connived at it. Throughout, there is an air of premeditation. The scene, the characters, the action pass as in a tableau of calm execution.

I noted that, if readers did not know when this was written, they would be hard-pressed to ascribe it to the second war. While one side of Lewis courted death, the other resisted it, and it is from this conflict that the tensions in his behaviour arose.

> I hope that my confidence in the question of suicide will not persuade you that I disregard them. On the contrary, the longer I study the work, the livelier they become.

In the showers episode, Lewis greets death exultantly:

> After much "groping and revulsion", attraction and repulsion, death is welcomed and happiness discovered to be

inseparable from it. That is what is celebrated in the snatches
of the song at the beginning and the fierce declamations of
love at the end.

I recalled that, at our first meeting, she had told me she was open-
minded about suicide; so was I. Accordingly, I came to the journal

without predisposition to either side of the argument, indeed
without any expectation that it would contain any evidence
that could help me make up my mind.

After the Billy Boy passage, however, I was in no doubt:

I remember most vividly your description of the attempts you
made to elicit information about his death and the prevarica-
tions you encountered and was convinced that I should write
to you without equivocation. That way, you need not suspect
any lack of openness, whatever you might think of my
opinions.

I reminded her there was a difference between what I said in the
privacy of our correspondence and what I might say in print:

Public discussion of a man's life should be no less honest
than a private one but it brings with it a different set of
obligations, pre-eminent among them the need to present the
reader with all the relevant facts and allow him to make up
his own mind without any undue bias on the author's part to
interfere with his judgment. While, therefore, the selection
and pointing of the evidence would obviously depend on my
understanding of events, they would do so in precise measure
to my commitment to present the facts of the story. If I were
to undertake any such work (and I could hardly do so without
your support), that would be my approach.

Gweno's reply was swift and to the point:

I know you are obsessed by your thesis, tracing the development of the poetic processes that, you insist, led to Alun's
death. You detach with your little forceps the fine strands of
what, to you, is unquestionable evidence and gather them
together to build up a convincing but wholly academic case.
Most of your evidence is derived from the period beginning
with his visit to the Nilgiris. For two whole months he is

knocked off balance by his love affair, from October onwards
he is adjusting painfully to a sense of rejection followed by
his crushing depression.

The 'rejection' is what Freda had told her had occurred – not what
happened but what Freda said had happened.

> Somehow, I feel your feet are no longer on the ground.
> Look at the actualities of the situation. Ever since 1940 Alun
> was never parted from a lethal weapon – first a rifle, then a
> pistol. For the first time now he comes into contact with the
> enemy, the real enemy at last, to within 25 yards range, and
> dosses down for the night with the company operating in that
> area. By this time they are all trained jungle fighters. They
> don't breathe, they don't talk, they daren't crack a twig. If
> you are asking anyone to believe that in *this* situation he
> decides to act out his fantasy and execute 'the order of a man
> you hate', popping his gun and thereby risking every man in
> that forward company and perhaps bringing about some
> action unplanned by the unit H.Q., you are being unrealistic.

But Gweno had gone ahead of herself here. The sesamum field
passage was written seven months *before* Lewis reached Burma.
Even then, his long-imagined encounter with 'the real enemy' never
materialised, so no 'jungle fighters' were involved. Rather, he was
testing himself against the time when – alone – he confronted the
enemy, not a Japanese soldier but himself. (Ironically, the Borderers
never trained in jungle warfare; raised as an infantry battalion in
1940-2, they were mechanised as an army corps in July 1942 and
reconverted to infantry on the 1st April 1943 in preparation for an
amphibious attack on Burma that never took place – everything but
jungle warfare.)

Gweno warmed to her theme:

> For you Alun is an interesting academic subject. You want
> to write about him – after all it is your job – and, with
> Sherlock Holmes detachment you set about proving your
> theory – you did write in your letter – 'the selection and
> pointing of evidence depending on *your* understanding of
> events' (her emphasis).
>
> Alun Lewis has been dead more than 32 years – probably
> longer than you have lived. I am the only person for whom
> his absence is still a painful reality. The 'grotesque' scholars

(Sylvia Plath's words) who pore over every line and every
shred of evidence all these years have effectively prevented
calcification of the lesion. Let the good things he wrote
perpetuate his memory, not a dissection smelling of
formaldehyde with all parts neatly labelled pinned out on a
board in the VIth form lab.

Evidently, the very care with which I had expressed myself counted
against me. I was the nit-picker who missed the essence:

I'm sorry I sound so cheesed off. By the way, you didn't
duplicate the letters and journal I sent you? I hope not. You
see, you don't seem to be able to distinguish between his
different – for want of a better word - voices. Knowing him,
I feel I am in a better position to separate what is genuinely
worthwhile interpreting from that which isn't.

As it happens, I had not copied anything, though I did take notes –
which is just as well, since some of the letters have gone missing
since (see Appendix One).

I was taken aback by Gweno's reply. Evidently, I had pushed her
into a corner until her temper snapped. In his (unpublished)
Longmoor journal, Lewis describes two Gwenos: one the quiet,
gentle woman who 'picked up the bumble bee in the lane in Gower
in April [1940, shortly before he enlisted] and the black beetle she
admired so for his handsome proportions and finish', the other the
one who played the piano 'showing that same coldness and embarrassment and spiritual irritation that is the sign, I know, not of short
temper, but of distress, of feeling something in the quick of feeling'.
I had touched that same quick of feeling.

What to do? I couldn't recant yet further discussion seemed idle.
As it happens, I had been making some enquiries for her about a
missing journal (of which more later) and had something to report,
so I wrote again:

You appear to have convinced yourself that I have an obses-
sion with Alun's possible suicide – at any rate, that I find it
a subject of inordinate interest. This is simply not so. All I
did was go through the material you loaned me and draw
your attention to the one matter that arose immediately to my
attention, as I had done earlier when discussing the short
stories with you. Then, you seem to labour under the impres-

sion that I could not write about Alun's life without pressing my view of him – this despite my assurances to the contrary.... If my words fail to carry conviction, perhaps those of M.R. Ridley, editor of the Arden 'Othello', might.

> I have, as will appear, some clear, if heterodox, views of my own, but I have tried not unduly to obtrude them. I have done my best...to put before the reader the data on which he can base his own judgment.

> The matter could not be put more plainly, as, no doubt, you will be able to confirm with any other prospective biographer.

That last remark astonishes me, appearing as it does to invite Gweno to appoint a new biographer – which is the last thing I wanted her to do.

She made one final attempt to convince me of the error of my ways. (Significantly, neither of us suggested meeting, though we lived barely twenty miles apart.)

> When you read that passage from the journal I showed you where Alun is singing under the showers, you interpreted it as his 'suicide note'! It was written immediately after his week with Mrs Aykroyd in Bombay. His elation and feeling of fulfilled manhood borders on hysteria and the purple writing with which he gives expression to his feelings is echoed by the emotional nonsense he wrote to me from the train on the way to his tryst in Bombay. The hardly suppressed excitement here too is similar in tone. Poor lamb, he would have been wild with me for showing it!

Once again, the emphasis falls on Alun's 'hysteria', his 'purple writing' and 'emotional nonsense'. But Gweno errs when she dates the showers episode to after Bombay; it took place a month before, on August 26th 1943. Perhaps she meant to write 'Coonoor' rather than 'Bombay'. Nor does she explain Lewis's remark: 'I could count the days that remained neatly'. What 'days'? Her reference to a letter 'from the train on the way to his tryst in Bombay' also intrigued me since no such letter appears in the published correspondence.

In 1984, shortly before transcribing his journals, Gweno reverted to the showers episode:

> Which brings me to that passage in his last journal which you

insist is his suicide note. It's what I call an outburst of post-coital hysteria, such as many a poet I could quote has given expression. Should you use this passage to prove your particular thesis you stand to make yourself ridiculous as the fellow who asserted that I had two miscarriages (the source of much merriment at our Christmas table) or the one who insisted that Alun tried to go to sea to prove himself to me!!

The jocular note struck me as odd, considering the subject and the intention to rebuke. Perhaps Gweno had not given up on me yet.

What follows is as strange as any other part of the story. So disturbed was she that she sought to join in league with Freda against me. She wrote to her asking for a meeting not to clear the air between them but to counter what she called 'profound speculation by a serious student'. She told her she

had a powerful feeling that we've got to protect Alun, if we can, from our little Dr Death and his unshakable belief in Alun's pursuit of his death wish – as far back as his early story – Attitude!

Accordingly, the two met for lunch and tea in Oxford at the Flag and Lamb in the company of Gweno's brother, Hywel. However, Freda made it clear from the start that she believed Lewis had committed suicide.

I must write to her again and dread it. Not about copyright [she remained as anxious as ever to secure Gweno's permission to use his letters in her memoir] – that I can't bring myself to mention now – but to tie off the loose ends left by our non-communication at our meeting, to say I realise it was a flop and am sorry that I can't and didn't help her as she'd hoped. Of course my setting you firmly in the centre of the lunch table as the person you are – honest and to be trusted academically – stopped her dead. In other words I was saying anything you wrote would be true and I would agree with it. So poor Gweno could hardly ask me to help her 'protect' Alun from what you might write, i.e. that he took his life. I still and always will find it strange that they won't accept this. So many other things, personal to themselves, weakening to his image – like some of the articles in Poetry Wales – I understand but not their terror of his suicide coming to light.

Writing to me, the nearest Gweno came to betraying her feelings about Freda was when she referred to her as 'F.A.'. At their meeting, Gweno told her that, had she known about them, she would have 'torn up his marriage lines', accompanying the remark with a tearing gesture of both hands.

A few years later, Gweno sent me a number of photographs for reproduction in the biography but forbade me from including any that featured her. I naturally regretted this, since I did include some of Freda, as I think was necessary. The lacuna has not gone unnoticed, though I managed to smuggle in a photograph of the Aberystwyth Students' Representative Council which included Gweno, Alun and Dick Mills in a sea of 37 faces together with one of the Lewis family in which Gweno is seen turning from the camera laughing, thereby blurring her image. Most revealing of all was a wedding photograph: all that remains of her is the tip of her left shoulder pressed against Alun's right one. She had shorn the picture in two.

Gweno's concern about suicide reflected her belief that a man might lose his head over a woman sooner than shoot himself. Suicide reflected on everyone – wife, family, friends, the battalion. There was also the implication of cowardice: Lewis died on Sunday 4th March, the day before the Borderers were due to launch their counter-attack on Japanese lines (contact was actually established on the 18th.) A Court of Enquiry concluded that his death was an accident, after which funds for her pension were released. Some I met felt that it would be better to let sleeping dogs lie on this score alone.

# II

Gweno's version of events needs to be tested against the evidence of his work and his correspondence with others.

As early as May 1943, he was expressing disillusionment with the war and the politics of his youth in that bible of British left-wing opinion, *The New Statesman*: 'Born and bred in South Wales, I thought I knew the face of poverty, but the poverty of India is like acid in the brain'. In India, 'everything is vaster and slower and less easy to alter or influence'. Nothing changes, nothing matters – *kuchh fikr nahin*. There was no chord of righteousness in him either for the Indians or the British. In 'The Jungle', which he completed in

January 1944, he refers to 'the humming cultures of the West', conjuring up an image of something busy but purposeless, despite the fertile associations of the bee. Writing to Gweno, he referred to 'us will-o-the-wisps of the West who never stay long anywhere'.

In his last letter five months later, he declared: 'the long self-torture I've been through is resolving itself now into a discipline of the emotions'. Gweno took to refer to his breach with Freda, though 'self-torture' could be read in a different way. Divided thus in his affections and trapped in the army, he longed to go 'beyond' but was prevented by his body.

> I wonder sometimes if there is a yellow-eyed beast in the jungle and that is me. I would be happier if I knew there was such a beast and it *was* me. Tell me, sweet, am I talking tuppenny rot?

The oblique reference to Bombay is promptly deflected by 'tuppeny rot' – he knew how Gweno would react to such talk. He then apologises to her for his last 'queer' couple of letters:

> It's only one of those cyclical expeditions that take place and take me willy-nilly with them,… these swings from the existing….

He was leaving her but implying he might return; first the admission, then the rider.

On October 12th, another possibility was canvassed:

> You should come to India and I'd get a job in Delhi in the Wounded But Brainy soldiers department, and you could have a punkah and a refrigerator and lots of servants in white uniforms dirt cheap and two gardeners and fruit trees and a horse and trap and a wine cellar and books and leisure and a baby daughter. And we'd be like the other Anglo-Indian aristocrats and let the war drift by without worrying how long it lasts as long as it doesn't inconvenience us. I'd take you for long journeys, and when I have a month's leave we'd go on the Frontier Mail and Srinagar and then by taxi into the lakes and snows of Kashmir and drift on a houseboat with a little cook's galley towed behind and a motor boat with surf boards for excitement and little shops full of fine carved woodwork, and beautiful shawls. And you would dress in a sari and be exquisitely cool and fine in the long quiet evenings!

Even as lovers' fol-de-rol, this is painful. Lewis's pen runs on, converting them into Raj-types. Since the purpose of fancy is to project wish upon reality, this is strange.

A more authentic note was struck when he said he sometimes felt 'as if I'm to blame for the whole world'. Back in hospital in October, he owned he was 'rotting in my mind' from 'the endless strain of estrangement and uncertainty and preparation for fighting – it's a long nausea'; his thoughts had grown 'too rancid': 'I'm not busy, you know. I'm just at something or other all the time'. Ill at heart and uncommitted, he railed against the 'phoney civilisation' (humming cultures?) of army concerts and 'the coarse swearing ranting violent and shallow atmosphere' of the mess.

On November 27th, he complained of 'a universal pining and regret that scarcely has any context or reference, so wide and purged is it. And it will increase more yet'. A week later, he wrote:

> I wish they'd leave Xmas alone. I don't want it. I simply want to clear my head of the darkness that has gathered there like water in a sump. But I don't think I'll ever do that until the war is over. It's grown there quietly and persistently since the day I made those awful blackout blinds for Elm Grove and you etc.

A signal admission, implying that his unhappiness had never really left him.

On December 6th he wrote: 'You try so hard to dispel my Doppel-ganger – you are very good to me'. Yet:

> I am aware always of forces more powerful than myself. They are the determinants and it's always been a hard fight for me to keep my self as an individual integrated against these forces. Some of them are integrating forces – like you: Some are destructive forces – it's quite true and sensible, too, there is a lot of destruction at large on earth and we survive as best we can.

He sees himself here battling against the forces of integration *and* destruction, 'death in life, the black water' *and* Gweno.

> ... it's a bad old world, it really is. And is it really getting better? In so many ways I feel it's getting worse....You chide me for being downcast and bedraggled of soul. I'm sorry for

> being like that. But I must go the way my imperative leads
> me – and I feel that this long trial and strain on the spirit is
> likely to be decisive for me. I believe I'm being true to the
> realities in feeling this way: India is really a great purgatory
> and so is the war, and so is the future we are facing. And if I
> could be light hearted and tranquil about it as I sometimes
> can be I'd be very glad. But just now the burden of it weighs
> hard and steady. I'm foolish

Again the confession and its prompt – if partial – withdrawal under
cover of self-deprecation. He knew she would not want him to
wallow in unhappiness.

The theme that links these letters is 'miserable volatile me'. In
them, Lewis projects himself as the self-absorbed student of his
Manchester days, a protective device that allows him to confess
despair while distancing himself from it. By the end of 1943,
however, he was, literally and metaphorically, in the jungle. His only
relief came from the 'coldness and pride of nature', so different from
'the hypercivilised world' he had left behind. In the simple rituals of
the peasants he found 'a humanity that imperialism and snobbery
haven't spoiled'.

> And I've got a feeling, dear, that another phase of my life is
> ending now, and the climacteric is near. I'm glad, and I feel
> something working blindly towards a position from which it
> can see and plan, and have faith and work enduringly, not
> among things that crumble as they are made and are
> meaningless in history and in the heart. Let it come: it's the
> old cry for the Saviour, let it come. We need it so much, thou
> and I.

Lewis alludes to Yeats's 'gyres', grand cyclical movements that trace
the end of an era and its replacement by a new, antithetical one. As
for history, so for the human heart. Where once there was love,
something different stirs:

> … everything is fluid in me, an undigested mass of experi-
> ence without shape or plot or purpose. And it is as well to let
> it be so, for it's a true reflection of this Now we scramble
> through.

On 23rd January 1944, he told Robert Graves:

> I'm as restless and fidgety as a man on a deserted platform…
> England is 'easy' compared with India – easier to corrupt &
> easier to improve. There are few deterrents at home: the incli-
> nation isn't continually opposed by the cosmic disinclination,
> the individual isn't so ruthlessly & permanently subject to
> the laisser faire of the sun and the sterility. India! What a test
> of man!

It broke him. Eleven months earlier, writing to Graves from India for
the first time, he referred to 'this amazing country with its fasting
saint and starving peasant and universal evil eye. The sun astounds
me'. Thoroughly astounded, he now told him:

> I want to go East & East & East, faire la tour; there is a
> consummation somewhere: after it is over, then I can be
> particular & exact; meanwhile I learn to fire a revolver with
> either hand and try to suppress the natural apprehensions of
> the flesh at a thing so long delayed & postponed & promised
> & threatened.

That 'thing' was Burma and death by a revolver.

On February 7th 1944, he confessed to Brenda Chamberlain what
he had confessed to no-one else: 'God knows where happiness &
spiritual safety lies: not here, not with me, not now'. He said it was
impossible to

> become a poet now, or let myself be. I'm on a hard rein,
> blinkered, mettlesome; I watch lest I bolt, and I look at the
> froth & the sweat of my noisy and clumsy living and I sigh
> very quietly and regret myself & let it all go on in its
> inevitable crashing drive into the headlines and the oblivions
> of this mammoth world.

After July, he was

> as deeply and innocently in love with life as I've ever been.
> Since then I've gone steadily downwards and a growing
> obscurity & introversion has come over me. As usual with
> such neuroses we don't do anything to stop them until the
> 'thing' has a very strong grip on you and then your realisation
> has a quality of hysteria in it and you tend to go wronger
> instead of righter.

Neither Dick Mills nor Harry Tudor, his batman, could release him from his 'neuroses':

> I talk lightly as I can of a bad business: not the first time it's happened: but just now I can't afford to have it: it's a critical period in my little existence and more depends on my balance and brain than ever has before.

He hoped he would emerge straight from it but was

> grappling & clinging a long way from the safe & fructifying life Gweno made about me & I made about her.

'Others' could no longer determine his fate: 'I've lived in vacuo too long & I want no more of it. But I'm not my master'. The letter ends with a promise to visit her in Snowdonia 'in flesh or ghost'.

Sixteen days later, on 23 February 1944, he told Gweno his long self-torture had resolved itself into a discipline of the emotions, which she understood to mean that his depression had lifted. Five days earlier, however (a day before the Borderers sailed from Calcutta for Chittagong), he wrote to his old Aberystwyth girlfriend, Wendon Mostyn:

> My Dear Wendy,
>
> I heard from Gweno that you are in hospital. This is to say how sorry I am and how deeply I hope you are getting over it and not distressed by it in your spirit. I've never been able to make a stoic out of illness. It's always excited and altered me into strange attitudes and I've a great fear of it & a great attraction to it. I do hope it's better with you, Wendy.
>
> I haven't written for a long time, nor heard from you for a longer time, yet I never feel 'out of touch' with you. I'm writing this at a very critical time in my own little existence and I'm not asking you to reply. You're always part of me and I know without your writing. I've been burning myself this week – your lovely letter from Presteigne when you stayed with Rogie has gone to ash – sadly. I've got nothing now except to fight with.
>
> I've gone a long way and I'm very tired. I've written little and felt much in India, and I think I've become more & more taciturn as experience intensifies. I won't write again until I can think as well as feel. Which will be when it's peace. If ever – . I've contrived to get a volume of 50 poems to press

– called HA HA AMONG THE TRUMPETS (you know the
lovely words from Job?). Please write if you can. Your letter
will find me in a strange wilderness. Do send it. If it doesn't
find me it will come back to you with my love.

Ever    Alun

Between the 18th, when he wrote this, and the 23rd, he may have
escaped his 'strange wilderness'. Or perhaps he had done what he
could to tell Gweno what had happened and what was about to.

# Part Eight
## *The Death of Alun Lewis*

### I

An Army Court of Inquiry sat to examine the circumstances of Lewis's death on 31st March 1944. It was presided over by Major I.G. Moon, assisted by Captain D.M. Morgan and Lieutenant D.L. Drummond (both of whom were killed in Burma; Moon died in Africa after the war).

The first witness was Lewis's batman, Harry Tudor, who attested he had called on him at 05.35 for stand-to parade, which lasted an hour before first light and again in the evening. He brought him his shaving water and fitted his equipment in readiness for the patrol he was leading at 09.00. He said Lewis was looking forward to it. After shaving and washing, Lewis left the hut with his .38 revolver in his hand in the direction of the latrines, 40 or 50 yards away. All ranks were under orders to carry loaded weapons at all times since leaving them in their belt holsters might render them inaccessible in an emergency. More than one soldier, though, told me Tudor had told them Lewis usually removed his gun belt after breakfast.

On returning to the hut, Tudor heard a shot from the direction of the officers' latrine. He ran towards it and saw Lewis had fallen down the khud (or hillside). His revolver had fallen from his hand and he had been shot in the head. He ran back to the officers' lines and summoned a party to carry the body back to the medical tent.

A second witness, Major R.O. Crewe-Read, attested that, on hearing the shot, he ran towards the latrines, where he met Tudor, who told him Lewis had fallen down the khud and been shot. Making his way down the steep path to the latrine, he saw the body lying on the ground about five yards away. Lewis had been shot through the head; his revolver lay nearby. There were no witnesses to the accident. He examined the pistol and found it was loaded, with one empty case and 5 rounds. He helped carry Lewis back to the medical tent and sent for the Medical Officer. Three-quarters of the way down the hill, Chalfont arrived and assumed command. Crewe-Read ended his evidence: 'Lieutenant Lewis was normal and was keen to go out on the patrol.'

A third witness, Lt. M.S. Qureishi, of the India Army Medical Corps and Officer Commanding B Company, No 1 Field Ambulance 26th Division, attested he had been summoned to offer medical assistance at 07.45 (there was thus about an hour after stand-to for Lewis to wash, shave, prepare for the patrol and go to the latrines). He found Lewis lying unconscious on a stretcher with a first field dressing to his head. He studied the wound and decided there was nothing he could do, so he applied another dressing. He said Lewis had been shot through the head, the point of entry being on the right temple. There was no charring of the wound at the point of entry, 'and in my opinion the wound could have been caused by the revolver going off when Lieutenant Lewis fell down the khud-side.'

The time of death was fixed at 13.25 hours on 4th March 1944, i.e. six hours after the fatal wound was received at 07.30 hours. Lewis was buried later the same day at Bawli Military Cemetery. The Court's verdict: accidental death.

In signing the report, Colonel Cresswell wrote:

> I have read over the Court of Inquiry, and have investigated the case, and am satisfied that the cause of the shooting was accidental and that no other person or persons were involved. It would appear that, while falling over the khud, the hammer of Lieutenant Lewis's revolver struck a stone or branch, thus causing the revolver to be discharged.

At the same time, Bernard Gutteridge, staff officer at Divisional H.Q., was told by Major Moon, President of the Court of Inquiry, that Lewis had killed himself, a view repeated by Michael (later General Sir Michael) West, 2nd i/c Brigade.

In 1980, I quizzed Cresswell about the Court's verdict:

> I cannot tell you exactly where in the head the bullet entered. I cannot imagine how this would interest the readers of your book. As far as I am aware Lewis died immediately.

In his official history of the 6th Battalion, Lt. Col G.A. Brett wrote:

> At Goppe Pass the Battalion lost one of its most popular
> officers, their first Burma casualty. Lieutenant Alun Lewis,
> the Intelligence Officer, was accidentally wounded by a
> pistol shot; he died in the Casualty Clearing Station at Bawli
> and was buried in the little military cemetery alongside the
> river near Bawli Bridge.

In the Battalion Roll of Honour, his name appears in a section titled
'Died from Battle Accidents', though there is another, 'Died from
Battle Accidents – Not Due to Enemy Action', which might be
thought more suitable. When I asked Cresswell about this, he said it
was a matter of terminology.

A War Office telegram expressing 'deep regret' that Lewis had
been 'accidentally killed' reached Gweno on the 15th March. She
said she would let me see the letter Cresswell sent her but, as so often
with material in her possession, it had gone missing:

> I still cannot find Cresswell's letter. I found it a few weeks
> ago and re-read the terse 'stiff-upper-lip' style of the man
> who simply told me how Alun must have lost his footing, the
> gun striking a stone and exploding, a few suitable compli-
> ments, message of sympathy, offers of any further help, blah
> blah. If it surfaces once more from the pile of manuscripts in
> my room, which from time to time I have to turn upside
> down on your account, I'll send it, never fear.

She never did, but I read Colonel Popham's letter of condolence,
dated 9th April 1944. Popham, the 6th Battalion's first commanding
officer when it was raised at Glanusk Park, Breconshire, in July 1940,
stayed with them until June 1943, when he transferred to General
HQ, but he returned to see them off to Burma. He said Lewis's death
had filled him with 'considerable shock': 'Alun I considered was one
of my best officers and from the day he joined the battalion I recog-
nized in him a man who would make his name anywhere'.

To help clarify matters, I asked Professor Bernard Knight, then
the country's leading forensic scientist, to review the Court of
Inquiry's report. He wrote: 'Obviously the whole point is the differ-
entiation of accident from suicide'. 'Sites of election' needed to be
considered whenever suicide was in question, specifically the temple,
mouth and chest. If the entry wound were at the back of the neck or
top of the head, an accident was more likely. He drew my attention
to the nature of the discharge. If a gun muzzle were held close to or

in contact with the skin, a substantial powder mark would result. However, the Court found no 'charring' of the wound at the point of entry, so the discharge would have had to be fired from over a foot away, 'though naturally the importance depends upon the accuracy of the observations'.

'Charring', however, was not to be confused with powder burning or staining, i.e. the tattoo-like implanting of burnt carbon particles and unburnt propellant powder from the cartridge into the skin. 'Charring' was the result of the application of heat to the skin, like a red burn. Even so:

> ...I must admit that it seems somewhat unlikely that the revolver should be discharged without the trigger being pulled, merely by the hammer being pushed back and then released from accidental contact with some object and that at the same time, the muzzle was pointing in exactly the right direction to cause a fatal head wound.

In his opinion, the mechanics of firing a service revolver from over a foot away meant it was unlikely to have been the means of delivering the fatal wound.

However, a tight contact wound would have caused less powder-staining:

> If it was a contact wound there may be no burning or powder staining.... What usually does happen in the contact wound is that there is a very large entrance wound due to the fact that the gases of propulsion blow into the wound, expand a dome of skin which then splits so that the entrance wound can be very horrendous. If the gun is fired from even a short distance away, this does not happen and the entrance wound is a small circular inverted hole.

He concluded:

> By and large the whole story to me smells of suicide but on the information available I would not think it justifiable to make any firm decision. If we had a better description of the wound and especially as to whether there was powder blackening rather than charring then interpretation would be easier. To the best of my knowledge I have never seen an accidental death with a revolver, though they are common with shotguns.... I feel strongly inclined to think that the statistical

chances of a single shot from a dropped revolver hitting
someone in the temple are very remote indeed and that
deliberate self-infliction is far more likely.

One further piece of evidence, though of a circumstantial and
imaginative kind, needs to be considered. Lewis's most popular poem,
the one that established his reputation, 'All day it has rained…',
makes specific mention of a death by bullet wound. It offers a deceptively simple account of a party of soldiers who are confined to their
tent by the bad weather. On its first appearance in *Horizon* in January
1941, its editor, Cyril Connolly, recommended it as a description of
army life as it 'really is', i.e. far removed from heroic soldiering.

Lewis paraphrased the poem when writing to his teacher friend,
Andrew Davies:

> Yesterday [i.e. October 6th 1940] a great gale came up from
> the sea & all day I watched the grey rain swirl and creep
> along the heather outside my tent, & the acorns pattered onto
> my canvas & the pine needles. Then the marquees we mess
> in soaked thro', grappling with the mad flapping things. Then
> nothing to change into, nowhere to get dry. Blankets damp.
> Darkness early. No lights. No desire. Sleep in warm moist
> blankets & dirt. Itching but tired, tired.

The poem, however, makes something else of it:

> All day it has rained, and we on the edge of the moors
> Have sprawled in our bell-tents, moody and dull as boors,
> Groundsheets and blankets spread on the muddy ground
> And from the first grey awakening we have found
> No refuge from the skirmishing fine rain
> And the wind that made the canvas heave and flap
> And the taut wet guy-ropes ravel out and snap….

Gone the documentary account; Lewis instead creates a languorous
atmosphere, the long, lilting lines reaching beyond boredom to evoke
a dream-like state, ennui shot through with yearning.

> All day the rain has glided, wave and mist and dream,
> Drenching the gorse and heather, a gossamer stream
> Too light to stir the acorns that suddenly
> Snatched from their cups by the wild south-westerly
> Pattered against the tent and our upturned dreaming faces.

Lines with a distinctly Romantic ambience: 'gossamer' recalls Tennyson, 'wild south-westerly' Shelley, the 'upturned dreaming faces' Rosenberg's 'our upturned listening faces' in 'Returning we hear the larks' (which Wilfred Owen thought the most impressive account of the First World War). What irks the soldiers turns out to enchant them.

'All day it has rained...' marks the moment when the war entered Lewis's imagination. On 1st July 1940 (his twenty-fifth birthday), he told Gweno:

> I'm not a pacifist any more. I'll be sorry to my dying day,
> but I won't shirk it. It's a new world to me, this world where
> war has entered the dream world of poetry.

'Dreamy' is what people called him – at Pengam, it was 'Jesus' or 'Dopey'. A teenage girlfriend, Iris Jones, said he seemed to be drifting towards a different destination without feeling the need to struggle against it:

> I knew he was different from other boys of his age. I felt
> some sort of sadness, and at times he seemed to be in a world
> of his own that even I could not share.

When John Petts called on him at Steep in early 1941, Lewis took him to the war memorial in Steep church. Petts, seized by a sense of occasion, felt Lewis was showing him something of great significance to him. When Lewis pointed to Edward Thomas's name on the memorial, he thought, 'Oh dear, you too!'. After, he completed the engraving of Lewis straight off onto boxwood with a burin, a hazardous enterprise. It captures the man to perfection: head bowed, eyes closed, body still, the death mask of the dreamer.

'All day it has rained...' is one of the new kind of poems Lewis began writing in his 'military backwater', 'very quiet poems', 'like Rilke's Bilder [Pictures]'. Though they are written in a time of alarm, they are not alarmed – the poet chooses his subject, not the other way around. Writing to Petts in March 1941, Lewis observed:

> It's peculiar, the fact that although I have never had to waste
> so much time, do so many distasteful things, I've been much
> more successful than ever before with the little I have
> written.

To Petts and Brenda Chamberlain, he confessed he was glad he had decided to 'drop into the Army':

> It's taught me many lessons I'd never have believed – how slow and out of date institutions can become, how happy the human animal can be with so little cause for happiness – isolated in a leaking tent, dirty and tired out in a packed army lorry.

To Renee and Bryan Hopkin, he proffered a summary of the poem's middle section:

> But how coarse and worthless this existence is. Men gathered together in thousands with little to occupy themselves, & no desire to read or do anything but the stock things – beer, cinema, dances, variety concerts full of filthy jokes, dirty talk. I've been doing technical training for 8 weeks – as a prospective railway clerk – and we've done no work at all after the first two weeks. All day they just talk sex, sex, sex…

Never mind; the good soldier Schweik had reserves enough to make good the contradiction between incompetence and its reverse.

Lewis's sensitivity to place is captured by Longmoor's 'perpetual dole'. Indeed, his career as a writer can be summed up in a roll-call of place-names: Cwmaman, Penbryn, Manchester, Longmoor, the east coast, Bovington, Nira, Lake Kharakvasla, Coonoor, Karachi, Bombay. The importance of Longmoor lay in its proximity to Edward Thomas's Red House. In the autumn of 1940, it is not too much to say that he was possessed by Thomas. The issue of *Horizon* in which 'All day it has rained…' appeared also carrried his review of Thomas's *The Trumpet and other poems*.

> I have been garrisoned for six months in Edward Thomas's country and walked his walks. I have sheltered from the rain in the beautiful house he built but did not inhabit. I have read his poems often and often in tent and hut. And now there is this little book to review. Of the book I can say it is well chosen and good.… But of Edward Thomas it is difficult to speak. Say that he was a wise and good man, even after one has realized the cause of his dark and divided personality –
>
>> 'I but respond to you
>> And do not love.' –

> His own words. Say his poetry has the quality of bread, or
> tweed, or a ploughed field; strength, simplicity and a natural
> delicacy that together can express the most complex and
> mysterious moods – what he called melancholy – and at the
> same time a tremendous reality, both of place and time and
> mind.

It is strange Lewis should say Thomas did not 'inhabit' the Red
House: he and his family were its first occupants and remained there
for four years, from December 1909. The house was built by
Geoffrey Lupton and occupies a commanding position on the edge
of the escarpment that overlooks the South Downs called the Shoulder o' Mutton, near Bedales, which the children attended and where
Helen Thomas taught for a while. Thomas disliked the Red House
but discovered it stimulated him imaginatively, as Longmoor did
Lewis. It was where he found he did not love his wife and children -
not because he lacked affection for them but because he could not
love, only respond to, people. Stranded in the house in the mist and
wind was the symbolic expression of his isolation. Perhaps this is
what Lewis intended to say when he asserted Thomas did not
'inhabit' the house: though physically present, spiritually he was
elsewhere, in the beekeeper's hut next door, his study-cum-bolt hole,
on long walking expeditions or visiting friends – anywhere but
'home', a word which had a provisional meaning for him.

In 1913, the Thomases left the Red House for Steep. Two years
later, in July 1915, Thomas enlisted, aged 37. His friend, Robert
Frost, remarked the coincidence of the outbreak of the war with the
poetry he started to write after a lifetime of prose. Nearly all
Thomas's 144 published poems date from after the onset of war; like
Lewis, he is a war poet in the sense that, whatever his subjects, the
tensions they reveal are those only war could resolve.

In his *Horizon* review, Lewis makes specific mention of
Thomas's failure to love and his longing for death. It is the complex
that defines him, too:

> …as war poet, say that he did not suffer as Sassoon, Owen,
> Rosenberg, and was not embittered beyond bearing in him –
> Death, the ultimate response that he, despite himself, desired.

Thomas's recoil from his loved ones appears at a critical moment
in 'All day it has rained…':

> And we talked of girls, and dropping bombs on Rome,
> And thought of the quiet dead and the loud celebrities
> Exhorting us to slaughter, and the herded refugees;
> – Yet thought softly, morosely of them, and as indifferently
> As of ourselves or those whom we
> For years have loved, and will again
> To-morrow maybe love; but now it is the rain
> Possesses us entirely, the twilight and the rain.

The hushed intensity of the lines is as impressive as their patterned cadencing. Men who are separated from those 'whom we/ For years have loved' discover they will 'maybe' love them again – a critical hesitation.

In the closing lines, Lewis describe his walk from Longmoor to the Red House. Though unmentioned before, Thomas has been present in the poem from the start. Indeed, his poem, 'Rain', is the model for it:

> Rain, midnight rain, nothing but the wild rain
> On this bleak hut, and solitude, and me
> Remembering again that I shall die
> And neither hear the rain nor give it thanks
> For washing me cleaner than I have been
> Since I was born into this solitude....

Rain imaginatively expresses the poet's alienation.

The walk to the Red House occurred on Saturday 5th October 1940. En route, Lewis passed the memorial stone to Thomas erected on the Shoulder o' Mutton by some admirers in 1937 with the inscription: 'To Edward Thomas, poet. Died at Arras 1917'. At the top, he turned left into Cockshut Lane, where he met the owners of the house, Bill and Leslie Sykes, who were inspecting a motorcycle Bill had just purchased. Leslie, another Aberystwyth graduate, invited him in and he was to return there often. It became his spiritual home, somewhere he could listen to records or the radio and meet new friends like the journalist Howell Davies, an ex-editor of the Aberystwyth student magazine, who admired Lewis's 'Attitude' when it appeared there.

Lewis's 'long lonely walk with a stray dog & children collecting conkers' was succeeded by a rainy Sunday every bit as 'awful' as the one Cathy Earnshaw and Heathcliff endured in Wuthering Heights:

> And I can remember nothing dearer or more to my heart
> Than the children I watched in the woods on Saturday
> Shaking down burning chestnuts for the schoolyard's merry
>     play,
> Or the shaggy patient dog who followed me
> By Sheet and Steep and up the wooded scree
> To the Shoulder o' Mutton where Edward Thomas brooded
>     long
> On death and beauty – till a bullet stopped his song.

At that, the poem comes to an abrupt halt: Thomas's end is its end. This resolution has divided readers: some (including, at one time, myself) believe it divides the poem into two, the first half focussing on the soldiers, the second on the poet; where it was raining, now it is not; starting in the Second War, the poems returns to the First. It is as if Lewis's 'shaggy dog' signalled Lewis's wrongfooting of his readers.

Yet it is surely this wrong-footing that goes to the heart of the poem, releasing a pressure that has built up from the start. The last line directly echoes Thomas's 'The Path' (which ends: 'till, sudden, it [the path] ends where the wood ends') while 'the schoolyard's merry play' recalls Thomas's 'The Manor Farm':

> 'twas not Winter –
> Rather a season of bliss unchangeable
> Awakened from farm and church where it had lain
> Safe under tile and thatch for ages since
> This England, Old already, was called Merry.

With one word, Lewis converts a walk into a pilgrimage.

Like Thomas, Lewis knew 'Moments of everlastingness' or 'melancholy', a gentle word to describe an ungentle condition. In early 1940, he told Gweno he had spent a night in 'the wet, shabby slums of misery' of Longmoor:

> I sat on the floor, and let the war filter through me, wave after
> wave after endless wave, into beyond time, endlessly.

Here is the music of 'All day it has rained…'. That suggests the poem's theme is not the boredom of the soldiers but one soldier's particular crisis, both dreary and captivating, initiated by his aware-ness that his separation from his loved ones might become permanent, drawn as he is to 'death and beauty' – the death that is beautiful, the beauty that lies in death. Rain is the metaphorical definition of the complex, which accounts for the fact that mention of death in the last line is not imposed but manifests a latent wish. Both Lewis and Thomas were susceptible to suicide but the latter resisted it out of a conviction that he did not need seek death; death would find him – and where better than on a battlefield? All he needed to do was put himself in harm's way.

Lewis makes another significant error when he says that it was a 'bullet' that stopped Thomas's song. It was not; a burst of shrapnel in the first hour of the Arras offensive precipitated his fatal heart-attack ; the body was left unmarked. The poet whose death was caused by a bullet wound was yet to come. Was Lewis consciously or subconsciously anticipating his end here? Whatever, by misde-scribing the older poet's death he inscribes his own in it. It is this creative misreading that grants the poem its substantial unity.

Writing to his sister, Mair, in 1942, Lewis remarked:

> I know I can go on writing – I'm not the sort to dry up. I can feel the depth of the mountain spring – only a bullet can shut it down.

## III

'All day it has rained…' was followed by 'To Edward Thomas' (subtitled 'On visiting the memorial stone above Steep in Hampshire'). Once again, Lewis begins, Thomas-fashion, with disarming simplicity, addressing the poem to the older poet in a manner that could not be humbler:

> Climbing the steep path through the copse I knew
> My cares weighed heavily as yours, my gift
> Much less, my hope
> No more than yours.
> And like you I felt sensitive and somehow apart,
> Lonely and exalted by the friendship of the wind
> And the placid afternoon enfolding
> The dangerous future and the smile.

Thomas is Lewis's 'Other', Lewis his continuation by other means.

In 'The Other', Thomas wrote of his pursuit by an alter-ego with whom he shares 'moments of everlastingness'. So again here.

'To Edward Thomas' echoes the first poem Thomas wrote, 'Up in the Wind', and, beyond that, *Adam Bede*. First Thomas:

> But the land is wild, and there's a spirit of wildness
> Much older, crying when the stone-curlew yodels
> His sea and mountain cry, high up in the Spring.

Then George Eliot:

> High up against the horizon were the huge conical masses of
> hill, like giant mounds intended to fortify this region of corn
> and grass against the keen and hungry winds of the north;
> not distant enough to be clothed in purple mystery, but with
> sombre greenish sides visibly specked with sheep, whose
> motion was only revealed by memory, not detected by sight.

And now Lewis:

> I sat and watched the dusky berried ridge
> Of yew-trees, deepened by oblique dark shafts,
> Throw back the flame of red and gold and russet
> That leapt from beech and ash to birch and chestnut
> Along the downward arc of the hill's shoulder....

The sunlight then goes

> slanting sea- and skywards to the limits
> Where sight surrenders and the mind alone
> Can find the sheeps' tracks and the grazing.

As Ian Hamilton says, 'a superb moment in Lewis's poetry'. A familiar tension erupts:

> Later, a whole day later, I remembered
> This war and yours and your weary
>
> Circle of failure and your striving
> To make articulate the groping voices
> Of snow and rain and dripping branches
> And love that ailing in itself cried out
> About the straggling eaves and ringed the candle
> With shadows slouching round your buried head;

And in the lonely house there was no ease
For you, or Helen, or those small perplexed

Children of yours who only wished to please.

In time, the 'voice that called you' became

More urgent as all else dissolved away,
– Projected books, half-thoughts, the children's birthdays,
And wedding anniversaries as cold
As dates in history….

Till suddenly, at Arras, you possessed that hinted land.

Once more, a poem about Thomas comes to an abrupt end with his death. It as if Lewis wished to test the idea twice.
    In 1935, T.E. Lawrence told a friend:

As for fame after death, it's a thing to spit at; the only minds worth winning are the warm ones about us. If we miss those we are failures.

Lewis also wished to be loyal to the 'warm ones' but eventually had to ask pardon from 'you who want us for ourselves' for the 'strange inconstancy of soul' that led him to reject the 'warm pacts of the flesh' for 'death and beauty'.

# IV

The question remains: why did Lewis go on to commit suicide after meeting Freda? In her, he had found a most powerful reason for staying alive, yet he did not.Why?
    The answer lies in the false assumption that he was centrally concerned with life and death. He was not. What he sought was the fulfilment of the self, and this is what Freda granted him. Thanks to her, he had become one of the 'yellow-eyed proud soft moving beasts that go their own way and in some clearing in the jungle sometimes come upon each other and become thereby sublime'. Gone his devotion to 'the warm ones about us' and the democratic ideals of south Wales; he had become an isolate in love, a creature of the existential moment. From that perspective, falling in love with Freda

was not the antithesis of suicide but its precondition. It *allowed* him die, to *choose* to die, in that way securing his identity. For Lewis, 'to be' meant 'not to be' – that was the only freedom that mattered to him. As he told Freda: 'I'm gasping for somewhere I can at least & at last *breathe*'; after meeting her, 'how different everything is from anything that went before'.

This strain of thought derives from 'Lance-Jack', the fictionalised version of his Longmoor journal. The opening section appeared in November 1940, the complete version in *The Last Inspection*, 1943. (The American poetry editor, James Angleton, called it 'the best single literary effort to come out of England since the war'.) In it, Lewis for the first time uses 'I' as other than a literary device. Like all his best his work, it was written in 'feverish mood' and expresses his ambivalence towards the army, which could be crude and coercive but oddly inspiring, forcing on the soldier an impersonality that was akin to that of a writer.

> In the Army you begin again…. Conventions go, respectabil-
> ity, narrowness, the suburban train and the Sunday best.
> Those who were trapped are forced to be free of the old
> routine. Those who were unhappy are forced to be unhappy,
> conscripted into a new way of life. Everyone will realise
> sooner or later that nothing is fixed, nothing inevitable. They
> will realise the possibility of change. Many long-standing
> abuses will no longer be able to conserve themselves.

And that is what happened after 1945. It constitutes the optimistic view of the war.

> But it is dangerous, too. The soldier doesn't bother. He
> is a migrant, an Arab, taking his belongings with him,
> needing surprisingly little of the world's goods. He leaves
> his violin and his Cezanne and his garden behind. His wife,
> too, and his children, as time passes…. Certainly the soldier's
> heart leaps for leave. But when I go home on leave I feel
> vaguely 'out of it'. The new carpet doesn't thrill me as it
> should; the troubles and little quarrels with neighbours are
> no longer my troubles; they are the preoccupations of
> strangers.

It was the same alienation that confounded Edward Thomas:

> [O]n guard at night at some outpost, somewhere, he can only

envisage the human past, the great centrifugal force of the
heart which draws into its orbit and unites in love all differences of people, mother and sweetheart, friend and pauper,
employer and baby daughter, I say he can only envisage this
great power of life as a swarming of bees on a bough....

And if you ask why a man appears to prefer what is
casual, rough, hazardous and incomplete to what is warm and
personal and loving, I suggest you read Edward Thomas's
poems again. It is, if you like, curious that the idealist should
live casually with regard to himself and the preservation of
himself, that he should find the haversack, the trench, the
journeying, most suited to the pursuit of high ends. Christ
had no home. Women dislike, even hate this quality in their
men. It is the overturning of all that was so hard and slow to
win, the gradual building up of friendship, love, mutual
knowledge, home, children, the rooted beauty of flowers,
budding and opening in petal and colour and curve *in one
place*. But it is a fine quality, in the best men. And there is
always, it seems, some suffering. There is Beethoven as well
as the nine symphonies.

When Freda released the artist in him, she inadvertently sealed the
man's fate.

In September 1940, typing out 'Lance-Jack' in Cwmaman, Lewis
told Christopher Cheney:

It was so very nice, all of it. Even the first odd unreal feeling
of not being in my own home with my own flesh and blood,
but in some kind friends' home whom I've not seen for years.
It wasn't at all nice then, but thinking over it I find it full of
implication. What was it all – the school I worked in, the
walks I always took, my sister, mother, aunt, Gweno; her
house and the fun we had in getting it and fitting it up? – a
way of life. Just as this is a way of life. What will be the next
mode for me? I don't like this line of thought.

He was detaching himself from home, felt 'out of it', though he could
not say as much to the women he loved. But he could to Freda
because, with her, he became 'Arab'. Very distinctly, she offered no
'*one place*', no possessive love, no crimping and crippling, no
distinction between 'thee' and 'me'.

... you are natural to me. Do you *like* being each other? I
know we are also ourselves, two separate historical beings,

> but I have this new feeling always that I can ask of you
> anything I can ask of myself....

T.E. Lawrence once told a friend:

> You guessed rightly that the Arab appealed to my imagina-
> tion. It is the old, old civilisation, which has refined itself
> clear of household gods, and half the trappings which ours
> hastens to assume.

That, in the end, is why Alun could let Freda go.

> The clearing again in the jungle. Go away from my water-
> hole. I am drinking. Drink with me. Go away. Stay. Go away
> that you may always stay.

Repeatedly, he offered her none of the reassurances he offered
Gweno. With her, he could bear/bare the truth.

Robert Graves understood why when he observed: 'the lost
rudiments of poetry...confirm the intuition of the Welsh poet Alun
Lewis who wrote just before his death in Burma, in March 1944, of
"the *single* poetic theme of Life and Death... the question of what
survives of the beloved"'.

> No Muse-poet grows conscious of the Muse except by
> experience of a woman in whom the Goddess is to some
> degree resident;... A Muse-poet falls in love, absolutely, and
> his true love is for him the Embodiment of the Muse.

Not that this necessitates a comparison between his two loves. Each
was true, though in different ways. Alun's letters to Gweno are vivid
but there is an element of compunction in them that occasionally
rings hollow. They are what an Arab might write while pretending
to be a Jew. Freda once told me:

> I have always thought that there was something *platonic* in
> his letters – the extracts we read – to Gweno and his poems
> to her. There is no passion in them. The only passion in
> writing of her to me was in his *fear* (as he wrote emphati-
> cally) for her, and a sort of low-toned, muted intensity when,
> as though forced out of him, he described her 'leaning and
> clinging' (when he wrote of his ideal of love), even, so
> surprisingly, of her 'crippling'.

She contrasted them with the letters she had written to me:

> Any extract that might be made from these letters of mine,
> however unconnected from ourselves, somehow conveys a
> reflection of the passion which existed between us....

Lewis's youth was characterised by home, respectability, self-improvement and moral responsibility. For him these were a powerful good, yet not the greatest good. When he accepted this, he could reconcile his guilt towards Gweno with his love for Freda, his disenchantment with the war and the West's cheap-jack civilisation.

Alert to the drift of his letters, Freda could not yet grasp their deepest implications:

> If I were reading now for the first time these letters as written
> to some other woman I might see more clearly their true
> significance in his life and death. But I gave them birth, as I
> gave his love birth, watched them and it develop and change;
> I have lived with them for thirty years – is it not understand-
> able that my sense of them was overweighted by the
> awareness of he and me?....

Looking back, she realised that, beneath the drama of herself and Gweno, lay that of Alun *contra mundum*. As an uncollected poem has it:

> What is love at least?
> A way of dignifying death....
> Love may have ravaged like a beast,
> Yet at the last it is at least
> A way of dignifying death.

No longer was it a regression to the maternal, a 'child at your breast'.

> I know that at some late stage I thought painfully that if I
> could go near enough to be with him for one meeting (it was
> difficult to do this sort of thing with soldiers in camp) I might
> comfort him. But one did not attempt that sort of compas-
> sionate undertaking during war... and, furthermore, I was
> expecting this child for whom we had waited for ten years. I
> was anxious about Alun, loving him in the romantic, isolated
> way that was our own, and at the same time preoccupied with
> the coming birth of the baby. I tried to comfort him in my

letters, to give him hope of some sort of solution to our divided loyalties – I tried very hard – but in the end I, too, lost faith in there being any solution.

He, for his part, fretted at his 'emptiness of personality':

The war comes uppermost. The self, & Love, & all warm nearnesses recede.... I want to get beyond this poverty of the imagination. I know there is a way – and intuition says the way is through Burma. Maybe it isn't, maybe that's only the bait on the trap.

Whichever, he was going to discover.

# II

India tested Lewis to the full. After docking at Ballard Pier on 18th December, 1942, he travelled to Nira, a hot, dusty village near Poona. Out on a walk with a friend, he stopped before a granite Buddha beside the track.

… the sun beating on my neck round which I'd slung my bathing trunks, I felt the refusal. A wall of darkness, hard, resistant, smooth-surfaced.

He had found something 'outside' himself that could not be mastered at the end of an officer-sahib's pistol:

For about half a minute and the only time during the week I've been here, I was aware of physical desire; a local itch, entirely local and thereby quite definite, in the sensitive inch or two of flesh that always has represented the simply physics of love.

Yet never did I breathe its pure serene.

Since it was the 'simple physics of love' that had previously confounded him, the event is notable. Stirring before the Buddha, he was taken out of himself, aware only of his body, which was granted a prominence previously denied it, conscious only of 'a service of perfect freedom, a sense of infinite space to be in, just to be in'.

In his aroused state, he wished to travel

> through lands whose existence I did not know but whose
> location I had been ignorant of till then. The map of the
> spirit's geography.

> Oft of one vast expanse have I been told
> Yet never did I breathe its pure serene.

These lines from Keats's sonnet on first reading Chapman's Homer
suggest that for him, as for Cortez, a new planet had swum into view,
one that promised him wholeness.

A month later, he was in Poona Hospital with a broken jaw; his
teeth had to be removed and wired back and a splint inserted. When
the fracture suppurated, it had to be reset. There followed an attack
of dysentery. In acute pain, he drifted towards

> the unknown place that Edward Thomas wrote of in his poem
> "that has not any book/ Nor face of dearest look"'....My
> mind has gone into such frozen, desolate wastes that I've
> been appalled; and the pain has been the taut enduring pain
> of being frozen by the whiteness and blankness of the scene
> and the failure to find any relief or hope or any familiar sign.

In 'Ward "0" 3 b' (a hospital story), he observes:

> The sick have their own slightly different world, their jokes
> can't afford to be morbid like the healthy, nor to be indiffer-
> ent to their environment like the Arab. The outside world has
> been washed out; between them and the encircling mysteries
> there is only the spotlight of their obsessions....

He explored these obsessions in three hospital poems. The first
of them, 'In Hospital: Poona (1)', ends with a vision of 'the lady of
the red yacht' (Gweno, the goddess in her kindly guise), with whose
help he 'survives the venom of the snake'. The second, 'In Hospital:
Poona (2)', opens with a description of the view from the Junior
Officers' Ward over the maidan (or parade ground) to the Towers of
Silence, where the Parsees (Mohammedans of Persian descent) leave
their dead for the vultures. His operation is once again associated
with Edward Thomas's 'unknown place', an out-of-body experience
which permits him to venture into the bourne from which no traveller

returns. At the end, the 'heart's calm voice' reasserts itself and a balance is restored.

The third hospital poem, 'Burma Casualty', is dedicated 'To Capt. G.T. Morris, Indian Army'. 'Charlie' Morris, from Newport, south Wales, lay in the next-door bed to his; he had had part of his leg amputated after receiving wounds in the retreat from Singapore.

> Lying in hospital he often thought
> Of that darkness, whence it came
> And how it played the enchantress in a grain
> Of morphia or a nodding of the head
> Late in the night and offered to release
> The Beast that breathed with pain and ran with pus
> Among the jumping fibres of the flesh.

Fine, edgy writing.

Morris's experience reinforced the reputation of the Japanese for ruthlessness and confirmed Lewis's belief that Burma was a 'bad' place for him. In the poem, a narcotically seductive 'enchantress' replaces his 'wife's sweet body and her wilful eyes' and their 'timeless love'.

> ...he lay in the lightness of the ward
> Thinking of all the lads the dark enfolds
> So secretly.
>                        And yet a man may walk
> Into and through it, and return alive.

– as Edward Thomas had imagined. A soldier enters the darkness that 'enfolds' his comrades yet comes back alive. Though tempted to join them, he resists but understands why they have succumbed – and why he still might.

> The dark is a beautiful singing sexless angel
> Her hands so soft you scarcely feel her touch
> Gentle, eternally gentle, round your heart.
> She flatters and unsexes every man.

Lines of immense suavity. In 'The Way Back', the White Goddess was a golden 'she' who turns into a Black Goddess in the closing liebestod, promising the lovers a reunion through death and dismemberment. So again here.

Lewis described the hospital poems to Dick Mills thus:

> As for the poems, I very much want you to see the ones I
> have written here: but I feel they are *wicked* poems. They've
> distressed me a lot in writing them and I shall be glad to re-
> establish my contact with solid things by leaving the dream
> world of hospitals & reentering the rough warm material
> Earth world of every day.

The India Lewis found when he emerged from hospital at the end
of February was both daunting and inspiring. It was where his
parents' progressive attitudes ran out of steam and he grew increasingly attracted to the peasants' dignity and forbearance:

> Every time I look at an Indian peasant, I feel tranquil,
> especially when we are on some fantastically strenuous
> exercise, for the peasant is so utterly different and settled and
> calm and eternal that I know my little passing excitement and
> worries don't exist in his world and are therefore not univer-
> sal and will disappear.

Like them, he was bowing before the inevitable.

In 'The Mahratta Ghats', the Indian scene is painted with a rare
power:

> The valleys crack and burn, the exhausted plains
> Sink their black teeth into the horny veins
> Straggling the hills' red thighs, the bleating goats
> – Dry bents and bitter thistles in their throats –
> Thread the loose rocks by immemorial tracks.
> Dark peasants drag the sun upon their backs.

Fertility is as much a burden as a blessing to them. Occasionally, he
was irritated by their impassivity, their inability 'to be anything
positive or to experience either defeat or danger or risk of loss; their
awful social complexes, their profiteering slickness as well as their
pauper passive suffering'. Nevertheless, the common man remained
the

> last repository of worth – not in the mass for then he becomes
> a blind force: but in himself – helpless in political terms, but
> inestimably worth the world in himself.

*That* much of the democrat survived.

> The sun has sucked and beat the encircling hills
> Into gaunt skeletons; the sick men watch
> Soft shadows warm those bones of rock,
>
> And the barefooted peasants winding back,
> Sad withered loins in hanging dirty folds,
> Mute sweepings from the disappointed streets,
> Old shrunken tribes the starving dusk enfolds.

Before the sun's unblinking eye, human effort fails.

In 'The Peasants', a group of soldiers pass a group of cowherds who are 'Stepping lightly and lazily among the thorntrees/ Dusky and dazed with sunlight, half awake'. They are followed by some pregnant women with stones on their heads engaged in road-making:

> Across scorched hills and trampled crops
> The soldiers straggle by.
> History staggers in their wake.
> The peasants watch them die.

Never has 'History' seemed less of an abstraction. Nature and time alike spell out the fate of the soldiers: '*And no returning*'. Lewis surveys the scene from a great height, like Hardy's Spirit of the Pities in *The Dynasts*, reducing the soldiers to mere objects in the landscape, beyond both pity and blame.

Only the Muse remained to comfort him. She first appears in Lewis's work in two Longmoor poems, 'Prelude and Fugue' and 'Peace'. In the former, she symbolises the darkness of a world where 'armoured monsters tremble' (c.f. 'iron beasts' in 'The Way Back'):

> The beautiful stranger
> Is singing the songs in which the larks are hidden –
> That music was always in us, farmer, collier, or sailor.
>
> What seemed a long way is not far to go.

The stranger's songs arise from earth and deliver us back to it.

In 'Peace', which Lewis sang as he crossed from barracks to cookhouse, a buried 'she'

> ... comes from the dead,

> Smiling, without mystery,
> Homeward slowly turning
> Century by century.
> And all the heart's deep yearning
> In her Being is burning, burning.

A Yeatsian annunciation.

In March 1943, the Battalion moved to Lake Kharakvasla, a six-mile stretch of water, to train in amphibious warfare. He wrote six poems there: 'My head seemed to develop a spasm of music and lovely phrases appeared in the water'. The siren was singing again. Returning the poems to Gweno, he assured her that their love was 'indestructible', as if the reassurance were necessary:

> your old husband is so terribly anxious to get back to you
> that he hits out violently at any suggestion the poet might
> make to the contrary.

Suddenly, poet and man pull in different directions.

The finest of the lake poems is 'Water Music'.

> Deep in the heart of the lake
> Where the last light is clinging
> A strange foreboding voice
> Is patiently singing.
>
> Do not fear to venture
> Where the last light trembles
> Because you were in love.
> Love never dissembles.

Moving lines, as epigrammatic as they are lyrical. The lady of the lake addresses him:

> Fear no more the boast, the bully,
> The lies, the vain labour.
> Make no show for death
> As for a rich neighbour.

*Sub specie aeternitatis*, nothing remains.

> What stays of the great religions?
> An old priest, and old birth.

> What stays of the great battles?
> Dust on the earth.

In 'Lines on a Tudor Mansion', Lewis referred to 'Samson dead/ And Delilah dirtying her hair/ In the dust of the fallen/ Faiths'. Old religions may repeat themselves but in vain; so are all the battles that have been fought.

The poem then builds to a powerful conclusion:

> Cold is the lake water
> And dark as history.
> Hurry not and fear not
> This oldest mystery,
>
> This strange voice singing,
> This slow deep drag of the lake,
> This yearning, yearning, this ending
> Of the heart and its ache.

All printed versions of the poem have a full stop after 'This oldest mystery', thus destroying the mounting effect of 'This...' - 'This... ' - 'This...' - 'This...', which climaxes on 'this ending/ Of the heart and its ache'. 'Ending' appears to end-stop the line but leads into the next, enacting what it describes. The heart *will* find surcease in the 'beautiful singing sexless angel', harlot of the imagination.

Water imagery appears often in Lewis's work. At the end of 'Ward "0" 3 b', Lieutenant Anthony Weston sits on the ledge of the pool in the grounds of the Junior Officers' Ward in Poona Hospital with his hand in the water:

> Circles of water lapped softly outwards, outwards, till they touched the edge of the pool, and cast a gentle wetness on the stone, and lapped again inwards, inwards. And as they lapped inwards he felt the ripples surging against the most withdrawn and inmost ledges of his being, like a series of temptations in the wilderness. And he felt glad to-night, feeling some small salient gained when for many reasons the men whom he was with were losing ground along the whole front to the darkness that there is.

'Salient' and 'front' recall the First World War. Weston believes he is protected from the darkness that has claimed so many of his friends but the 'temptations in the wilderness' come to him 'softly' and

'gently', as if an angel were hovering nearby who rendered all protection futile.

In July, shortly before Lewis left for Coonoor, he completed 'The
Orange Grove' in a 'kind of drunken frenzy'. It is his masterpiece in
the short story form, based on a reconnaissance trip into 'this
mammoth jungular world of the East' 200 miles from Bombay,
enjoying

> the freedom, the new sights, the utter disconnectedness of
> each day.... It satisfies the nomad in me. ... I haven't got an
> address now, I'm just a gypsy.

He could go on travelling like this for years, experiencing

> the infinite feeling of a star in endless motion, a sort of lack
> of connection, as though no yesterday and no tomorrow
> could affect this steady Now.

Six months later in 'The Jungle', he wrote:

> The act sustains; there is no consequence.
> Only aloneness, swinging slowly
> Down the cold orbit of an older world....

In 'The Orange Grove', Staff-Captain Beale's reconnaissance trip
takes place the week after Ghandi and Nehru's imprisonment for their
'Quit India' campaign, designed to expel the British from India
despite the presence of the Japanese on the border. In an atmosphere
of heightened tension, he finds his driver has been knifed in the back.
Placing the body in the back of his truck, he drives off but soon gets
lost – he who prides himself on his efficiency and his nose for danger.
Eventually, he halts in a ford which is just then being crossed by a
tribe of faun-like gypsies; he hands the driver's body to them before
joining them himself. First the *sarkikos* (or carnal man), then the
pneumatikos (or spiritual man).

Aboard *The Athlone Castle*, Lewis had told Gweno about

> ... little George, the boy who wanted to divorce his wife in
> Southend because she was whoring, and who joined the army
> at sixteen after trying to go to the colonies, he gave the loveli-
> est talk I've ever heard, in his singsong illiterate unaspirated
> Welsh voice, about the Jewish collective farms of Palestine

which he'd seen when he was shooting Arabs out there. 'No one grows for money, they breeds beautiful 'orses and they got lovely orange groves an' the doctor don't ask for money for 'is services but you pays 'im with food or clothing or whatever you do make. An' I never seen a 'appier people in my life an' by God I wished I could 'a stayed with them'.

The collective ethic of the Jewish kibbutzim echoes the democratic socialism of south Wales. Like his creator, Beale chooses the jungle over the orange grove.

On July 8 1943, Lewis told Gweno he was engaged on a search 'as deep as childhood' for existence 'in the clearer less bounded incorporeal space of endlessness'. A week later, he wrote to Dick Mills:

I'm in a mulish & grieving mood in secret these days – grieving over something I've lost, something unbearable it is. I dream very intensely and do my work with the efficiency of an automaton, whether it's running the Eisteddfod or acting Adjt for a battalion move. But I can see through the mirror all the time – at the *emptiness* behind.

He wanted to go through and beyond. Having interpreted the war previously in terms of fitness, feats of endurance and proud muscles, Beale finds himself in a rising state of panic and turns to Lawrence's 'old, old civilisation', as figured by the gypsies:

Once Life had been nothing worth recording beyond the movements of people like these, camels and asses piled with the poor property of their days, panniers, rags, rope, gram and dahl, lambs and kids too new to walk, barefooted, long-haired people rank with sweat, animals shivering with ticks, old women striving to keep up with the rest of the family...

He wished, though, that he knew where they were going. They only smiled and nodded when asked. Maybe they weren't going anywhere much, except perhaps to some pasture, to some well.

'Maybe', 'perhaps', 'some pasture', 'some well' – noticebly ambivalent language.

In his Karachi journal, Lewis originally concluded the story with an account of Beale's 'feverish excitement' in 'this mort of history, this after flux of ancient and mass migrations'. 'Mort of history' is a magnificent phrase, evoking the graveyard of time. Late that night, a gypsy child dies and is burned together with the body of his driver. Soon after, Beale leaves, fretful at 'not having some Army form or accident report' to fill. Back in the battalion, he is reimmersed in a 'world of detail & formality & necessity with chagrin' and has to contend once more with his chancy character:

> Thinking back now he cdn't see why he cd get nowhere with one girl & why it had to end with another – & the erotic absti- nence of two years had not sublimated so much as deceived him. And in buying a woman & letting her more & more share in his day dreams in conflict with his wife he was going beyond the possible, without yet realising it.

By mid-1943, Lewis was conscious of his false position in India:

> There is such a thing as freedom, and in Europe *we are* liber- ators at the moment. In the East it is less so, alas. Liberty isn't the point at issue, and neither side offers it. That's what makes it so hard to accept.

– which grants the British as little justification for waging war as the Japanese. Evidently, there was little left of his enthusiasm at the time of his enlistment. As early as autumn 1941, he had told Dick Mills (then about to embark for India):

> I wonder whether you will have to support the British Raj against the democrats who demand the same rights as Joe Soap 'ave got. I hope not. But it must be very difficult to soldier where the unarmed have got the moral victory.

It was a difficulty that came back to haunt him when he, too, became a representative of the Raj, and it irked him as much as

> the conventional life of the Mess, the officer mind and its artificial assumptions, the rigid distinctions of rank which so rarely go with quality or character, the backbiting and watch- ing each other that is a seething obligato to our daily bread.

He realised he was 'miles & miles' outside India – not as far as a civil servant, perhaps, 'but hopelessly far for a poet to be' and took care not to write in his 'outside moods':

> My chief salvation is the awareness of this, and the strange feeling that comes sometimes, & swings me into an immediate & brief communion with this country.

Even so, he was uneasy:

> It really is an amazing, spectacular land but something seems to have gone wrong at the root of it. I sense a perpetual undercurrent of mockery and hostility towards us among the people. I've been reading a book by Edward Thompson on India, a deep careful and disturbing book which caused me to think that there'll be no peace with the Indians until we've fought them – I feel very sad about it all, for my heart is in the right place and I don't agree with the Britisher School nor the Churchill School. I feel this problem is too vast for us. I wish I had come here as a doctor, teacher, social worker: anything but a soldier. It's not nice being a soldier in India.

How to defend a country against the wishes of its inhabitants?

> I don't mind joining a movement to kick them [the Japanese] out but I don't want to play at belonging to them [the Indians].

A pox on both sides.

Once, when travelling by train, he passed a waiting civilian train in which 'all the Indians booed & booed & booed'. Stung, he said he 'loathed the whole gambit. I could be happy in India but only if Britain and India could be friends'. But, in 1943, that was impossible:

> I can't ever grow used to the idea that this is ours. I feel utterly strange here, and I sense a perpetual undercurrent of hostility among the people.

Even so: 'I can never be just English or just Welsh again!'. National identity seemed irrelevant to one caught up in 'the sprawling gamble of big empires grappling for blood and oil and palm nuts'. That was all the war meant to him now. He may have seen possibilities in it for him as a writer, but he lacked 'the deep brooding silences that are necessary to this trade of poetry'.

# Part Nine
## *The Jungle*

### I

Early in 1976, Freda met Lord Chalfont, whom she found tough and touchy. When she told him: 'I am and always have been convinced that he [Alun] took his own life', he replied: 'Oh, you are, are you? Well, it is a point on which I have always refused to commit myself.' With defensive belligerence, he told her that only two people knew the truth – himself and Harry Tudor, and Harry was dead. Freda told me:

> I have wondered since whether there is not some sort of embargo set upon him as first Alun's adjutant, and secondly as Minister of Defence – he spoke of the dread of the army to be involved in any sort of scandal and this somehow still holds good with him. He never actually admitted the suicide to me but only when I spelled it out – for instance by asking him where the wound was, or rather by telling him I'd asked Gweno this – spread his hands or nodded or some such indication of agreement. And he talked of the 'classic place' – the temple – for suicide. Never actually agreeing. You would, I know, run into trouble (and I wouldn't like to be on the rough side of his temper) if you made any attempt to 'get him to commit himself to an opinion'. Oh heavens! I shiver at the thought. He wouldn't.

Her last comment refers to my hope he might help clarify matters once for all. He told Freda everything 'suddenly came to me clearly' when he read a description of manic depression: 'He had all the classic symptoms'. Gweno might have agreed without accepting that he had committed suicide. Her incredulity on the score was only marginally affected by the rumours to the contrary. In certain circumstances, he might be tempted but his caring self would always have prevented him. Her brother, Hywel, believed his eagerness to go to a forward position on the fatal day was the result of the 'galvanic' nature of the occasion rather than reveal any personal inclination. He might have fallen victim to sniper fire.

Freda wrote:

> ...I don't believe in her [Gweno's] 'sadness' after all these years but the years do not make a difference to other terribly complicated and entangled emotions, rooted in self-esteem, self-pity, self-torture of various sorts, and in the fact of loss. Gweno had and has and is the sort of person who never would have had anything other than her marriage to Alun, and out of this comes heaven knows what tortured and probably unrecognised motives and emotions.

Such love was a powerful weapon in self-defence. Had Gweno read the letters he wrote her, she might have come to a different conclusion but Freda had misled her about their contents. Was Gweno deceived? I doubt it, but she was grateful for any suggestion that Alun had returned to her in the end – if, that is, he had ever been away.

Freda, on the other hand, believed he belonged to no-one. When he admitted her 'within the charmed circle', she knew exactly what he meant:

> I had said, after the many operations etc. I'd had, that if it came I would not be so unwilling and as though we suddenly entered together a country until then only known to him. He drew me in with joy.... And his last letter clearly describes the dead man – 'heart failing, eyes, lungs etc.' Wallace read it then and thought the same, and Gilly since and of course the same. I remember my distress at reading it. Death-wish is the name of that which compelled him.... I myself wrote to her to ask her [Gweno] why she felt it matters so much that it should be known, pointing out that it never affected the respect and admiration people felt for other poets who died by suicide or wished to or who invited death. She never replied to that.

Even so, she thought Gweno knew the truth, even though she would not admit as much.

> Gweno isn't one to go into the deep psychology of creatures,

or the mystic or romantic or despairing. People are men and
women with certain facts relating to *what happens* to them,
not what goes on inside them. Alun is either cheerful,
'breezy', buoyant, or ill, depressed, not himself. He is stating
things categorically, overstating them – not feeling them,
unaware of what is driving him or torturing him. I think she
knows he died by his own hand.

'The Jungle', Lewis's last poem, is a 99-line poem concerning a
party of soldiers who fall asleep beside a jungle pool. At once gnomic
and confessional, rhetorical and lyrical, its tone is elevated but
exhausted. That Lewis should have wrested such noble expression
from his dire circumstances is a tribute to his resources as a writer.

The poem's closing lines register the approach of death in heightened theatrical fashion:

> ...if the mute pads on the sand should lift
> Annihilating paws and strike us down
> Then would some unimportant death resound
> With the imprisoned music of the soul?
> And we become the world we could not change?
> Or does the will's long struggle end
> With the last kindness of a foe or friend?

For a last time: what survives? The 'mute pads' might be those of a
tiger or panther and conjure up an image that is at once terrible and
picturesque. 'Annihilating paws' is a sumptuous phrase that strikes
terror while leaving one awestruck by that which terrifies. The paws
are poised to attack but promise the ennoblement of the victim by
raising the him above the struggles of life. Will the poet's 'unimpor-
tant death' resound with all he leaves unfulfilled or does death merely
signify termination?

Earlier in the poem, the soldier senses 'time is swept with a great
turbulence,/ The old temptation to remould the world'. In 'The Earth
is a Syllable', completed on March 5th 1943, a dying soldier recalls

> the queer consolation of the other things he'd tried and
> written off for failures and now recalled – the little meetings
> he's tried to run, debates round a hurricane lamp on the
> FUTURE, talks he'd carefully put together on RECON-
> STRUCTION, gramophone records he'd borrowed and
> played for the lads, the choir he'd tried to make something
> good of; naturally it was no good for a few odd men to sit

round and discuss how to prevent another war, naturally they
couldn't 'succeed'. Still, it was all right to remember it.

Not now. What Longmoor nurtured, India destroyed. As 'The Jungle'
puts it, the 'distant world is an obituary':

> The act sustains; there is no consequence.
> Only aloneness, swinging slowly
> Down the cold orbit of an older world
> Than any they predicted in the schools,
> Stirs the cold forest with a starry wind....

The 'warm' ones vanish, along with the world of mediaeval theologians with their notions of transcendence, to be replaced by the absurd universe, in which nothing exists but the recurrent present. The 'humming cultures of the West' disappear into the jungle's 'trackless wilderness'.

From this perspective, death is 'the last kindness' of a friend or foe – friend for ending life, foe for denying individuals their fulfilment. Like the sesamum field, the jungle reveals the eternal doubleness of things – foes as friends, friends as foes. In the opening lines, a crocodile slides into the water from the ochre sand, driving the translucent fish under the boughs. Once more, a predatory action is granted picturesque expression. In the poem's third section, quail and teal migrate from Turkestan across the Himalayas to Kashmir and the south. Such is life, a coming and going, bringing existence here, termination there. Such images, far from inducing despair, dignify the inevitable.

1915 was not a good time to be born in Cwmaman. The scars it left lasted a lifetime. Whatever else was the cause of Lewis's depressions, they could not have been only personal. In his memorial broadcast to him, Dylan Thomas described him as

> a healer and an illuminator, humble before his confessions,
> awed before the eternal confession of love by the despised
> and condemned inhabitants of the world crumbling around
> him.

It is the poet of social justice who penned the outstanding retrospect of the Hungry Thirties that opens the poem's second section:

> Wandering and fortuitous the paths

> We followed to this rendezvous today
> Out of the mines and offices and dives,
> The sidestreets of anxiety and want,
> Huge cities known and distant as the stars,
> Wheeling beyond our destiny and hope.
> We did not notice how the accent changed
> As shadows ride from precipice to plain
> Closing the parks and cordoning the roads,
> Clouding the humming cultures of the West –
> The weekly bribe we paid the man in black,
> The day shift sinking from the sun,
> The blinding arc of rivets blown through steel,
> The patient queues, headlines and slogans flung
> Across a frightened continent, the town
> Sullen and out of work, the little home
> Semi-detached, suburban, transient
> As fever or the anger of the old,
> The best ones on some specious pretext gone.

The fact that Lewis was one of the 'best ones' lends poignancy to the description. But if he left the valleys, they never left him. His account of Depression Wales is at once indignant and austere and not the least of its virtues is that it should be an 'imitation' of W.H. Auden, the poet who, more than any other, defined the 'low dishonest decade'.

What Auden does from the outside, however, Lewis does from within. His is no mere pastiche but a homage and criticism, from pupil to master, by way of emulation and rivalry. In Longmoor, the type-poet was Edward Thomas, in Bovington T.E. Lawrence, in India Auden, champion of political engagement and preacher of enlighten-ment in the cause of social and psychological health. The poem echoes to his rallying cry of 'a new architecture' and liberation from sexual repression, emotional neurosis and political injustice as expressed in vivid panoramas of a land in crisis. But when, for him as for Lewis, the tide turned, he recanted. The future he had once envisioned perished in a 'dive' in New York's Fifty-Second Street in September 1939, which Lewis alludes to with 'mines and offices and dives'.

Auden's influence on 'The Jungle' is overpowering. (In Part III, it is Yeats, the private retrospective there balancing the public one here). Lines like 'As shadows ride from precipice to plain/ Closing the parks and cordoning the roads' come effortlessly to mind without compromising the poem's originality. This is not so much Depression Wales as Depression Wales *as Auden might have envisioned it* surveying 'Glamorgan's glove-shaped valleys'. Lewis describes Cwmaman 'as the hawk or the helmeted airman sees it' but without Auden's levity, all passion spent. Where Auden fixes a scene preparatory to leaving it, Lewis stays in Cwmaman.

'The Jungle' tells of a group of exhausted soldiers who, having fallen asleep by a jungle pool, never waken from their 'little death'. The poem is their dream reverie, 'Where sleep exudes a sinister content', 'sinister' suggesting evil (if the accent falls on the first syllable of 'content') or relief which, though kindly meant, is evil in effect (if the accent falls on the second. Such verbal play occurs again in 'quenching', which refers either to the slaking of their thirst or death: 'As though all strength of mind and limb must pass.'

Asleep, the men desert 'those who want us for ourselves'

> And all fidelities and doubts dissolve,
> The weighted world a bubble in each head,
> The warm pacts of the flesh betrayed
> By the nonchalance of a laugh,
> The green indifference of this sleep.

It is Edward Thomas's recoil from his loved ones again. 'Pacts of the flesh' and 'fidelities and doubts' hint at Freda and Gweno. Six months earlier, he had told Freda:

> The war comes uppermost. The self, Love, and all warm nearnesses recede. And I say only Frieda, Frieda, and many things that happened to us are happening again in this liberation of the Indian jungle, in me. The element that nags and vitiates is absent. I'm simple again and like a stream, it may be deep, it may be still and swift, it has its own nature. Oh God, how lovely it is, this interim of peace.

In Raymond Williams's *Border Country* (1960), the conductor at an Eisteddfod concert welcomes each child performer by name and by reference to their families and/or place of residence, treating them not as individuals but members of a community and the event a 'ceremony of identification and memory.... This, centrally, was the meaning of life'. When Lewis severed his ties with his loved ones, he lost the ground of his being.

> The killing arms uncurls, strokes the soft moss;
> The distant world is an obituary,

We do not hear the tappings of its dread.

Like Othello, the soldier loses his occupation; like Hamlet, he finds
sleep – if

> ... by a sleep to say we end
> The heart-ache and the thousand natural shocks
> That flesh is heir to, 'tis a consummation
> Devoutly to be wish'd. To die, to sleep;
> To sleep: perchance to dream: ay, there's the rub;
> For in that sleep of death what dreams may come
> When we have shuffled off this mortal coil,
> Must give us pause.

Thus severed from the past, he forfeits recognition and rootedness
for the repetition of acts that are themselves devoid of significance -
the ultimate absurdity. The historian in Lewis never worked to deeper
purpose than when he wrote 'The Jungle'.

Towards the end, the dream of death exalts the soldier's 'bowed
and golden head' ('golden', naturally). Gweno thought this referred
to the men sitting at a trestle table but the more pressing reference, I
think, is to Narcissus. A man stares at his reflection in the pool:

> Oh you who want us for ourselves,
> Whose love can start the snow-rush in the woods
> And melt the glacier in the dark coulisse,
> Forgive this strange inconstancy of soul,
> The face distorted in a jungle pool
> That drowns its image in a mort of leaves.

More Auden: 'glacier', 'coulisse'; these gravely beautiful lines form
part of the chain of water images initiated by the jungle pool. 'Mort'
might signify a large number or death. (In his schoolboy story, 'The
End of the Hunt' (1931), Lewis tells how 'the mournful horn sounded
the mort'.

> And I, who sought humanity
> Within myself, and found a lie,
> Turn to the heart of things at last
> And know the way we live and die.

'The Jungle' tells how he lived and died.

1. Brynhyfryd Villas, Cwmaman. The Lewis family lived in the end house.

2. Alun with his brothers Huw and Glyn, 1922.

3. The Lewis family, probably 1924. From left to right: Mair, Gwladys, Laurie Phelps, Tom, Alun, with Huw and Glyn in the foreground.

4. On holiday in Penbryn, 1932. Alun, Gwladys, Glyn; Mair, Huw.

5. Cowbridge Grammar School First XI Hockey. Alun is standing on the left. The team included four Welsh internationals.

6. Aberystwyth Students' Representative Council. Alun is third from the right, back row; on his left is Chris Germanacos. Gweno Ellis is second from the left, third row, and Dick Mills is fourth from the right, front row.

7. Alun in 1938.

8. Alun, July 1942.

Wood Engraving : Debris Searcher.                    John Petts.

# TWO POEMS *by Alun Lewis*

## RAIDERS' DAWN.

Softly the civilised
Centuries fall,
Paper on paper,
Peter on Paul.

And lovers waking
From the night—
Eternity's masters,
Slaves of Time—
Recognise only
The drifting white
Fall of small faces
In pits of lime.

Blue necklace left
On a charred chair
Tells that Beauty
Was startled there.

## SONG OF INNOCENCE.

Pyrotechnic shells
From the blackened fair
Break like meteors
In the careless air.


Dancing girls and singing birds,
Poets' and crooners' platitudes
Violently die.


But the simple words
Spoken in shelters, crypts
  and wards
Where the disfigured lie


Are swans in the sky.

Published by the Caseg Press, Llanllechid Caernarvonshire
and printed at the Gomerian Press, Llandyssul, S. Wales.

9. Caseg Broadsheet Number One, featuring Alun's poems 'Raiders' Dawn' and 'Song of Innocence', with an accompanying engraving by John Petts.

10. In India, with his friend Jack Gush, at Poona Hospital in February 1943. The hospital provides the setting of the story 'Ward 'O' 3(b)'.

11. And with Gush at the Poona rifle ranges, April 1943.

12. Highfield, the Aykroyds' home.

13. Freda Aykroyd.

# Part Ten
## *Portraits*

### I

Freda believed Gweno's reaction to my interpretation of the Karachi journal disclosed a deliberate intention to wound: 'Oh lord! How difficult it is to read or remember his letters about Gweno and think of the letter she wrote to you'. She said Chalfont '– who, I should judge, is not the nicest of men himself! – immediately recognised the character she seems now to have revealed'. Nevertheless, she wished to remain on friendly terms with her. Gweno had recently written:

> Are you going to develop the theme of Alun Lewis's Muse in India and record your love affair? I'm asking you this because I want you to feel perfectly free to do so.....Knowing you I feel your book will be sensitive, compassionate and deeply sincere, but if you are going to portray his great love for you, I beseech you, omit his breastbeating on my account and any reference to me. The young man 'doth protest too much, methinks' as people will say. And anyway actions speak louder than words.

The letter combines generosity with resentment. While encouraging Freda to write, she stipulates a condition which would have made it impossible for her to do so: not to mention her. She knew Alun loved Freda (something she was at other times at pains to deny) but asked her if she had given him 'the basket, as they say in German'.

This, of course, was a bind of Freda's own making, as she recognised:

> ... how in the world can I write the truth when I have been at such pains to convince her of the untruth?

Gweno had told her:

> I shall always feel sour in my heart that he did not choose to
> tidy the nest before he went to Burma. During the time he
> was in Karachi, he was in a state of high-hearted happiness.
> After one of his many avowals of eternal love, he seems to
> be justifying what has happened to him since his visit to
> Highfield as a kind of compulsion of a creative spirit 'to go
> where the cross currents and tides take me, and I know that
> I always seek for wider and deeper experience'. Then on the
> Frontier Mail on his way to his assignation with you in
> Bombay, he writes '...that now I can go where I *must* and
> where I *will* – and always be certain of us!'

Interestingly enough, this letter is absent from *Letters to my Wife*.
Freda wrote:

> When I say I felt humbled by this letter I mean it, but I did
> also, once again, feel strongly the essence of what he'd
> described: a sort of insensitivity to the finer shades of feeling,
> a persistent reality which does not allow for anything other
> than the obvious reality.

She had not mentioned Alun's poems to her and felt their correspondence had run its course. 'She knows I believe he killed himself and
I wanted her to accept the fact from you'. Gweno had told her:

> You are right about John Pikoulis. If he does write anything,
> and I must gird up my loins and see him before he does, he
> may well err on the side of being too positive.

Which is to put it mildly. Evidently, she was in no hurry to pass
judgment on me.
    I did not how to proceed. Freda told me:

> Wallace, quiet and not giving out much, said: 'It would
> depend how he writes it. Anything can be written with tact
> and skill.... One can't prevent anyone from writing what they
> want to write.

Yet how write when every word must be gravel to Gweno's wound?
Several people I interviewed asked me not to repeat what they had
said if it would harm her.

Ironically, Gweno herself had pointed a way out of my difficulties. There was no doubt I had hurt her but, by the same token, she was now beyond further hurt. Disapprove as she might of my conclusions, she wanted to retain some influence over me while I, on my part, wanted to defer to her without assumuing she could not defend herself. She had, in effect, dared me to publish and I would do so, conscious of the harm to Lewis's reputation the continuing lack of attention was causing. Once, in cynical mood, I told Freda that no-one reads, mindful of how 'The Way Back''s declaration of love had escaped detection. The general reader seemed not to know much about him and wasn't keen to find out more.

Freda saw the biography as an attempt to honour him while correcting the false interpretation she had palmed off onto Gweno.

> I think you are very right to go to see Gweno and not to try to write. You will most certainly come nearer to her and make yourself more subtly understood than in any further attempt to do so by letter. I want you to know that you may tell her that my explanation of Alun's and my love was not really true but how you are to do this you must judge for yourself. It will be terribly difficult. But I do not see how you are to put all the illuminating factors leading to acceptance of his suicide without doing so. Perhaps you think it is not necessary? Perhaps you can *suggest* it, making it seem it was there but unrealised by me – if this will make it more acceptable to her. Oh, I don't want to hurt her again, nor set her back in the shadow from which I truly believe she has emerged. This came to me when she wrote about her task now being to record, collate and make some whole of his journals etc. and then ended with a cry of relieved joy in the thought 'And then I shall be free'.

Evidently, she was as subject to contradictory feelings as Gweno.

This became more apparent when Wallace's health began to fail. Previously, she had not discussed him with me but now wrote:

> It is a beautiful story and set down sensitively can do no hurt. BUT there is one thing which is the main cause of my hesitation and it is this: Wallace never knew about Bombay. I think Gilly does – she must do as she read the letters. I don't think Juliet does. But Wallace did not.... you see, he knows there was this romantic love affair, that Alun was probably (in W's mind) deeper in love than me, but he doesn't know and it

would hurt him that we were ever lovers.... He never knew
the real truth about Alun and me. Guessed he loved me (knew
it) guessed I loved him but, I am sure, because that was the
way he behaved, thought not very seriously, not remotely
coming into my real life. He couldn't have imagined that at
all. I was not unattractive and he was used to these things,
but for me to have physical love for any man – consummated
love – would be outside his understanding.

Lewis had once written: 'That other life haunts me inescapably & I
desire it ineluctably. It makes the rest of living sad'. That is what she
felt, too, and it explains her neglect of him at the end for she was
rooted in *her* 'other life'.

[Wallace] realises I always loved him and would not have left
him for anyone else. I always knew this in my deepest heart...
.Wallace always came first. Always. He was the rock on
which my life had been based for more than ten years – a long
time when one is young.... Alun became less and less important and, I feel great guilt about it, I neglected him. I didn't
brood over his need for me. I should have. I had felt wildly
happy about the romantic love affair with him but that is what
it was for me. For him it was something much, much more.

When they fell in love, he finally left 'home base'.

The root of his life was poetry – the writing of poetry. The
soil in which it thrived was the love of his parents and family
and his wife Gweno. And the love which came to him during
the short time he was in Coonoor, when no word of it was
spoken, could be called, I suppose, its fruit.

Until now, she had thought of herself as 'an instrument in all this
discussion and research, not as myself':

Now I'm talking of me as myself. I loved Alun; it was a
romantic love, a poem, a realisation of some ineluctable
longing people like me – and him – have, mainly women.
(Or is that not true? Men too, then.)

The version of events she had given Gweno eased both their hearts
but revealed an inner truth in favour of which no more persuasive
voice could be raised than her own.

Freda's belief that she had neglected Lewis at the end was sincere. Caught up in preparations for the birth of her third child and secure in her love for Wallace, she did not write as frequently as he wished. To say what, though? Both of them understood that reality had placed a limit on their romance – indeed, positively demanded its submission. But romance placed its limits on the practical, too. If there were to be no more Freda and Alun – or Gweno and Alun, come to that – it was because *they* had determined it should be so.

Freda once urged Lewis to 'be careful'. He responded:

> Love is one of the few things we can't be careful about. It lives and dies in its own nature. Care cannot foster it, nor lack of care kill it. All it asks is honesty. That is all I'm trying to give. Honesty and love.

Freda believed that love was for him a repetition of the maternal tie in a different key and that his attachment to her was greater than hers to him: 'my love for Alun was a romantic love that was apart from the existing love, intense though not eroding it.' She had tried telling Gweno as much. She may even have believed it herself.

## II

I knew Wallace Aykroyd only a little. When I visited Freda, he kept himself to himself and joined us only briefly before leaving us to our excited speculation. A tall, lean man with aquiline nose and drooping shoulders, a ghost of a smile played on his lips. He was unfailingly polite and spoke mildly and tersely. Evidently, his labours had taken their toll.

At the time, Wallace was employed by the Nestle company in their defence against critics of their provision of dried milk to mothers in the third world with their slogan: 'Nestle kills babies'. It is easy to understand why they should have wanted him. Wallace Ruddell Aykroyd was born in Dublin in 1899 and trained as a medical practitioner, specialising in the diseases of malnourishment. After two years with the Lister Institute in London, he joined the League of Nations in Geneva and in 1935 published *Three Philosophers*, which included an assessment of the founder of the science of nutrition, Antoine-Laurent Lavoisier.

In the same year, he and Freda moved to Coonoor. Each morning, he would put on his white coat and tour the laboratories and animal houses of the Nutrition Research Centre. In 1943, he served on the Inquiry Commission into the Bengal Famine and, after India, spent 14 years with the FAO in Washington and Rome, ending his career as Senior Lecturer at the School of Hygiene and Tropical Medicine in London. His chief work from this time was *Sweet Malefactor* (1967) (subtitled 'Sugar, Slavery and Human Society'). He also wrote a novel, which remains unpublished.

Increasingly ill and tired, he died in February 1979, a few days short of his 80th birthday. He was notable for his research and organising the research of others as well as creating practical solutions to the problems of malnutrition.

# II

I met Lord Chalfont in late 1976 in the hope that he might clarify the circumstances of his death and thus help repair my relations with Gweno. Freda wrote:

> He likes to think of himself as being the one *army officer* who knew A.L. and who had his confidence and was a sort of father figure.

As it happens, I had been in contact with Chalfont about Lewis's last journal, which was passed to him for safe-keeping on March 3rd 1944 before the latter left for Goppe Pass. In August or September the following year, Chalfont gave it to Glyn Lewis, who was also serving in India at the time and copied it on the train carrying him to Burma. On his return, he gave it back to Chalfont, posting the copy he had made to his mother. Chalfont packed the original up with Lewis's other effects and forwarded them to Gweno in the usual way. After that, it disappeared.

Some time during the family holidays in 1946, Gwladys Lewis handed Glyn's copy to Gweno, who until then had been unaware of its existence, since all his other papers had been returned to her the previous year. (So anxious was she about them that she visited Chalfont in Shrewsbury at the end of August 1945 and extracted from him a promise they would reach her shortly.) When I queried him about the journal, he made his displeasure plain.

I must add that I am very reluctant to become involved once
again in these rather convoluted transactions. I have never
understood Gweno's approach to this – from the beginning I
have made the facts absolutely clear, namely that as Adjutant
of the Regiment it was my responsibility to send *all* his
effects through the proper channels. This I did. If Gweno
received a copy of the notebook from the Army, presumably
they must have been in possession of the original.

Gweno, however, insisted she had seen neither the original nor the
copy. It seemed odd no-one in the family was familiar with it. – the
terms are interchangeable) mentioned Freda and showed Lewis to
be in a state of despair and instability. Someone – perhaps Major
Moon, the Battalion's second in command, a civilised man – may
have suppressed it.

Chalfont began the interview by remarking that Lewis was 'dull'.
Freda took exception to this and protested that Lewis disliked
Chalfont and was never close to him. During their meeting, he had
told her he did not understand his poetry. Perhaps 'dull' referred to
Lewis's awkwardness in the Mess, when his natural liveliness was
suppressed under cover of abstraction – Siencyn, again.

Chalfont stressed that anything he told me was off the record but,
as it happens, he said very little. When he found Lewis's body, there
was a pistol clutched in his right hand; a single shot had been fired.
There was no massive disfigurement to the head: the bullet had
entered the temple and exited from the rear. When I asked if he were
willing to be cited as authority for these facts (though not decisive,
their tendency is clear), he said he would speak on the record only
to an official biographer. Since I was one such, he was insisting on a
distinction without a difference. Chalfont's gift for obfuscation had
been well-honed over the years. Freda thought he wanted to encourage an air of mystery as cover for the possibility that someone had
seen Lewis shoot himself. Whether or not, it was apparent that, if
Gweno were to be disabused, Chalfont was not the man to do it.

He then said (as he had told Freda) that he was thinking of writing
something about Lewis himself, so his caution might have been
related to his desire to hold something back for later use. Freda
surmised:

It is possible that he is just plain jealous of the fact that you
clearly have every intention of writing one and doing it

thoroughly and, since he feels himself to be the doyen of
Alun's military career (rather as Dick has felt for years he is
of A's literary one!) he is making a thing about having information about him which he just has not.

Despite Chalfont's penchant for Delphic utterances, I found him
charming. He told me nothing of significance but wanted to say it in
person, as it were, mixing reticence with veiled significance, now
and then adding a dash of worldliness, as when he remarked that all
married men were liars and the Welsh the biggest of them all.

In his autobiography, *The Shadow of My Hand*, Chalfont devotes
a few pages to Lewis. They are a masterpiece of saying something
while saying next to nothing.

> We had been in position for a few days when Lewis came
> to me and asked permission to visit one of the companies on
> the hill just above our headquarters, with the quite reasonable
> purpose of reconnoitring the situation for himself instead of
> just basing his intelligence assessments entirely on periodic
> reports from outlying companies. I was a little uneasy about
> this request, as he had seemed depressed and distracted for
> some time and was obviously in some kind of emotional
> turmoil – not an ideal frame of mind for someone proposing
> to go on a jungle reconnaissance. However, I eventually gave
> in to his pressing arguments and agreed that he could go and
> spend a few days on the hill, on the strict condition that he
> attached himself to the troops already there and did not go
> thrashing about the jungle on his own.

Years earlier, however, Cresswell had told me:

> Lewis did not request to join 'B' Coy which was guarding
> the Goppe Pass. I sent him. It was good practical experience
> for the I.O. to go with patrols into enemy held territory; and
> to collect & collate information for my use at Bn H.Q..

After launching a surprise attack on the British lines in February
1944, the Japanese had received their first check and fell back,
though pockets of resistance remained, so that, by the time the
Borderers reached Bawli Bazar on 26th February, the atmosphere
was jittery.

Chalfont's account hinges on the notion of Lewis climbing a hill,
from where he could enjoy a better vantage point for intelligence-

gathering. In a BBC interview in 1994, he recalled that 'something was really bothering him and bothering him is a silly word to use – something was weighing very heavily on his mind'. When he charged him with it, he said something about Freda and gave him his papers for safe-keeping:

> I don't know what the nature of the relationship was, but it was clearly worrying him. Whether it was giving him feelings of guilt, or what the feelings were, I don't know. But he was deeply depressed. I suppose at that stage I should have thought more deeply about this and thought more deeply about the wisdom of sending him on this particular mission. But quite honestly I thought that he was just in one of his 'downs', one of his depressive moods, so I took the papers as a simple precaution....

Lewis then climbed his hill.

> He had only been gone a day or so when I received a radio message from the officer commanding the company on the hill that there had been 'an accident' and that they were bringing Lieutenant Lewis back to battalion headquarters. [In the broadcast version, Chalfont added that the message read 'that Lieutenant Lewis had been killed'.] Sensing that something really serious had happened, I quickly assembled a small patrol and set off up the hill. About halfway up, I met a stretcher party carrying the body of Lewis, who had an obvious gunshot wound in his head. Everyone subsequently involved in the enquiries into the circumstances of his death was anxious to avoid any more distress than was necessary to his wife and family and the official version was that his death was the result of an accident, although those on the spot at the time were convinced that he had taken his own life.
>
> The incident had a dispiriting effect on the troops, especially at battalion headquarters where, as intelligence officer, he had become a familiar and popular figure. I experienced especially acute feelings of depression and guilt. As adjutant and therefore his immediate superior, I felt that I should have probed more into the emotional problems which had clearly been preying on his mind in the days before his death; and, of course, I blamed myself for letting him leave battalion headquarters and go up the hill where he was exposed, not only to possible attack from the enemy, but

more dangerously to whatever devils were at work in the
depths of his own mind. Perhaps I should have read more
carefully the poem which he wrote for me and gave to me
on our first Christmas in India in 1942 and of which I still
have the stained and crumpled manuscript. It ended:

> The nearness that lies waiting in my bed
> The gradual self-effacement of the dead.

The lines come from 'Song', which Lewis wrote after seeing dead
bodies float off the Cape of Good Hope. In the poem, a soldier's wife
laments her husband's death: 'he sleeps well,/ Though cell by cell the
coral reef/ Builds an eternity of grief'. The concluding couplet – the
one cited by Chalfont – anticipates how his memory will fade though
his presence remains vivid. Once again: what survives? ('Self-efface-
ment' refers to the steady erosion of memories of the dead.)

It is not clear why Chalfont should say the poem was written for
him – perhaps he meant that Lewis had copied it for him – nor why
he should want to assume responsibility for his movements on the
fatal weekend. Lewis would have been in danger whenever his devils
struck; in any case, Goppe Pass is not far from Bawli Bazar. It might
have suited his purpose better to quote 'The Suicide', which tells of
a man who has been crushed by the 'Too much' of life as by 'The
immaculate Gestapo of his brain'. Sitting in a Soho restaurant, he
contemplates his end:

> He would not make our Cause his own;
> He slipped through every clause in every plan –
> Yet he who wouldn't tie two bits of string
> Now lies serene and serious as a Man.

Death enhances him as nothing in life has done, granting him peace
and dignity. (His inability to 'tie two bits of string' anticipates
Chalfont's description of Lewis's ungainliness.) *That* much survives.

Chalfont ended his interview:

> When I was up there, of course, I met the company
> commander concerned and I met Tudor, Alun's batman, and
> I examined the general scene. And I came to the conclusion,
> although it is not the conclusion of the Court of Inquiry, I
> came to the conclusion that he had taken his own life…. First
> of all there were the circumstances. I saw his body with the

gunshot wound in the head. Subsequently I saw the place where he had died, which was a field latrine, with the holster of his pistol hanging on the pole with the revolver – service revolver – removed from it. And then there was the circumstantial evidence of the kind of mood he had been in when I last spoke to him.

He said Lewis was

a very, very unhappy man at the time, a deeply unhappy man at the time, and, of course, that depth of depression can almost be suicidal in itself.

The imminence of the Japanese added to his depression:

I don't think he was afraid of being killed himself. What I think he feared most, and indeed this came out in one or two of my conversations with him, was the possibility of having to kill. I think that worried him more than anything else....

Lewis was a puzzle to the Army:

It was very strange to have someone like that in the battalion, so very different from everybody else in his attitudes and in his approaches and in his concept of his duty and what he was doing for the world. Very strange to have someone like that in an infantry battalion.

This was, by any standards, a remarkable interview and would have made a considerable impression had it been broadcast but the remarks above survive only in transcript form. Chalfont may not have seen any harm in speaking out but others apparently did.

His remarks about the impact of suicide on the battalion – himself included – are particularly noteworthy. One soldier said a sickness spread through the ranks when the news came through. Another recalled that Lewis

always shone like the sun for me. His external cheeriness (happiness) and seeming certainty concealing his depressions. The shock and rumoured nature of his death just before our first clash with enemy troops cast a pall of gloom over anyone you talked to – and our preparations for attack (and capture) of the Mayu Tunnels.

He said suicide was the worst thing a soldier could do, short of desertion.

Lewis's hankering to climb Goppe Pass recalls an aspect of
Cwmaman life that is charged with significance. On the Graig
(mountain), one could find relief, forgetfulness, inspiration. As Eliot
has it in 'The Waste Land', up there you feel free. After graduation
in 1935, Lewis told his Aberystwyth Professor, Reginald Treharne,
that he was contemplating 'something more definitely social and
economic' for his Master's thesis: 'I've spent one or two evenings
right up on the whinberry fields on the mountains thinking the matter
over'. Years later, he told Gweno:

> ... it's more fun really to live in a little town and organise
> your own life, if you want a theatre build one yourself, if you
> want music save up for a piano, if you want to think climb
> the mountain and look down on the quiet little town.

That is what he does in 'The Mountain over Aberdare'. This common
motif among Welsh writers of the period counterbalances the loss of
peace and beauty in the valleys – and who is to say this was not as
significant a deprivation as any other they suffered? – with the
freedom of the heights. Up there, one could court, walk the dog, sit
and think or listen to the birds.

Mair Lewis once described how her mother ensured the children

> never went to chapel or church or anything. Everybody –
> 100% of the other people – did, but Mother always used to
> say, 'You'll learn more about God on the mountain top than
> you will in the valleys'.

Symbolically, then, climbing the mountain signifies a breach with
'100% of the other people' in favour of personal freedom; psychologically, it reveals the 'darkness' shared by mother and son. Like
Edward Thomas stranded in the mist and rain of the South Downs,
Lewis is beset by ineffectuality and self-reproach, lost to love, lost
even to himself.

Though devoted to Cwmaman, he was increasingy absorbed by
his concerns, at the point where 'self' merges with nature. In an essay,
I once wrote:

> However much the writer in him may strive to make the
> place real, he can never forget his separation from it, never

recover from the feeling that he has come into existence only at its expense and therefore his own....

As the short story 'Attitude' shows, he understood very early in his career how opposed was his sympathetic self to his poetic self and how the latter could flourish only by killing off the former.

From time immemorial, climbing a mountain has been linked to visionary experience. In 'The Mountain over Aberdare', Lewis frees himself from the quotidian and confronts his destiny. I noted that the title

is not 'Cwmaman' or 'Aberdare' but 'The Mountain over Aberdare'. That is, the subject of the poem is not the suffering of a Welsh mining valley but the suffering of a poet as observed through the related suffering of a Welsh mining valley.... He can do no more tell us...that life in the Welsh mining valley consists of ... this mysterious relationship, at once binding and separating, between the place and its would-be describers, now drawing them into the details of its crabbed, ugly yet homely streets, dark and crowded, now urging them away to the surrounding mountain heights as to the freedom of open air.

As late as August 1943, Lewis tried to heal the breach in himself by rejecting the offer of a captaincy and staff officer's job. En route to his Battalion, he broke off his journey at Lahore to visit the family of an Indian naval officer he had met on *The Athlone Castle*, Lieutenant Khulla,

a nice Indian R.N.I.R. sublieut. who is very cultured and happy and is going to teach us Hindustani. He talks about philosophy, the Vedas, Urdu, knots and cards.

From Lahore, he took a tonga to Khulla's village and

found the old father, who had a face like Hindenburg, sitting in a shirt and dhoti under a pear tree. They made me very welcome and paid me most careful and courteous hospitality, the eldest son pouring out lime water for me, and emptying ice cold water over my head when the heat grew intense.They fed me on fresh limes and grapefruit and melons and bananas from their own garden and talked intel-

ligently and without reserve on India and us and the war. The
only son at home now 'Jaggi' is a master moulder at the
railway foundries, one son is in England and 'Kuchie' in the
navy. He told me of many exciting tales of his battles in the
N.W. Frontier where he was a station master for thirty five
years: how once he killed three robbers with an axe when
they tried to rape his wife, and expounded his doctrine of
celibacy to me in careful English. The women of the house
never appeared but the old man sent for his tiny grandson to
play with me. Then they sent for 'Jaggi's' friend. He's a
remarkable pilot of the I.A.F. with an O.B.E. for bravery in
Burma. He's a very forceful boy – took an engineering
degree and then joined the Air Force in the ranks – and being
in the ranks in India is a dog's life. He was a big Congress
man in his college days and did his turn in jail. Now he
believes India must be made strong and will never attain or
deserve Independence till her own boys are pilots, generals,
admirals and India can really defend herself.

So Saturday was a rare and valuable experience, to share
the home life and confidence of an Indian family. It cheered
me immensely.

As it does the reader.

'The Mountain over Aberdare' is a misnomer since the view
described is over Cwmaman, not Aberdare. The poem is a reworking
of 'On the Welsh Mountains' and represents his farewell to the land
of his birth.

From this high quarried ledge I see
The place for which the Quakers once
Collected clothes, my fathers' home,
Our stubborn bankrupt village sprawled
In jaded dusk beneath its nameless hills;
The drab streets strung across the cwm,
Derelict workings, tips of slag
The gospellers and gamblers use
And children scrutting for the coal
That winter dole cannot purvey;
Allotments where the collier digs
While engines hack the coal within his brain;
Grey Hebron in a rigid cramp,
White cheap-jack cinema, the church
Stretched like a sow beside the stream....

The last image refers to St Joseph's church, whose five side-chapels viewed from above resemble a sow with her farrow. (Lewis had used the image again in 'The Housekeeper'). Here is another powerful panorama of Depression Wales, as terse as it is intense, as Dylan Thomas acknowledged when he paraphrased the poem in an essay on the valley poets: 'They spoke… of the Wales *they* knew: the coal-tips, the dole-queues, the stubborn bankrupt villages, the children scrutting for coal on the lag-heaps, the colliers' shabby allotments, the cheap-jack cinema'. The iambic tramp – four stresses to the line -lends the poem a sombre air that goes beyond the documentary to capture a whole way of life.

The diction is patched, now decorative ('jade', 'purvey'), now colloquial ('scrutting', 'cheap-jack'), as one would expect from someone in Lewis's liminal position. On the mountain ledge, he is divided between what he sees and what he feels, sympathetic to Cwmaman but with a personal edge to his suffering that prevents him from identifying with it completely. In 'Preludes', T.S. Eliot evoked 'The notion of some infinitely gentle/Infinitely suffering thing', and that is what Lewis does in the poem, too, stretching his soul tight across the sky as he considers Cwmaman's poverty and its attempt to find release through the movies, gambling or religion. An overwhelming sense of hopelessness fills the poem.

In 'On the Welsh Mountains', Lewis recorded a wish 'Deliberately to understate;/ To pare down to the quick/ Reality'; that is what the poem does, too, but in the final lines he strikes a more introspective note:

> I watch the clouded years
> Rune the rough foreheads of these moody hills
> This wet evening, in a lost age.

'Rune' might refer to the scratchmarks on the rocks resembling a rudimentary sign language but also to a poem or verse. 'Rough foreheads', 'clouded years', 'moody hills', 'lost age': all these hint at the poet's melancholy. In the Welsh tradition, he speaks for his people at a time when the compact between them is fracturing.

The phrase 'lost age' recalls Hemingway's 'lost generation', the generation that was slaughtered in World War I. Lewis absorbed something of the trauma of that conflict (as in the closing paragraph of 'Ward '0' 3 (b)') while his youthful years were clouded by the threat of approaching war, as summed up by Leonard Woolf in the

title of the second part of his autobiography: 'Downhill All the Way'.
As if by instinct, on his last night, Lewis climbed his Golgotha. At
that moment, the lost generation fused with the lost age.


# IV


Gweno once observed that all Alun's male friends were tall and fair,
and Dick Mills, his oldest friend, was one such. Born two years before
him in Dolgellau, and raised by his mother after his father's death in
the First World War, he was 'a lion of sympathy', 'funny, philosophical & patient'. Alun thought their friendship was 'one of the few
things I count as valuable'. After graduating from Aberystwyth, they
went on a walking tour of northern France, when Dick emerged as
an 'ideal travelling buttee', a 'very balanced boy' who served as 'a
ballast in my mind'. Both enlisted at the same time, Dick going to
Sandhurst, from where he could meet Alun regularly at Longmoor.
Both served in India, Dick with the Royal Welsch Fusiliers.

I first met Dick in the London offices of the Gulbenkian Foundation, where he served as Deputy Director in charge of its social
welfare programme. He spoke in a quick, whispering way that made
catching what he said difficult. Though voluble, he said little of any
consequence. He was the enthusiast without discernment; all he
managed to convey to me on that day was appreciation of a general
kind. Unlike Freda, he could analyse neither the man nor his work.
Freda, who had kept in touch with Dick over the years, referred to
him as 'poor Dick' in that exasperated, indulgent way of hers as well
as 'obtuse', but that is too harsh. He implicitly accepted what had
happened and was proud of his part in bringing them together. He
told Alun he was glad he and Freda had become 'us'. Reporting this
to Freda, Alun remarked: 'Dick was born in heaven'. He was 'either
amazingly brave or amazingly ingenuous. In either case amazing'.

Dick thought that, had Alun survived, he would have been
abandoned as being too stupid – indeed, he was surprised he had
thought sufficiently highly of him to make a friend him in the first
place. But in this he was being over-modest; friends, like lovers, are
chosen despite as well as because of their qualities. He knew he lived
outside Alun's 'magical and infinitely complex private world' and
would have floundered had he tried entering it but remained sensible
of the honour his friendship had bestowed on him.

I think I must have made Dick uncomfortable by my assumption that he was eager to exchange views about Alun. In his letters, he is always apologising to me for responding tardily to my 'exciting' and 'stimulating' remarks and explaining why, even now, he cannot do so. Or he postpones a previously-arranged meeting due to pressure of work – anything rather than having to face the challenge of discussing Lewis with me. His letters are breathless, dashed off in an almost unreadable scrawl, as if he were intent on covering his own tracks; they are urgent but empty. However, when the subject was anything other than Alun, a different Dick emerged: practical, efficient, far-sighted, considerate. Friendship, it seems, can daunt as well as inspire.

Freda believed she and Dick had failed Alun.

> I didn't know anything about [manic depression] at all. People got depressed – fed up with circumstances they disliked, frustration – but as a darkening of the lights of existence, as an irresistible calling to death – this I never for a moment comprehended. It sounds very obtuse & stupid not to have, especially now all the unearthed signs & signals, all the proven intuitions make so clear the awful road he had to take. I shrink often, sometimes moved unbearably, at the realisation of what that poor, poor darling boy endured. What he had to face *alone*. Perhaps this is why I feel a not very clearly comprehensible irritation, even anger, with Dick whom I really love. He failed Alun so signally and is so enragingly unaware of the fact. Once only I glimpsed an inkling of the realisation of insensitivity in himself when he told me, not very long ago & to my utter amazement, that he had been in love with me 'in my own way'! Poor old Dick – he knew his way was a candle held to the sun of Alun's passionate nature.

On 29th November 1943, Alun reported to her Gweno's remark that

> I work either on romantic wishful-thinking or an obscure disbelief in myself, and so she says I'd better disregard my own judgment & take that of the nearest normal man – meaning hers.

To Dick, he expressed a hope that Freda's new baby would 'steady & appease' her:

She's always got the deep complex of being disregarded or maltreated by those nearest & most important to her – I'm sure it's from her childhood – she'll never outgrow it now, and it gives her much of her wildness and freedom because she compels herself to be independent & self-strong against its next assault.... I don't think she needs [a child] as much as Gweno, though. Or maybe me, too. I don't want perpetual reassurances that I can exist & be and create. When I know I'm nothing I manage to scrape through the chaos of my mind without reassurances. They don't seem to affect the mood, but fall off from it.

On 30th January 1944, five weeks before his death, he met Dick in Poona '& I told Dick what is wrong with me'. Separately, Freda and I pressed him to record what had passed between them but he could not remember. However, the flavour of their conversation may be reflected in Lewis's last letter to him, dated 14th January 1944:

I have lived a whole life with Freda. The kind of life that one lives for ever. I have grown up with her, fought for her against the bullies & the people who wanted to take her away & me away, written her poems, though only a poor few, loved her, made a whole world with her & loved the world as it passed us. And we've known the end all the time, the joy that ends in loss. A life is a finite thing. It finishes, corporeally. That is the pain of the flesh.

I haven't lived one life: but two. I've lived a life with Gweno that will go on in me & her. I can't explain these two lives. It's distressed me deeply & it's inexplicable to me. I am Gweno's, not out of obligation but out of love. I would have had children with Freda. Perhaps I'll have children with Gweno. I want them. I can't write about this, Dick. There is no infidelity in me, no deceit. Only love, love, love.

I myself, physical me, am much more transient & ephemeral than these loves that have inhabited me. I don't want to analyse and draw conclusions. Can I let it be at that? Am I fair? I feel no guilt, no wrong. Only all the time this love. It's too much to bear & I hide it, suppress and don't listen to it, can't write poems or stories, no, nor be a good I.O. – yet I wouldn't have had it otherwise. It hasn't swerved. What there is of the worldly wise in Frieda & in me will have to do the rest, is doing the rest. It must be like that.

Lewis summarises his life before moving on from – or out of – it.

Neither Freda nor he could prevent what was happening. Should he survive, he will return to Gweno, though he cannot imagine having a child with her as easily as with Freda. The only certainty is that joy will end in loss. Love will have to be put away for the duration, together with his writing.

Of Dick it might be said that, though Alun remained beyond his ken, he managed to win his trust.

# V

Around this time, I met Alun's brothers, Huw and Glyn, and exchanged letters with Mair. Their brevity, however, together with the distance between us (travel to Ireland was not as easy as it is today) discouraged further contact. Mair said she was not close to him – he was 6 when she was born and at school and college by the time she reached 'an age for remembering'. She called him 'a holiday brother with whom I had a pact never to quarrel and never did':

> The fact is we were both 'seekers', inherited from our mater-
> nal grandfather Melchizedec, who used to sit breathing
> through alternate nostrils while his poor children starved
> around him! That's how seekers go on, when they really pick
> up a strong scent – total self-centredness, justifiable because
> the goal is total selflessness.

Mair was proud of Alun's achievements while he always thought of her as his 'beautiful sister', a type of the feminine ideal. When he wanted to express his feelings for Freda, it was to Mair he compared her: 'I love her and she loves me and we've been as simple as that ever since I can remember'.

Mair died in 1993. Freda wrote a memorial poem to her called 'Gilly and Mair'.

> Tender love her brother had for Mair.
> And tenderly he loved that other child
> He met in Indian hills so long ago.
>
> To Mair he wrote in answer to her poem:
> 'The longing for – oh what? – oh where? Is it
> Ever – really? Yes, but not for ever.'....

> Here the children loved by him as women met
> Sharing not only him but spirit's tune,
> Not knowing that, too soon, the one would stand
> Beside the other's grave.

Alun's younger brother, Huw, was 'a cocksparrow', a 'queer kid
– very serious in a way, but a devil with the girls & a rapier with
men. He writes to me as if I were his confessor'. He was the lively
one in the family:

> … since he went to college he's been as thick as thieves with
> mother; every morning while she made the beds he followed
> her from bedroom to bedroom, telling her endless anecdotes
> about 'Coll' and 'Rugger'; she was bored by them but loved
> it.

During the war, he became an RAF wireless operator 'guiding our
fighters to enemy planes'. When he was posted to a bomber
aerodrome near Longmoor, they got to know each other better. Alun
wrote to his friend, Leslie Sykes, at Edward Thomas's Red House:

> His work is dangerous & it has made a great difference in
> him. He was a proper little rake before – an adolescent rake-
> – now he is a man. And a rake – but the rakishness is reason-
> able now – it's his jaunty answer to the threat of Death. We
> had a nice afternoon together last Sunday at a little fishing
> village on the coast. A white frost on the low sea-meadows
> turning to mist on the harbour waters & the sun red & the
> planes warming up their engines. Then we went to Chichester
> cathedral and wandered round aisle & cloister & garth. Huw
> said, 'Didn't the monks use the cloisters for training for the
> annual sports?'

In India, Huw forsook his 'rebellions and mitchings' and was 'in high
form in the wilds, developing a conscience at last'. For the better part
of 1943, he helped defend Imphal by the visual reporting of aircraft
in a forward observation post 7,000 feet high in the Chin Hills, the
rugged terrain having rendered radar ineffective.

I met Huw only once, an occasion made memorable by his wife's
habit of putting her head around the door and saying after I had put
a question to him: 'What do you want to know that for?'

Glyn Lewis was very different. Freda thought Alun disliked him,
'probably from jealousy', though of what she did not say. Mair said

he had led a restricted life: 'he married a little girl from a chemist's shop', she wrote to Freda. Even so, I found him the most sympathetic member of the family. As Gweno observed, he had 'the stillness and deep inner strength of his father', a compelling modesty and sincerity as well as a mental toughness born of loss and disappointment.

At the time, Glyn was 63. He said he could not account for the time that had passed; here he was, nearing the end of his life, and it had all passed in a flash. Like the other Lewises, he was a small, spare man with bony face, high cheeks and sallow skin (one reason, perhaps, why Alun's men friends were tall and blond). In 'The Reunion', Alun describes him thus:

> … raw, hair strong and ungroomed, little almond eyes, broad
> cheekbones, such very thick eyebrows, hunched shoulders,
> funny little private soldier….you can't tell his age any more
> than a tortoise's. The world has hit him. He's taking it, he's
> got a good stance, must have been there all the time. How
> we used to fight, hate each other, refuse to share things, he
> resenting having to wear out my suits while I had new ones,
> he rejecting the opportunities, failing the exams, indifferent
> to jobs, capricious and wary of any gambits to tame him…
> some gentleness in his nature sees injustices and inequalities
> as if they were human maladjustments, the tragedy of a bad
> marriage, not to be condemned.

The fairy godmother had run out of gifts by the time she came to Glyn's cot but, by dint of sheer strength of character, he had made something of himself. After a four-year apprenticeship with Boots and college, he worked in a munitions factory until the excess of sulphuric acid in the atmosphere began to affect his health. His first child died in infancy while he was on embarkation leave, something he found impossible to accept. The rest of his life was spent as a dispensing chemist and he had recently retired to a village near Carmarthen.

Very consciously, Glyn was the family's remembrancer and defender of its interests. Once, when I approached one of his cousins for information, he wrote: 'You should have the wit to know that the only person who can give you any authoritative information about the Lewis family is myself'. I did not make that mistake again.

In January 1979, Gwladys Lewis, by then 93, suffered a stroke in her bathroom at midnight. She somehow managed to climb down to the sitting room, put out the lights and fire (singeing her right hand

and forearm in the process) and haul herself back up again. After much shifting and stumbling, she put on her nightdress and got under the bedclothes, where she spent the rest of the night, unable to remember any telephone numbers. The next morning, she put a call through and spent five days in Cardigan hospital, after which she returned with Glyn and his wife, Olwen, to their home.

> And now she'll stay here & not go back to her cottage. She's very happy & warm here & getting less trouble every day as we get our routine sorted out. Things are not really as bad as they might have been. She's not confined to bed & eats all her meals with us at the table. She can get about the house on her own as long as Olwen or I have a hold of her in case of accidents. She has some paralysis of her right side, arm & leg, but it's improving every day with exercise.

In a postscript, he added:

> Mother's mind is as acute as ever though she has some problems in expression which are also passing slowly.

Glyn's sense of responsibility was induced early. While Alun was still at primary school, he was diagnosed with a heart murmur (which later disappeared of its own accord). In *Alun Lewis, Poet*, Gwladys Lewis recalled:

> Because of Alun's supposed 'heart' a sacred trust was laid on our second son Glyn. He was told the secret that we assiduously kept from Alun, and we conjured him that never, if he were on the spot, must he let Alun swim out to sea alone – that he would always accompany him no matter what other plans he had made. As far as I know he never failed this trust.

Glyn was the last family member to see him alive. They met in Poona on the 12th December 1943 after Glyn had travelled from the other side of India for six days in a fanless third-class compartment, sleeping on a wooden rack. They stayed in the Napier Hotel, the Taj (Alun's usual haunt) being out of bounds to other ranks. Meeting Glyn reminded Alun what life was like for troopers. As a private, Glyn received 40 rupees a month to his 250 plus. (Had he accepted the Staff Officer's post at Karachi, it would have been 1,000.) He had access to the Mess, Poona's clubs and Bombay hostelries, but

Glyn had to make do with bully beef and biscuits.

> Glyn touched me deeply. There was real pathos in his narrow
> short cheap trousers and simple shirt issued by the grateful
> government: and his quietness amongst all the toffs. He told
> me how he sees things – the authentic and bitter view of the
> ranker who has no mercy for his superiors and revels cruelly
> in criticizing them - which is all he has the power to do.

Metaphorically speaking, Glyn was still in short trousers. He told
me:

> I've been plugging away at this end ever since you were
> down here but I find Gweno a most unsatisfactory subject in
> many ways. She's very difficult to tie down to anything
> concrete and the more you press her the more she insists that
> everything is going according to plan. The only trouble is
> that I don't feel there's a plan to accord to. I've spent hours
> with her on the phone – she talked almost without let up
> tonight for a good hour – and I don't feel any the wiser at the
> end of it – perhaps any more informed might be a better way
> of putting it. I suggested back in November that we might
> get together again to talk things over & her reply was 'Yes,
> I'll see you some time in the new year'.

Glyn's exasperation arose from the fact that Gweno had for some
time been encouraging a London journalist to write a 45,000-word
biographical account called *Lieutenant Alun Lewis,* drawn from
published accounts and interviews. The Lewises decided his
approach was too 'thin' but Gweno took up with him again after her
disappointment with me.

> His whole approach was too pedestrian to be of any great
> moment was the general consensus. Not having seen any of
> his work I was obliged to take Gweno's opinion & Mother
> was in the same position. So all we had to go on was
> Gweno's opinion. Tonight I find, greatly to my surprise, that
> he is submitting each chapter to her for revision & correction
> after which he finalises what he's written. Gweno agreed that
> his work lacked any substance but felt it might stimulate an
> interest, which is a complete reversal of all we'd agreed
> previously. However, I find that much in keeping with
> Gweno's character as I am beginning to find it.

The implication that no regular contact was maintained between the Lewiscs and Gweno surprised me, especially since Glyn and Olwen had lived with her after their marriage, from spring 1940 till mid-1942, until Glyn joined the army.

> Please, for the sake of family unity & the fairly delicate position which exists, don't quote me on that to Gweno. You can probably appreciate that the onus of seeing that Alun's work is fully appreciated has passed out of the hands of those who knew him best to someone who knew him for a comparatively short time but who is, perhaps, more emotionally involved with things.

This characteristically forthright passage reveals Glyn to be a blunt but not insensitive observer.

His interpretation of my part in the affair was equally blunt:

> There are several things I would like to say to you. Firstly I'm afraid you have alienated yourself from Gweno. She says that she is not going to give you any more help because 'you overinterpret things'. To some extent I must agree. When you were here I tried to give you some insight into the thoughts & emotions that were uppermost in the minds of most thinking people at a time & under conditions of which you have no experience & probably find it very hard to imagine; of a country almost beaten but fighting for its very existence under what looked like hopeless conditions; of men newly married with their lives before them separated from all they loved & transported, in a man's world, to a harsh & alien land with possibly no future in front of them as it turned out for many & indeed for Alun. Such conditions gave rise to unusual, uncharacteristic & sometimes even morbid thoughts. Some, the more sensitive, were more deeply affected than others & it is against this background & not against that of an inborn death wish that you must interpret what you read in Alun's poems. I sincerely hope that I convinced you of this because that is where the truth lies I am absolutely & irrevocably certain.
>
> The second point is one which we scarcely touched on when you were here – that of Freda Ackroyd [sic]. Mother I know is fighting hard not to have her world (and Alun has been her world for most of her life) punctured & deflated. It was an episode in the context of my previous paragraph which, while it will explain one poem yet has little or no bearing on practi-

cally all of his work & practically the whole of his life. And it would be rather shabby to use that one fleeting episode to explain one poem whereas all his other have a totally different background & explanation. However the modern world in general may look at it as being not in any way abnormal the feelings of a mother reared in the rather puritan atmosphere of a country parsonage at the turn of the century & of a newly married & probably starry eyed young soldier's wife cannot & must not be ignored. What it would do for literary honesty is miserable compared to the hurt it would give to good people were it to [become] common gossip.

I discussed your desire to write a biography with Gweno &, as she says, she cannot stop you writing what you like & you probably have enough material to write what you want but she is quite adamant about not giving you any further help. I believe she is really getting down to editing the journals now but also believe she has been putting it off for many years possibly subconsciously. One shortcoming about your relationship I feel has been your eagerness to dig down below the surface & to plug away at things until you get deep down into unknown layers. Possibly Gweno feels as I do that good poetry & prose should speak for itself & stand by its own efforts without relentlessly trying to collate & find hidden meanings, reading into things, as has so often been done with Shakespeare to the detriment of generations of grammar school boys' appreciation of great literature, thoughts & interpretations which were probably not in the mind of the author. It may sound a very tame approach to you but I think it is very valid.

I have been as frank & open with you as I can so that you'll know as well as I do what is going on & how difficult it is to make any constructive progress. And I'm quite sure that progress could only be made along the lines I have outlined.

The rough eloquence of this letter is typical of the man. All Glyn's characterisations strike me as convincing: Gweno is one who prefers to go her own way and can behave contradictorily. A month later, he offered to help her with the journals but she 'definitely declined':

She said you are quite welcome to get on with doing a biography but not to expect any help from her.

This was as unexpected as it was puzzling since she certainly could have stopped me by refusing permission to quote from his work. Coupled with an appeal to family and friends not to co-operate, this would have finished me off. I doubt whether even Freda could have resisted such an appeal.

A few months earlier, I had approached Gwladys for an introduction to Glyn and she told me: 'Glyn will answer any question that will help you in what we believe to be a legitimate quest'. Again, I noticed the way she didn't include her daughter-in-law in the family. The Lewises, it seems, still trusted me.

Glyn's portrait of me as a researcher who was intent on pursuing the truth regardless was also convincing. At this time, I felt like Gregers Werle in Ibsen's *The Wild Duck*, forcing the truth down people's throats whatever the cost. Yet, if I drove too hard, I can only plead that the pressures on me were great. The Lewises wanted me to avoid Freda, Gweno wanted me to avoid suicide, though neither could be ignored, even on grounds of compassion.

Glyn's remarks about the effect of war on soldiers arose from his knowledge of the impact of war on men who had been transported to a 'harsh & alien land' and faced an uncertain future. Some of them might well fall prey to 'morbid' thoughts, the more sensitive (including his brother) being more 'deeply affected'. But though Alun may have contemplated suicide, this was not because he had an 'inborn death wish'. Circumstance, not character, determined his end.

Glyn's portrait of his mother was more defensive. He saw her as hailing from a different era, having been raised in a sheltered country parsonage in a rural environment and being both puritanical and idealistic in temper. She would be distraught if her favourite son fell victim to 'common gossip'. The difficulty lay less in the fact of his adultery than in her inability to countenance it, which would have forced her to revise her opinion of him. Where previously she had viewed the world from a position of moral superiority, now she would become subject to its opprobrium.

Glyn repeats his mother's view when he asserts that Alun's love for Freda is relevant only to 'The Way Back' but this would have impressed me more had he not added: 'Alun has been her world for most of her life', thus quietly accepting his demotion in her affections with Huw and Mair and raising questions about her treatment of her children, questions he would never have raised with her. From early on, Glyn understood that his mother's affections were for the most part directed toward her eldest son and accepted the situation without complaint. There is real poignancy, therefore, in his devotion to them, a dogged love. The fact that they did not return his love was neither here nor there. He was a loyal footsoldier, unflinching, unassuming, upright.

This embattled quality drew me to him – that and his unvarnished sincerity, his flinty honesty. When he corrected me, he did so not so much because I was wrong (which he believed I was) but because my errors were worth correcting, as it were. He neither hectored nor belaboured, stating his reproofs bluntly but working into them a measure of understanding. When, for example, he accuses me of 'digging' too hard and thus missing the truth, the colliery image carries a charge of meaning. I had been candid with him and he would be candid with me, and the basis of his appeal was: 'Can you see this from my point of view?'.

Glyn's description of grammar school boys who lose their love of literature because of over-ingenious readings like mine touched a raw nerve: who better qualified than he to point this out, for he was precisely the kind of boy he was writing about, without the gifts of his older brother, the derring-do of his younger brother and the aetherialism of his sister. He was just an ordinary man married to an ordinary wife who was as caring as himself.

Glyn's description of life in Cwmaman during the Depression is as memorable in its way as Alun's. Life had bitten him hard. A year after our exchange of letters (1978), he wrote expressing sympathy after our eldest daughter contracted meningitis, aged 18 months; for a while, it was touch and go.

> That's one thing that has yielded up its terrors to modern medicine. I remember cases in Cwmaman when I was small – blinds all down, a sock tied over the knocker on the door & children forbidden to play anywhere near the home while everyone passing walked on tip toe & even then it was more often than not fatal. At least you've been saved all that.

Even now, Glyn's sock was tied over the door-knocker and he still walked on tip-toe.

After a year fighting a painful cancer, he died in 1984.

# VI

After selling their French house, Freda and Wallace moved from Charlbury to Woodstock. There was now less time for 'the endless pursuit', as she called it, preoccupied as she was by Wallace's deteriorating health, her failing eyesight and anxious preparations for the birth of Juliet's first child. 'I think of you working at this book which means so much to me and am solaced'. She thought several others could be written, two by herself ('a muse-love one according to Gweno's recipe' comprising more-or-less innocuous excerpts from Lewis's letters with linking commentary, and a second, more truthful version of the same) as well as 'the authentic one by you'. Yet another might be fashioned 'from our combined correspondence which I still think fascinating'. In a sense, this book is that.

Playfully, she added a fifth: an account of individuals like Marjorie Walters (later Lady Linstead). She and Alun had met during vacations while she was at Cambridge and he at Aberystwyth. When I approached her for an interview, she asked me to send her copies of my articles and approached my Head of Department 'for his view of whether I should do this, or not. You will appreciate the position. I have a lot to do and do not undertake extra pressures'. Her letter ended: 'I am in some difficulty, as you do not say who referred you to me. Perhaps you can elucidate this, at the same time?'

I never did get to meet her but benefited from a memoir she wrote for Gwladys Lewis in 1964, in which she explained how she and Alun had met in 1935 when her aunts, who happened to be the Lewises' next-door neighbours, took her on holiday with them to Penbryn, where they became

> tremendous friends out of common necessity because we had such a lot to talk about and time seemed very short.... We thought that everyone should have *enough*, in a sort of William Morris ecstasy. Enough beauty.

Alun tried to get her to take a greater interest in world affairs:

> He taught me how to look at things carefully from the outside and carefully from the inside. And how to suspend judgement. He was far more tolerant than me. He was always sorry for people; ugliness hurt him but never offended him.

In Aberdare, they strolled across the fields to Llwydcoed for tea with Miss Bromham, an elderly lady in Crossbychain. They made an attractive couple, she short and dark (some thought her haughty), he 'tidy', with his loping walk, soft- and slow-spoken, a touch gaunt, with curly, dark hair and deep-set hazel eyes that off-set his pallid complexion. She thought he might have been handsome save for an irregularity of the mouth, which had been scarred by hockey accidents. A plated tooth had replaced one lost in a match in Manchester.

> He used his hands to pat the air with his fingers as if it were painful….In contemplation he had an Oriental air. He could remain perfectly still, unwinking as if he had stopped partic-ipating. On such occasions he was particularly perceptive: he had been identifying himself with an object. His smile, when it came, was quick and full of delight.

At other times, though, things went 'dead' on him.

Alun used to call on her 'in what I used to think was rather a courageous way'. If a poem were 'on', his jaw would become more definite and his facial lines bolder; his skin would stretch and his eyes turn inward: 'an air of resignation hung about him then'. At such times, he would cycle to a vicarage in Penderyn, at the foot of the Brecon Beacons, to write: '…it must have been like having a cross angel to stay'.

She last saw him early in 1942, when he called on her at the Ministry of Information wearing battledress. Whereas he was usually preoccupied with death and hated violence (their mutual friend, Mansel Davies, once noted: 'Poor old Alun. He thought a lot about death. And dying'), on that occasion he was preoccupied by mundaner matters: 'He had tried to teach a man to read and write and the man had asked him not to muck his life up. This had been a great shock to him.' She called him a fine man, a very good person and a good poet.

Two episodes in Alun's life involve Marjorie. The first relates to a 'hurt' he caused her which she responded to with 'a stinging nettle' of a letter. The second concerns a telegram he sent her on her marriage while he and Gweno were staying in Kenilworth. Gweno was so offended by it that she sat up all night knitting. At this point, memories diverge. Some say it was signed 'Don Geraldo', after Gerald Brennan, Dora Carrington's suitor, who travelled to Spain after her rejection of him, where he became Don Geraldo, but Walters recalled it was signed 'Dom Leclercq', after Dom Henri Leclercq, the Benedictine mediaevalist whose work Lewis knew. At the outbreak of war, Dom Henri sat next-door to Marjorie in the British Museum Reading Room working on his dictionary of scriptural antiquities. Lewis's offence appears to have been less the appropriation of the saintly man's name than the addition of a quotation from *The Tempest*: 'And now farewell my Ariel'. Marjorie wrote: 'It reduced him very much in my estimation'. Gweno must have been disconcerted to discover that he considered Marjorie his Ariel.

Freda and Marjorie met over tea. She told her that, though Alun loved her, she did not love him – indeed, found his company 'claustrophobic'. Ironically, this may only have served to encourage him since the one thing he disliked was clinging love. After his death, she destroyed his letters and had 'closed her mind' to him. 'He was a good writer. Not very good letters', she recalled. He could also be 'very up and down', but this was understandable, granted the times. When Freda raised the subject of his death, she replied: 'I don't understand it – he was, of course, very clumsy – with guns and things'.

The prospect of the biography filled Marjorie with apprehension.

> If he [that is, me] is going to write his conclusions, I shall stop it, I shall write to the *Times* – I am a quite powerful person, you know.

Freda attributed her anxiety to her devotion to her husband, Sir Patrick Linstead, an academic scientist, who had died in 1966. As his widow, she may not have wanted to be reminded of a youthful attachment, even if to an intellectual sibling. Nor would she want her modest origins to be revealed, for she considered herself a person 'of ideas'. On her marriage, Nancy Astor sent her a telegram (another one!): 'Now you won't be able to get on with your work'. Freda concluded that her ego was 'intact'.

Their meeting was followed by another when Freda was summoned by the persistent ringing of the front-door bell downstairs in her dressing gown and unmade face to find Marjorie on the doorstep: she had been trying to ring but her line was out of order. She was even more agitated by the prospect of publicity but Freda managed to calm her by reminding her she was only one of many I had wished to interview. She told me:

I'm sure she thinks of herself – or thought – as the central and vital thing in the poet-hood of Alun Lewis, her possession, her creation, even.

Marjorie kept repeating: 'I am an intellectual', 'I am a quiet person', 'I am an experienced reader', 'I have read a great deal', 'I have a degree in –', 'I do know a lot about'. Freda sent me this fragment of their conversation:

> 'Why were you [Freda] upset when I said I'd write to his wife?'
> 'Are you going to?'
> 'Oh yes.'
> 'Why?'
> 'To ask if she approves of your writing this memoir.'
> 'I've read to you on the phone her letter [giving her permission to do so].'
> 'I'd like to see that letter sometime. You could bring it over. You can just go ahead and write it. She could do nothing.'
> 'But of course she could. And it would be dishonest.'
> 'Oh no. I don't see why you shouldn't go ahead and write it.'

Freda and Wallace agreed this would be their last meeting.

## VI

My relations with Gweno took a further turn for the worse after my essay, 'East and East and East: Alun Lewis and the Vocation of Poetry', appeared in 1978. In it, I contended that there was a tension in him between the creative and human which proved fruitful to him though, in time, he rejected his parents' humanism in favour of the imagination as 'the only guarantee of certainty, of positive life'. Gweno objected to this, as to much else, in my analysis of 'The Mountain over Aberdare':

> Page 2. Alun wasn't *exiled* from his people. He wasn't an outcast in any 'poetical' way. He had left this little community [of Cwmaman] years ago.
> Page 4. 'The Christ being crucified is himself – the poet'. In

> the whole passage containing this idea I really think you push
> it too far. My brother, whose criticism I value, agrees with
> me in this – this 'simple extension' (line 6, page 4) is only in
> your mind. Of course the poet is a 'high priest' & suffers but
> not in the context of this poem.

By 'high priest', I was alluding to the Welsh bard as conscience of
the tribe.

> Page 6 (line 7). 'Indeed if the truth be told, he would much
> rather be left by himself high on his ledge.' Yes, every now
> and then perhaps, certainly not forever.
> Then again, 'the subject of the poem is not the suffering of a
> Welsh mining village, but the suffering of a poet.' I do not
> agree. I suppose you call it 'critic's licence' to delve too
> deeply and thereby distort the truth.

I had remarked that the passage about 'mute pads on the sands' in
'The Jungle' is more picturesque than factual, citing Lewis's description of the crocodile that 'slides from the ochre sand/ And drives the
great translucent fish/ Under the boughs across the running gravel'.
The allure of such images showed how far he had strayed from 'The
old temptation to remould the world'; in the poem, this exalts his
'bowed and golden head' for a last time, like the flashing of a sword,
an image suggesting ritual decapitation. The 'mute' pads belong to
this excited apprehension of death. Gweno disagreed.

> Page11. The 'mute pads' were not as unrealistic a form of
> death as you think.

Again:

> Page 11. 'He has chosen perfection of the work by making
> his life into Art and needs death to seal it.' If by this odd state-
> ment you mean Art for Art's sake, then you are not discussing
> Alun Lewis but somebody else. Somebody you insist on
> mythologising.

I was here alluding to Yeats's farewell to the young in 'Sailing to
Byzantium' as he crosses the mackerel-crowded seas to find occupa-
tion for his soul in a city contemplating 'golden' (naturally) craftwork.
    More Yeats comes in 'The Orange Grove' when Staff-Captain
Beale attaches himself to a tribe of gypsies straight out of 'Lapis

Lazuli':

> On their own feet they came, or on shipboard,
> Camel-back, horse-back, ass-back, mule-back,
> Old civilisations put to the sword.
> Then they and their wisdom went to rack....

When John Lehmann read the story, the image of Beale carrying the body of his dead driver in his truck reminded him of Yeats's soul 'sick with desire and fastened to a dying animal'.

Gweno took exception to my identification of Beale with Lewis. True, Beale is no naïve projection but his concerns are nonetheless his author's, as Lewis suggested when he remarked that the story was 'flesh of my flesh'. Both men are attracted to the image of an orange grove in Palestine and both come to a fork in the path when Beale is stranded in a river. Crossing it suggests rebirth, a movement to the farther shore, completed only when the body is shed. Lewis described a similar scene to Gweno:

> Usually there were despondent busloads of Indians on the bank unable to proceed further, or tribes of nonchalant gypsies camping with their mules & camels till the river might choose to subside & let their Mosaic concourse proceed.

'Mosaic concourse' is a magnificently Yeatsian phrase that prepares for Beale's descent into Hades.

Gweno's three typed pages of 'corrections' ended with the following note written in her own hand:

> Mrs Lewis sent on your article. She cannot see very well now as she has developing cataracts on both eyes unfortunately. But I rang her up & discussed various points with which she agrees. I do hope you don't mind my sending you these notes & points of clarification.
>
> Searching around for a suitable envelope to return this article I found this old one containing Broadsheet No. 5 with Brenda's drawing of Ann Jones. Please keep it if you wish.

An unexpectedly magnanimous gesture in a letter characterised by much disagreement. Once again, I pondered Gweno's contradictory character. The generosity of the gift may be measured by the fact that the broadsheets have long since become collectors' items.

Lewis launched the Caseg Broadsheets in 1941 with Brenda Chamberlain and John Petts at a time when his socialist fervour was at its height. Writers like Forster and Orwell were moving in the opposite direction – had not that grand apostate, Auden, announced 'Art is not life and cannot be/ A midwife to society'? – but that is not how he saw it.

> ... there are two urgent needs for me:– one, to write for: the other, to educate *The People*. In practice, they work together – my writing is an expression of all the comfort, all the hope & faith & despair & love that is humanity.

The element of strain in this passage in no way detracts from its sincerity.

In February 1942, after Petts had sent Gwladys Lewis a hand-coloured print of his engraving of Alun's head, she told him she welcomed the broadsheets as 'a splendid venture made in the spirit of the real crusaders':

> I tell Alun that when the war is over, all you young Welsh artists of every sort, who believe in the eternal goodness inherent in the heart of things, must join together and make yourselves felt in a forward drive to establish all that you stand for and so make life holier and happier for the people who up to now have had a bad deal.

Once again, she speaks not only *for* her son but *as* her son.

For Lewis, the broadsheets demonstrated the 'continuity, almost identity, between Wales sixteen centuries ago & Wales today'.

> I think the war theme is the best for us – since the early poems of the 9th century poets are all war – & they establish a direct continuity of suffering and stoicism with Wales today.

Writing to Petts and Brenda, he observed:

> If we start with ourselves and Wales: if you understand all that is inarticulate, all that is potential in ourselves and Wales – not in us alone: nor in Wales alone. Nor yet anything merely patriotic....

The broadsheets were to speak for Wales, though in no nationalistic sense. He did not want too many bilingual sheets since support for the venture would come mainly from the '*English*-Welsh' and he did not want it to fall between two stools. The focus was 'the peasant, the soldier, the land. It's for the people, to show them the continuity and courage of the race, see?' He wished to reach them 'with beauty & love'.

Each broadsheet was both art object and literary statement, the texts accompanied by woodcut illustrations. Lewis acted as editor and planned to recruit Glyn Jones, Professor Gwyn Jones, A.G. Prys-Jones, Henry Treece and Davies Aberpennar (the bardic name of Pennar Davies) as Board members. He sent Chamberlain and Petts frequent ideas for the woodcuts and urged them to seek inspiration from 'the quarry, the pit, the slum streets & the bench in front of the Workmen's Hall'.

At the time, Chamberlain and Petts lived in north Wales as part of their revolt against D.H. Lawrence's hated machine:

> We had outlawed ourselves, though we had never heard of 'beat' or 'off-beat'. We never drank alcohol, and had never heard of narcotics. Free love was our creed and password, though we had married towards the end of our student days at the Royal Academy Schools. We had gone to live in an old stone cottage above the village of Llanllechid in the slate-quarrying district of North Carnarvonshire. The property consisted of a sloping field at the top of which stood a haybarn joined to the cottage, then a stable, a cartshed, and a pigsty. The place was said to have been owned by drovers in the old days of pony transport over the mountains. The main room had a big chimney open to the stars.

Lewis told Rene and Bryan Hopkin:

> They farm a bit of furze on the side of one of the big carneddi below Nant Frangcon & are a fine couple, a rare couple, living miles away, alone with a white goat, a black pony & a piebald sheepdog.

At the outbreak of war, they created a private press with their little Adana machine in the hope that it might make them some money and named it after the river that ran nearby ('caseg' = 'mare').

The idea of a series of individual publications like the pedlars' chapbooks may have been inspired by the work of Lewis's tutor, Christopher Cheney, whose research included the popular press of the eighteenth century. Cyril Connolly's *Horizon* issued the occasional broadsheet while Keidrych Rhys printed a letterpress leaflet (without illustrations) in *Wales* with poems by William Empson and D Kighley Baxendall. Lewis told Brenda: 'We'd have to choose the poems carefully – let them be universal poems, not obscure modernities such as Keidrych Rhys floated'. He wanted them to be sold for a penny or two but, as costs rose, this became fourpence. 500 copies of each were printed, Lewis bearing the cost. He told Gwyn Jones (who incidentally gave the project its name in his letter of support) that it was 'entirely a friendly project not a business racket'. However, when the Pettses' Adana duplicating machine proved unequal to the task, they were produced by the Gomerian Press, Llandysul. Harri Webb remembers seeing one of them,

> a tattered, treasured possession in an otherwise very ordinary working class home where it obviously meant something precious outside of daily experience.

Six of the 20 projected sheets were issued; proof-copies of two more exist. The one Gweno sent me, number five, dates from June 1942 and carries an extract from Dylan Thomas's 'In Memory of Ann Jones'. Since Lewis did not have the text with him at the time, he asked Glyn Jones to check it for him.

The project ended when Lewis joined the South Wales Borderers. From Woodbridge, he told Lynette Roberts and Keidrych Rhys:

> By the way, the broadsheets aren't going to survive, I'm afraid. We're losing a lot on them and can't afford it indefinitely. Sad. But it was pretty hopeless to try and organise a thing like that from 200 miles distance.

# VII

In view of our latest disagreements, I am surprised to find that I met Gweno early in 1979, on which occasion she said Lewis was attracted to married women – she had not been the only woman in his life. This will come as a surprise to readers of his letters, which give the impression of uxorious devotion.

One such married woman – and the most innocent of them – was Renee Hopkin, a fellow-student at Manchester, who wrote him long letters and appeared in 'wild erotic dreams, very immoral'. Then there were Marjorie Walters and Brenda Chamberlain, whose art he admired more than her poetry. The most significant, however, was Lynette Roberts, born Evelyn Beatrice Roberts in Buenos Aires on 4th July 1909 and so six years older than himself (as Freda was four and a half). Marjorie thought her 'a most unreliable informant', but she came nearer him than anyone save Gweno and Freda.

Lynette was a gifted poet, quirky and original. Her *Poems* appeared in 1944 and *Gods with Stainless Ears* in 1951, though it was written in the same period, 1941-3. On both occasions, her timing was unfortunate: few readers in 1944 were interested in life in a remote village in west Wales while in 1951 even fewer wanted to be reminded of events a decade before, particularly now that an era of peace and plenty beckoned. Memories of the war had faded while their popular exploitation had yet to come.

T.S. Eliot, Roberts's publisher, admired her skill in lyrical forms and her terse, economical idiom. Like him, she was 'difficult', using erudite words and allusions. At his suggestion, she added 'arguments' and notes to *Gods with Stainless Ears* which, like his own to 'The Waste Land', added to rather than clarified the confusion. Even so, Eliot thought her '*readable*', for she possessed the quintessentially Eliotic quality of being able to communicate before being fully understood. After 1945, however, the Muse deserted her and he rejected her third volume, *The Fifth Pillar of Song*. From the mid-Fifties on, she suffered a number of breakdowns and quickly sank from view. Her *Collected Poems*, edited by Patrick McGuinness, appeared as late as 2005.

Lynette's parents, Cecil and Ruby Roberts, were both of Welsh extraction though born in Australia. After marrying, they emigrated to Argentina, where Cecil became manager of the Mechita railway station, near Buenos Aires. Their house, in the vicinity of the station, was a pillared colonial bungalow with duck pond, chickens and geese. Cecil was a notably outdoors man and owner of a Bentley and yacht, which he himself had built. After the war, he became Director of the Western Railways and moved with the family to Ramos Mejia.

Relations between Cecil and Ruby were never easy. She had a boyfriend who asked if he could buy her a ring, to which Cecil replied: 'Yes, so long as she doesn't wear it'. For his part, he sang songs and played tennis with his girlfriends, Ruby looking on enviously since she did not own a white dress and couldn't sing. At the outbreak of war, he joined the Western Front, bringing his horses with him and leaving Ruby and the children with his parents in Bournemouth. Since Cecil's sister (and Lynette's godmother) was Lyn, she was called 'Lynette'.

During the war, Ruby and Cecil parted. She found employment as a waitress in London while boarding Lynette and her two younger sisters with a Mrs Barwell in Norwich. A fourth child, Dymock, who was born in 1914, stayed with her. Lynette described Mrs Barwell as a drunken, lesbian teacher of music and dancing who proved reluctant to let them go when the time came since they had become the mainstay of her income. Ruby rescued them from what became a virtual kidnapping, the children waving to her from an upstairs window.

After the war, Ruby and Cecil were reunited again and in 1920 returned to Argentina, where she died three years later of typhoid fever, contracted from drinking contaminated water from a well. Lynette's lament for her, 'To a Welsh Woman' (1939), was part of Lewis's fourth Caseg Broadsheet together with her 'The Circle of C'. In it, she appears as a sad, broken woman, lovely in defeat, who dispatched her 'cam' (crooked, bent or false) burdens 'to the sun':

> Gentle as stardust and as little known
> She strained to the Future always remote
> Faded the image at too early a date
> Blurred – now pale –
> Lone cymry.

Ruby's fate emblematises the Welsh experience and, by a strange coincidence, anticipates Lynette's own.

A further blow came when Dymock was diagnosed schizophrenic while still a schoolboy and committed to an asylum in Salisbury suffering from a species of religious mania. He was to spend the rest of his life there. Once again, his fate anticipates Lynette's.

In the 1930s, she enrolled in the London Central School of Arts and Crafts, where she learned to design and print textiles, carve and sculpt, do gesso work and apply gold leaf. She made skirts for herself with French pleats or patchwork with embroidered pieces of mirror or fully-gathered round the waist in tight belts and reaching down to the ankle, Hungarian-style. Afterwards, she trained with Constance Spry as a floral decorator and interior designer and, with Sonia

Brownell (later Mrs George Orwell), set up a florist's business called 'Bruska' (her nickname). In her partly-published autobiography, she states: 'I knew nothing about business but simply added 100% to everything I sold'. She was always anxious to impress her father and craved his good opinion.

In 1939, while engaged to another, she met Keidrych Rhys, whom she took to be 'county' as he thought her an heiress or 'that upper-bourgois capitalist bit of fluff', as he called her, affecting to despise what he intended to profit from. 'This is the first time an affair has Got me Down: she is such a darling, so sweet so funny so warm!' She was all those things but, if she had a fault, it was her inability to tell the good apart from the bad in people. Three years earlier, Keidrych had been convicted in the Central Criminal Court for robbery and carrying an offensive weapon.

The couple wed in Llansteffan in October 1939 without telling their parents. (Cecil, by now remarried, was still living in Buenos Aires while Keidrych's parents farmed in Bethlehem, near Llandeilo); Dylan Thomas was best man. So uncertain was she about going ahead with the ceremony that the wedding march had to be played three times before she could pluck up enough courage to enter the church.

Keidrych Rhys, a journalist and poet, was born in 1913 and christened William Ronald Rees Jones ('Ronnie' to his schoolfriends). According to Glyn Jones, he

> used Keidrich Rhys as his *nom de plume* or more accurately in his case as his *nom de guerre*. The Rees, Rhys, explains itself and the Keidrych comes from some natural feature – a valley or a spring – near his parents' farm near Llandeilo in Carmarthenshire.

Some thought his name was the best poem he ever wrote. Keidrych was an ardent – and ardently Welsh – man of letters, combative, adventurous, wayward and with a talent for the higher gossip; he carried many plans in his pocket. Alun Richards, who was not above calling a spade a spade, thought him 'large, eccentric and farouche'; Lewis called him Lynette's 'neurotic surreal husband'. To Dylan Thomas, he was 'the best sort of crank'. Glyn Jones, though, was more impressed by 'a Welsh-speaking grammar school boy who talked with the accent of the English public schools, tall, blond, well turned out and very handsome'. Though chary, he found him 'chatty, lively, combative, sometimes contradictory, but full of a sense of life and energy and a desire to achieve something for himself and others'. Thanks to Glyn's *The Dragon Has Two Tongues* (1968), he has been granted a central role in the promotion of Welsh literature in English; indeed, the hero of Glyn's remarkable novel, *The Island of Apples* (1965), Karl Anthony, is created in his image and is characterised by the same romantic braggadocio and air of exotic adventure. The non-Welsh 'K' in both men's names is a talisman of their extraordinary presumptuousness.

Rhys began the magazine *Wales* in the summer of 1937, drawing his material from the first generation of Welsh writers to use English as their medium of expression (and the second to enjoy universal public education): Dylan Thomas, R.S. Thomas, Emyr Humphreys, Glyn Jones, Idris Davies, Lewis and the like. Until then, there were no literary publications in Wales and no meeting places for its writers. When they sought publication, it was to Dublin or London they turned. The boldness of his venture is implicit in the title, which flourishes Wales both as a location and a source of values, assertively and defensively. In the preceding fifty years, the country had become a Klondyke of coal-mining and industry, in the process weakening the influence of chapel and the notion of parental authority that underpinned it. *Wales* proposed to take the measure of this new Wales, whose young were likelier to be drawn to authorship than the pulpit. In the events of the 1920s and 30s, they found a rich seam to work but laboured – where it mattered – in isolation. Their success may be gauged by T.S. Eliot's remark on the fly-leaf of *Gods with Stainless Ears* that 'English poetry of our time, as in the first half of the seventeenth century, is greatly indebted to poets from Wales' while in 1943 Cyril Connolly was assuring readers of *Horizon* that 'there is already a Welsh Renaissance in being'.

In his first editorial, Keidrych proclaimed that the 'greatest of present-day poets are Kelts' and that the burden of English literature had fallen on them since

> we realise the beauty of the English language better than the English themselves, who have so shamelessly misused it. Though we write in English, we are rooted in Wales.

That contention has confounded many, especially those for whom only Welsh-language writers can contribute to an authentically Welsh literature, English-language Welsh literature being a contradiction in terms. Nevertheless, writers like Idris Davies, Gwyn Thomas and Lewis Jones were no less Welsh for using English as the language of their imagination.

Rhys saw such writers as saving the English from themselves, being more English than the English because more Welsh. He argued that literature in Wales was the preserve of 'the small shopkeepers, the blacksmiths, the non-conformist ministers, ... the miners, quarry-men, and the railwaymen'. Unfortunately, the man he chose to launch his magazine, Dylan Thomas, was none of these.

Thomas was Rhys's star and each made good use of the other. For the press, they were the stormy petrels of Welsh literature, enfant terribles of the new school. In 1939, Dylan co-edited two numbers of *Wales* and became Keidrych's drinking companion, much to Lynette's displeasure. He called her 'a curious girl' with 'all the symptoms of hysteria' while she complained that Keidrych failed to protect her from his slights.

Rhys published an elegy on Alun Lewis in *Wales* (not included in his *Collected Poems*):

> Going forward on detachment in the Arakan,
> Carrying the usual revolver loaded at the time,
> He tripped and fell and the hammer struck a stone.
> He died on a Sunday in March at eight o'clock.

William McGonagall would have approved.

# VIII

Without insurance stamps, Lynette and Keidrych could not claim the dole and the only place they could afford to rent was Ty Gwyn (White House), a two-roomed stonewashed cottage in Llanybri that had been condemned as unfit for human habitation before the war. It lacked running water (the Council well lay 400 yards down the hill), was cramped (the kitchen was barely wide enough to fit a hob, fire and oven) and had stale air (to avoid window tax, the windows measured 18 by 12 inches, excluding 'deadones' or fixed skylights). Compen-sation came from the bowlful of light rising from Carmarthen Bay and the two rivers running either side of the promontory on which the hamlet sits, the Towy and Taf. It was a light that magnified, clari-fied and cleansed.

After serving with the Home Guard, Keidrych was called up on July 12th 1940 and posted to coastal defence on the East Coast with the Royal Artillery, leaving Lynette behind in a fragile condition. In March that year, she had suffered a disastrous miscarriage and bled alone for six days in the cottage. In the spring of 1941, he wrote to say he was seeing another woman (there were rumours of several others) and she travelled up to Dover to confront him; en route, she called on Lewis in Longmoor. She had been in correspondence with him on Keidrych's behalf before. He told Gweno:

> Lynette Roberts – do you know her name? – sent me a funny drawing on a postcard asking for some poems for an anthology of war poetry her husband is editing. A soldier with a squint and a cauliflower ear, yelling like hell. I laughed for a whole afternoon at it, off and on; giggled in the back row. And sent her some poems forthwith.

The two met in a field near camp, Lynette wearing her trademark red flannel cloak and carrying as a gift Gigli's recording of 'Una furtive lacrima' from Donizetti's *Elixir of Love*. Lewis then inititated her into his circle by holding up a stick for her to pass under and practised his skill in falling, which he said was a secret from all bar herself and Dick Mills.

At Dover, she managed to win Keidrych back:

> I was worried about the consequences but admired his openness. I thought the best thing to do was to give him a tremendous kiss and I did this and he asked me to do it again.

Rhys's joy at their reconciliation is expressed in 'Letter to My Wife':

> It was in the White Cliffs, my own, that we renewed contact
> Your image, flesh, bone, thought, again became a fact
> Fine temper, home, and all unchanged yet stronger than
>       imagination
> Unearthed, conjured – too much with the destructive tools
>       of reformation!
>
> O marvellous personality – again we *found* each other
> A living testimony of honeymoon outings together!...
> Life before meeting you was a drifting chaos, pretty
>       purposeless
> Needing your sturdy Argentine warmth to fire me on, loveless!

After film-dawn halos, a too short union, now we've been 9
    months parted
By circles of lust, still threatened but O how amazingly lion-
    hearted…

You are my front-line love – and always will be – with *ease*
Oh I can see you at your window in the cottage through the
    trees…

O my darling and my own
    Remember the willows by the river in summer
    Remember always our love in wintry weather

    Remember the cottage the bridge the flowers the fields
    O never forget the power love yields and wields…

She never did. Whenever I mentioned Llanybri to her in her later
years, she would lift her head and sigh: 'Ah, Llanybri!' In *Gods with
Stainless Ears*, Keidrych becomes 'He, of Bethlehem' (his own
designation of himself) and is seen floating in clouds, his 'fleecy
cade' or pet animal beside him.

Lewis was something of a godsend to Lynette. Here was someone
who understood her, despite their many differences in character and
situation. While she was entering Wales, he was just leaving it and,
far from being a socialist, she preferred the aristocrat-cum-peasant,
believing that the cultivation of taste would do more for democracy
than any middle-class notion of social welfare. Nor was she any
kinder to pacifists and gentle Jesus: 'I only like Christ when he
thrashes the old traders and moneylenders out of the synagogues'.
She told Alun her childhood was 'too elusive, unbelievable':

> …quite frankly I am frightened to go over a lot of my past
> life even in my mind I have drowned it as much as I can.
> Later, very much later I may use it but not now. I have a mad
> brother alun; was kidnapped & badly treated in my youth;
> starved even; had a miscarriage & was for 6 whole days
> without a doctor working and worrying all the time and
> nobody cared. Christ it was awful.

He, for his part, assured Gweno nothing had passed between him and
'the red-cloaked one':

> She's an exciting and strange creature, very vivid and Welsh

and restless I should think… You will like her when you meet
her. She's not a vampire or anything like that at all, and she
lays no siege to my heart. She's a human being with a world
of disaster and courage in her, that's all, and she has great
powers of helping the soul of people. I got a wretched letter
from her today…. She's in awful trouble. Keidrych hasn't
written for ages; the villagers have started horrible lies about
her saying she's a nazi spy. When the plane crashed in her
garden a month ago she ran out and pulled the dead boy out
of the cockpit although the ammunition was going off; she's
the head of the First Aid in Llanybri, finding him dead she
ran back to her cottage and was sick. And they say she ran
out to steal plans from his pocket and she's expecting to be
arrested. But she thinks she'll separate from Keidrych unless
things improve. And that is and always will be Lynette, a
strange uncontrollable simple living being.

Even so, Gweno never took to her.

In September, Keidrych sent Alun a 'charming' letter to tell him
that he and Lynette were 'still together' (!) and 'very happy at last'.
There is no doubt that Lynette depended on him, both as woman and
writer. In 'The Shadow Remains', she describes 'Two angels pinned
to the wall – again two' (an allusion to Sonia Brownell's wedding
gift to her of a print of angels). Keidrych was to use the same image
in 'Third and Fourth':

> But here your dear warm afternoon body remains
> Proud against pillowslips cross-colour pains
> Three wardrobe gargoyles stare at where
> Two golden-winged cupids look down from above in
>       their rare profusion of hair
>
> Look down upon what cut our bed of love
> My love my love what is to be done….

A great deal, apparently, and most of it by Lynette. Alun told Gweno:

> As Keidrych wrote, it's no good breaking one's heart or being
> childish these days when so much is needed and so little has
> been asked.

But break her heart he did. Alun to Gweno:

> A very worried letter from Lynette asking me to see Keidrych
> [in Yarmouth at the time] who is suffering from his hate
> neurosis and turning his embitterment into insults to her.

The two were 'always "fighting" against the pacifists – rather a pre-war sort of fight it is, too'. Or perhaps Keidrych was simply restless again: 'Keidrych... had such a dose of London that he can't deflate himself to the quietness of Llanybri'.

While she admired Alun, Lynette kept her distance from him:

> I like your letters Alun but I should be frightened if you came
> too near. I might be disillusioned. Of the two I prefer the first.
> The second is horrible.

Years later, she wrote to me:

> There was no physical contact with Alun & myself. What
> existed between us would be for the letters, both of ours.

Her best-known poem, 'Poem from Llanybri', takes the form of an invitation to him to visit her:

> You must come – start this pilgrimage
> Can you come? – send an ode or elegy
> In the old way and raise our heritage.

The 'old way' is the bardic way, an amalgam of literature, nature, history and myth fashioned by her to replace Argentina. Llanybri, she declared, was 'an offering of peace and security for the soul. A pastoral root which is wholesome...'. It represented a folk culture under siege, one that had survived many battles and for which many had died. (Emyr Humphreys calls it the Taliesin tradition, after the sixth-century author of *The Book of Taliesin*.) Mention of the lover's spoon, on the other hand, lends the poem a personal complexion, one obscured by the courteous elegance of its phrasing and which both were at pains to deny.

Lewis response to the invitation was 'Peace', which he said came to him crossing from barrack blocks to cookhouse quietly singing words and music:

> The wind blows
> Through her eyes,

> Snow is banked
> In her whiter thighs,
> The birds are frantic with
> Her last distress,
> And flutter and chatter over
> Her nakedness.

Despite the sexual imagery, he said the poem represented a 'dream of peace' and he became obsessed by its 'Beautiful ice cold death images of perfect poetry'.

> 'Can't you see?' the words said. 'Alone – come alone.' This is the home of the soul, its freedom to wander, alone and released – released from the body and the situation. A spirit world....

Roberts protested she had been prematurely buried in the poem:

> Funny isn't it, we must have written a poem to each other on the same day.... My poem is real i.e. true of the everyday things I do. Yours is mythical.

The two were to meet twice more. The first time was in late 1941 in Llanybri, after he had visited Brenda Chamberlain in Llanlechid, when she told him that his praise for her art meant almost more to her than her painting. John Petts remembered things differently:

> I remember too, vividly, when Alun made his journey to Ty'r Mynydd, he had travelled the length of Wales from Llanybri, and he brought warm greetings from Lynette, – such a smiling courier! He had been lit by her personality, clearly, saying: 'She was lovely, – as I left in the bus, she stood there waving, the wind blowing her scarlet cloak...'

Evidently, he was excited by her presence.

Their last meeting was in Gloucester in summer 1941. Gweno remembered that he mentioned Lynette's sheathed 'claws', virtually admitting there had been an element of attraction between them, though now he was glad to see the back of her and knew that he loved Gweno alone. 'Perfidious, wasn't he?', she told me.

After Lewis's death, Lynette told Robert Graves Lewis had been over-praised:

> ...there was [a] young airman who was killed as his plane
> crashed into the meadow behind my cottage. And Alun
> Lewis, the poet who had spent days with us and his girl
> [Gweno] in our village. He too died in Burma. Not one of
> these was suited to the climate of war. Some men are suited.
> These were not.

According to her, three-quarters of the poems in *Raiders' Dawn*
contain a 'death-wish', which she attributed to 'the lack of action in
his physical and spiritual life'. The clue to her interpretation may lie
in the figure of the beautiful-deathly Goddess in the poem that she
herself had inspired.

## IX

Keidrych's army career ended in 1942 after he refused to be posted
overseas. He went awol for five days before turning himself in. Lewis
believed he had mishandled the whole affair and was more likely to
be charged with desertion than idealism: refusing to serve abroad
was different from refusing to fight 'in vacuo'. For a while, he was
held at Woolwich Arsenal and then posted to the army psychiatric
hospital at Northfield, near Birmingham. Herbert Read and Bonamy
Dobree tried to have him declared insane so as to avoid charges being
brought against him but eventually he was discharged. He spent the
last three years of the war in the Ministry of Information.

> K. has been discharged from the Army ('health reasons', she
> says Maclaren Ross and Rayner Heppenstall are in the same
> mental home as 'K' was. What's the matter with the boys?
> Can't they take the same knocks as everybody else? I feel a
> bit cross with them. Don't give K any new poems, Gwen.
> He's 'funny'.

Lynette divorced him in 1949 and moved out of Wales with her
young daughter and son, only to return two decades later, spending
the rest of her days in an increasingly fragile state in Carmarthen as
an active supporter of the Jehovah's Witnesses.

# Part Eleven
## *Searching for Alun*

### I

In 1979, after finishing transcribing Lewis's journals, Gweno gave me permission to quote his letters in the biography. Having received similar permission, Freda decided to recast her memoir as a more truthful account of her relations with Lewis than had at one time seemed possible. All the work of the previous five years – 'a travesty of what happened' _ went into the wastepaper basket. Skirting reality, she decided, was as bad as distorting it. 'Why don't I write my book? Any book? I write it all to J.P.'. At the same time, she asked me to arrange the deposit of his letters in the National Library of Wales but eventually placed them in the Bodleian, where they would be nearer for her to consult. After Freda's death in 2005, Gweno expressed a wish for them to go to Aberystwyth and Juliet, Freda's literary executor, agrees.

The years of work and fret had taken their toll. Freda thought I was in danger of whittling away at the subject until it snapped and urged me to get on with the biography rather than publishing articles like 'Alun Lewis and Edward Thomas', which appeared in *The Critical Quarterly* two years later.

> From the very first letter I wrote you I had him standing behind my back and I was inhibited. I sometimes have the feeling still, that he is not at all liking all our discoveries, all our digging. 'Must you dig so hard and deep?' he wrote me once. I never knew why. I think he felt a sudden recoil, out of his growing need to cut adrift – that curious need which yet catapulted him back all the time, longingly….
>
> I'll admit now that when you wrote to me, so soon after we met for the first time and I'd told you so much in the Randolph which was for your hearing alone and to which

admonishment you had answered 'of course, of course,' so
soon after a letter came from you beginning: 'Gweno and
Mrs Lewis now know all about you and Alun'. I reeled. But
I had to accept it and I realised, after much thought and great
anxiety and personal worry, that if you were to enter into this
story truthfully you had made the necessary beginning.

So I took it. But I was, while admiring your singlemindedness, agape at your ability to jump in at the deep end, to
hurl yourself into the scrum and heaven help those in the way
of your boots! I forgot it – or nearly – and have been, as I
say, with certain uneasy moments of wondering what he
himself would think of all this. (Sometimes I think he'd
HATE it, other times, when I contemplate the fact that he
wrote triumphantly about me in his journals knowing they'd
be read after his death, included in his Ha! Ha! Among the
Trumpets all the most revealing poems about us – and wrote
to me: 'You want to be in the book, don't you Freda? – then
I am comforted thinking perhaps he *wants* all the anguish,
all the unrecognised, unadmitted form of his terror and
torment to be set down, to be understood by sympathetic,
loving people who, above all, rejoice and are illuminated by
his poetry.)

On one subject, she remained firm: I must make no mention of the
episode in the woods at Coonoor.

Nothing one can write can produce the realisation of how
gentle that scene was; how quietly and on a gentle impulse
it happened; how very little I actually had to do with it! It
was some need of his, not a physical one, and a wish on my
part to help him, hardly knowing as he led me quietly into
the wood, what he was intending.

This presented a very different image of her from the 'sexy harlot'
who seduced a young poet and led him to an early grave.

It was this sort of attitude in much of the reading public in
regard to some mysterious female who probably caused his
suicide which really started me off writing to you when you
saw, so incredibly, what The Way Back meant...I was afraid
of hurting all sorts of people but so loathed wearing the
scarlet dress.

Even so,

> I did regret telling you at our first meeting. Why I did it I
> can't imagine. Something to do with his gentleness, and the
> quiet conduct of our loving. NO. To show how why Bombay
> meant so much. I don't know.

She herself did not believe his impotence was a spur to his creative
writing, despite what he himself had said on that occasion; it may
have contributed to it but, even then, his sexual malfunctioning was
not clinical.

Lewis's sexual difficulties reflect on his introspective character,
so different from the four-square image of masculinity associated
with the miner. Lithe of frame and 'dreamy' in manner, he epitomised
vulnerability, not one of the young who went looking for a start of
work at a time when work was non-existent. The least hint of
violence disturbed him, as when his brother, Huw, sparred with the
boy next door when they lived in Abermaman, en route to Aberdare.
Thomas Jones, the boy in question, was a retired miner by the time
we met and precisely the kind of man Alun might have measured
himself against. He considered Alun unusual, though he valued the
exception – he said he 'left a fragrance in the air'. This phrase was
reproduced in my biography in the hope that the context would
protect it from the unintented double entendre, but one reviewer took
exception to it, not believing it could be unironical.

The example of Alun's 'Orphean uncle' Ned should give us
pause. Alun deviated from the norm of masculinity in certain obvious
ways – as graduate, writer and exile – but it was a deviation the
miners themselves might have wished for, reflecting as it did the
fineness they had had to suppress in themselves. To this extent, he
was not so different from them as themselves in disguise.

One aspect of Lewis's sexuality became apparent to me much
later, thanks to Lewis's artless frankness and his tendency to scatter
his love poems through his collections rather than group them. John
Petts first alerted me to it:

> By the way, the other day I remembered Alun's telling me,
> during a walk in Surrey [Petts was a conscientious objector
> and ordered to work on a farm near Longmoor] of a night he
> had spent with a prostitute. It stays in my mind as a very
> beautiful & moving short-short-story. Have you come across
> an account of this in any of his writings or letters? If not, I'll
> jot it down for you, for it has stayed in my mind as simply

and as clearly as Alun told it.

In Alun's voice, he composed the following account:

> I went with a street-girl the other day, she took me to her
> room. Oh, she looked so *tired*, gaunt and drawn under her
> make-up. She sat on the edge of the bed, bent, round-shoul-
> dered, tense, exhausted. I lay down beside her and held her
> quietly in my arms. Her head was on my shoulder. I said
> nothing; just held her. She gave a long, shuddering sigh, and
> then sank limply into sleep. I held her all night long, and she
> slept like a child. That's all.

The episode reveals his regard for the 'street-girl', whom he
embraces platonically and with whom he regress to an infantile state,
free of the necessity – and anxiety – of sex.

In Manchester, Lewis found himself stranded among strange
people. The city made him shiver with disgust: '…ugh. Oxford Road
and its syphilitics', he told Christopher Cheney. Its grimy streets,
sooty railings, hard pavements and wheezing wind oppressed him.
In London, where he moved to to be nearer the Public Records Office,
conditions did not improve. On 18th April 1939, he told Cheney:

> I also, in the few hours remaining to me – alone – was as
> wretched as sin – it's a soulless place, and I nearly sought
> relief from the whores of Picadilly – my Puritan ancestry
> prevailed, and my modesty, and – well, that's enough of that.

His life, he said, consisted of

> …[t]ubes and lectures, the Tate, the National Gallery, ballet
> and Proms, and people, people, people. Conversations
> growing taut and hysterical, or flopping like clumsy dead fish
> into your lap. You couldn't be sure. Rembrandt, Leonardo,
> Beethoven, Van Gogh, Brahms – all so important, all to be
> weighed and included in the necessary plan, all reacting on
> each other like chemical agents till the mind was in a vapour.
> And work, the diurnal, unmanageable – bending over
> medieval charters and accounts, transcribing, copying, collat-
> ing. And all the time trying to make it remote and scientific,
> this long-dead Thirteenth Century, that must resurrect itself,
> swell and lour, assume nebulous shapes, of fish and animal…
> [ellipsis in the text] and then suddenly to see it for the clod

> of dry dung that it was, and try to kick it off the sole of your
> shoe, and kick and kick in a vain nightmare.

Freda Thomas, in 'Attitude', could not have put it better. In 'Last
Leaves of a Long Journal', Lewis wrote:

> I was without interest in the long thesis at which I was so
> meticulously working for my M.A.. I loved no one and only
> desired one thing – love.

'The Soubrettes' tells where he found it. According to the OED,
a 'soubrette' is a maidservant in a play, 'usually one of a pert, coquet-
tish, or intriguing character'. Lewis was to use the word again in a
letter of December 30th 1943 when he described collecting eight
Eurasian and English female performers from Poona for the battalion's Christmas concert:

> It became ultimately an invitation to irresponsible pleasures.
> I find occasional irresponsibility almost a necessity
> nowadays – as a kind of laxative – no, as a necessary relief
> from the unending burden of earth but not that kind of dissi-
> pation. I keep thinking of those soubrettes – to them every
> evening is routine, to their hosts (every evening different
> hosts) each evening is an occasion.

The word's French ambience suggests the poem was written in
Pontigny, site of a student conference he attended in May 1937, going
via Paris. The poem first appeared in my *Miscellany* (1982) and tells
how 'a boy's spontaneous smile' disrupts the 'simulacrum of delight'
displayed by ladies whose 'clients changed from night to night'.
Where once there was shame and yearning there is now 'a shudder
and a scream'. Sex is no longer a matter of unsatisfied lust and decep-
tion but simply expressed.

'The Desperate' (section two of *Raiders' Dawn*, 'Poems in Love')
reads:

> When the soul is mad
> With foiled desire,
> And whirls the flesh
> In an arc of fire;
>
> When the mind's a fever
> And the grey brain drips,

> And the virgin seeks
> Polluted lips,
>
> O man and woman
> In that hour of need,
> Fling wide the sluice,
> Release the seed;
>
> And Love, poor Love,
> Must bear the ache
> Of lust grown holy
> For the soul's sweet sake.

A 'virgin' seeks release at the 'polluted' lips of a prostitute, thereby salving his conscience as well as his body and soul. Interestingly, the sex described is indoors, as it is again in 'The Soubrettes'. Apparently, the domestic taboo applied only to women of a certain class.

'Threnody for a Starry Night' (written in September 1939) includes this by-now familiar vignette:

> The boy who climbed the creaking stairs
> And floated on a couch at last
> In that sordid attic found
> His soul was rifled. Stumbling down,
> Sobbing in the street he fled
> Familiar things. His body
> Suffers in khaki.
> He disapproved Christ's chastity,
> Chose warmth
> Of loins, afraid to burn
> Obedient martyr to a rigid creed;
> Yet found
> Christ crucified bequeathed
> His agony to us.

A boy hurries from his assignation in a 'sordid attic', guilty at betraying his chastity. ('Khaki' suggests he is in uniform; the first section of *Raiders' Dawn*, which deals with the war, is called 'Poems in Khaki').

'Encirclement' dates from the autumn of 1940.

> Wrapped in the night's diseases,
> Haunted by streetwalking fancies

Of Coty and hunchbacks and sequins,
In the nameless dugouts and basements
Of Everyman's darkness,
I seek in the distant footfalls
The elusive answer of love,
Till deeper than any appearance
Or any one man's failure,
The shrivelled roots touch water.

And on this abandoned frontier
Where many visions falter
And youth and health are taken
Without complaint or reason,
I strive with the heart's blind strength
To reach the mild and patient place
Where the lamplit room awaits a stranger
And suffering has sanctified your face.

When two strangers meet in a lamplit room, something holy results.

'Compassion' (1941) tells of a man's bliss when a woman draws his matted hair to her breast, where he 'shivered' and grows still. Having banished his terror, she taps his 'dark will'.

Nor did she ever stir
In the storm's calm centre
To feel the tail, hooves, fur
Of the god-faced centaur.

She has released the man-beast in him. However, the sex involved may not be anonymous since the same image appears in 'War Wedding':

The fragile universe of self
In all its fine integrity
Becomes a cosmic curve, a thrust
Of natural fertility;
And Gods who shivered in the dust
Have found their lost divinity.

Lewis's recourse to prostitutes dates from his undergraduate days and continued at least until a year before his marriage. In Part II of 'Lance-Jack', a soldier wanders through a city's streets late at night: 'Not in my sweetheart's bed, for she has locked her father's door in my face'. There, he meets a group of 'loafers at the street corners' who tell him of 'the places where you may forget; they are easy to find and there everyone is agreeable, out to please; and it is not too costly'. Three years later, Lewis assured Freda 'the sex-hunger wretchedness' of 'Lance-Jack' was not autobiographical since, at the time, 'I was living in the most divinely satisfying sin'. 'Sin' contrasts with 'the other world, the hungry pale planet of loneliness, the natural failures' and releases him from 'loneliness' as from 'failure' in his 'natural' relations with women.

> I don't want to make too much of them [i.e. 'the natural failures'], Frieda; I never do, except when suddenly someone makes my whole life swing into one single orbit and I am compelled to integrate these worlds more closely because I feel all their strength swinging me the way of that person. And that doesn't happen often. How many times in a life time?

For him, twice.

> Innocence is a hell of a damned thing to suffer from; it's much easier to be a doggy man & slink about with a nice natural greed & the intention of satisfying it.

In his work, Lewis treats the whore with compassion verging on indifference. In 'Southend at Dusk', one cries: 'Oh why does my heart no longer leap/ When men come creaking up my stair?/ O why do I feel *so mean, so mean*?'. Demeaned by her trade, she cuts a sad figure. In 'The Island' (an Indian poem), a 'young patrician' casts his houseboat off an island: 'Do you step off fastidious as a virgin,/ Or with the mute complaisance of a whore?' 'By the Gateway of India: Bombay' describes 'the aching knots of lust/ In the harlot's clinging breath'. In 'The Orange Grove', Staff-Captain Beale recalls 'the popsies and the good-timers, the lonely good-looking boys and the indifferent erotic women' of Bombay:

> the girl behind the grille, in the side street where they play gramophone records and you pay ten chips for a whisky and you suddenly feel a godalmighty yen for whoever it is in your arms.... Why had he failed with this woman, why had it been impossible with that woman?

One who has known sexual frustration finds relief with 'the girl behind the grille'.

Beale recalls the school gardener, Mr Turvey, telling the boys that 'woman wasn't clean like man'.

> And when the boys demurred, thinking of soft pledges and film stars and the moon, Mr Turvey would wrinkle his saturnine face and say, 'Course you young gentlemen knows better than me. I only been married fifteen years. I don't know nothing of course.' And maybe this conversation would be while he was emptying the ordure from the latrines into the oil drum on iron wheels which he trundled each morning down to the sewer pits in the school gardens.

The association of female sexuality with uncleanliness appears earlier in the story with the tale of the seduction and betrayal of Beale's driver by his coarse 'barmaid' wife.

Nor that any of this necessarily contradicts Gwladys Lewis's view:

> Like his father, and a certain type of Welshman, Alun possessed what I can only describe as an affectionate indulgence towards women in general, almost a universal compassion, though that is hardly the correct word; maybe tenderness is nearer what I mean to convey. Their devotion and loving protection make them perfect lovers and ideal husbands. A friend of Alun's once told me that Alun could never be rude to a girl: and that about sums it up.

He could not be rude *as well as* kind to girls – not nice girls, anyway.

'Fever' is written in Lewis's best superheated style and relates a 'dream' that comes to a man when he is lying in bed with his (female) lover. The poem was sent in a letter to his girlfriend, Megan Lloyd-Jones, in which he complained about her sexual timidity and broke off relations between them. The two used to meet most Saturdays in 1935/6 in Chester, midway between her home town, Bangor, and Manchester.

Lewis's sexualisation of colliery life in 'The Rhondda' is also interesting in this context. First, the scene is set: a shaft-wheel whirs and steel hammers 'din down' ('drown out' as well as 'echo along the length of') the river Rhondda, whose bubbles resemble a 'Water-hag's slander'. The greasy water leaves scum-marks on the boulders, coal dust 'rings the scruffy willows', 'unwashed' colliers gamble and children float tins down 'dirty' rapids.

Into this filthy scene emerges Circe, the enchantress who makes swine of men:

> Circe is a drab.
> She gives men what they know.
> Daily to her pitch-black shaft
> Her whirring wheels suck husbands out of sleep.
> She for her profit takes their hands and eyes.

When the colliers enter the pit, they go down Circe's 'shaft', leaving behind their 'fat flabby-breasted' wives with their scrubbing, making tea and peeling potatoes – a very different 'drabness'. The poem invests the colliers with a terrific sexual frisson: their traffic with their 'drab' (or whore) proves their virility, domestic life being no more than the residue of pit life. When Lewis turned to his own 'drabs', he became a collier, freed at last from contradiction. Joining the female 'other' made him no longer 'Other'.

'The Rhondda' demonstrates again Lewis's habit of choosing fictional parents who are unlike his own: his mothers flabby, exhausted, flat-breasted 'mams', his fathers colliers. His actual parents' imaginative value to him was apparently nil.

From this perspective, it is easy to understand why what at first appears over-heated in his work ('Love cries and cries in me', 'I within me holding Turbulence and Time', 'he sought…/ The bleating wounded beast that was his voice') is no more than an accurate reflection of his distress. Similarly, his treatment of women as virgins and whores arises not from prejudice but inhibition. His whores are neither angels nor demons and his attraction to married women motivated by the suggestion that they treated his difficulties with greater understanding. Psychologically, they repeat the bond with mother.

Lewis's idolisation of children belongs to the same complex. 'Raiders' Dawn' describes the burial of young victims of an air raid:

> The drifting white
> Fall of small faces
> In pits of lime.

Rarely has the pity of war been more poignantly captured. (Compare the 'dying children' and 'joy/ Of luckier babes playing' in 'After Dunkirk'.) These lines were glossed in his 'Last Pages of a Long Journal':

> Like the insipid exhaustion of 'flu, the civilised centuries lapse and the houses fall in the night, paper on paper, and children fall like snow softly into the lime-pits of oblivion. The lovers remembering the nakedness of the first night know now that they do not after all possess mastery over time. But their mastery may be over Eternity. That is the hope in us, a little germ in us, the seed that is in us we do not know how, and not all the irreparable cruelties and blind malignance and loss of the war can kill the germ, the seed of humanity.
>
> This is the seed of the writer. Words are seeds, semen. And the writer must gradually work forward, stubbornly and without ever surrendering to the temptation of failure, though he must include this temptation in his work and in his penultimate word. Lovers progress slowly and by failure to their consummation. Everywhere there are lovers, in all countries, friends. Goodness is like sex.

As is writing – and attended by the same difficulties. That explains why he worked at it so 'stubbornly', despite the 'temptation of failure'. Each 'consummation' was hard-won but the 'seed' eventually released was productive. 'Odi et Amo' defines the soldier's plight thus:

> My body does not seem my own
> Now. These hands are not my own
> That touch the hair-spring trigger, nor my eyes
> Fixed on a human target, nor my cheek
> Stroking the rifle butt; my loins
> Are flat and closed like a child's.

The soldier is a child – a spoilt child but a child nevertheless, both tarnished and doted on. He keeps alive the notion of goodness, victim of the contest between innocence and experience.

# II

Some see Lewis's departure for India as his exchange of one colonial situation for another, the British being the colonisers in Wales as in India. His predicament is thus said to derive from his 'so feeling partly British and partly Welsh that he can feel neither fully British nor fully Welsh'. The British part of him rendered him imperial, the Welsh one of the wretched of the earth.

The difficulty here is assuming that 'British' and 'Welsh' are distinct and antithetical terms, relying on an essentialist definition of 'Welsh' which underestimates the ambiguity and complexity of life at that time. Indeed, being neither fully British nor Welsh might itself be regarded as characteristically Welsh. If the Welsh really were a subject people, it would be difficult to account for the part Welsh coal, religion, politics, cabinet secretaries, teachers, nurses, district commissioners and the like played in the Empire, not all of whom could be considered victims of false consciousness. As Gwyn Alf Williams has contended, Wales was 'the central directive force' of Empire.

> Welsh identity has constantly renewed itself by anchoring itself in variant forms of Britishness.... It was in the British Empire that a Welsh intellectual could find fulfilment in the sixteenth century. The pattern has proved recurrent.

In the light of this, it is difficult to posit a 'Welshness' that does not to some extent involve 'Britishness' and a 'Britishness' that does not to some extent involve a separate – and separating – notion of 'Welshness'. Single allegiances in a plural world are difficult to come by. History and Utopia (or Dystopia) flank the Present. Certainly, Lewis never regarded himself as a victim of colonialism and opposed it in South Africa as in India.

The culture of alienation in the modern era created by movements between dependent and dominant countries suggests that the colonial experience – however culturally defined – is normative rather than a departure from 'belongingness'. Far from limiting, it has proved extraordinarily creative. When Lewis applied for an officers' training course in March 1941, he declared: 'I am Welsh by birth, have lived in South Wales all my life, graduated at the University of Wales, and taught in a Welsh County School'. In a review for *The Dublin Magazine*, he defined the problem facing authors like himself as one

of interpreting the life of one country in the language of
another. English is our medium; Welsh…life our raw
material. And the resolution of this problem is our literary
mission. It is a problem which at once checks and inspires,
denies difficulties and supplies the energy to remove them.

French was his second language and English one of the many
'Englishes' available to writers.

Unsurprisingly, therefore, language is foregrounded in his work.
Some regard his prose as securer than his verse because less exposed.
After enlisting, he started writing in a simpler style under the influence of Edward Thomas and the war. 'The Soldier' marks the
transition.

> I within me holding
> Turbulence and Time
> – Volcanic fires deep beneath the glacier –
> Feel the dark cancer in my vitals
> Of impotent impatience grope its way
> Through daze and dream to throat and fingers
> To find its climax of disaster.

By the end, this excited style of writing has moderated, as if part of
the poem's burden were the contrast between hyperbole and simplicity:

> Yet still
> I who am agonized by thought
> And war and love
> Grow calm again
> With watching
> The flash and play of finches
> Who are as beautiful
> And indifferent to me
> As England is, this Spring morning.

Lines all the more effective for contrasting with the preceding 'agony
of thought'.

Lewis first started writing under the influence of Auden and
Dylan Thomas but soon forged a style of his own that was more
modest but still saturated with feeling. It has has proved influential,
as Ted Hughes attests:

When I first began trying to cure myself of the hangover
from the adolescent surfeit of poetry, I went on a diet of sane
herbs, so to speak. Alun Lewis was one of the few I found.
Something in his essence supplied a vital mineral that exists
nowhere else. I still think so…. The sterling thing is evidently
in *him* – the prose manifests it as clearly as the poems.

He can go from the Movement-like:

> Framed in a jagged window of grey stones
> These wooded pastures have a dream-like air.
> You thrill with disbelief
> To see the cattle move in a green field.
>
> 'Corfe Castle'

To this:

> Three endless weeks of sniping all the way,
> Lying up when their signals ran too close,
> – 'Ooeee, Ooee,' like owls, the lynx-eyed Jap, –
> Sleeplessly watching, knifing, falling back.
> And now the Sittang river was there at last
> And the shambles of trucks and corpses round the bridge
> And the bridge was blown. And he laughed.
>
> And then a cough of bullets, a dusty cough
> Filleted all his thigh from knee to groin.
> The kick of it sucked his face into the wound.
> He crumpled, thinking 'Death'. But no, not yet.
> The femoral artery wasn't touched.
> Great velour cloaks of darkness floated up.
> But he refused, refused the encircling dark,
> A lump of bitter gristle that refused.
> The day grew bloodshot as they picked him up.

Such Hughesian lines marry acute observation with a steadily-
mounting rhetoric - 'And' - 'And' - 'And' - 'And' - 'But' - 'But'. The
violence that attracts also repels. A decade later, Hughes reflected
similarly on the cycle of life and death in *The Hawk in the Rain*,
Christian teleology yielding to repetition within a process that is
endless. For both poets, nature is less a locus of feeling than a revelation of fate.

'The Mahratta Ghats' opens:

> The valleys crack and burn, the exhausted plains
> Sink their black teeth into the horny veins
> Straggling the hills' red thighs, the bleating goats
> – Dry bents and bitter thistles in their throats –
> Thread the loose rocks by immemorial tracks.
> Dark peasants drag the sun upon their backs.

The harsh consonants create a grinding music – 'crack', 'black', 'rocks', 'tracks', 'dark', 'backs'. Yet everything is as formal and ceremonious as in a poem by Yeats. It is Lewis's ability to stare into the heart of light that is his greatest poetic attribute. India revealed life to be a punishment and a burden, beyond all illusion. The 'dark' peasants rehearse a tragedy in which 'the sun is always brilliant and violent, like an ancient god'.

'Lady in Black' opens:

> Lady in black,
> I knew your son.
> Death was our enemy
> Death and his gun.
>
> Death had a trench
> And he blazed away.
> We took the trench
> By the end of the day.
>
> Lady in black,
> Your son was shot.
> He was my mate
> And he got it hot.
>
> Death's a bastard
> Keeps hitting back.
> But a war's a war
> Lady in black.

An astonishing anticipation of Sylvia Plath's mature manner.

Another aspect of Lewis's work is his ability to carry words musically across the page, the bloom of freshness on them:

> Last night I did not fight for sleep

> But lay awake from midnight while the world
> Turned its slow features to the moving deep
> Of darkness, till I knew that you were furled,
>
> Beloved, in the same dark watch as I.

This is a precursor of the confessional style popularised by Lowell and Plath. As in a poem by Yeats or Edward Thomas, it is the witching hour of midnight when Lewis turns to Gweno in thought and motion. 'Night', 'fight' and 'midnight' enact the tension of the moment. 'World', at the end of line 2, chimes with 'turned' at the start of line 3, pivoting the turn on two successive stresses ('world', 'turned') and disrupting the iambic rhythm.

More enjambment comes in lines 3/4: 'moving deep/ Of darkness'. The alliterative 'deep/ Of darkness' and the trochaic rhythm (stressed syllable followed by an unstressed one) carry the reader over the line-break. A bolder enjambment follows in lines 4/5 over both verse and line breaks: 'you were furled,// Beloved'. The caressive 'f' in 'furled' mutates into the 'v' of 'Beloved'; the former suggests the embrace of the lovers and the spinning of the earth on its axis which makes it possible - 'furled', 'world', 'turned'. Such sonic finesse is extraordinary.

These instances of 'turning' imitate the coiling of a snake and, indeed, a real one appears in the last line:

> …Time upon the heart can break
> But love survives the venom of the snake.

'Break', at the end of the line, refers to the heart's ache but also to the line-break and releases a powerful head of feeling. The snake opposes love and Time but the lovers survive, having made an eternity of their love. Time can be beaten, as the stresses on 'love', 'survives' and 'venom' insist, the soft 'v' in each caressing the ear. The metaphorical snake that has been winding its way through the poem rears its head at the end only to be repulsed.

This hopeful resolution was promptly questioned by 'Burma Casualty', where the 'Beloved' gives way to the 'beautiful singing sexless angel'. The dark drift of the transformation is ironically emphasised by words like 'Lucency' and 'effulgent'. When linked to spoken rhythms and formal rhyme schemes, they can be impressive. It is as if, in a sea of Hindustani speakers, Lewis's English grew more self-conscious. In 'Mahratta Ghats', he asks:

> Who is it climbs the summit of the road?
> Only the beggar bumming his dark load.
> Who was it cried to see the falling star?
> Only the landless soldier lost in war.

Gnomic lines, simple and profound. The falling star bodes ill luck to the 'landless' Indian poor and the differently 'landless' poor soldiers.

As Intelligence Officer, Lewis frequently engaged in 'motion and mileage and tinkering', 'furled' in 'vast migrations' harking back to a time

> When history was the flight of a million birds
> And poverty has splendid divagations.

'Divagations'! Ah! *that* kind of poverty! Lewis here essays the paradox of a journey that is rich in meaning but empty of direction. History yields to space-time. In this context, 'divagations' is not only not incongruous but thought-provoking.

# III

Despite our differences, Gweno and I continued to correspond. One of her letters ends: 'With good wishes' and 'Kindest regards'. She provided me with letters of authorisation for the National Library of Wales and the Army Records Centre as well as samples of Lewis's unpublished work, drafts (written in her own hand) of 'All day it has rained...' and 'To Edward Thomas' and Lynette Roberts's letters. I told her the last-mentioned struck me as 'certainly unique, full of a quirky intelligence, charm, even, despite the flurry of typing errors and the hailstorm of opinions, injunctions and exhortations. How maddening! And how vivifying!'

Freda believed Gweno's contradictory behaviour proved she had 'truly criss-crossed mental equipment'. At their last meeting in Woodstock, she felt there was acceptance, even magnanimity and laughter, though there was 'steel in the smile'. One reason for Gweno's continuing to correspond with me, she thought, was her desire not to be excluded from a process both the Lewises and she approved of. She saw herself as playing a cautionary role, neither obstructing nor admitting me into her confidence. Gwladys Lewis told me: '…she [Gweno] said don't tell him but I'm now willing to help him'.

The unpublished material included 'The Miner's Son', written at the end of August 1937. This describes the Edwards family: an ailing mother, unemployed collier father who is champion of social justice and Meirion, their eldest son, who wants to turf the capitalists out 'with a pitchfork rather than a bayonet, though'. A neighbour says he is ''anging about the mountainside all 'is days'. After graduating from Aberystwyth two years before, he has been unable

> to write and philosophise, and drowning my failure by reading and running off to the mountain to brood and brood and brood. I've fed on my thoughts till I've eaten myself hollow. I used to believe in goodness, in human perfectibility, in socialism, in progress. Now I don't know what to believe…. I'm shallow – and undersexed – I don't *feel* anything.

An old girlfriend, Menna, tells him he has 'got something of Paul Morel' in him; his new one, Muriel, taunts him for not making love to her, playing Clara Dawes to his Paul Morel. He confesses: 'I've never properly wanted to – I couldn't until I feel whole inside myself'. Not that he was any happier with Menna: 'Well, he knew himself for what he was, futile, useless, small-minded, immoral'. A more wounding self-assessment it would be hard to imagine.

The unpublished material also included two novels. The first of them dates from Lewis's last year in Aberystwyth (1937/8) and concerns Adam, lately returned from two years' research in London in a state of virtual invalidism, having suffered a 'sort of annihilation, a sword cutting through all your sinews, leaving your emotions hamstrung and impotent'. Occasional episodes of reasonless joy punctuate his despair. He recalls

> the cruel barren anguish of last year and the year before when his soul had been an ooze of black putrefying matter inside him and he had been alone, alone; God, yes, alone.

He tells his girlfriend, Nest Scudamore, of a recurrent dream he has in which something 'slimy and irresistible' pushes him into a tunnel, 'a sort of sewer, through which you've got to crawl if you want to reach the sunlight on the other side'. She tells him he is wearing

himself out with love, life and thought: he *will* try to attach a meaning
to everything (an echo of Marjorie Walters complaint that his
company could be 'claustrophobic', just as her 'reserve, her over-
sensitive avoidance' recalls Megan Lloyd-Jones's 'principled' refusal
of sex).

Nest's timidity is explained by a recent diagnosis of tuberculosis.
Eventually, she breaks with him, treating him thereafter as her best
friend. In effect, they have entered a sexless marriage.

> They tried to short-circuit physical love and be perfect in
> each other without performing the necessary act. They tacitly
> set themselves to undervalue it, to consider it as an unneces-
> sary matter of form, like signing the marriage register. *Their*
> love should be unconventional. *They* would not desire, until
> desire came back to the numb body.

That, however, is of little comfort:

> *He* had never been innocent, never. There had always been
> the secret sense of guilt, carried about in the heart in a
> capsule that was leaking, leaking, a black drop each year of
> his puberty, his adolescence, his young manhood.

In despair, he turns to a 'barmaid' for sex.

Out on a walk one day, they fall into an embrace and their feelings
soon get the better of them, 'tossing their limbs like so much wreck-
age'.

> But he knew almost at once that he had done the wrong thing
> in attempting to respond physically to her. When he covered
> her with kisses he hated himself; and hated himself more and
> more as his lips became more frantic. And revulsion dried
> up his seed, all his vitality, and held him as if he were a dead
> fowl and choked him closer and closer the more his lips
> writhed to find the impossible release.

Though wishing to make love, Adam fears sex is an imposition, and
guilt and embarrassment cause him to fail. The image of the 'dead
fowl' accurately reflects his deflated desire and his frantic attempts
to revive it. Lewis infrequently disproved what the novel proposes:
'The last thing we learn is that we cannot love'.

The second novel, *Morlais*, written in the summer of 1939, opens on the day before Morlais Jenkins is to sit his scholarship examination for entry to the County School (the 11 Plus). A sensitive boy, he is nauseated by the casual sexuality displayed by his teenage sister. When his best friend, David Reames, the colliery manager's son, is killed in an accident, his mother visits him in the middle of the night and offers to adopt him. She offers him a new, clean, cool, safe environment 'swimming around him like sea water, green and exciting'. Here is a way out of his hesitations, the whole pressing world of pits, teenage gangs and political strife. Despite being his mother's pet, Morlais's parents agree to give him up. They foresee advantages to him in the new arrangement, though he is disconcerted by their failure to keep him. He has been sacrificed on the altar of 'getting on'.

Four years later, Morlais meets his mother by chance in the street and begs her to take him back. She refuses:

> 'It's the only reason I'm not sorry you're living in the big 'ouse. You got a chance to get out of it all.'
> 'No, I haven't,' he said, clenching his teeth with the strife that was in him. 'I'm here, here.'
> 'No, you're not, not for good,' she said sharply, stamping her foot. '…. No, you keep at your lessons now, and go to College, see?' She stood in the path and commanded his eyes with her burning ones. 'You go on, see? You'll be a teacher, or a minister, something where you can be yourself, see?'
> 'I want to come home with you, that's all I want,' he said quietly. She caught her breath; he sensed her hardening.
> 'Don't be daft,' she said curtly. 'We don't want you.'

The refusal is final.

Morlais tells Mrs Reames 'there's nobody wants me' but she warns him against his sensitivity which, though it grants him unusual understanding, is 'a terrible power'; the only good is love. But how love when the mere mention of sex brings a sweat out 'on his forehead and under his arms and round his loins'? One night, he overhears her reciting Keats and imagines he is listening to his own voice spelling out his destiny:

> When I have fears that I may cease to be,
> Before this pen has gleaned my teeming brain.

The novel then switches to Aberystwyth, where Morlais, standing before the ocean, finds the problem of sex resolved:

> ... the sea was coming in naked and wild with music,
> washing away the roughness of the earth and casting its
> marriage veils over the bridal beach. Earth and sea, water
> and stone, eternally in intercourse, the thrust of the inward
> flow, the caress of the ebb, the renewal in whiteness of foam
> and smoothness of rock. And he perceiving it with all his life,
> like Shelley. He tossed his head back, tasting the salt on his
> lips, and for the first time felt his manhood respond to the
> attraction of Being without at the same time being tormented
> with shame.

He can finally enjoy an erection without embarrassment. This
episode is an uncanny anticipation of one that occurred shortly after
his arrival in India, when he stood before a shrine of the Buddha and
experienced a sensation of physical desire without purpose,

> a local itch, entirely local and thereby quite definite, in the
> sensitive inch or two of flesh that always has represented the
> simply physics of love.

> Yet never did I breathe its pure serene.

Freed from inhibition, Morlais rejects College and rejoins his
family, who are now in straightened circumstances. Mr Jenkins has
lost his job and is standing for election to the Council, but he
manages to get Morlais a post as library assistant in the Workman's
Institute: 'It's Karl Marx with me and John the Baptist & William
Williams Pantycelyn with your mother', he remarks. (Pantycelyn,
Wales's most famous hymn writer, was a leading figure in the
Methodist revival of the eighteenth century.) Once again, Lewis's
fictional parents are unlike his own.

Between Mr Jenkins's politics and Mrs Jenkins's religion,
Morlais tries to find his way. There are two Morlaises in the novel:
Morlais Jenkins is a product of the valleys while Morlais Reames is
attached to the muse-like Mrs Reames. Like so much of Lewis's
writing from this time, the resolution to this division in himself is
optimistic: Morlais reconnects with his community. It is a consummation devoutly to be wished.

In the context of Welsh nationalism, it is pertinent to note that
neither Morlais Jenkins nor Morlais Reames is 'Welsh' or 'British'.
Their plight concerns class, that whole nexus of forces – psychological, social, sexual – that writers like Hardy and D.H. Lawrence had

to contend with when trying to establish themselves as writers in a world which had not seen their like before.

The last of the unpublished works, 'The Tunnel', is a four-act play with epilogue. The title refers to the rite of passage which the young have to pass through before they reach the light. The cast-list is a familiar one: dominant father, a collier-promoted-undermanager, his thin, stooping wife and their 23-year-old son, Gron Roberts, a final- year student at university. His father says of him:

> E's spent 'alf 'is life on that mountain, though what 'e sees in it, I don't know. If Gron don't know 'is way about it, the foxes don't neither.

His mother comes nearer him when she remarks:

> 'e's different from the rest of us somehow. Seems to live inside 'imself – as if 'is thoughts won't let 'im be…. You can't get near 'im, sometimes. 'E'll sit there and talk to you, and all the time 'e's quite alone, some'ow.

Up on the mountain, with the wind blowing through the ferns, he is nobody at all.

Gron lacks the usual Lewisian protagonist's angry radicalism. That is reserved for Harold Watkins, a collier impatient of intellectuals like him, whom he regards as a Hamlet who would let the Poloniuses and Claudiuses of the world get away with the profits. Gron is no more than 'a heap of old flywheels and screws and springs, which don't work no matter how much I oil them with with reading and thinking'. He sees himself

> … walking across a desert, when the wind obliterates the footprints you've just made, and you don't know what direction you came from nor where you're going to. You just stand there impotent, and inside you and all around you it's all arid and dead.

Sex fails to come naturally to him and he senses he harbours the germ of death. Noting the way children are brought up, he observes:

> Teaching them to be Christians and suppress all their natural desires. Telling them to be good, as if they know what good means unless they've been the other thing. And telling them

to work hard, as if they were machines, not strange sensitive
live things.

Spoken like a true Lawrentian, though he cannot quite bring himself
to mention the 'other thing' that is not 'good'.

In the Epilogue, Gron's father lies dead following a pit accident;
his wife joins him shortly after. Their deaths leave Gron feeling
'purified somehow' and he senses afresh the power of the enemies
of the working class as well as – more Lawrence – something 'flame
inside me, running through my veins'. Phoenix-like, he rises from
their ashes. The political temper of the conclusion is qualified by a
sense that his liberation comes at the expense of his parents - they
die so that he might live. And though he feels he can strike out on
his own, he is only following the path they have laid down for him.
The Oedipal hero becomes more socialist by liberating himself from
the arid state induced in him by the suppression of his loving self by
his loving parents.

# Part Twelve
## *Writing Alun*

### I

In 1966, Ian Hamilton, the most influential critic yet to have rallied to Lewis's cause, published *Alun Lewis Selected Poetry and Prose*, the first anthology since *In the Green Tree* (1948). For all his merits, Gweno took against him: she agreed he showed 'considerable ability' but complained he had failed to return all the manuscripts she had lent him, some of which she believed later appeared in the catalogues of rare and antiquarian second-hand booksellers. Freda also took against him, referring disparagingly to his 'cold' Scottish ancestry.

In a 50-page-long introduction, Hamilton explained he had conceived his selection out of admiration for 'a writer as good but as uneven as Lewis' – not exactly a clarion call.

> My main editorial aim has been to chronicle the life and recommend the work of a writer who seems to me to have been shamefully neglected in the twenty-odd years since his death.

There is no logical contradiction between the two statements, though the contrast in their tone may have been confusing.

Hamilton placed his emphasis on a central dilemma:

> commitment to one's art, to the solitary routes of the imagi-
> nation, to the steady personal quest for a fulfilment that will
> transcend, although it may be occasioned by, 'the warring
> elements', or commitment of a practical, energetically loving
> kind to 'the warm ones about us'? It is the crucial conflict...
> Lewis could never finally accept that these pursuits need be
> distinct, or that a choice must be made between them, but he
> was often consumed by that failure of energy which can arise
> from their antagonism, and often enticed by thoughts of a

death in which they might be absolutely reconciled.

That is acute, though its effect was limited by his concentration on the work he did before India, regarding the latter as a coda rather than its culmination. But then he knew nothing about Freda. The only poem of hers included was 'The Way Back', without comment.

This was followed in 1981 by *Selected Poems of Alun Lewis*, edited by Gweno and Jeremy Hooker, an Aberystwyth lecturer. Her choice of Hooker doubtless reflected on his abilities as teacher and poet but also had something to do with her disappointment with me. When I heard of the venture, I argued that it would jeopardise the more comprehensive publishing programme we all agreed was necessary. No publisher would want to do anything more until the *Selected* had sold out. Hooker, while not unresponsive to my arguments, felt he had given his word and that, if he withdrew now, Gweno would find somebody else. Better to reach out to a wider audience, paving the way for my biography.

Towards the end of his life, Lewis told Freda that he had included 'Wood Song', 'Peasant Song', 'Ways' and 'The Way Back' in *Ha! Ha! Among the Trumpets*:

> May I, Frieda? You are willing to be in the book, aren't you darling? Please.

Since then, critics have done their best to take her *out* of it. Hamilton and Hooker at least had the excuse of ignorance. The only Freda poem in the *Selected* was 'The Way Back', but what could Gweno have done? This suggests why it was unwise of her to be involved in the project in the first place. The *Selected* appeared just as the wartime editions of his work were going out of print. Set as an A-level text by the Welsh Joint Education Committee, it stimulated a great deal of interest among schoolchildren, though its wider impact was more limited. Certainly, Allen and Unwin did nothing to follow it up. Their attitude to it may be judged by their inclusion of Robert Graves's preface from *Ha! Ha! Among the Trumpets* from 36 years before – a dubious bit of bookmaking. Hooker's contribution was an 'Afterword' and again concentrated on the Longmoor poems, a reflection of his belief that Lewis's death was accidental, which held out the possibility of his eventual return to Wales after the war, when he would have re-engaged with all the issues that had previously exercised him. It is not what happened but what might have happened.

My *Alun Lewis, A Miscellany of his Writings* (1982), comprised a selection of fugitive and unpublished pieces with linking commentary. Most of the material was early – I didn't think this was the time for revelations. Gweno called it a 'very attractive venture' but thought it would reach no more than the usual audience (she was correct, of course). Freda was much less enthusiastic, believing it to be an attempt on my part to curry favour with Gweno. Jealousy and pique had something to do with her reaction, but she was genuinely dismayed that another incomplete account had been added to the ones that already existed.

In the *Miscellany*, I included samples of Lewis's student stories (which are more interesting than the usual juvenilia, e.g. 'Attitude'), magazine articles, journal extracts, the *Horizon* review of Edward Thomas (the starting point for Thomas criticism), some poems (mostly late) and the correspondence with Robert Graves, amusing because written at such cross-purposes. Where Graves dispenses obiter dicta blithely, Lewis is heartfelt and humble. The exchange was initiated by him after he heard a radio talk by Graves in which he remarked on two lines from 'The Soldier': 'But leisurely my fellow soldiers stroll among the trees./ The cheapest dance-song utters all they feel'. Graves called them courageous and thought they exemplified the difference between the poets of the two world wars. Lewis wrote to disagree:

> It seemed to me you were using it to express a point of view I don't endorse, to wit, the isolation or difference of the poet….the isolation is not that of a cultured gent timidly roughing it with a blunt gang, but the simple, cosmic loneliness that is natural to a man today as to the old Ecclesiast.

'The Soldier', in other words, is not about war but the human condition.

As a tailpiece, I reprinted John Berryman's 'Elegy, for Alun Lewis' (*Poetry (Chicago), January 1950*). Berryman had been rejected as unfit for service and, in 1972, committed suicide by jumping off Washington Avenue Bridge in Minneapolis. His elegy begins:

> Little attention we paid each other alive
> But Death has made us friends. Your death, not mine.
> I am dying slowly.

The courteous but stealthy tone makes an immediate impression. Evidently, Berryman treats Lewis as a kindred spirit, one who has beaten a direct path to the desired end:

> Now envious I hear of that exploit
> And sit down to these poems of yours and grieve.

The 'poems' are those of *Ha! Ha! Among the Trumpets*, published five years before.

Berryman regrets his inability to imitate Lewis's 'exploit', a word that gives his death an atmosphere of daring:

> Grieve for a stranger made strangely a friend,
> 'Killed in an accident on active service.'
> All, all an accident?

This is the first and only time anyone had publicly questioned the Court of Inquiry's verdict of accidental death. Berryman had no grounds for doing so other than his conviction that he understood the 'stranger' whose death had made him a 'friend'. Like him, he knew what it felt like to be embattled:

>                                    Familiar glowers
> The universal furnace, restless and careless powers
> Who club us wall to wall ahead of them
> In brightening darkness through the harrowing hours.

The 'universal furnace' is an apt description of a world at war, suggesting some Hardyesque President of the Immortals who impassively surveys the 'brightening darkness'.

> You died a strange way. Your blood on my hand.

Lewis becomes Berryman's blood brother, a stranger both intimate and haunting, an Edward Thomas-like 'other' who bequeathes his death to him, in that way rendering him complicit in it. The hand tainted with Lewis's blood is the one that inscribes this tribute to him:

> – Hand flexing so, white hand of this age
> Heart stops to look on, what have we done?

'We' might be Berryman's heart and hand, or Lewis and himself, not so much guilty beings affrighted as poets sharing a mutual end. A strange death has taken place in 'familiar' circumstances, revealing unexpected connections.

The last verse gives a twist to the notion of the stranger who is a friend:

> Only the death to come can make us friends.

Their kinship will be fully realised only when Berryman, too, commits suicide:

> But hesitate (soul quicks) grotesque amends
> To the dissolving slain.

The closing lines encourage him to

> Take up your nature for
> The future which these strangers from their minds
> Clouding – dismissed with horror and courage.

Having begun by addressing Lewis, Berryman ends by addressing himself, urging him to prove true to himself by imitating the action of one who, having 'dismissed with horror' the future, had the 'courage' to do something about it. Lewis's accomplice turns out to be his successor.

Berryman's tribute poem was uncollected, as is R.S. Thomas's, 'Alun Lewis' (*The Stones of the Field*, 1946). It bears the influence of 'In Hospital: Poona (2)':

> You with your reference frequently to the rain,
> Sharp as spears to prick the mind alive,
> Or silver, suggestive of the wealth of grace,
> God's grace showering on the parched earth,
> Breaking the arid season of the flesh:
> I salute you, Alun, knowing your thought, born
> Not of our climate, where excess of rheum
> Blurs the clear image and enlists the heart's
> Ready commerce. It was the sun's glare,
> Harsh as the land, whose white bones prompted
> An alien creed, that wakened in you the soil's
> Naked perception of the rain's worth.

In watery Wales, heart feels more than the eye can see – 'excess of rheum/Blurs the image', an uncanny repetition of Berryman's 'clouding' of Lewis's mind by a hostile future. In India, the sun clarified his perceptions, revealing to him a metaphysic rooted in annihilation. That made the arrival of the rain all the more precious – a virtual reprise of 'The Way Back'.

## II

After publishing the *Miscellany*, I started writing the biography. Freda thought one phase of our friendship was ending:

> There is, no doubt about it, a telepathic something between us: I had been thinking about you yesterday after forgetting you for quite a long time. I love you for learning to love me – of course you do, I gave you Alun. And you know I have always loved you because you became a sort of surrogate Alun for me. I thought in my bath this a.m. that I can say truthfully that the only thing in the past six years which filled me with creative reality, was the Freda-John-Alun dialogues. I was sad when they seemed to have ended with the beginning of your book.

I returned her sentiments with equal affection, though this did not mean we always agreed, as Freda revealed in her reaction to my Miscellany. We had both shown we were proof against encouragement and discouragement and wrote all the more freely because of it.

Freda's regard for me as Lewis's surrogate touched me. Discussing him with me, back and forth, I believe she found herself falling in love with him again, an experience as painful as it was magical. In the past 30 years, she had led a buried life, one overshadowed by guilt; it was a species of grieving without end. Now, the stone on her heart, which had depressed her natural vitality, began to shift. My article on 'The Way Back' must have struck her with main force, holding up a mirror to her frozen feelings, and throwing the years between into relief. In her long, passionate letters and equally long telephone calls and meetings, she relived the past, both in its diminished and augmented forms. Free at last to confront the joy and grief in her life, feeling began to flow in her again, all the tenderer for having been suppressed so long and relieving her of a pressure grown so habitual as scarcely to register as such. What followed was the flowering of her natural and emotional intelligence. Able to express her sorrow, she entered the most testing experience of her life, having to submit the personal to external discipline and analysing it with a measure of objectivity.

At one stage, she asked me to return her letters to me so that she could use them in her memoir; as a quid pro quo, she returned my own letters to me:

> My letters to you came back this morning. Thank you so much for them. I'm rather downed by the fact that I wrote so much better then, (even so short a time ago) than now. Time, and the nasty blows life deals one, has taken its toll. The letters bring back, as yours did to you, the struggle to convey the truth (in yours to find the truth) and are also moving because of the quotations used to do so. We really must seriously think about putting these letters into chronological form and launching them. I mean this because they do make a most fascinating journal, our styles and emotions different but the attitudes to most things and the goal quite the same.

Perhaps her notion will bear fruit one day.

As she worked on, I made two new contacts. The first was Philip Unwin, Lewis's publisher, whose interest was both personal and professional – Alun was his protégé. In *The Publishing Unwins*, he explained that his firm stood for 'a fairer distribution of the country's wealth, a better regulated economy, wider educational opportunities, the ideas of Karl Marx, Hobson, Keynes, Laski, Beveridge – each of whom we had published!'. Lewis could not have found a better home.

It was Clifford Makin, then business manager of *Horizon*, who first drew his attention to Lewis when 'The Last Inspection' appeared in the February 1941 issue of the magazine. Both responded to its sympathetic humour – here was the authentic voice of the ranks. As it happens, 'The Last Inspection' is one of Lewis's few satiric pieces and is the product of his frustration at the way the Railway Centre at Longmoor was run. So critical was it that he expected a reprimand, though none came. The story focuses on a Brigadier who, having come out of retirement at the start of the war, is now about to retire again and goes on a farewell tour of the loco sheds:

> He was going to see everything today, for himself. It's only
> natural when you're retiring, you want to see for yourself
> whether any work has been done during your tenure of office,
> how things have been getting along, sort of thing; because
> when you're at the helm you haven't any time to go dashing
> into the stokehold to supervise the trimmers, have you?

The tour of inspection is planned to end at the point where the two
ends of the railway have been joined but, needless to say, they have
not. When lunch takes longer than expected and the weather turns
cold and wet, the tour is abandoned.

> Then the Brigadier said he had one last toast to propose.
> Silence in the diner.
>     'To Victory!'
>     'To Victory!' they all replied.

At that, the fireman, Morgan Evans ('Mogg'), says to the driver,
Fred: 'We've dug for Victory and saved for Victory. And now they're
drinking for it'. Just then, a messenger arrives to tell him a telegram
is waiting for him at the office. At that, he goes grey, thinking of his
wife and children in Shoreditch; Mogg takes him gently by the arm.
For some people, the war is real.

So moved by the story was Unwin that he asked Lewis if he had
a novel to submit. He is not the only reader to have been impressed
by the novelistic endowment of his short stories. Lewis, he said,
'responded with the roughish little collection of poems which became
RAIDERS' DAWN'. He could not hide his disappointment. Here
was someone who could express Tommy's point of view, though not
necessarily in Tommy's own words, but, in truth, Lewis was in flight
from Tommy's war. *Raiders' Dawn* is suffused with a dreamy
restlessness that suggests a deeper suffering. As irritated by the Army
as he was, it inspired in him an element of idealism; reading 'The
Last Inspection', Unwin thought of Rupert Brooke. It was a creative
misreading that was to prove lucrative for him.

Lewis picked up on it when he asked him to reproduce John
Petts's 'sulky engraving' of him on the front cover: 'I feel it makes
the whole thing rather Rupert Brooke-ish', to which Unwin replied:
'Rupert Brookeish it may be but I shouldn't at all mind your becom-
ing in your own particular way the Rupert Brooke of this war'.
'Post-script: For Gweno' begins:

> If I should go away,
> Beloved, do not say
> 'He has forgotten me'.
> For you abide,
> A singing rib within my dreaming side;
> You always stay.

The Brookeian echo ('If I should die, think only this of me') shows how much Longmoor stirred a capacity for sacrifice in him, one that was to carry him to the infantry and India. En route, he assured Gweno she was still 'deep deep deep in me'.

Freighted with such feeling, the poems are inevitably more subjective than objective. A university friend recalled:

> There was always this impression of suppressed emotion in him. However still or thoughtful, whether talking or laughing, there was this intensity, a suggestion of waiting, which communicated itself however remote he remained, however near he came.

Like Edward Thomas, he expressed emotion with disarming simplicity. Unwin called him a 'true sensitive Welshman' and never lost his faith in him. He had a real sympathy with people and a slow sense of humour that poked fun at many of the things that amused him:

> ...my word, I still find some of the stories infinitely touching – after all these years! .... I can still see him as on his first visits he was in the rough khaki of a corporal, his gentle Welsh lilt in his speech, the wonderful green of his eyes, dark almost swarthy complexion and the half-humorous outlook in so much that he said. It must be said, however, that – when all is said and done – I met him only at rare intervals during his few visits to London from Wales and from the East Coast during 1940 to 1942 before he was sent to India. There was never the stage when he could 'drop in' frequently, or when we could lunch together and chat at leisure.
>
> I never knew just what his matrimonial situation was – married, of course, but someone who knew him intimately (on Service I think) spoke to me of his not being 'conjugally happy' and I believe that he and Gweno had lost a baby. I had that impression myself but have no firm evidence, not surprisingly.

When *Raiders' Dawn* appeared, it had unprepossessing paper covers and was priced 3/6. A few years later, Lewis wrote 'almost timidly' to ask Unwin if he would consider selling *Ha! Ha! Among the Trumpets* for 5/-:

> … it seemed quite a lot by book price standards in those days, but of course he was quite right. All prices were going up then and it was no good for us to go on thinking that it was a virtue to keep book prices as low as possible. It went up to 8/6 later!

There was also a 'de luxe' edition of 25 numbered copies, set on smooth 'Cartridge' paper, whiter than ordinary, with a gilt top and gilt lettering on the spine, the whole bound in dark blue buckram. Unwin possessed the only copy he knew of.

At the time we met, he had long since retired from publishing. A gentle, thoughtful man, he was puzzled by Lewis's failure to attract larger sales after the initial success of *Raiders' Dawn*, which went through six impressions in four years selling 9245 copies; the first impression sold out in the year of publication. *The Last Inspection* (1943) sold 7005 copies in three editions and remained in print until the 1980s. *Ha! Ha! Among the Trumpets* sold 7507 copies and went out of print only in 1977. *In the Green Tree* (1949) sold 3780 copies and went out of print in 1979. Over the years, Allen and Unwin had received increasing numbers of requests for permissions to reprint. By any standard, these figures are remarkable but gradually the blight set in. Unwin had high hopes for Ian Hamilton's *Alun Lewis, Selected Poetry and Prose* (1966) but it did not even cover its costs.

Unwin's dealings with Gweno were never less than uneasy. In 1944, shortly after Lewis's death, he wrote enquiring after the novel he felt sure had been left behind. 'About the novel,' she told him:

> It's a very nebulous affair I'm afraid. People used to ask about it, but as far as I know it never existed…. Alun developed so much in the last year or two that I shouldn't like anything to be published that looked backwards instead of forwards.

That makes it unclear whether or not there was a novel. First, she denies its existence, then calls it a throwback to his early years and so not worth publishing.

As it happens, his relations with her had got off to a bad start when she allowed extracts from Lewis's letters to appear in Gwyn Jones's *The Welsh Review*. Unwin, alarmed that as many as 18,000 words were to be reproduced, claimed first rights and could see no commercial advantage to him in the arrangement. Nevertheless, anxious to secure her co-operation, he tried to remain interested. The extracts were then issued in book form as *Letters from India* from Jones's Penmark Press (1946). Again, Unwin protested but Gweno assured him only 500 copies would be printed and that no reviews would appear outside Wales. As it happens, one did, in *The Observer*, adding to Unwin's chagrin. By way of compensation, she suggested he publish *The Collected Letters of Alun Lewis*, but nothing came of it. Its time will come.

In 1946, just as *In the Green Tree* was being prepared for the press, Gweno wrote asking for a delay: she said she was 'waiting for a reply from one of Alun's fellow officers, who, we have just been told, has been keeping back his last journal for a keep sake!' (A reference to the Chalfont affair.) The next year, despite repeated requests from him to expand the text of *Letters from India*, she said she had decided on a straightforward reprint with some minor excisions: 'Gleanings from his other letters and journals can be left to help a biographer'. Unwin had to accept her decision.

After the war, the austerity conditions governing book-publication were relaxed and, anxious to benefit from the altered situation, he suggested they include John Petts's line-drawings; Gweno agreed; in turn, she asked him to add Vernon Watkins's 'Sonnet on the Death of Alun Lewis', first printed in Keidrych Rhys's *Wales* in June 1944. (The book gets its title from it). Unwin felt it was 'far below the standard of Alun's work', but Gweno insisted: 'We do feel it is its own justification' ('we' being herself and her brother, Hywel).

While proofreading the book in the summer of 1948, she wrote to say she was 'rather puzzled' by the inclusion of Gwyn Jones's obituary notice from *The Welsh Review* in 1944. She said it needed 'bringing up to date' and asked him to exclude it. Now it was his turn to dig his heels in. He said the book had already been set and could not easily be altered; besides, he thought Jones's notice useful. In it, Jones recalls first meeting Lewis in 1941:

> He was, of course, in khaki. He was dark and lean, with a
> long South Welsh head narrowing downwards from a noble
> forehead to a sensitive mouth and strongly moulded jaws. In
> height and build and colouring he was the very symbol of

> the Valley folk he loved so well. He had that slightly 'foreign'
> look which many handsome South Walians have, both in
> their own and others' estimation, but was native to the nail-
> ends. Our talk was of the Army and personalities, and then
> of books. I recall so clearly the expressions of amusement,
> tolerance, indignation, contempt, which kept his features
> always alive.

This is done in Jones's best florid style and captures Lewis's mixture
of forthrightness and reserve.

> He had, and I think this worth saying, a detestation of those
> assorted exhibitionists who hang upon the edge of honest
> writing, and was modest about his own work.

Not that any of this would have upset Gweno; but this might:

> His term in India had clearly produced a new Alun Lewis –
> the poems are there to prove it. They are not happy poems,
> nor can I think him a happy man out there.

Or this:

> The comfortable assumptions, if he ever held them, were
> gone; he saw a continent of four hundred million people
> where Nature's indifference and Man's stupidity made life
> as cheap as dust. It was a cosmic revelation for one who
> believed in the dignity and inviolability of the individual.

Gweno, however, believed that he went into battle fully restored.

Gwyn Jones was a phenomenon. A tall, burly man with whispy
grey hair, a bristling, shandy-coloured moustache and tortoiseshell
glasses, he was the very model of a 60s university Head of Department and a law unto himself (though without the element of
self-promotion this might imply). A scholar of Nordic and 18th
century English literature, he was also a novelist, short story writer,
translator, anthologist and editor; he had the air of an impresario and
believed in the humanising influence of literature, so mocked at in
these post-structural days. When I joined Cardiff University, it was
to him and his friend, Glyn Jones, that I turned for advice, but
whenever the subject was Alun Lewis, he clammed up. Perhaps he
felt he had said enough already.

Unwin was further taken aback by Gweno's failure to respond to a letter of his in April 1949 suggesting the publication of a book of poems and/or stories to succeed *In the Green Tree.* The initial sales figure of 1500 copies had not been particularly encouraging but he wanted to capitalise on the publicity that had been created. He wrote to her again in 1952 but, again, no reply.

After reading a draft of my biography, Unwin said it confirmed his belief in Lewis's 'exceptional quality'.

> I relived so much of those war years – the 'phoney' part and the years of waiting – blackout journeys – rationing etc. The arguments amongst left-wing intellectuals – then those Saturday morning visits of his (we always worked on Sats). Then, once or twice with Gweno, and, later on, the sad meetings with her over the publication of *Ha! Ha! Among the Trumpets* and *In the Green Tree.* And that awful day when I saw in the evg paper the bald announcement of his death 'due to an accident'.

Unwin wanted the book to be published by his cousin, Rayner, then in charge of Allen and Unwin, but his sudden death in 1981 put an end to that. His widow, Evelyn, wrote to say how 'greatly interested' he had been in our discussions and I, too, had the impression that, as we talked, he revisited an aspect of his life which, though valuable to him, was more valuable than he had imagined.

My second new contact from this time was Elizabeth ('Lisa', pronounced 'Leesa') Berridge, a well-known novelist and then chief fiction reviewer for *The Daily Telegraph.* (She died in 2009.) Her husband, Reginald ('Graham') Moore, founded *Modern Reading* in 1941 to profit from the wartime interest in short stories and Lewis occasionally contributed to it; Freda's 'Some Letters of Alun Lewis' appeared there. He was also editor of *Selected Writing*, an annual anthology of published work, and (with Jack Aistrop, another of Lewis's friend from Longmoor) of *Bugle Blast*, a Forces anthology.

In 1943, Lisa, Graham and their children left London for the Oswestry/Welshpool area only to return in 1950. Shortly afterwards, she discovered that 'Alun Lewis' was speaking to her.

> Neither I nor my husband met Alun Lewis, although we were in correspondence with him and published some of his work. I imagine that Gweno has told you of the 'sympathetic communication' I had with him for a very short period. In fact she has all the writings that came through at that time.

> Since then I have given up – or been given up by –
> automatic writing, because one doubts oneself.

I met Lisa at her Hampton home. Afterwards, I noted that it was one of the most disorganised interviews I had ever conducted, though I can't imagine why. She struck me as eminently sensible – a considerable tribute, in view of what follows.

In the autumn of 1953, Lisa and Graham were part of a small group experimenting in psychic communication. One night, their leader said someone called Alun Lewis was coming through. Did anyone know him? Lisa, a Londoner by birth though of part-Welsh extraction, had been in brief communication with him when she posted him a copy of *Selected Writing* in Felixstowe in 1942 with a cheque for his contribution. He replied:

> I don't think I'll have any new stories by the end of the
> month, I'm afraid. I'm full of unwritten stories, lacking time
> and typewriter. If I do manage one, I'll send it along.

One Sunday evening in their Regent's Park flat, she wrote 'Alun Lewis' down several times. The following afternoon, a soundless exchange occurred with a presence she sensed standing beside the bookcase. On that occasion, he said he wanted to dictate some poems and stories to her and she agreed. They included two poems for Gweno, which he asked her to forward to her. Lisa hesitated, fearing to intrude on her grief with material of such doubtful provenance. 'Why me?', she asked herself. Why become involved with Lewis, or Lewis with her? She had only passing knowledge of his work and feared she was joining something either fraudulent or mad.

Eventually, she wrote to Gweno and explained she would understand if she reacted with 'indignation, grief, incredulity':

> Very recently, I have discovered that I have the power of
> automatic writing…. You know, you sit down and try to
> 'blank out' your mind and see what comes. I did this, and
> found that I had 'Alun Lewis' several times. A message then
> came through 'Will you write to Gweno and tell her I am
> happy'. This seemed so extraordinary that I tried to get some
> proof that it was in fact Alun Lewis who was doing the
> writing. *My* mind was completely blank, I had not been
> thinking about him. Again the message came 'Tell Gweno
> not to weep for me, love'. I expostulated, saying that it would

upset you, even if you had a belief in life after death. He said
you did not believe, but to write all the same. I asked him
why he had come through to me, and the message came 'You
are a writer'. The proof I tried to get was this: I asked how
many children he had. He said a son. I asked his name. he
said Curig. I asked when he was born. He said 1944. I asked
his birthday, he said June 21st. I don't know whether these
facts are correct or not. But you will. I asked if you were still
in Wales. He said yes.

It may be difficult for you to understand – or accept – but
he told me he wants to start writing again and cannot until
he has reassured you as to his well-being.

I do want you to know that this is no idle hobby of mine
and that I write off to people with fake messages! This is the
only thing that has ever happened to me and I was in a
complete dilemma as to whether to write or not. Then last
night an urgent message again: 'Be a dear girl and write to
Gweno tonight'. I feel there will be no peace for him
wherever he is until I pass this message on to you, whatever
your reaction. It will be damnably painful, I expect, and you
will curse me....

Do please forgive me if I have made you unhappy, and
believe me when I say that this is quite the oddest and most
compulsive letter I have ever written in my life.

There was, of course, no 'Curig'. When Alun contemplated the possibility of children, he used the names 'Sian' ('Shan') and 'Nevin'.
However, Wallace and Freda's daughter, Juliet, was born on the 16th
May, 1944; her name is related to a minor Celtic saint, St Curig, who
is always venerated with his mother, Juliette. When I pointed the
coincidence out to Freda, she was much struck by it and thereafter
referred to Juliet as 'The saint child. Wallace's child, Alun's wish-
child'.

A further significance attaches to the date June 21st 1944, which
is both the summer solstice and nine calendar months after Alun and
Freda's meeting in Bombay on September 21st 1943.

In an appendix to my biography, I reproduced transcripts of Lisa's
'automatic' sessions and 'communications', the latter amounting to
four poems and two stories. One of the stories, 'The Lost Man', deals
in ironic fashion with a group of army officers in India; the other,
'The Boychick', is set in a Welsh coal-mining valley and is comic in
vein. Both turn on affairs of the heart. The poems included 'Tell not
the fearful piper I am dead' and 'Time is no stream to get fixed in'.

In the former, the poet addresses his 'bride of green':

> My garden girl, my mountain-crowned love.
> Above the trees she lingers. Not for me now
> As of old she hesitated in the grass.
> Wedded now to bracken and to ash
> She leaden walks the paths upon the hill
> My gay and gallant one, my girl of joy.
> To greet you tardily my verse now comes.
>
> At home nowhere, nowhere to rest
> My phantom head upon your solid breast.
> No more the robin on the gate
> Will sing us his warcry. For too late
> I'm gone, another warcry fetched me forth
> And left poor robin on the bitter earth
> To dig, to sing for worms
> I shall not dig.

The imagery recalls 'Bequest', first published by Ian Hamilton in 1966 and so unread by Lisa. Written in India, it is addressed to Gweno as one who can quell his anguish:

> Tonight this anguish hurts my hands,
> This Eucharist I cannot see,
> Your pale distressing image in my grasp....

'Bequest' also mentions Lewis's father, Tom, his uncle, Ned, and Gweno's father, all of whom are said to 'have lived and died within my blood' (though all were alive at the time). They 'will live on/ Whatever may betide'.

> I leave you in their company,
> The winter snow heaped on your door,
> In the dark house in the mountains
> With a robin on the floor.

Gweno's 'mountain-crowned love' plays on the name 'Mountain Ash' while her hesitation 'in the grass' recalls the Bedgellert episode in 'In Hospital: Poona (1)'.

   The second poem, 'Tell not the fearful piper that I am dead', again associates Gweno with mountain walks and nature ('Mountain Ash') in Cwmaman and Aberdare and holidays in Snowdonia and the Black Mountains.

The transcripts of Lisa's 'communications' included dated from October and November 1953 and continued for another year and a half. Lisa forgot how persistent they had become. In them, 'Lewis' revealed his principal concern was for Gweno: she could not be left behind grieving. Amends had to be made if he were to make spiritual progress.

> I try to take care of Gweno – she does need rest poor darling.... Gweno knows I am with her but also she must lead her life in her own way. There is nothing more I can tell her or do, really.... Lisa thinks I ought to speak to Gweno through a medium. Believe me, that would never satisfy her. She would want to probe and become immersed in it or disbelieve completely. I feel she must be left alone.

This repeats sentiments expressed in his letters. He said life was

> all a complicated interweaving of passions, actions, reactions – like sound waves spreading out into the atmosphere widening, thinning but never actually dying completely away.... I am glad to be free of that parcelling up of time.

During one session, he dictated an inscription in the fly-leaf of Lisa's copy of *Raiders' Dawn*:

> Alun Lewis, in memory of one who is kind and gentle and takes trouble over the so-called dead and salutes Lisa and Graham Moore, 1953.

The exchanges ceased in 1956. Lisa never doubted their authenticity but felt inadequate and scared. Nothing she was writing at the time bore any resemblance to his and, since she had not been reading or thinking about him, there was no question of unconscious influence.

One further coincidence attaches to the story. At the time, Graham and Lisa lived in the upper half of 3 Kent Terrace, Regent's Park, owned by the poet, John Hall. It was to 3 Kent Terrace that Lynette Roberts came in 1952, occupying the rooms immediately beneath. Lisa remembered meeting her at parties, in particular the skirts she wore with bells on and her strange, intense manner, but they never became friendly. Neither mentioned Alun Lewis to the other.

In April 1944, a month after Lewis's death, Freda, too, visited a medium in Coonoor and was told: 'Don't go my way, Frieda'.

After reading a draft of that part of the biography that concerned her, Lisa wrote: 'I must say it has been quite a useful exercise to think about these past events and get my own mind clear'.


# III


At his request, I sent Lord Chalfont a draft of the biography and, shortly before Christmas 1981, he replied:

> I have read your typescript with very great interest. Of course the full story of Alun's death is still not told. Perhaps you would like to have a private word with me before you finally go to print.

We met early in the New Year and a fortnight later he wrote again:

> I am bound to say that I am not prepared to engage in any further correspondence or discussion about the matter of Alun Lewis. All I am prepared to say is that in the version of your book which you have sent me the circumstances concerning Alun Lewis's death are inaccurately stated.
>
> I am returning the manuscript under separate cover and I hope you will understand if I say that I would prefer not to be any further involved.

Somewhat to my surprise, I find I replied to this and, even more surprisingly, received the following:

> I must apologise, in turn, if my last letter was framed in any unfriendly way. I certainly did not mean it to be. The fact is that I have been subjected to a certain amount of 'harrass-ment and embarrassment' from other quarters about the whole Alun Lewis saga and I have decided that it would be better on balance to say no more about it. I am sorry about this but I hope you will understand and also accept that this reflects no unfriendliness on my part towards you personally.

It was now clear why Chalfont had blown hot and cold in this affair. A strong-minded man, he could see no harm in speaking out, but others did. Significantly, he was the only officer who granted me an interview – all the others cried off, for one reason or another. Evidently, he was chosen as their spokesman but turned out to have a regrettable tendency to exceed his brief. The more I pressed him, the more he was tempted to break ranks, only to have to beat a hasty retreat. In any event, it was unlikely I would go into print saying Lewis had killed himself. All I wanted was private confirmation that he had, but Chalfont couldn't take the chance, though he was unhappy at having to connive in an untruth. Alone of Lewis's fellow soldiers, he had a taste for literature as well as a highly-developed sense of drama. The Foreign Office mandarin, keeper of the army's conscience, contended with the litterateur. The result: oracular obscurity.

# IV

Dick Mills who, after taking part in a Radio 4 programme about Lewis, renewed his acquaintanceship with Gweno, now wrote to say that he realised 'just what a fine person she is':

> I would not wish to hurt her in any way, & must therefore ask you not to quote from any of my letters in any reference your book may have to Alun's relationship with Freda. I now hold strongly to the view that the relationship is not necessary for an understanding of Alun's poetic development; but even if I did not, I would not wish it to be discussed in any book published during Gweno's lifetime. I think Alun would share this view.

He was here repeating views previously expressed by Glyn and Gwladys Lewis. I naturally appreciated his wish for discretion but was nonetheless surprised he should want to jeopardise his long-standing friendship with Freda, though I doubt he saw the matter in those terms. His notion that 'Alun would share this view' was plausible but failed to acknowledge that Lewis himself had broached the subject with Gweno. Nor could he know that Gweno had encouraged Freda to write her memoir. Like Gwladys, he wanted to protect her from the knowledge that she already possessed. Such quixotic gallantry was typical of the man; lacking guile himself, he rallied to the side of those he imagined lacked it. This was odd, considering that my article on 'The Way Back' had long ago disproved the notion that Alun's love for Freda was irrelevant to an appreciation of his 'poetic development'.

I replied to him as emolliently as I could, but he persisted:

> I have to ask you for a firm undertaking not to use my letters
> in any reference to Alun's relationship with Freda. Anything
> less precise would, I fear, mean withdrawal of permission to
> make any use of the letters.
>
> I'd be very sorry if it came to that, as I believe in your
> ability to produce the sort of biography we've all been
> waiting for.

John Petts proved more encouraging, allowing me to reproduce
his frontispiece portrait of Lewis *en profile* from *In the Green Tree*
as front cover of the biography; inside pages carried his wood-
engravings from *Raiders' Dawn* and *In the Green Tree* and two Caseg
Broadsheets, nos. 1 (featuring two poems by Lewis) and 5 (the one
Gweno had sent me).

Freda's copy of the draft biography arrived on the 30th September
1981 and she read it in a state of high excitement. It represented
everything she had worked for over the past seven years. She said
she was enthralled by it and that the portrait of Lewis that emerged
was a true one. She was particularly struck by the chronology, which
allowed her to clarify her impressions. More than ever, she was
convinced he had committed suicide.

Freda's emphasis on chronology is a reminder that, in a sense,
biography is chronology, tracing a sequence of events that illuminates
a writer's work without implying it was either necessary or
inevitable. Freda now could trace Alun's development clearly and
set her own part in it in context. This led to a renewed crisis of
conscience. She feared she had misled me by implying Alun had
replaced Wallace in her affections. She had anguished about this
before and reading my typescript reawakened her old qualms. She
insisted her pride in Wallace kept her feelings in check and asked me
to understand that Alun had not played such a prominent part in her
life after all.

This then led her to accuse herself of a vast vanity in helping me,
burnishing her image at the expense of others by proclaiming that
her hold over a remarkable young poet was no mere infatuation. She
had been wrong to allow me to quote his letters and feared their effect
on Gweno. Gweno had given her permission to cite them but that did
not entitle her to pass her permission onto me. Gweno had told her:

'knowing you I know you will be compassionate'. Was it 'compassionate' to let me use them? She must have been tempted to prevent me doing so even then, yet something stayed her hand. Had she done so, she would have dealt me a fatal blow. After all, the central revelation of the biography was their love and nothing demonstrated that better than his letters.

Freda was, in fact, suffering a species of stage-fright. Just as the auditorium lights were dimming and the audience settling down in their seats, she was seized by nerves. She asked me to make numerous alterations – a word here, a line there, concentrating not on the text nor even Lewis's letters but her letters to me, which emerged as a special source of irritation. First, she alleged I had not quoted them accurately, then she regretted the freedom with which she had expressed herself. Reading them in the cold light of day, detached from their context and unprotected by the assurance that the person receiving them would know how to interpret them, every nuance of thought and emotion she had invested in them seemed to vanish. Torn this way and that, she asked me to remove one letter in particular, which would be too bitter for Gweno to read. Then again, part of it might stand. No: all of it would have to go. Yet – perhaps not.

Freda's letters from this time are a whirlpool of uncertainty. For example, discussing p.199 of my biography (second edition), she writes:

> ...John, I *hate* all the protestations: 'I loved him always, always... Never for a second ever did I not love him...' (Did I really write that? How melodramatic! You must have writhed.) It sounds as if I'm trying to prove something which wasn't true. *PLEASE* take it out and 'I loved him... but I drifted unhappily away, in the practical world I lived in, etc.' The other sounds quite false, and, in fact, was. This is what I meant at the beginning of this letter when I said I misled you into an over-emphasis which is not true. A quiet statement of the truth is much more convincing and impressive. Just as, I don't like at all the letter on the same page which says histrionically 'Love had been such an ecstasy...' It's cheap and it's a cliché and doesn't convince – and anyway it isn't true, as it sounds. Please cut it. 'Love had been such an enchantment... so tender, close, fraternal almost, winged with such joy', ...all that is absolutely true. It *was* an enchantment and after all he was enchanted by his muse, i.e. spell-struck. I can't let 'such undreamed of fulfilment' go in

as it suggests there had not been fulfilment with Wallace. It
was undreamed of fulfilment for him, but something different
for me. Oh John, how difficult this is! And I am trying so
hard. I'm so afraid you'll be angry, hurt, puzzled. I feel rather
ill! I had to get up and go out for a walk to relieve the giddy
feeling just now. You DO understand, don't you? And  this
is what you wanted me to do, isn't it? Give you my reactions.
Again, I love the book; it moves and amazes me – amazement at so much you tell of him (and others) and seeing the
whole picture. But I must die without guilt at perpetrating a
wonderful story which is just off balance.

As it happens, all the passages complained of appeared unchanged
in the book – she left me to make my own decisions: 'don't be
disconcerted by my comments on the book,' she wrote. 'It's lovely'.

Shortly afterwards, she came to stay with my wife and myself
and we visited the David Jones exhibition at the National Museum
in Cardiff, which she was particularly interested in since she was
preparing an article on Jones and Lewis, followed by an essay on the
poets of the two world wars.) It was on this occasion that she paid
her first visit to Cwmaman.

On her return to Woodstock, she wrote:

I know you are re-writing the biography and know that I
asked you to change it, however slightly, when we met and
that I was a bit nervous (not seriously at all) that you might,
in trying to fulfil this lean a little too far (for my horrible and
unworthy possessiveness) in Wallace's direction.

The pendulum was beginning to swing in the opposite direction.

What a maddening old fool I am! Do bear with me, John, and
forgive me. I know how tiresome I am. But the truth about
ALL THIS, about so desperately important a thing as his
deep, deepest feelings, what was there in his profoundest self,
the self he covered with all the rest, that a whole world (as,
indeed, he once wrote to me) was being lost while he and I
could not come to each other for ever.

One thing consoled her:

He killed himself with my ring on his finger and though he
burnt my letters for fear they'd hurt Gweno, he yet kept my

ring on his finger. All this, to anyone outside our love, must
sound petty, childish, mean-spirited. But these things have
brought me comfort.

Plagued by anxiety, her old unhappiness at the *Miscellany* resurfaced and, for a time, she fell silent.

I'm a bit of a twanging instrument where he [Alun] is
concerned, sounding strange chords at the least touch.

In her less fretful moods, she could see how the Miscellany foreshad-
owed his genius, despite the pangs of womanly possessiveness it
caused her:

...this is all silly. Let's stop it. It is amazing, when I come to
think of it, that you and I have never had a really sharp
disagreement before! After all these years I look back on that
as a sign of real respect and affection on the part of both of
us. I'm sorry I cast the slightest mist over it. To tell the truth
you have put your finger on the truth (one aspect of it) as you
often do when you say every line of my letter cries: 'he has
gone over to Gweno...he who was my ally, the one who
could tell the truth of me and Alun'. You are quite, quite right.
I did feel that.

Yet her faith in me remained:

I love you enough to trust you even if you ever showed signs
of being untrustworthy, and you have never done that. You
are one of the most honest people I have ever met, and
fearless – look how you approached Gweno and his mother
with the truth!

Nor was she resentful of Gweno:

In fact I have a sort of rather terrified affection for her! Much
tinged with guilt. But I loathe the reduction, by her, of Alun
to a silly boy with tiresome and daft ways and a little trick of
writing poetry. This I do hate.

In a draft of her memoir, she described Gweno thus:

She was a proud girl, reserved and pragmatic by nature,
though with a tremendous sense of fun. Cautious of hurt,

wary of life generally and inclined not to trust it, she did not
give her affections easily – though she was a devoted and
dutiful daughter and sister. She was intensely single-minded:
once having chosen giving unshakeable and steadfast
commitment to whatever her affections or dreams might
encompass. Perhaps the absolute quality of her singlemindedness narrowed the range of her emotions causing them,
thereby, to acquire a greater simplicity and intensity....
Undeviatingly direct, with a sharp critical mind, there was a
purity in her attitude to life, an uncompromising reality. A
friend who knew her intimately, searching for the right word,
said 'there is a...*virginal* quality about her'.

The 'friend' was Lewis.

Freda could not help contrasting Gweno's sanity with Lewis's
depressions. She knew he would have floundered without her help
but feared implying her love was of a different order or revealing
that he had asked her for a ring. In rising panic, she accused me of
tricking her into granting permission to quote his letters. Worse, I
had broken my pledge of confidentiality concerning the episode in
the woods. Reading my account, she winced. She asked me now to
vow that, should Gweno complain, I would say I had used the letters
without permission. They were not in the draft I had sent her – better
still, she had seen no draft.

As it happens, the only person who did not receive a draft was
Gweno; there seemed little point. I felt she had, in effect, dared me
to publish and be damned and certainly never stipulated prior sight
as a condition of publication. However, she made her displeasure
plain:

> I would be very grateful if you would now clear your Alun
> Lewis file and send me the rest of the material which
> belongs here.
>    I think you would have been wiser to have sent the proofs
> of the book to me first before publication to clear up a few
> errors. I have only skimmed through the book superficially
> as yet but in doing so I have found much fudging and
> nudging of little details which, however unimportant, do
> discredit a fastidious biographer. For example, Page 132. we
> didn't live *stormily*, I am not a *stormy* person, ask any of my
> friends. Then you mention the ring [a reference to the
> engagement ring Lewis gave her.] *Mrs Lewis* insisted that
> Alun should present me with a ring. She felt she had to insist

on the proprieties of the occasion. Then you go on to remark 'which she promptly lost' giving the impression I did not value it. I cherished it for two years before it disappeared.

You also give the impression I married Alun out of pity…

Page 197. You give the impression that Alun was sometimes impotent. That too was news to me.

On page 235 and 263 you have used passages from the letters I forbade you to use. You obviously photocopied the letters and I beg you, be a little gent, and send them back to me. If you read those letters carefully you would have found the poem 'A Fragment', which Alun sent me in November. Check again. The wild beast was a symbol for love which he first used in an unpublished story I showed you once. Do you remember the short story about a fellow cadet who had had a battle experience and suffering some trauma or other had killed another cadet on a night exercise? 'Midnight in India' was written about this time and he sent this to Mrs Akroyd. Although still in the toils he did realise there was no future for them together and the 'mysterious tremors stirring the beast' – his love for her is how he expressed it. That love had to die however painful for him.

The burden of her letter was plain: Alun had given up Freda by the time he went into battle. She ended her letter:

I must now give my mind to reading the book in more depth now that I've got these irritating things off my chest. Hoping you are all well.
Gweno.

Not the least remarkable aspect of this remarkable letter is her belief that Lewis's impotence was a 'little detail' I had 'fudged and nudged' and which she wanted to get off her chest before settling down to read the book in greater detail. The passage she was referring to read:

He recalled her efforts to dispel the 'atrophy' that overtook him in their lovemaking, saying it was 'another instance of the contrary trust we always meet sooner or later in our fascinations'.

Her unflustered reaction to what she took to be a false imputation certainly proved her contention she was not 'stormy'.

Gweno's conviction that 'A Fragment' and 'Midnight in India' proved Alun had returned to her is one I had had to contend with before. To repeat: 'Midnight in India' was written *before* Alun met Freda while 'A Fragment' was written for Freda and posted to Gweno on December 3 1943. Because it was sent to her, she assumed it was for her.

My remark about Gweno and Alun living 'stormily' together derived from one of Lewis's letter to Jean Gilbert, librarian at Pontigny, and ascribed as such. However, I erred when I asserted it was Gweno's mother, Anne, who insisted he give her a ring: it was Gwladys Lewis. Nor did I mean to imply she had married him out of pity, only that she visited him in Gloucester out of pity; perhaps it amounts to the same thing. Nor had I photocopied the letters, though I did take notes, which is just as well, since some of them have gone missing since (see Appendix One).

Gweno's reaction to the book drew the attention of my editor at Poetry Wales Press, Mick Felton. She wrote to him shortly after asking if the Press would be interested in publishing Alun's letters and journals.

> I also got the impression that she didn't like the biography too much, partly because she felt you weren't very accurate about details of Alun's life in Wales. Other parts which might be expected to raise her temperature weren't mentioned at all. Rather odd.

Odd, indeed. Alun's sister, Mair Fenn, told Freda that she liked the book, adding: 'Gweno was very upset. She hated the book and threw it in the dustbin'. Freda expressed her amazement at this, whereupon she replied:

> But Freda, she is a lovely girl but you must remember that she has lived all her life in Mountain Ash, she is very unacquainted with the world. You must remember this.

# V

Five years after my biography (1989), Gweno published *Letters to my Wife*, her edition of Lewis's letters from the time of his enlistment in May 1940 until a week before his death, 278 in all (including aircards). Since I had read only a sixth of these, it necessitated a second edition of the biography in 1991.

The text of *Letters to my Wife* was not set from the originals; Gweno provided typed scripts with a few brief annotations and a 16-page introduction. Remarkably, not one complete letter is included: all salutations and superscriptions have been shorn off. They simply begin *in media res* and break off. In a disclaimer, she owned to making a 'very small number of cuts' indicated by ellipses, though several pass unnoticed. It says much for the quality of the letters that they make an impression even in this truncated form.

Gweno's Preface is, in effect, her riposte to my biography. It begins with an account of the 'apocalyptic night' at Whitsun 1941 when a German air raid damaged her house and goes on to describe their visits to Chepstow, Llanthony Abbey and Abergavenny later that year. The last took place on a Saturday at the end of June:

> ... we climbed the steep embankment near the station and there we called upon the four winds to witness our most solemn oath to each other for ever and ever.

That oath was made good the following month, when they married.

> As we left the building, Alun jumped up snatching a bunch of rambler roses growing over a high wall. 'Here's a bouquet for you, Gwen.' I still have them pressed in some book.

'Some book' strikes the familiar note of ambiguity whenever items of his in her possession are mentioned, thereby unintentionally diluting the value of the keepsake. (In *If I Should Go Away*, a radio 'drama documentary' of August 2007, she said she kept the roses until they fell to pieces.) Later at the New Inn, Gloucester, Alun scattered petals on their pillows which he had stolen from the hotel's flower baskets.

Gweno calls Gwladys Lewis her 'dearest friend' and 'a good Yorkshire housewife'. This is surprising, considering that she spent her entire adult life in Wales. Nevertheless, 'Yorkshire' she remained, just as Glyn regarded her as coming from another era, having been raised in a distant country parsonage. Above all, Gweno admired 'Mutti''s devotion to family:

> When her youngest son returned from lengthy war service,

he applied for a special refresher course at a well known college. He had completed his studies and training before being called up to the R.A.F. and he felt in need now, after demobilisation, for just such a course before applying for any posts. He was turned down and Gwladys was furious. Tom, in authority himself, felt he couldn't question another's authority, but Gwladys had no scruples and wrote forthwith, trouncing them hard for their attitude towards boys who had helped win the war, and whom now they evidently considered expendable. By return of post came a humble acknowledgement and the much desired acceptance.

There follows an account of Lewis's depressions, which began in Manchester in 1935-7 and lifted only to return in November 1941, when he joined the Borderers. At such times, he was plunged in 'unwarrantable despondency' – 'unwarrantable' because without rational foundation, which is rather to miss the point. Like his parents and friends, she accuses herself of 'unforgivable ignorance' in allowing him to struggle on without medical help. The depressions could be devastating, as a hitherto-unpublished poem from his Manchester days illustrates:

> When I lie down, above me the sky
> Is vast and still
> Two words for one quality,
> And instead of the thrush's wild music
> Or the sublimation of the skylark
> That makes the mind follow
> It upwards till it is spirit
> And the body an unneeded
> Precipitate, the spirit's dregs,
> There is nothing but the slow
> Strong pulse of silence
> The throb of waiting in silence.
> Then comes the tread of feet, the
> Clatter of mattock and spade
> Over me.
> The terrible presence of the sexton
> The living man with a purpose
> That must be performed upon me.
> And the silent bell screams
> Out as his hand tugs the rope
> Which he pulls till the bell,
> Tormented, beyond bearing,

> Turns over and swallows
> Its tongue and suffocatingly falls.
> And when I at last dare
> Lift my terrified eyes to
> Confront the sexton
> I know the features, the eyes,
> The mole by the drooping
> Mouth, the white uneven teeth,
> The twisted grief
> The terrible presence of the
> Lover
> Whom I do not love.

This poem bears a striking resemblance to the sesamum field passage: in both, a man witnesses the death of an Other whom he loves but does not return his love, being both corpse and gravedigger. One self buries another, his mortal self, in an act of kindness (compare the sesamum field's 'unforgiveable sorrow' and 'The Jungle''s: 'does the will's long struggle end/ With the last kindness of a foe or friend?')

The sexton appeared again in an unpublished notebook of 1941:

> Lying under the wall of the church I
> feel the terrible presence of the Sexton,
> the living man with a purpose that
> must be performed upon me
> The silent bell strains as he tugs
> the rope: he tugs till the bell
> cannot endure it & fall over
> Swallows its tongue and suffocating
> falls. And when I dare at last to lift
> my terrified eyes to confront the sexton
> I know the features, the mole the broken
> teeth, the hanging mouth, the ['?'] grief
> the terrible presence of the lover
> whom I do not love.

As an unpublished poem of 1941 has it: 'I would have died quite easily,/ If my strange enemy had come'.

Gweno insisted there were long stretches of 'equilibrium' between his depressions during which he proved himself as teacher (Pengam, 1938-9), conscript (Longmoor, 1940-1) and officer (from 1941). He was in good health in Bovington in 1942 and for the following twelve months (i.e. until he met Freda in mid-1943). On their last night together in October 1942 in Liverpool, she gazed at him while he slept. Even now, she writes like a woman in love:

> ...there was something so angelic, so ineffable there, I felt my heart would break. I studied his high smooth forehead and soft dark hair, his dark fringed deep set eyes and the little lines that ran away from them, deepening when he laughed and the hazel eyes disappeared altogether. The fine skin above the beard line was slightly flushed with fever; and his dear mouth still bore a scar from some game of hockey long ago. I prayed for the safe return of my dainty duck, my dearest dear, and, fearing to wake him, I switched off the bedside light and snuggled close.

Freda used similar terms describing their staring at each other at a dinner-dance in Bombay with iced gimlets in their hands:

> His deep-set dreaming eyes, the beautiful architrave of his brow, the black hair and the tentative lips which looked always as if they were about to speak or to smile and above which was a tiny scar.

Gweno sees the damaged archangel, a 'dearest dear' threatened by time and chance, Freda the yearning dreamer with an accidental wound.

Gweno's account of Lewis's time in India begins by referring to his disapproval of soldiers who sought sexual relief in casual encounters with Eurasian girls, prostitutes and 'bored and discontented expatriates'. For all that, he 'helter-skeltered deep into the toils himself'.

> It was obvious he was living on a high emotional plane. When I asked what was the matter with him, he recollected himself and henceforth wrote in a more sober vein.

He had been called to order.

In her mind if not in her heart, Gweno can understand how home-ties weakened 'in the stony wasteland' where 'the signposts for so many only point in one direction'. His 'romantic rendezvous' in Bombay precipitated his worst depression yet, as if he were being punished for his sins.

> We must have seemed to him like figures behind glass
> making meaningless gestures for all the help we were to him.
> If only someone wiser than we were could have guided him
> to a source of help and healing.

That there *was* a cure for him she was in no doubt:

> ...it is possible that the root of his periodic distress lay in the
> realm of the pathological or in an imbalance in the chemistry
> of the brain. Why should someone who, when well, was so
> bright, active and able, descend to such depths of despair
> about himself?

It is a question the well often ask about the unwell, puzzled that despair should come to them as naturally as contentment to themselves. In Gweno's view, Alun's depressions belonged not to the man she loved but some strange morbidity that assailed him from time to time prompted by who-knows-what malfunctioning of the brain's wiring. One minute he could be fit and active, the next prey to his 'strange enemy'.

Concerning the 'sesamum field' passage, she observes that the threat from 'the man I hate' came from an enemy soldier and made him determined to prove himself, thereby ensuring his survival. His depression of late 1943, she says, lifted in December, as 'A Fragment' (which 'he said he had just written for me') proves. By mid-February 1944, there was

> now no trace of the complicated emotional life of the past
> months, and although his last letters to me continued to be
> loving and intimate, in his journal he wrote, 'I only think of
> Gweno pragmatically now', for the sight of his weapon was
> a constant reminder of the realities ahead.

Having freed himself from Freda as from the vagaries of despair, he focussed on the task ahead.

As ever, Gweno relies on Alun's letters as authority for her views:

> It was reassuring to think that Alun had reached a kind
> of equilibrium within himself at last and showed no trace of
> the melancholy undertones which had so weighed down his
> letter writing of the past months.

To support this contention, she cites his last letter to her, which recalls their visit to Snowdonia at Easter 1939, 'his most cherished of remembered landscapes'. (This letter does not appear in the book.) She says his death was accidental: rushing to 'complete his morning routine', he fell heavily and shot himself, a view confirmed by his death certificate and the Brigadier commanding 72 Indian Infantry Brigade.

> I don't believe it was 'the Sexton' or 'my strange enemy' or 'the man I hate'. He had long since come to terms with them. At the moment he had more urgent things on his mind; the patrol was getting ready to set out and he was in charge.

In a 'Coda', she describes visiting his grave in the Taukkyan Cemetery, near Rangoon, his final resting place after temporary field burials at Bawli North Cemetery, Maungdaw and Akyab Military Cemetery.

> It was distressing to think of these graves being disturbed so often. [The head gardener] [v]ery patiently explained the policy of the War Graves Commission and of course I could well understand why. 'But how was it possible? What remains? 'Only the long bones, Madam, only the long bones'.
> Oh Best Beloved – only the long bones?

She added the following inscription to his headstone:

> Lieutenant
> A Lewis
>
> The South Wales Borderers
> 5th March 1944  Age 28
> (cross)
> And what's transfigured will live on
> Long after death has come and gone.

The lines are from Lewis's 'Song' (*Ha! Ha! Among the Trumpets*).

While preparing the poems for publication, she added the following epigraph, 'from me to him':

> Kann dir die Hand nicht geben,
> Bleib du im ew'gen Leben

Mein gutter Kamerad!
*March 5th, 1944*

This comes from of a German soldier's song which is usually sung at military funerals. Composed by the nineteenth century poet, Ludwig Uhland, it tells of two soldier-friends; when one of them is killed, the other is too busy firing to help: 'I can't give you my hand, but you must remain in eternal life my good comrade' ('Kamerad' is what Lewis occasionally called Gweno, recalling the time she taught him German folk songs). This was a brave gesture towards one who had fallen fighting the Axis powers. The date 'March 5th, 1944' is puzzling; it is not the date of his death. Perhaps it signified the start of her new life. Gweno never remarried.

# VI

Two years after (1991), Freda published 'An Exchange of Love Poems' in *The New Welsh Review*, including Lewis's poems for her: 'The House', 'Love is never born complete', 'The heart compels', 'The Transmigration of Love' and the opening lines of 'Beloved when we stood'. She also included five of her own poems: 'The Exquisite Moment', 'The Parting', 'It Matters Little', 'To Alun' and 'Speak in Me'.

Preparing the article induced in her the usual anxious introspetion. It was designed, she said, as a 'a quiet and *truthful* reply to Gweno's shrill finale' in her Preface and is remarkably candid:

> My love was simple: I loved Wallace and I loved Alun. I did not feel guilty towards Wallace perhaps because I married him when I was very young and he was older than me. He was as surely a part of me as life itself and I knew, in a deep, very deep unquestioning way, that nothing could ever change that... 'My little craft afloat upon your sea,' I once wrote in a poem for him.

It was, she concluded, 'a strange truth that more than one love can inhabit the heart'. With Alun, she had experienced the total fulfilment, as I never thought could be, of a dream love:

> romantic, responsive, articulate in an acutely sensitive way.

> I don't now remember whether I immediately fell in love
> with him or whether it was that love grew over the following
> days. I remember being very moved at the sight of him, so
> much so that I could only murmur his name – Alun? – and
> that I was aware of the colour rising in my cheeks.

The only guilt she felt was for Gweno.

She then made a gesture in her direction by remarking that, in the
last weeks of his life, Alun struggled to overcome his guilt and return
to his first 'invulnerable' love. However, the impression was
somewhat blurred by her remark that, in his last letter, he 'seemed
weighted with some portent, some helplessness in the face of an
inevitable destiny'. He was returning to Gweno but also steeling
himself for a final act.

Freda once told me Lewis wanted 'to get back to where his
conscience did not torment him':

> … it was a decision of the mind & not the heart. He is still
> grappling & clinging, he is still trying to come out 'straight
> & new – at whatever price'. All in the present, the decision
> is still not yet entirely made. He knows he will make the right
> decision – but of the mind.

Gweno, on the other hand, had 'woven a protective garment for
herself', and who was she to remove it?

> Yet when I read her preface [to *Letters to My Wife*] I felt an
> anger & revulsion which made me want to strike back at her
> – & still does when I think of it. Yet I remember all the time
> our meeting in Oxford & her saying quite simply & rather
> sadly 'Oh no, it was not a passing attraction. He loved you
> *very deeply*'.

Writing the article had made her even more aware of 'what a very
sweet, humane creature' he was:

> But the depth of his understanding – of *all things* – was
> astounding. And he was only a boy. Again, I brood over the
> fact of his being almost permanently emotionally ill.… Yet,
> I do see what he loved in [Gweno] and made her into in his
> mind. I myself saw something of it in our meeting in Oxford
> – some strength, something one trusted if one *were prepared
> to go entirely her way*. A frightening woman and yet.…

In a passage later cancelled, she added that, whatever her guilt for Gweno, she was, like Alun, powerless to kill their love. He told her that writing to her

> kept alive the marsh light of some nebulous hope in which I
> half imagined all of us could resolve the imponderables.

After this, Freda returned to work on her 'opus minimus'. A few years earlier, she had told me:

> ...whatever I write or don't write it won't cut across your
> book. It should, I rather think, lead into it. If I can dignify
> what I have so often said will be a non-book (like my
> meeting with Gweno was a non-meeting) with even a mask
> resembling a book. If I quote you, which isn't likely, I'll ask
> your permission. And will you, if you quote me, ask it – it
> will be given in most cases – and, more important, acknowl-
> edge me. I don't know quite why I want this but I do. It is
> perhaps that I may feel it is all I will contribute to Alun
> Lewis's image.

She continued working on it despite her various ailments (the most serious being her failing eyesight) and the usual busy round of family and social engagements. Every morning at 8, she would sit at her desk in the little room adjoining her living room without ever losing her sense she was jeopardising her Catholic soul. It was all very well for her to write – she hadn't been the loser. At one stage, she asked me to edit the letters while she concentrated on her preface.

Now more than ever, she was struck by the intensity of Lewis's depressions:

> I'm writing about this and realise more and more (though I
> always have, always and powerfully) that they are the secret
> of so much which is puzzling or disconcerting. I've always
> known this and have always intended writing somewhere
> about it. They were havoc in him. A dread beyond realising.
> She brought him through them, suffered them with him. His
> fear, his pity for her, his love for her – they are all based in
> the depressions.

This is typical of Freda's habit of analysis. She liked returning to a subject, each time drawing fresh insights from it. She never tired of a topic – if it were true, it stayed true. Something in her rejected the notion of the final formulation of a final idea. She would have had a hard time of it as an academic. She liked exhausting every nuance of meaning  not in a flash or series of flashes but by a process of immersion. The result was rather like a set of musical variations, in which a theme is transformed until it is difficult to tell where the original ends and variations begin. She was at her best in her letters to me, writing with sensitivity and concentration. While she repeated herself, she was never repetitious. Reading them, I suspended everything without realising anything needed to be suspended.

Freda observed that working with me

> has been so exciting and stimulating. The sight of your handwriting on the door-mat always set a reality on what was often a dull unreal day. It has, you may not believe me, been the only true reality in my life for a very long time.

Our collaboration gave her

> a sort of glimpse of what life should have been for me if I had given up everything else to writing, to the intellect rather than to the foolish worldly enticements.

Freda's formal education ended early; over the years, her energies had been diverted into various channels. Now that they had to be submitted to an external discipline, she went back to school and I don't doubt that my being an extra-mural lecturer helped. When it was all over, she wrote:

> It was such fun, wasn't it? Such joy. It quite simply kept me alive when my life was rather grim – fun, and exciting and rewarding.

And the end result? She came to embrace Alun. Previously, she had placed a limit on their love, arguing that their time together was too brief and her devotion to Wallace too deep-rooted. She knew better now:

> Poor, poor little lamb. I am worthy of this love now, though too young, too full of exultation then. Only two emotions, I have decided, bring human creatures nearer the gods: sorrow and love. All other are negative: ambition, jealousy, fear, even happiness. Only sorrow and love *really* deepen under-

standing of what it is all about. It has just struck me that Alun
Lewis knew this – he said so in so many ways.

If he wanted to protect Gweno from the truth, she would adopt his
scruple as her own. Hurting Gweno was, for her, tantamount to
hurting him.

Even so, another impulse remained 'sovereign':

> the life he needed his poems to achieve, the gift of his tender
> appreciation & love of humanity and of Life itself to be given
> and accepted. For this reason Gweno, Freda, Wallace took
> second place in the final offering.

That is a noble conclusion. Gweno, Wallace, Freda, their children –
all were subject to the 'final offering' and that, in the end, is why she
was able to set aside the personal, thus squaring the circle. The
personal was not to be the logic of this story, after all - the poems
and stories were. That, too, is why she eventually acknowledged that,
in the showers episode, Alun's cries of joy mark the moment when
his love for her became inseparable from his acceptance of death. He
who had said 'yes' to her in Coonoor now said 'yes' to whatever was
about to happen to him

It was at this time that Freda asked me to attest her will. Since
witnesses to wills cannot be beneficiaries of them, she offered my
wife and myself some tokens of appreciation. To my wife, then a
furniture restorer, she gave a prentice (or demonstration) rush-cane
chair painted black and decorated with floral motifs, a miniature of
the one she had seen her working on before. The two stood juxtaposed, one on the mantelpiece, one beneath, for many years.

My gifts were two-fold: a photograph of Lewis she had taken at
Highfield and a copy of John Piper's *British Romantic Artists* (1942),
which Alun bought at the Modern Book Store, Poona and inscribed:
'Because you'll like it./ With love from/ Alun./ Xmas 1943', to which
Freda added: 'To John Pikoulis,/ forty years later, with/ love from/
Freda Aykroyd.'

> I'm *so* glad my thought of Alun's present to me should, in
> becoming my present to you, please you. It becomes, I
> thought, a sort of present from him. It is now a difficult thing
> to describe the closeness I feel for you. The young man
> bouncing excitedly about in the kitchen as I cooked years
> ago, bringing lively mice to my feet; the pleasure of seeing

exactly the same implications in our mutual discoveries
(yours mostly, my *brooding!*), the letters sending yet another
discovery, exciting always, sometimes dramatic, and the
response to my own, belonged to a very young man, one
who, like Alun, was finding his way. I couldn't think of you
as a son because in some way I identified you with Alun –
young, teaching, literary, eager – & as Alun remains to this
moment, so I remain in thinking of him, young. So you were
a sort of buddy! Of Alun & me. Now you are mature – it is
very moving to see how the publication of the book has intro-
duced you to a real critical responsibility or rather to a grave
approach to this responsibility. It is difficult to describe but
it is there: maturity taking over from youthful excitement.
And it is very nice for me now I am in declining years to
have a mature friend who feels so much about Alun Lewis,
one who has journeyed so far with him & me. Do you think
Fate had in view these remaining years when I first wrote to
you, these years when Alun should be brought out of limbo
and his voice be heard and thereby accompany me when I so
much need a companion? I have lately thought (very often)
that Alun is helping me to die.

Re-reading his poems, she travelled back to Highfield. Like the
faintest breeze or haunting fragrance, they revived the purity and
longing of their love, joy and sadness fused.

I have this year comprehended what you seem always to have
realised: that this love went to the grave with him.

Previously, her guilt had prevented her acknowledging this. Not now.
    In my introduction to the biography, I wrote that it was conceived
as 'a homage and a rescue'. That is what it was for Freda, too, and
she pored over it with the devotion previously reserved for his letters.
The experience had changed us both, she said:

I thought the other day with a certain awe that I must have
affected your life quite considerably, in one way and another!
…most readers will read the book without the trembling
intensity we feel for every word of it.

She went on:

Am I to say again what your book means to me? I asked

my 'daily' to fetch it from upstairs, the other day – feeling
very low, dispirited, at the end of my courage. I wanted to
check the date of his death so that his name can go down on
the list for prayers for the dead on his day. (You'd think the
date was seared into my mind, wouldn't you?) She brought
your book and I opened it and, as always (and as I have done
for forty years with his letters) I began to read; forgetting
everything else, all the things I should be doing, the reason I
asked her to fetch it for me, and the wonderful comfort and
the bringing of him near, and the truth about him which only
you have seen and which I have carried about in me all these
years, alone, and the love you have for him and the respect
– all flooded over me again and, miserable as I was, I was
quite comforted and fortified. And I made up my mind that I
just will not give way to this horrible mortality but press on
and do my little best to pay him homage and show him,
somehow, gratitude and here I am back at the typewriter and
writing to you which is a sort of beginning of writing about
him. Yet again I thought: I'm not worthy of him, or rather I
wasn't worthy of him then. I am now. In fact I realise and
often have that there was only one woman for Alun Lewis to
love as he wanted and needed to love and that was me! That
sounds so very vain but I mean it in its simple literal sense:
I had in my own nature the exact elements which composed
his, though heaven knows in so very minor a degree; the
needs, the exaltations, the comprehension of one knew not
what, the sadness which no one suspected (in me), the
strange awareness of that which was outside reality, and the
joy in it all. You feel in reading Gweno's letters, poor girl,
the total apartness from all these – and many more – things
in him. But we grew from the same root. Yet, I can even say
that if by some means we had come together and given up
everything and everyone else the possibility is that he would
have wandered away again in the course of time. He said he
was not a monogamous creature. Nor was I – though I doubt
I'd have left him ever. I don't know. Perfection is difficult to
nurture and sustain in this jagged world. Yes, I wasn't worthy
of him and he probably loved me more than I did him –
though my life was sweet then, in a way that it never was
before or after, sweet with a love made somehow innocent
by its newness. For such a very short time. But is that all that
my life was then? It was so filled with reality, life, children,
Wallace. The especial sweetness Alun brought belonged only
to he and me. Every word he wrote and which I read and re-
read speaks to something very deep and grafted in whatever

it was we shared and shared with no-one else.

I long to answer these letters of his *now*. I understand every syllable of them, every coded line, every obscurity and every attempt to express the unknown, the guessed at. In some untellable way I inhabit him.

The letter shows that she, too, was touched by greatness. Having accepted Alun, a new recognition sprang up in her, one that was quite unattended by remorse. For her, I had been the essential inessential, a catalyst who helped form her views. When I told her how moved I had been by her letter, I added that the biography was written for her – not that it was against anyone else but in recognition of her help, without which it could not have come into being.

Lewis once told Dick Mills that Freda believed no-one could ever love her. Now that she had finally accepted Lewis's love, the effect was overpowering:

> I'm a bit of a mess. I admit these things now. The Pope, in one of his more acceptable pronouncements, said: "The truth will set you free." How true. The old boy has it in one…. I think I am worthy of him as I have grown to be now. I think that is true.

Beyond wavering, she added:

> I sometimes think I should write Gweno an IMMENSE letter! I often compose it when I should be sleeping. If I tell her the *absolute* truth (thus setting myself free!) of how I have collaborated with you in a work which has hurt her very much, revealed so much she would rather not know or be known, lied to her in saying our Bombay idyll was only an occasion when I needed to eat bananas, being pregnant, and nothing very profound – all the lies I told her – and put to her that Alun belonged to us both, loved us both, but – as I have been trying to convey in this letter with my thoughts about love – in different ways, each consuming, but God knows! very different one from the other. Would it help to write thus? And to ask if she can be further hurt by the reading of and publication of his letters to me? Because they have to be given to his readers, his admirers – he is a little misrepresented unless they are shown to the world. They MUST be published. Can she take that, d'you think?

At the same time, she felt increasingly uneasy about the letters she had written to me. These, she felt, had served their purpose and struck her as bigoted and biased. 'Bits' of them might be acceptable only if one could overlook the 'whining and excuses and eulogies'. What she admired most in Lewis was honesty – was it honest of her to parade her feelings so?

Evidently, Freda never lost the habit of the confessional and was even now offering up the letters on the altar of humility. But her doubts faded in time and she even encouraged me to write something called 'The Making of a Biography', a tribute to Lewis and her children. In a sense, this book is that.

My last memory of Freda is of her standing outside Woodstock House watching me leave, her hands behind her back, her head tilted to one side, her toes splayed. She stoops beneath a head of cropped white hair. Her prominent, watery eyes lend her face an expression of mild grace. I always regretted leaving her, fearing it might be for the last time. As my car went over the gravel of the circular drive, I glanced back to catch her in the rear-view mirror before setting out on my long journey home.

# VII

Lewis's *Collected Poems*, edited by Cary Archard, appeared in 1994, 50 years after his death. It is a straightforward reprint of his two collections of verse shorn of his introduction to *Raiders' Dawn* and Gweno's epigraph to *Ha! Ha! Among the Trumpets*. Also excluded were Lewis's grave poem from *Letters to my Wife*, Freda's poems in *The New Welsh Review* poems and those I included in my biography. Twenty-seven 'Uncollected Poems' were added.

The virtue of the *Collected* is its availability; its defect (apart from the omissions I have noted) is the absence of any critical material barring a 'Biographical Table'. No considered estimate of him is offered nor of his relation to the age nor any information about the composition of the poems, the impact of Longmoor and India on him and the influence of Yeats, Auden, Edward Thomas and the two Lawrences. The reader is unable, for example, to trace the relation between 'The Mountain over Aberdare' to 'On the Welsh Mountains' or penetrate the disguise 'Peasant Song' wears or the significance of 'The Way Back'. Indeed, Freda is absent from the volume, barring some innocuous mentions in the 'Biographical Table'.

Cary Archard was a teacher at the time and moving spirit behind Poetry Wales Press (now Seren). He had succeeded Jeremy Hooker in Gweno's affections and it was thanks to him that a programme of publishing was finally begun with her *Letters to my Wife* (1989), the *Collected Stories* (1990) and the *Collected Poems*. In his preface to the *Collected Stories*, he comments:

> Most books about Lewis [Ian Hamilton's anthology and my biography included] have implied that he is pre-eminently a poet and the tendency has been to play down his achievement as a short story writer.

The stories are indeed neglected, particularly that deceptively subtle study of a terrorist outrage in India, 'The Raid'. But, though memorable, they remain a poet's prose. In his introduction to *The Last Inspection* (also excluded from the *Collected*), Lewis notes that they are 'rather personal observations than detached compositions' which puts it fairly. This has not prevented some from preferring his stories to his poems, and it is certainly true they came more easily to him and prove him to be an unusually sympathetic observer. In 1942, he told Lynette Roberts:

> I'm growing more & more into a mere short story writer, Lynette. I *love* it, just *love* it. I get all the feeling of poetry, with something less miraculous and more credible in the act of writing. I can never believe I write *poetry*. I can draw comfort and power from knowing that I can write short stories.

'Mere', however, suggests that, though he excelled at it, story-writing represented a lesser activity, consolation for the poetry that reached him with such attractive difficulty.

# VIII

In 2006, my revised edition of *In the Green Tree* appeared in the Library of Wales. It included the letters in Gweno's edition of 1948 shorn of the numerous errors that had crept in: parts had been repeated, spliced together or appeared out of sequence. Also removed

were some 'improvements' made by an unknown hand. The General
Editor of the series also decided to exclude A.L. Rowse's introduction and Glyn Jones's obituary, though John Petts's illustrations were
retained. In an 'Afterword', I gave a description of them based on a
letter of his on 5 October 1980.

# IX

Freda's memoir, 'Remembering Alun Lewis', appeared in 2006 as
the preface to her edition of his letters, *A Cypress Walk*. Not surprisingly, the sheen had come off her writing by then, thanks to all the
effort she had put into it. Dogged by the shadow of the past and the
prospect of death, she doubted whether it would appear in Gweno's
lifetime but, when it did, it was she who had died. According to
Juliet, there was very little religion left in her at the end. Years before,
she had entered a 'sort of bargain' with God when she feared one of
Juliet's children might be born a 'mongol'. She prayed that, if she
were spared, she would sacrifice her book. Nevertheless, she continued to slave over it in a complex of loss and grief. I received
numerous drafts over the years, all of them rejected as unsatisfactory.
Her letters have the bloom of freshness still on them, carried on a
stream of eagerness; when it came to the memoir, she toiled without
hope. At one stage, she converted it into a play called 'The Syllable
of Love', an acted reading of which took place in Juliet's home.
(Juliet is a playwright and for several years was a member of the
Royal Shakespeare Company.)

Ten years previously, Freda had told me: 'Remember, I wrote it
with a dozen ghosts at my shoulder, a million inhibitions, and a
mountain of guilt'. The memoir lifts that mountain but the effect is
far from liberatory. Exhausted by memory, she appears forlorn,
wreathed in the past and shifting from topic to topic, reverie-like.
For a last time, she counts what she has lost. Alun is lovingly, gently
treated, Gweno with compassionate respect. Nonetheless, there are
flashes of steel when she comes to the subject of his suicide. Like
Gweno, she goes over the history of his depressions, emphasising
the 'remorseless way' he drove himself into 'a final depression' in
the autumn of 1943. With immense sorrow, she has to admit their
love may have contributed to it:

The possibility is anguish to me and I have prayed that it is only half true, knowing what all who knew him accept: that he would in due course have brought himself by his own hand to that world he wondered and dreamed about, which called him irresistibly.

The phrase 'knowing what all who knew him accept' was immediately arresting. Had Gweno conceded to her what she had conceded to no-one else? Or was Freda implying that she did not know him? She then records how dismayed she was by

his last two letters for they were clearly written when the decision to take his own life had been made. In both he alternates between acceptance of the fact that he is going to die and slipping back into fleeting thoughts of a possible future. They are a testament of his agony. He was in the deepest depression, helpless yet determined to leave those he loved certain of his enduring love.

Lest this be confused with a soldier's resolution before battle, she goes on:

The threat of death itself would not have obsessed him: all soldiers face the possibility of death. The cause of his inner frenzy lay in knowing the action he was to take in obedience to the relentless force which guided his will.

In her most forthright declaration on the subject, all deference to Gweno was cast aside:

In physical and emotional chaos, and with the terrifying and certain prospect of confrontation with the Japanese, Alun yet found time to write to Gweno to reassure her and tell her, heart-breakingly, that his 'reason was taking control and working carefully and methodically'; that 'my grasp is broader and steadier than it's been for a long time'; and that their future must be 'full of sunlight and growth and health'. In fact, far from his reason taking control, he was on the perilous edge of breakdown. His journal shows that he was drawing nearer to suicide, counting the remaining days as 'twelve days that remain in a neat pile on a white cloth'.

I cannot say where 'twelve days' comes from. In his journal, Lewis wrote: '...I could count the days that remained neatly, in a neat pile on a white cloth', immediately versified to:

> Counting my days upon my fingers
> Neat pile of days on a white napkin....

A precise figure is added few lines later:

> And this sweet joy of writing is the right spending
> Of one day that remains out of seventy...

'Seventy' is then crossed out and 'ninety' substituted for it – but not 'twelve'.

In a final thrust, she adds:

> To me he wrote in an agonised attempt to prove that so 'worthless' a creature as himself could 'belong' to no one. He wrote of 'returning to the revelation and inacarnation'', and that 'There is no end to all this, except the accidental end'. He then clearly describes his death. 'Oh the *thrill* of myself to thyself, sweet swordsman,' he wrote, 'the dancer & the dance, the wind & the cry of the wind'.

Lewis here refers to Yeats's 'Among School Children', in which the dancer and dance, symbol and fact, fuse into a romantic unity of being. Lewis hints at the self's fulfilment that will follow once the deed has been performed.

Lewis's letters to Freda are the most accurate record of his state of mind in his last months. They reveal him in all his pain and sensitivity, sustained by the 'uncanny understanding' that existed between them ' – so close it becomes invisible, immanent, unnecessary'. The letters are thus less an exchange of views than a simultaneous flashing of signals.

> There are situations, obligations, yes, yes, yes – but not now: nor when we meet again.... Frieda, come to me. It doesn't matter when.

However, the obligations never went away and he counted the cost. It was a burden willingly borne and did not detract from their love. Whatever the complications, they had discovered something thrilling and rare.

On the 24th August 1943, he wrote about 'the huge thing that had happened to me' in Karachi when he cried 'I am glad & I am in love and I don't care', a quasi-Yeatsian expression of tragic joy asserting love in the face of extinction, towards which he hurries crying 'Ha! Ha! Among the Trumpets'. On the 31st, he told her he was pining for her 'real presence':

> Otherwise I ache only for oblivion, the desert, fighting & the laughter of a spirit grappling with brutality. All bad things: it's ugly, this silken fascination that evil has some times.

He could not write the poems that belonged to her and would not

> until long after this is over and it is part of me & I have made myself see the world again with my new eyes that you said were blind, as of course they are, as a newborn animal's are.... But of course I can't write the real real real poems yet. A very big thing happens & after it, under its impact, one is for a long time apparently smaller. Like concussion....Oh I wish I could write the poems now, darling, it would be such a relief.

These early letters are written in a daze of desire, joy mixed with frustration. At Bombay, 'enchantment sealed my forehead':

> Tomorrow I shall see the window at which we sat: I shall be the horizon we contemplated. Last night, lying in the dunes I thought how we let the the breeze make love between us in the luminous freedom of the last darkness before dawn, and how by moving closer and locking our arms a little closer we excluded the breeze and were front to front and cool and simple together.

Back at Lake Kharakvasla, he was 'dwarfed & stilled & humbled' by his new-found love; everything lay 'behind a gauze'.

> I know it was something more than either of us, that it is a directive force which will achieve itself in us whether we oppose it or not, whether it brings pain or not. And I am content perforce to wait.... I haven't slept for two nights on this exercise & I've sweated & exerted myself hugely, & yet I'm not tired because of this sleepless longing for the veil to fall off, the reality to come. It grieves & worries me, too;

> Frieda, beloved, the untamed wildness is away in the jungle about its own ways & we must let it be so. It's the only really fundamental truth we mean. It's the only miracle over which we have no control.

The 'untamed wildness' recalls the parable of two lovers who meet and part,

> yellow-eyed proud soft moving beasts that go their own way and in some clearing in the jungle sometimes come upon each other and become thereby sublime.

In the autumn, the 'armour [sic; 'amour'?], the tenderness, the afterglow' turned into hopelessness.

> I feel such a dolt, Frieda, and whatever it was that happened, now seems to have been so swift & so beyond me & greater than me that I sit like a lump in my chair.... If it had happened slower, so that I needn't have closed up like this & excluded my bewildered self like this. Did it happen too quickly for *you*? I know it did. And it now seems incomprehensible that we were in a window, high & unassailable and perfected & you spoke of goddess & god; and I knew only the charm and not the hardness that succeeds it. Yet I *did* know of the hardness because it is always my ancient enemy, and has an old claim on me. But you'd so spirited it away that I couldn't – I get no nearer by talking, Frieda darling; it's the old childish hankering for a continuous happiness. Happiness brings its own nemesis; feeling its own atrophy.

Such happiness as he had known was part of a sequence of finding and losing, 'atrophy' hinting at the sexual withering that lay at the root of it. Even so, Freda made him wish to 'burn and defame & fight'. They had come 'from an old negative world into the simple & supreme syllable of love'.

'Syllable' has a particular significance in this context. (Lewis had also used the word in 'The Earth is a Syllable'.) In the *Upanishads*, it is part of the search for spiritual enlightenment; like Yeats, he was drawn to its account of the stages of enlightenment seekers must pass through before death. The earth is the mystic absolute 'Om'; in life, people are absorbed by their relation to their surroundings but, as death approaches, this yields to true knowledge. The aim is unity with the universe, an expansion of the self's consciousness.

However, by now, Lewis was finding it difficult to utter the syllable of love: 'One way or another I make a lot of shadows where I
go. Everywhere I go, inevitably'.

> It's only now when I think of Frieda Aykroyd in Coonoor, &
> Alun Lewis in the South Wales Borderers going their
> disparate & necessary ways that I grieve for the poverty and
> nakedness of spirit in which we became minute and splendid
> as a grain of sand and were capable of surpassing whatever
> had & does now prevent us.

As if steadying himself before the end, he told her 'an "old" feeling'
had returned to him, one first sensed in Bombay as they prepared to
leave when she remarked: 'It seems such a wrong & so wasteful that
we must go different ways', to which his 'oldness' replied: 'No, it
isn't a pity, Frieda'. A year earlier, he had sensed it again when he
heard the engines of *The Athlone Castle* pounding out a truth
displayed by D.H. Lawrence's blue gentians: '*And I knew I had
gone!*' At Poona station, he bowed his head before the inevitable:
'That's a tremendous truth, darling, to know one has gone'. Everything that had not begun to begin in them would now never do so.

At the end of October 1943, he was immersed in an 'absurd flap
of work', poring over maps, planning reconnaissance trips and route
marches, joining physical exercises over mountains, fighting mock
battles and launching amphibious dawn attacks. It was a 'bastard'
existence of blisters, iron biscuits and dates and meant little to him.
Only Freda relieved the oppression he felt. As 'The Way Back' anticipates, he had gone through her golden gate and rejoined the
'gladiators and levies/ All laconic disciplined men'.

One day, he swam in the lake only to find its usual tonic effect
failed to materialise:

> I went on then to the lake where I was quite alone and
> stripped by the brown flood water under the bushes and let
> the sun smooth my body and my genitals. And my body was
> thinking of you and me. But my mind said very remotely,
> like an arbiter 'Body is captivated, but the mind is not at one
> with the body.' And at that antilogy the body withdrew its
> thoughts & its desire as if rebuked and I went and swam my
> body and came back wet & fishlike & insentient.

The use of 'I' in this passage is arresting: mind and body are separate entities obeying separate commands. Presently, it is the mind holds sway, reducing the body to a subservient role. 'I went and swam my body': 'I' does not swim; it takes the body for a swim, observing its activities before reasserting control over it once the anticipated relief fails to appear. 'Self' is associated with mind rather than the body and binds the two into an uneasy alliance:

> I I I I I I I I I – silly word. I'm not very I, darling: it's only
> that I'm not objective, and events are significant only through
> their passage through me. It's a pity: but there it is.

'I' is the spectrum that reflects the world, a filter for everything that happens to happen and only proof of what lies beyond, but it cannot influence or prevent events. In his next letter, he sends love to Gilly – 'And to you my self. Do you want it? Alun'.

In the sesamum field passage, there is no 'I'. The scene is set: 'you' is a man who kneels among yellow flowers and also the man who orders him; there is no 'I', only two 'you's, the one who does and the one who is done to, both embraced by the narrator. Shortly afterwards, one 'you' bends over the other, whose life is bleeding away. This is what suicide does: allow the alter ego to cancel the ego.

> You were afraid of something that might turn into resent-
> ment in me and of something in me that cowardice and for
> peace of mind would shut away this love, this burning image
> and deep reflection of you in me & in the world. But it could
> only happen like that if I died also within myself: and I need
> to be as terrified of that as you, or more than you.

He and she had achieved an 'IS' which would survive the disappearance of 'I'.

In the following months, the world's demands took their toll. Back in Poona hospital at the end of October, he complained of 'the lack of toughness of my mind which I'm afraid isn't half as strong as I'd hoped and has really behaved very badly of late'. Again, 'my mind' is separated from 'I' and exerts limited control over it. Nothing was coming in to replace what was going out of him.

> I've never been so cast off, so worthless, purposeless,
> unresponsive. I loathed myself for it and was anxious about
> it, too....it's a long time since my ancient enemy made such
> a determined assault on me. Damn his bleary eyes.

The letter ends: 'And this from Alun', his signature enclosed in a
maze of coils. 'I've been wandering in tedious unrhymic circles &
spirals in the wilderness of the last few weeks'. It was as much as he
could do to lift his head.

Oppressed by such 'leadenness, the persistent oppression', he
waited for something to happen and told her his depression

> always manifested itself in an intense awareness of the waste
> that I'm causing or suffering. And what is waste? I think it's
> the feeling of dissatisfaction with one's deeds, the feeling of
> incompetence, of being hustled into inefficiency by the daily
> rush of trifles & duties, none of which give any feeling of
> accomplishment or fulfilment.

He had recovered before but

> ... it's all I can do not to cry out with sorrow & hurt. At other
> times in these long inadequacies I suffer I think I want it to
> go a little further, a little further, that I might explore the
> fields of insanity. That is a temptation  that attracts & repels
> with like force & I don't act towards it: it's just a thought in
> me, not an impulse. I know it's danger: but it's very closely
> connected with the bit of poetry there is in me, the writing &
> creating mystery that wants to break down the last barriers
> and explore the deep involutions of trouble and complexity
> & relationship of things. But I don't really know whether the
> great poems were really written in madness. I think they were
> written in intervals of sanity. Madness I fear is chaos, a
> greater bewilderment, a worse darkness. Has any apprehen-
> sion of the mystery of everything and the mystic varieties &
> interconnexions of the universe ever come to anybody except
> in a moment of exalted lucidity? I don't know.

It is a confession he could have made to no-one else. As at the conclusion of 'The Way Back', he anticipates a reunion with Freda after 'I'
has been 'squandered' and 'hurled' in a violent impact.

Lewis's last story, 'The Reunion', based on his meeting with his
brother, Glyn, in Poona in December 1943, shows how precariously
things were balanced. Glyn recalled that the meeting was friendly
but Eric (Alun's alter ego) finds it hard to connect with his brother.
Late at night, some revellers in the next-door hotel bedroom create
a disturbance; he reacts in a fashion recalling Edward Thomas's
description of

> a sort of nervousness, a continuous palpitation and sense of
> something approaching that never comes.... I don't mean a
> sense of approaching good or bad luck, but merely a sense
> of *something* coming, as if I had heard a report and waited
> for the other barrel.

Worked into it is a larger sense of failure:

> I can't settle down, I can't sleep, life is being wasted in me,
> going round and round on its empty repetitive journeys,
> avoiding the encounter, identifying itself with nothing, avoid-
> ing love, refusing socialism, rejecting a better world because
> my self is worse, worse, worse, but doesn't matter, my self
> doesn't matter....

Listening to the partygoers, Eric projects his brother's experiences
in Burma into his own imagined encounter with the enemy:

> He could have shot me, but he didn't. All the time I was
> crossing the clearing he could have got me with his pistol.
> But he didn't. He waited until I was right by him, till he could
> make his magnificent thrust. Then he leapt out of the brake
> and his sword was raised over his head.
> So near me I could not miss. I've never hit anything with
> my pistol, except him. It was absurd. Just the reflex action
> of my trigger finger, before I thought about it, before I
> screamed. I wish I hadn't screamed.

Another version of the sesamum field's encounter with a Japanese
soldier, again more ceremonial than realistic. In the latter he carries
a sword rather than a pistol, more samurai than conscript, and his
'magnificent thrust' as he 'leapt out of the brake' is decidedly theatrical. Eric fires cackhandedly at him (as it happens, Lewis was a good
shot), after which comes a real or imagined break-in to the next-door
party, when his brother collapses hysterically:

> Oh God, oh God, they got him first. He wasn't awake, was
> he, he wasn't aware of what goes on in the world. Listen, I'm
> screaming again... I'll kill ... I'll kill. Kill now. Kill.

Lewis was disappointed by what he made of the story:

> Should I start it objectively, writing it from the outside, disci-

plining it? Or should I let it rush over the weir? It's bad for a
writer to feel emotional   he floods & corrupts his sentences
& themes with his own emotions.

By contrast, 'The Jungle' was written in a 'moment of exalted lucidity', its diction purified, its tone eloquent, its cadences hieratic.
    Shortly before Christmas, he posted 'A Fragment' to Freda:

> The wild beast in the cave
> Is all our pride: and cannot be
> Again until the world's blind travail
> Breaks in crimson flower from the tree
>
> I am, in Thee.

There *would* be a flowering, after all, though it was presently beyond
'tedious fatigable me'.

> ...I am doing nothing except, read, write letters, sit & think,
> worry, do odd jobs, wait for the pistol. Only I feel I'm
> rushing it.

Earlier that autumn, he had sent his poems to Robert Graves, who
now returned them with his approval. By now, however, he had lost
all his faith in them.

> I feel all the time that I'm either washed out or waiting to
> start. It may be either. I'm waiting to see. It's boring, being
> nothing. And I am nothing here somehow. Nothing of any
> importance at all.

He wanted to be with his men when the day came; after that, he
would be stabilised.

> I'm far away in nowhere & no compass could locate the way
> I got here.

He could not avoid contemplating the 'gruesome':

> I was very conscious of the hotchpotch we make of life in
> the Army, the bad way we do a lot of jobs because we're
> doing them all at the same time and for a purpose that is intol-
> erable. And I had a wicked sense of dissatisfaction with

everything I put my hand to, & in consequence did them worse than I needed to, because I had no faith in myself doing them. And I'm clumsy & dreamy in matters of memory & administration. I forget details or slur them, and condemn myself like a Dickensian Bumble. And the whole vast enterprise the world is engaged on falls into doubt in me and I go under a surge of bungled violence & released irresponsible harm. Have you ever heard a battery of artillery laying down a barrage of shell? It's a terrible experience philosophically & morally, all that crushing dreadful arbitrary violence. Physically it's just a bloody row & a reflex fear or shudder. But to think of the impersonal evil it implies is terrible.

At the end of January 1944, he wrote: 'I want to be less I but I can't lose myself in anything else not here, not now, not yet'. 'I' wanted out. He was wavering, and so was the cause for which he had enlisted. For its sake he had become a 'harrassed subaltern', uncertain of performance and nervous of the demands placed on him. But that mattered little now, though he hoped battle would 'activate the submerged instinct of humanity in me':

I'll fight much better for peace than I can for war. I'll write better, too. When it at last comes my slow way.

By now, he was 'impatient to have a showdown with fate'. Highfield was a long way away:

The first evening when someone called to take you (me thrown in) to Gloria's dinner party, I remember the spontaneous unquestioning feeling I had that the man who called was from outside and that it had happened to us & we didn't belong except to each other. A marvellous feeling of blood relationship, not then of a lover (but of a brother, not only a brother): and I'll always have that, though there are so many imponderable antagonistic forces and so many weaknesses in me that prevent & prevent. I wish I hadn't this capacity for pain. It so wearies me. I wish I was strong like oak. And less aware of the waste & the going wrong of things and mea culpa in it all. But not in us.

*They* would survive.

I want you to know I love you in as many ways as I have

moods & failings, and that I cannot come to you is in conso-
nance with everything I've lived.

It was now that he asked her for a gold ring, which he wore on his
little finger. He said he would not see her again until her baby was
born but 'I will come, somehow, I will, will, will'.

> … what has happened is us. I can hardly believe in it: it is as
> miraculous as God or the nativity. It will go on happening
> again, God knows when. I can hardly bear to imagine it. It
> *did* happen, darling, it *did* happen. It was thus & thus, beyond
> speaking.

At the end of January, he packed his kit, sorted out his papers and
burned her letters –

> oh with such trembling & gentle but fierce sorrow. I watched
> the words fade from your letters, each one as I burnt them.
> They grew nearer & nearer to me all the time.

He asked her to mark any future letters '"*If undelivered return to F.A.
Highfield etc. –* " lest they go the weary round of effects to be disposed
of and break a heart in the end'. He also burned letters from Wendy
Mostyn, his Aberystwyth girlfriend, the last of which arrived a few
weeks later; he then revised his poems over three nights and transferred his estate to Gweno. 'I've made everything so tidy', he wrote,
'tidy' being South Walian for 'correct', 'proper', fitting':

> The poems will be out in the Autumn: I've asked Gweno to
> send you a copy: so you've got one Xmas present being
> made ready for you next year. But I can't look at the future
> – I can't see any distance at all. Oh well, the time I've wasted,
> dreadful….
>
> And for yourself, know I am conscious all the time that
> a whole life is being thrown away all the time we are denying
> & are denied each other. That other life haunts me
> inescapably – & I desire it ineluctably. It makes the rest of
> living sad.

His last letter, dated February 10th 1944, was written in

> the impersonal, imperturbable mood which comes after a
> danger or an evil experience, when there is no clear emotion

or sense of peril or failure or escape but just an insulated
quietness from which one acts and considers & waits. I don't
mind what happens now: I've got myself in rein, I think I'll
be what I'm expected to be & do what I ought to do and that
in itself is a scriptural simplicity. For the rest I feel it's out of
my hands now: and I feel no distress at having to go
unresolved as it were....

There is soldierly fortitude here as well as chronic unfulfilment. He
had not discharged his duties as well as he wished 'because I plan
inwardly & not objectively'; nonetheless, he still wanted to prove
himself:

> There is no end to all this, except the accidental end, the bulb
> fusing, the mind failing, the body ceasing to function, lungs
> & hearts & eyes. Don't be fretted with loss, Frieda; I feel
> wonderfully happy whenever the certainty moves in me that
> I have lived indestructibly in thee. And in mother, & Mair,
> and boyhood, and Gweno, and words sometimes joining in
> flame. So I try not to shiver when a cold gout strikes me & I
> feel a collapse in the nervous clocktower of my being.

Freda was alarmed by this. It was so obviously a farewell letter. The
'accidental end' might be a soldier's but worked into it was an abject
sense of breakdown.

The letter ends with his familiar imagined return to Highfield:

> For you I wanted to come & see you first, but it will be
> very wonderful to come in the end. Don't worry over the
> hairs on my head. May you not be tried harder than you can
> bear. And I'll surely come up through the trees to the lawn
> to the splendour & the homecoming & the child & Gilly &
> us.

With which compare 'The Way Back':

> And in the hardness of this world
> And in the brilliance of this pain
> I exult with such a passion
> To be squandered, to be hurled,
> To be joined to you again.

As in 'The Earth is a Syllable', a man's death coincides with a reunion with the beloved

> in the only way possible, the spiritual way, having passed
> first through the spiritual experience of death.

The letter bearing news of Alun's death reached Freda at the end
of March. After reading it, she dropped it on the bed beside the
unborn child's christening robe and turned to weep in Wallace's arms.
About to give birth (she was seven months pregnant), she was experiencing another kind of birth in the womb of death. In 'Another Death
is in this Death', she wrote:

> This weariness of grief,
> More constant than the quietness of love
> Which asks for no relief,
> Is a burden grown with each day's passing.
> The generous hands of love can never move
> My heart again to tears,
> Nor pity gently touch my mind
> Which has grown too hard, nor fears
> Imagined and too real, quicken my calm breath.
> Another death is in this death.
> This grief
> Beats black wings throughout the lonely night
> And hangs, a stale despair, in each awakening.
> The lonely hours drag, the sun's unmeaning light
> Reflects an empty world.
> It is that you were there,
> In everything, and now are not
> So naught has meaning. Where
> You were in my mind and heart
> Is void and I a ghost
> Who has no more a part
> In this changed world. Time,
> Oh time, stand still, return!
> Let this moment be
> The one before I knew the dread
> To be a truth, before I knew that he
> Is forever dead.

Freda once told me:

> How awful, truly awful to want to [die] when young. Except,
> that it is, of course, a love of death rather than a hatred of

life. I can understand the love of death – I always could.
Having seen it close to fascinates and moves one to strange
longing: the peace, the mystery…. You know, when Alun
died I thought of it as the fitting end to a passionate, important love shared, an awful selfish thing to think, but I did
though it broke my heart. He had died and I thought of it as
a sort of transcendence, the dead poet, romantic, Shelleyan
– and somehow still with me, eternally. I've felt that ever
since – that somehow he's around, so to speak! Especially
when I read his letters which is why, I suppose, I read and
re-read them for countless years, the strange, sweet enchantment, the reassurance of total identification with each other
so that, as he said, we thought things at the same moment in
our leagues-away lives, the certainty of my love being as
desperately needed as I needed his – though he needed mine
more for I had Wallace. All this was part of his death –
somehow the story of he and me had to end in death, his
death. I can't imagine it going on – nor, I know, could he
though he talked of new beginnings, cast-off present. Nor
could I imagine that it had to be me who'd die. So his death,
though all my poems of the time show the anguish of it, was
as it should be.

One of Emily Dickinson's poems may serve as his epitaph:

Left in immortal Youth
On that low Plain
That hath nor Retrospection
Nor Again –
Ransomed for years –
Sequestered from Decay
Canceled like Dawn
In comprehensive Day –

The Dawn brings the Day it will not see. Lewis, too, was 'Ransomed
for years'. As Gwyn Thomas puts it:

Men move dimly towards what in their essence they wish to
become, and the things that happen to them have already
been planted by them in the waiting darkness ahead.

Freda once wrote:

Have I ever told you this: you know there were long

years when Alun was a far memory in my life. After writing the (awful) article in Modern Reading in 1952 I put his letters away & spent the next decade or two making a new life in Washington, another in Rome, & finally in England. The children, especially Juliet, with her T.B., seemed to take all my time – though that isn't really true: they were at school or University or married & I was very busy being an actress or caught up with people whose names often became public property, or searching for some way to God. Certainly having what is known as a good time – though more desolate at one time than ever before or since when Wallace was in love with his secretary. Or seemed to be. But having – not exactly forgotten Alun but putting him aside from my life – has often made me feel a fraud. Ridiculous, I suppose – I could hardly wear a near-equivalent to widow's weeds. I cherished him in my heart, though not many have had such a love. There is one photograph of him, standing with a glass in his hand & smiling very shyly, which brings back that pellucid ten days in Coonoor, the quality of which is expressed so vividly to me in his poems written then: 'the pine trees cast their needles daily', 'I have only this small plough...'. Reading them I can *feel* that clear, champagne-sparkling air, & am wrapped in that exquisite mystery. Strange.

# X

Early in 1995, Gweno invited me to lunch. I was naturally curious to know why she wanted to re-establish contact after so many years. Freda believed she was trying to draw me from her and said that, if there were to be a rapprochement, she wanted to be included. 'Wouldn't it be lovely if her determination to die in grace also extended into a long, forgiving letter to me!'.

I travelled to Aberystwyth with my wife, who pursued business of her own in town. I cannot remember now what Gweno said but it was not to any great purpose. It appears she wanted to part in peace from me and I greatly appreciated the gesture. It would have been painful if we had parted in any other way.

After lunch, my wife joined us and we travelled back to the

Chateau for tea. As we made to leave, Gweno handed me a copy of *The Last Inspection*. Since then, we have neither written nor spoken, save for two postcards she sent me, the first concerning some discrepancies I had noted between the texts of the letters in *In the Green Tree* and *Letters to my Wife*. These, she said, were the result of Gwyn Jones's wish to exclude any crude colloquialisms and 'sloppy syntax'. The text of *Letters to my Wife* was taken 'directly from the actual letters…exactly "as they was wrote, warts an' all, an' no kiddin"'.

The second arrived after I had undergone an emergency operation. It showed the Shwedagon Pagoda, Rangoon, a relic of her visit to Lewis's grave.

> This is just to wish John a speedy recovery & to say I hope
> you will both come to Aber again & if the weather is kind
> we might even enjoy Fish & Chips on the prom together!
> I do hope all goes well.
>                                    Best wishes,
>                                         Gweno.

The last refers to the meal my wife enjoyed on Aberystwyth prom.

I do not believe Gweno and I were ever in fundamental disagreement. Glyn Jones once told me (at a time when such reassurance was needed) that I was 'entirely innocent, only a revealer of resisted truths'. Perhaps that is how she came to see it. She had tried resisting those truths but always understood them and, when the time came, absolved me of bad faith.

Freda once wrote:

> Darling John, don't think me a daft old woman. I have a deep
> dislike of many of my own faults, and (not only religiously)
> hate myself very often. I hate myself for the vanity in letting
> you say all you did in your book which so hurt [Gweno] BUT
> do recognise that you were trying to write the truth, which
> you did, and also recognise that the book is an important and
> valuable addition to the literary world, setting down Alun
> Lewis and what he was as a man and poet and what influ-
> enced him in his life and his death. All that is vital. You and I
> are the only people who really knew, know him. That is true
> in every respect. And that is why I feel so close to you. I like
> you very much but that is the essential truth. Only you will
> stand as guardian of the truth relating to this complicated man.

...I don't mean by the above that I feel guilty about
bringing him into your life – far from it. It has been a powerful experience for you, hasn't it? From the time I first wrote
to you about your article on The Way Back. Oh my dear, you
really understood him then, and do always. I sometimes think
he would have been upset – being Welsh! – by your book
because it would hurt Gweno. I always knew this. And
sometimes worried about it. But he would have been so grati-
fied and proud of the fact that you showed the world what
his work really is and what sort of man he really was.

She continued:

You and your family mean far, far more to me than you can
know. I'll tell you: when I cut a slice of bread – and that is
very often obviously – I remember you saying, with a laugh,
that you always have to 'square it off'. So do I but never can.
When I eat strawberries I always think of Lorraine, heavily
pregnant, stooping to pick them in the pick-your-own near
here and your writing to say you were having strawberry jam,
tart, and cream, everything a strawberry can be. When I shop
in a certain toy shop in Oxford for various children as I
sometimes do I remember the real effort it was to find Eliot
Batman paraphernalia, and I remember your describing how
he dressed himself up in every sort of 'Western' thing he
could lay his hands on when he was very small. And then I
think of him in that sweet little house sulkily kicking – rather
nervous – the wainscot as you say 'No! No!'. And the big
Nanna dog walking with Lorraine and little Eliot on the
opposite side of the road and she calling to you the first day
I went there. And I often sit talking, talking, at the white table
in your dining room in the new house. How deeply satisfying
and exciting those talks were! How often does one have those
intellectual voyages of discovery in this life? We can't, we
mustn't set them aside.

Five years after the publication of the biography, however, she
complained that I had not sufficiently acknowledged her help during
the 'happy days of exploration and conjecture and conclusion'.

I think, as far as I remember, I said something about it, again
half-teasingly, when your book came out and you replied that
well, that is for the next book? letters? Something like that.

If I had not discharged the debt, I do so gladly now.

Let Freda have the last word:

> But I am intrigued by your hint about a memoir. Goodness!
> Tell me more – much more. Do you intend to write write the
> story of you-and-me-and-Alun (as he wrote to Dick) and if
> so I suppose my letters would come into it? But I have
> always said I won't allow them to be published, haven't I?
> I've even taken some frail steps to prevent them or any other
> written word which might twist the knife in Gweno's
> wounds. But you know how weak I am. I certainly won't be
> around to read all about it as you rather sweetly suggest. So
> I beseech you TO WRITE IT *NOW* so that I can read it and,
> possibly, help you. (The latter I doubt as you know it all.)
> Please *DO* write it now.

# APPENDIX ONE
## *Letters*

I reproduce below my notes on the letters Lewis wrote to Gweno from July 21st 1943 until his death. Some are silently excluded from Letters to my Wife or appear there with different wording or punctuation. All my quotations are taken from the originals. Lewis addressed his letters variously to Mrs A Lewis, Mrs Gweno M. Lewis, Mrs G.M. Lewis, Mrs Gweno Mererid Lewis and (once) Gweno Mererid Lewis. The first came when she was in Aberystwyth during the school holidays and he about to go to Coonoor.

The extracts make plain the persistence and intensity of Lewis's depressions and his reliance on Gweno. Her belief that his unhappiness was temporary and curable was influenced by his repeated protests of love.

**21 July 1943** (not included in *Letters to my Wife*)
Lewis notes that 'sometimes something *smothered* me, & us as a consequence, but that it wasn't anybody's fault and had no power over simple Love'. He recalls the times they had enjoyed together, including once in Swansea when 'I sat in your warmth and your deep certainty *like your own child*'. She

> rescued me and assured me, and given me that calcium which
> my spiritual home lacked and couldn't knit without.

Their love was indestructible and he would rather die than hurt her. He says he is travelling to the 'Aykroyds'.

**26 July 1943** (not included in *Letters to my Wife*)
Lewis writes from the Officers' Hostel, Ootacamund, where Freda sent him ahead of Wallace's return from America. He describes Highfield and says he 'felt guilty about staying there: and so I pushed off for a few days'. He says Freda has just returned from a sanatorium and is

a very brilliant woman who has been forced to live the deadly
false life of the Anglo-Indian society that dominates the hill
stations, and she's found it a cynical task.

He admires her 'vitality' and 'reserves of strength'.

**4 August 1943** (this appears, with variations, in *Letters to my Wife*)

I don't know why it was, but up in that brilliant cold
mountain country I was dissociated somehow from anything
before or after and I lived in a strange new way – angelically
almost.

Free of the army, he once again enjoys music, books, woods and
lakes as well as talking to Wallace Aykroyd. Gillian Aykroyd is fun
and Freda was 'brilliantly & mercilessly rude' to a man in the club.
   In a passage excluded from *Letters to my Wife*, he muses on

this strange world in which I move by predestined & haphaz-
ard ways. Why are you so afraid for me? DON'T for Christ's
sake. All my love Alun'.

**9 August 1943** (written en route to Karachi; it appears in *Letters to
my Wife*)
In an unpublished passage, he says he has sent her two stories by air,
'Ward 'O' 3 (b)' and 'The Orange Grove'. (The letter of 20 August
confirms they were sent in the third week of July.)

**12 August 1943** (this appears in *Letters to my Wife)*
'I feel now that the only place worth going to is the jungle'. He wants
to be with 'my own Welsh boys' and chastises her for her fears for his
safety. He feels tougher now and has too much 'to write & fight for'.
   In an omitted passage, he recalls an episode in London when she
suffered a 'bad night':

I felt horrified when I found you on the floor – oh Gweno
darling, that your young husband should drive you out of
bed!

**16 August 1943** (included in *Letters to my Wife*)

I see in strange things my own growing strangeness, and

nothing perturbs me now in the world of movement and
voyage and activity.

**20 August 1943** (not included in *Letters to my Wife*)
He is concerned for her and wishes she would stop teaching and buy
a flat rather than live in her house.

**23 August 1943** (not included in *Letters to my Wife*)
He proposes 'The Voyager' as the title for what eventually became
*Ha! Ha! Among the Trumpets*. The collection will be divided into
four sections: 'England', 'At Sea', 'India' and 'The Land of The
Heart'. The last-mentioned might be 'too fanciful' but contains the
'purely love poems which don't belong to any single place or time'.

> ...wherever I am Love relates itself softly to the physical
> influences of the land and when the mood & the place are
> fully integrated I write & send you the poem. It's lovely to
> have you to receive them, Gwen.

**24 August 1943** (included in *Letters to my Wife*)
He begs her not to fret:

> Make yourself separate from the necessities & accidents of
> the war, as I am making myself separate. I can feel myself
> growing more indestructible, more self-reliant and complete
> & inviolable, and I will *not* let myself be intimidated or
> destroyed – my true self, Gwen, you understand? But without
> separateness separation is dreadful. Can you feel what I
> mean, Gweno? It's very important, darling, to feel this differ-
> ence. Between oneself & what happens to one. A mouses's
> life is no life!! Give me the mouse that accepts the necessity
> for cats....

**28 August 1943** (not included in *Letters to my Wife*)
He wants to know why she was so angry with him at Kenilworth
when she sat up all night knitting.

> Oh, Gweno, don't you know how wide the world is, how
> many cross currents and tides there are and how all life is an
> enrichment and a proof, not a renunciation nor a forgetting
> nor a perpetual narrowing down? I can't find words, but I
> know that I seek always for wider and deeper experience and
> on all the planes and in all places you are present and can

meet me and help me profoundly and my response is always to you if you come without fear and without that cold clutch round the heart that makes the nerves hot and jiggery. Two things, love & understanding, are the end of all experiencing.

**1 September 1943** (included in *Letters to my Wife*. Gweno was now back in Mountain Ash)
He describes the poems for his new volume as

a queer batch, written in queer moods, over a long period, transplanting myself from India to Longmoor and Burma and never never Land and living more lives than one so that they're a sifting of imagined lives and other people's experiences as much as my own.

In a passage omitted from *Letters to my Wife*, he says the war will last until 1949 and explains that he rejected the offer of a staff officer's job at Karachi in order to be with 'my own Welsh comrades'.

**5 September 1943** (included in *Letters to my Wife*)

I was delighted with your vituperation...against the sexual preoccupations of my typewriter – breasts, breasts, breasts, you roar in a splendid Presbyterian Wesleyan rage. Well, unfortunately the world is full of breasts. I can't help it any more than you can. And where there are human beings, there's sex. And I just write how I see things and I see a lot more sex than I ever write. And as for the Welsh miner's son – I'm sorry you're cross with him. (There's a delightful little tree squirrel running down the fire escape, quick and beady.) He may be a bore but he's authentic.... And I make no apology for repeating myself any more than I would blame D.H. Lawrence or Spender or Hemingway for repeating them selves. It's unavoidable. So if you want to sever connection with the firm of Lewis & Lewis & join the Herring Society, well – solong!

In an unpublished passage, he says he has altered 'Like a lark within its nest/ Laid my hand upon your breast' in 'The Way Back' to 'I forgot the world's disease/ Among such branching harmonies'. (For 'world's', he once considered 'my young'.) 'You see, your rebuke is effective already'.

**9 September 1943** (not included in *Letters to my Wife*)
Lewis refers to a letter in which she

> spoke of my stories & poems and the necessity for me releas-
> ing my writings from my personal preoccupations, which
> is so true, and so difficult to achieve.

Cyril Connolly's acceptance of 'The Orange Grove' for *Horizon*
has left him 'absolutely gurgling with delight'. (After some hesitation, Connolly earlier rejected 'Ward '0' 3 (b)').

> 'The Orange Grove' means a great deal to me; I wrote it in a
> kind of drunkenness of composition, completely gripped
> & convinced & compelled by it.

He relates a dream in which she is due to arrive in India on the 26th
and he is 'almost scatty' because he is going into battle on the 24th.
He refers to their unborn child as 'Shan'.

**12 September 1943** (included in *Letters to my Wife*)

> Your longing stirs me darkly & grievously, I long futilely to
> soothe you sometimes, to shake you & rebuke you (with all
> the gentleness in the world, though) at other times, and I feel
> a dark & melancholy confusion rise in me like a turbulent
> mist.

The following passage appears in edited form in *Letters to my Wife*:

> Thank you, Gweno darling, for so much love and thought:
> but oh Gweno PLEASE be easy. Don't fret at it like this,
> sweetheart, please, please, please.

He himself is full of 'confidence & tranquillity'. In an excluded
passage, he protests at the difference between the 'final version' of
'Bread and Stones' and the troopship poem  in *The New Statesman*
and their originals.

**16 September 1943** (not included in *Letters to my Wife*)
He says he is suffering from the 'same doubts & travails &
hardnesses'.

I can feel them in me a little now: and it's such a pity, for you rid me of them so completely, Mererid dear. Will you, again.

**Undated** (not included in *Letters to my Wife* and written en route to his meeting Freda in Bombay)
He recalls their courting days and says he is 'quite certain of us'.

**Undated** (in *Letters to my Wife*, this letter is dated 30 September 1943)

> Darling Gweno, I'm sorry you had to go & marry me. It would have been so much simpler if you'd been charmed away by a fireside faun with a job of national importance such as doing statistical research or editing a literary magazine. Anyone rather than me, darling, for I'm just some animation the world has set flowing and compelled to develop into and out from myself. I learn new things everywhere, all the time; new things form in me & bud & flower & flow out over the streets & deserts & roofs and fishing boats and beggars and poems I encounter or rather find myself amongst. And I know they are necessary and vivid, all these things, and they do something to me and in a queer deep unchained way I belong to them and see & feel with their eyes & nerves. And also in a queer deep unchained way, I've made my peace with life and am willing to go on and into and through and beyond. The only thing that prevents me is my body, which grows tired, and my mind which grows dull, and my heart which has a grief and a love that these things, these perpetual heres & nows, do not permit to exceed them. And it gets constricted and crowded....

**3 October 1943** (not included in *Letters to my Wife*)

> I haven't given the poems a chance to write themselves. I feel like a young mother who has been gadding about & harmed the baby inside her.... I feel some strange poetic recession taking place in me, a withdrawal into some safer fastness. I can't help feeling it's a good event, this inarticulateness I've been feeling more & more in me lately. As for my gay tilt at your outburst against the collier boy & the erotic vision - maybe they've been chastened in the darkness. Only I know somehow that they are fundamentally ME as Hywel's brother motif [Hywel was Gweno's brother] or D.H.

Lawrence's mother and no man should cast off his true self.
It moves him, for better or worse.

*Letters to my Wife* prints a continuation of this letter, dated 30
September: 'I dread the long dry merciless months ahead'. He likens
them to the drying up of his poetry.

**8 October 1943** (not included in *Letters to my Wife*)
Lewis wrote at least twice a week but Gweno wanted him to write
more frequently. He said he could not, not through lack of love but
because of 'this wilful darkness that is my ancient self':

> I wonder sometimes if there is a yellow eyed beast in the
> jungle & that it is me. I would be happier if I knew there
> was such a beast & it was me.

He apologises for not sending her a Christmas card but says he
'couldn't' – 'I don't know why'. (In the letter of 21 November, he
includes a photograph of himself in lieu of the card.)

**11 October 1943** (parts of this do not appear in *Letters to my Wife*)
Lewis recalls the anniversary of his departure from Liverpool. In the
previous letter, he had described their meeting thus:

> It was a mysterious & miraculous event, that. My dark
> dreams breaking into the real flesh of petal and sepal &
> heart & touch overnight.

The occasion was beautiful but left him sad.

He has not been at Lake Kharakvasla long enough to recover the
'communion & sympathy' that led him to write the 'Water Music
and Shadows sequence'.

> I'm sure there are several deep water poems swimming about
> below the surface. And there's a whale of a story in the
> air, something big-boned and definitive, placing objec-
> tively the balances that swung in the monsoon of the
> Orange Grove.

This refers to a project he and Freda thought of collaborating on.
(See the letter of October 14th in *A Cypress Walk*, pp. 159/60)).

In *Letters to my Wife*, the final paragraph of the first part of the letter ends with an ellipsis. It originally continued:

> But oh I'll be glad to come back to you, sweetheart, and to
> lie beside you and need to ask no questions because your
> arms & lips and love have once again become the world &
> the heavens to your child.... God bless you & give you some
> of the love I carry with me in this tropical heat.

In a continuation headed 'Next day', he fantasises about the life
they might have led in India and says fighting against the world is
done 'at a cost':

> I know I'm paying, and sometimes I feel like asking you not
> to expect too much of me. If I bring myself back to you,
> Gweno dearest, I'll have done as much as I've the strength
> to do. If it's worn we out a little in the wear & tear you
> mustn't be grieved.... all my effort is to preserve what you
> want me to preserve, & to find what you say is worth
> finding – that betterness in me that you value.

**17 October 1943** (not included in *Letters to my Wife*)
Back in camp after an exercise, he is overjoyed to read her letters.
He is 'fit & brown & glad'.

**21 October 1943** (included in *Letters to my Wife*)
He recalls visiting Bombay and the books by war-time writers he
bought there. The tone is resolute.

**26 October 1943** (not included in *Letters to my Wife*)
In more reflective mood, he says he has begun writing poetry again.

**29 October 1943** (not included in *Letters to my Wife*)
Ill in bed with a fever, he discusses the grouping of the poems for
his new collection. It is to be called '*Ha! Ha! Among the Trumpets*'
and finish with a section including 'The Journey', 'The Run-In' and
'Bivouac'. The love poems will be scattered through rather than
gathered into one section. He wants to omit 'Sacco writes to his Son'
on the grounds that it is too literal a transcription of Sacco's letter to
his son. (Ferdinando Sacco and Bartolomeo Vanzetti were executed
for murder and armed robbery in Boston in 1927.)

**1 November 1943** (not included in *Letters to my Wife*)

He is back in Poona Hospital with malaria.

**2 November 1943** (not included in *Letters to my Wife*)
Once again, he has fallen prey to 'depressing thoughts and morbid reasonings', like 'the horrible slumps & no man's lands I used to stray into' when '20 – 21 – 22'. [Shortly after he joined the South Wales Borderers in December 1941, he told her: 'these days have re-opened old wounds and I can't think without a cold sweat of the terrible anguish I lived in once, when I was 19, 20, 21. I feel I could never live through it again: but perhaps I will, perhaps the next couple of years will have all that and more in store.]

The world appears 'chaotic & brutish and pretty grim & hopeless' to him and he is tired and could not care.

**5 November 1943** (not included in *Letters to my Wife*)
Still in hospital with a bronchial cold, he has 'queer and unpopular thoughts' and feels depressed by the 'Slowness & vastness of the war'. He asks her for photographs of herself – he cannot recall her face. More than anything, he would like to travel back with her to Llanthony, which 'has the dark secret that is our kernel of faith and danger'. He no longer courts danger and values balance instead:

> But I believe we will need to seek very near the origins of love when I come back to you: and in them we'll find all that we've missed. I'm sure that in the end we'll find the physical satisfaction that so eluded us & the harmony of our bodies that will produce Shan & Nevin & Alun & Gweno.

Her love is 'the most real thing I possess'.

**9 November 1943** (included in *Letters to my Wife*)
He is back in camp.

**13 November 1943** (included in *Letters to my Wife*)
The letter ends: 'Yours for better or worse Alun', the first time he signs off less than fulsomely.

**18 November 1943** (included in *Letters to my Wife*)

> I'm in the mood nowadays where it isn't wise to sit and think: my thoughts turn too rancid.

**21 November 1943** (included in *Letters to my Wife*)
(See the first paragraph in *Letters to my Wife*.)

> When will I have time (& the mind & the peace of mind) for
> all that is suppressed, jockeyed & heckled and spoilt? Oh
> hurry up, sweetness of all that & heaven too. Does it lie for
> both of us in the same place, the same pursuits? It lies in Shan
> more than in me for you, I think.

He is out of sorts but the 'fundamentals' have been 'solidly laid'.
Even so, 'I'll never be able to take myself for granted'. He thanks
her for the photographs of herself she sent him.

**27 November 1943** (included in *Letters to my Wife*)
Swimming gives him the 'lovely bodily feeling of being well and
balanced upon the earth'. For the rest,

> it's just either sleeping or waking and a universal pining and
> regret that scarcely has any context or reference.

**29 November 1943** (included in *Letters to my Wife)*
In a passage excluded from *Letters to my Wife*, he notes his irritation
at her remark that he 'can sit under a palm tree & contemplate my
navel in the front room'. He tells her 'Love is freedom' and outlines
an idea for

> a sort of symphonic arrangement of people & moods &
> antagonisms within a battalion built round the posting of an
> officer away from the unit just when they're due for action.
> I want it to be lighthearted, satirical and varied – not moody
> & rapt like the others I've written out here.

**3 December 1943** (this appears in amended form in *Letters to my
Wife*. Gweno was back in Aberystwyth again)
He describes 'the darkness that has gathered there [in his head] like
water in a sump' and has grown

> since the day I made those awful black out blinds for Elm
> Grove & you & I had had that queer premonitory holiday
> together in Llangranog.

The letter ends:

And you & I being made for ever & ever in the darkness we couldn't pierce or bear. Goodbye, darling. My Love, Alun.

**6 December 1943** (included in *Letters to my Wife*)

I am aware always of forces more powerful than my self. They are the determinants: and it's always been a hard fight for me to keep my self as an individual integrated against these forces. Some of them are integrating forces – like you: some are destructive forces.

**11 December 1943** (not included in *Letters to my Wife*)
His meeting with Glyn in Poona

seems to bear out the feeling of drifting away from many old and established things that I get so often – and the knowledge that I don't know where I'm drifting to or how much I am diminished in the process. I only know that you are there, in the beginning and in the event, and that just by being you you steady me and subtly attract and call me, and that I am moving towards the unknown destination in your company.

He thinks 'personal existence seems a luxury now'.

(*Letters to my Wife* prints a letter dated 15 December; I read no such letter.)

**18 December 1943** (not included in *Letters to my Wife*)
He sends 'lots of love' to 'sweet sweet Gweno':

And although I know that whatever I do & whatever becomes of me I can not wrong you or betray or leave you ever, ever, yet this daily drifting & accepting is cruel & harmful & takes incessant toll.

He continues:

… we won't stop singing & loving & burning in the heart whose parallels move unswervingly within us like the clean rush of steel railway lines to infinity & in nearness. Oh Gweno, Gweno, Gweno, I love you & hug you and love you & hug you & lie softly & blessedly with you – I know it matters when, but also it doesn't matter when, on the level

of apprehension where to have been is to be for ever and the
'once upon the time' is the 'happily ever after' of our true&
undeniable myth. I'm real, you're real.

Their love is his 'bulwark'.

**Undated** (not included in *Letters to my Wife*)
He fantasises about their meeting again in Bryngwyn in Mountain
Ash. They would read, wash up and go to bed,

> warm as fieldmice all the night of sleigh bells and wind &
> rain & old simple stories. And that'll be a night attractive to
> Shan and she'll perhaps then come & inhabit us.

The letter ends: 'A lover's Christmas... & a husband's thoughts'.

**15 December 1943** (included in *Letters to my Wife*)
He concludes his account of his meeting with Glyn. *Letters to my
Wife* omits the fact that he has finished typing a story based on it.

**22 December 1943** (included in *Letters to my Wife*)
He describes his first 'unique' experience of the jungle:

> You enter a separate world, remote, unperturbed, indifferent,
> serene:and it makes your own troubles & fears fall away &
> remain outside in the world of roads & spaces.

**25 December 1943** (included in *Letters to my Wife*)
There is a possibility he may be promoted but he insists: 'Alun's
main reason for living is to write'.

**28 December 1943** (included in *Letters to my Wife*)
He has started to shed his despair.

**3 January 1944** (included in *Letters to my Wife*)

> I wonder how we'll react when we're together again? Will
> we be suspicious of Life and wary & thrifty? Or will the old
> exultation and magic enclose and transmute us again? I
> suppose we'll burn as long as there's sulphur in the match,
> won't we?

The published version excludes a comparison of her with Bette Davies.

**5 January 1944** (included in *Letters to my Wife*)
He reports that 'miserable volatile me' is 'this January in the wilds'.

**9 January 1944** (included in *Letters to my Wife*)

> And I've got a feeling, dear, that another phase of my life is ending now, and the climacteric is near. I'm glad, and I feel something working blindly towards a position from which it can see & plan, & have faith vand work enduringly, not among things that crumble as they are made and are meaningless in history & in the heart. Let it come: it's the old cry for the Saviour, let it come. We need it so much, thou and I.

**15 January 1944** (included in *Letters to my Wife*)

> But everything is fluid in me, an indignant mass of experience without shape or plot or purpose.

In an omitted detail, he writes: 'I'm sorry I can't write another Orange Grove'. He has, though, completed five new short poems and a story.

**18 January 1944** (not included in *Letters to my Wife*)

> I become so dry & brittle here, I don't know how to overcome it.

He longs to be with her

> to save myself & be enlarged. All I want is to become natural again. When? For how long? Make me come out of my grisly shell and stop hunching up in myself, please.

**22 January 1944** (included in *Letters to my Wife*)
She must decide whether or not to include 'Letter from a Long Way' in the 52 poems of *Ha! Ha! Among the Trumpets*. If she excludes it on the grounds that it is too personal, he suggests replacing it with either 'Renewal' or 'The Soubrettes'. (Gweno omitted the poem but replaced it with neither of these alternatives.)

**24 January 1944** (not included in *Letters to my Wife*)
He wonders what will happen to his 'effects' should he be imprisoned
or die. Should he survive, he might become a foreign correspondent.
'It's funny, my sister & my wife have the same name, isn't it?'

**26 January 1944** (included in *Letters to my Wife*)

> I've put a huge burden on you always through my poems
> which have spoken more openly of the dangers & the jeopard-
> ies than either of us could or would with the living voice. I
> don't want them to mean foreboding to you or to me. They're
> universal statements if they're anything. They feel the world
> & they mean all that is involved in what is happening.

Their peace

> will stand in despite. So deep down we have no need to
> worry. I know we do: naturally: like hell: but I can't tell you
> the peace you planted in me any more than I can tell you I'll
> come back, Alun to Gweno, in the end.

In a passage excluded from *Letters to my Wife*, he notes that his
new friend in Karachi, Michael Clark, has been wounded and is now
in Palestine. Clark told him that

> people hide in their depressions & use it to excuse
> themselves from being energetic & bold when the situation
> is perilous or difficult. There's a lot in what he says – he was
> telling me off really & I've taken his words to heart. But a
> neurosis isn't easy to cast off. It has a life of its own & justi-
> fies itself, too.

**31 January 1944** (not included in *Letters to my Wife*)
He is

> wondering how such grace should have come to me who am
> so fitful and dubious a puff of wind. Have I been a man since
> you've known me, Gwen? I was always sure that you were
> the truth & the way to me: when I lost you I lost myself; and
> now that I'm losing myself again I want you more than I can
> let myself realise. I've always been accursed in some part of
> me: there's been an unreliable element, a vagueness, an
> embryo surrender, a feeling of worthlessness in me.

He says 'there've been times today when I could hardly keep myself in bounds'. She must not fret if his letters become irregular:

> Let us have room & time – we're not a short-term process of life, are we? O believe there is room in the life we merged into and guessed at and touched for infinities of failure & loss, going away and spiritually dying – and returning, returning, how, when, where? I don't feel now nor ask you to feel any faith in the chance sof time & war – but there is much, very much, that can't be touched now, can't be disturbed, can't be reached. That's safe, anyway. No matter what – .

**6 February 1944** (not included in *Letters to my Wife)*
He has been back to Poona for a day and a night to meet Dick Mills. In the last six months, he has finished one story and poem: 'The Reunion' and 'The Jungle'.

> I seem to want to avoid [writing], minimise its worth, dissociate myself from it. I shouldn't, but somehow I am compelled to. If I gave it rein my mind would become even dreamier & more tentative than it is.

The war makes writing impossible. 'So the writing goes by the board'.
    He has been asked to choose a poem of his for an anthology. Dick believes his best poem is 'The Sentry' and he agrees, though 'All day it has rained…' is the 'safest best'. He thinks she might have chosen 'The Unknown Soldier'.

> I'll never be a good soldier, which is sad in a way; but I wasn't made of that cast. I've been a long time finding it out – & I'm humble with the knowledge.Let me get back to something I am more natural to, please, please, please.

**9 February 1944** (not included in *Letters to my Wife*)

> …you know the cloud that comes over the mind: I'm in a useless phase now.

He wants to make something of himself. His love for her has

> always a richness of its own, and a strong pillar that is strong and beautiful like the pillars of Llanthony whether I am strong or weak.

He recently saw 'Now Voyager' with Bette Davies and was 'terribly moved'. Davies played a neurotic who fights for 'sanity & liberation'.

**11 February 1944** (not included in *Letters to my Wife*)
He sends her some 'precious manuscripts':

> I've been like a limping man lately, hoping to run and giving it up & trying again & being angry with his limp. It's a bad old mood.... Every morning for weeks I've wakened into the crazy machinery of anguish: and it's a colossal task to cast it away & be free & give myself a chance. It's because of all these failures that I tell you I'm an unsatisfactory husband: and because of them also I shrink from committing myself to any great task. [He refers to his refusal of a staff officer's job in Karachi.] Oh yet sometimes, sometimes Life leaps & exults & is exquisite in vein & nerve & cell: then I can truly love & create. But these darker cycles make me with-hold myself.... I know...that you see me otherwise and know you can make me in your image. But I've literally had to go away from you, darling, and in this no-man's land into which I press with a sober reluctance and a careful sadness I'm bound to be lost from time to time. I hate to think I am increasing your burden, your letters have been so brave these few months. And I want to be telling you that it's my way, always has been & always will be. And I'm telling you there are these limits, these vagaries in me. And these silences when I neither write nor know nor have joy in what I do. I know when they're over that they're the making of me, but oh God they're hard to endure..... I've got a hunch you'll not need to come out. I don't think I'll be away from you for the duration.

He might become a prisoner of war: 'I've always wanted to escape ever since mother sent me to Cowbridge!'

He asks her to omit 'Pastorals', 'Indolence', 'The Soubrettes' and 'Renewal' from *Ha! Ha! Among the Trumpets* (they were excluded) and to include 'A Letter from a Long Way', though he leaves the final decision to her.

**12 February 1944** (not included in *Letters to my Wife*)

> ...darling wife, be happy as far as Alun is concerned, for you've made him Alun.

**17 February 1944** (included in *Letters to my Wife*)
He believes the war will continue for another two or three years, so
she might consider coming out to India after all.

**20 February 1944** (included in *Letters to my Wife*)
Writing to me on 10th June, 1981, Gweno quoted the following
extract:

> I'm sitting in momentary comfort & peace under a fan with
> electric light & I've been reading 'Wales' quietly to myself.
> There's a lot of thought in Wales isn't there? It's a very inter-
> esting country, I do declare, & I hope I see lots more of it.
> And write more of it, though you find my collier-student-
> socialist such a bore! Maybe he'll grow up into someone
> worth marrying, Gwen, one day.

This is absent from *Letters to my Wife*, though the following is not:

> ... you've rid me of the black mood & distress of mind I have
> been labouring under [.] I'm just steady & square now & give
> as good as I get.

**23 February 1944** (his last letter; in *Letters to my Wife*, it is dated
'End of February 1944'.)

> ...the sun is bright and gay and everything sparkling and
> scrubbed, and if it were ten years ago or ahead I'd have a
> very gay scrubbed heart as well.

He cannot speak of his love for her:

> ... it's of no consequence to the fighting world, the world of
> telegrams and troop trains and supply columns. But it's
> singing out in my heart.... The darkness & the threats are for
> another part of ourselves. And the long self torture I've been
> through is resolving itself now into a discipline of the
> emotions of you & me and Shan and the Remington baby....
> I feel that my grasp is broader & steadier than it's been for a
> long time. I hope it's true, because that's how I want to be:
> and the rest of me, is invulnerable. I want you to know that,
> Gweno, sweet wife.

The letter ends:

I must run now, darling. Sorry I am to go. And god be in our heads & in our eyes & in our understanding. Buy me a typewriter when somebody has one to sell and I'll buy you a beautiful beautiful emerald or maybe a sapphire or maybe something neither of us know. For keeps for you for love. All my love: Alun.

The reference to typewriters arises from the fact that typewriters were scarce during the war and so more than usually valuable.

# APPENDIX TWO
## *The Karachi Journal*

The following extract from Lewis's Karachi journal contains a number of draft poems that appear in a stream of reflection containing related images and thoughts; several poems were later drawn from it.

Underlined words signify authorial cancellation. Query marks indicate uncertain readings.

The extract begins with a draft of 'The Journey' which differs from the version in *Ha! Ha! Among the Trumpets*.

There was also the memory of Death
And the recurrent irritation of ourselves
Two of us had wives, you know.
But our loins were only a thread of silk
Spun endlessly, breathlessly & simply,
Beyond & beyond this living, this loving,
This calculation & provision, this fearing.
We remembered their shrugs, but knew
Nothing is final, and needed no singing,
Needing no couches, zithers & cinemas,
Derek he curled up nightly like a dog.
I being a romantic stubbed my eyes
With stars & the great wheeling shapes of fate
But the wind so wound its ways about us
We neither of us heard
The voice calling us, calling us,
The anguish like rain softening & rotting the gourd
                                        The kindling wood,
And the night's appeal was drowned in the
Susurrance of insects
The cricket's loudness, the rolling automatic roar of
                            The endless insect.
How could we guess, oh Life, oh suffering
& patient life,

We among the camels & donkeys & waterfalls –
Oh how could we guess?
[*page break*]

The following appears to be a new poem which Lewis drew on for
'The Orange Grove'.

And she whose song is the world spinning
                    cosmetised
Whose age is <u>buried</u> (?) in the paints of space
indolence is endless space
How many centuries will argue & battle over
            which century will forget to ponder
her unknown, world famous, implacable face?
                              blind
        The <u>unknown</u> lineaments of her unknown face
                              None may kiss

        white & sloped      the <u>onward</u>
Her <u>grey bent</u> shoulders <u>glass press</u>
            casting round her lambent streams
But <u>those who drown in</u>        <u>waves</u>
        sl in with her seething      grace
<u>She takes with hunger & indifference</u>
Of this Magdalene of our dreams.
Upon the bleating queens [?], the weary slaves.

She has a [?] on God & pursues him
                    Of our frightened dreams
This Magdalene fiction of <u>despair</u>
But in the Satanic languor of her bed,
        An olden monster.
[*The last three lines above are scored out*]
<u>A child she did not want</u>
            And from her wild demonic languors grew
            She sought

But he – oh he is the terrible one
The silence behind the thunder, <u>the</u> after the guns,
He is the owner of the screeching cosmos.
                Heart-beat <u>throb</u> [?] drums & drums
His multiengined monstrous

                    word chagrin

In The inescapable insistent <u>wage</u>
From which no living brute may turn,
   The ineluctable vegetable God Will
<u>And his smile is muscular</u>
   And in the croaking night I hear him groaning
And with my dying ears I hear him still.

Ho


And     mad
<u>Oh in</u> this / dinning vortex of our error
        the
          <u>wade</u> flesh stone
Those The two ancestral
           Columns of her thighs
Swirls round the bladed/
        [?]
[?] <u>The sleep stone flesh of eternity</u>
    petrified splendour of eternity
Whose dust is love,
And the hard opals of her tranquile eyes.
Flash from the tranquil opal of her eyes

Her wild demonic languors lie
Silent behind the thunder, [<u>before</u>] beside the guns
And when some mortal plucks her swirling garment
Her multi[?] engined heart beat drums & drums.

The inescapable insistent word
From which no living brute may turn
The chagrins of the croaking night
The livid torrid suns that blood or burn
      em ness   <u>void the dead suns</u>
        passions
Corruptions that her splendours burn
        sure moods
And so the dinning vortex of our error
Swirls round the fluted columns of her thighs
And all
The petrified splendour of eternity
<u>Flashes</u> flames from the tranquil opals of her eyes.


The following is a draft of 'The House', the first poem to Freda.

It seemed there
No cessati
                    we
Beloved when I stood
And saw each other standing there
Suddenly, I did not know that all
That all The ordinary days
Had [?] in my better shell
Had vanished from
                    the earth,
Had fallen from my
And in my heart again
The glittering delight
That knows how the trees
The passion, the pain
          And the – dearth. [? 'death']
That releases
What did I know but you
Had brown eyes, tawny hair,
And that you also were standing
With the calmness that protects
A foreknowledge of what must be
[*page break*]
So we could talk in the window
Of other people other things
          And wait softly &
(No-one) While we waited tranquilly
For delight [?] that time brings.
                    that  brought nothing
I know  I  came poorly
                    had lost
But                         closed
Heavily
The roads closed, the seas mined,
The   And all else ignored
That [?] child grieved

And did my hands dream
Of the touch of your hair?
And did you know then
How
That I had been closed
By the steady expectation
And preparing of death?
          How      hope

[What?] did you plan
Of  That hardness to break
[*page break*]
Of the man who no longer asks
For love & its ache
Did you know his calloused hands
Would grow mild in your hair
And all he had renounced
Would  More steadily then in despair
Would live
Wake again answer when you spoke.


The next lines come from 'What is love?'.


At best
What is love at least?
A way of dignifying death
                their
So the poor must lay a wreaths
And the last letter before the battle
        Is no confessor to the priest
Is one of love the instinct breeds.
But             simplest impulse prompts
                    Instinct breathes
And that which ordinary days
Have fortified, the certain end
Is or seems to be denied
By.
I kept nothing but courage
And sufficient laughter
[*page break*]


At the foot of the next page, the following appears:


I kept no thing that mattered hitting back
Having put away the map]
What is love at best?
This silence that accepts the world
This child at your breast.


Beloved I ask not
                fruition
For time nor assurance
I know that in writing

And thinking I die
That to look at your photograph
        To deny
Means it is gone        cessation
        Proves the cessation
Beloved I ask of you nothing now
Of the living certainty.
But   The living delight
        so
The truth suddenly
                        over us
of love that flung, I know not how
        Ask we not why
Its glowing veils about a vanished Now.
        The vanished Now in which I dream
But is [?] Beloved I am not
        Across the battle lines, the famine?


Then comes a draft of 'The Map':

I wrote your name upon the map
then I laid
and let the map away indifferently
        map because
because the world rep  the world
And danger & diseases
        Every risk became a death
And every pause a [black? blood?] disease
And   And I was willing that the world
                pleasure with my breath
should have its will with me
[*page break*]
I laughed to keep my spirits up
Having put away the map

And fought my way into the world.
        And I thought everything had changed
        Until on the fifth day
        Our other activities demanded us

But   How could I know your name had
changed
And then your name became yourself
        the world became your name.

And  And you yourself were standing there
Among the <u>ordinary deaths</u>
                                        shame
                        teacups & the <u>deaths</u>
Your brown resisting eyes, your tawny hair
                wide brown
I know your eyes, <u>your lips, your tawny hair</u>
Your
<u>Beloved</u>  <u>I did not desire</u>
                [<u>nother</u>? mother?]
And map & world & death & space
Meant little                when I saw your face
                Released me


This is followed by what appears to be a new poem:

The days destroy us
And the nights assist

And never lean, exhausted so
With love & gentleness & pain
<u>Within that</u> tall & slender
Among the <u>eucalyptus</u> trees again?

That we must kiss & then must go
                single
<u>Dash to a separate joy, acting to pass us</u>
<u>- Eternity exhausting</u>        so
All And must never see ourselves again.
[*page break*]
I lay in sickness in the world
And heard that you were lying sick.
I dreamed In sickness I forgot the world of the map,
                The battle & [famine?]
But you And you became another world
                <u>Revolu</u> unapproachable in space
                        And  I did not know your silken lap
                <u>The red c</u> Now your animated face


The next lines are a draft of 'Ways' (in *Ha! Ha! Among the
Trumpets*).

                        Trees so tall & [gl?]
                Tall & slender <u>blue gum</u>

        & with      exhausted so
With tallness slenderness, that each <u>on each</u>
      Leaned on the other, as the
They leaned, as breathless loves do,
<u>Who sit: we</u>
As I on you.

The following lines are written vertically along the inner margin:

    I know not anything beside
    And when you lay within my arms
    The human passion in me cried
With the voice of
    <u>As many men</u> every man
Who [?] had that wound within his side
    And knew the beauty of the world
    And hated that by which he died.

The poem continues:

    What else but slenderness & death
    Could we two lovers ever know
          summer
    Swaying in the drifting rain
    Save that Time has made it so
    And would not do again
        What will not
           Although the trees remain.

    Tallslender eucalyptus trees,
    Tall & slender & young
        The trees surrounded our embrace
            We were there
    There were the trees & we <u>you & I</u>
The pale blue
    Trees exhausted so
    With tallness & with slenderness they leaned
        each     <u>as lovers do</u>
    Each on the other, And did we know
    What else could we, beloved, know
     waying
    <u>Standing</u> in the drifting rain
    <u>But that lovers must kiss & go</u>
    <u>And only the</u>    remember with

I would rather have it so
Love & all its bitter pain
[*page break*]
I had the h
For long I had made it my purpose
To be a good officer in the battalion
To be serious & yet always laughing
     the   of men
To be equal  and to understand
                          kill
And to go with friends to the ending.
         task
I know this  had hardened me
                & hard & strong
And I was humble in [this?]   hardness
I knew your hands could stroke it all away
Could            your
    Hurting me with gentleness
              your
Could Breaking me with tenderness
    Bringing into the agitated [plantations?].
    The wheel of wind and the white birds in the branches
    The perpetual shimmer & excitation of peace
    Instead of the coldly stern tranquillity of war.
    The rock you touched became a stream
    And all reality an ugly dream
    I know you kissed me in my sleep
  And        waking or in dream
    Always, you will be
    [*page break*]
    You bend above
            the
    Bending over my blindness in my head
        Raining    all your    all your
    Your grace bestowing a quickness, beauty
        Dark plantations of the dead
    On the morose, the taciturnly dead.

Next comes 'Hands', another of the Freda poems.

    I love the hands of children & old men
    The barber's has hands in my hair
    The barber's hands in my hair
    And the masseur has hands

<u>Friends and enemies' hands</u>
           the hands of friends
Hands soothe and ease and enemies of war,
The great painters were fascinated by hands
Gnarled & beautiful as trees
That wind & storm & time have twisted
To see the
Into loves & agonies
That now are flowing from your hands
That hold my face between your knees
          lonely in too many lands
And <u>I have sought in many lands</u>
And hardened by strange enemies
And I have wandered for your hands
For their restless singing ease
The lines upon your small white palms
And the long white [beeches?] of your arms
And the young plantations of your heart
Where we meet & cling & part.
[*page break*]
Life became
   grew
It <u>never</u> too simple to dissemble
Being among soldiers & peasants
I had <u>their</u>  the                              lives
       Learnt endurance of their ways
And ordinary suffering      for
And <u>the</u> a shelter of leaves <u>to sleep in</u>.
And the sharpening of knives
       grinding fine a thrust

How could I help but tremble
       gate
Entering your <u>house</u>
And discovering you there
Among <u>With</u> the tall <u>clear</u> windows
           blue
<u>And the children's laughter</u>
Oh more beautiful than fate.
With sunlight on your tawny hair

    I did
Yet did I not dissemble
Nor did I hide myself from you

Remembering the soldiers & peasants
        told you of their        ways
And I talked of them to you lives
And the endurance of their      alas
And you were the peasant & I the soldier But we
We
An  And x the clear blue sky of love because the sky was blue
Each Forgot the darkness & the knives
                sowing
(I knew your gentle hands held all my days.)

Next comes a draft of 'Peasant Song'.

The seed is costly
(And Plant it carefully
I have only the mighty earth
[*page break*]
Will you kiss me now
And With mysterious birth
Will you give me birth?
Long ago I built this hut
Of bamboo poles & leaves
        [thin?]
The leaf has turned
                Rod & reed
For Bless this hut of stick & leaf
This shelter to sleep in
        And while you are sleeping
I will turn the mighty earth
And lie beside you, till you wake
                lift
The fields will sing & rear their lovely heads
                with rustling corn
[?] the sun & rain one kind
And we shall go reaping.
        the
And If sun & rain are kind
The fields will be abundant in my heart
                the love within my
And plenteous as my mind.
Oh, why are you weeping?
You are my woman, m
And I your man & you my woman always
Oh why are you weeping?

[*page break*]

The following is part I of 'Ways' (in *Ha! Ha! Among the Trumpets*):

It had been easier, not loving.

I knew I had grown harder than the trees
In which I held you all the afternoon,
The tall blue slender saplings leaning
Each on each, their strength outgrowing.
And suddenly we two were swaying
Each upon the other leaning.

It had been easier, not loving.

The draft continues:

Why did you stroke away my hardness
            impetuous
Why with your            gentleness
            sin cured[?]
Why with burning tenderness
            headstrong      stubbornness
Did you Excoriate my bitter hardness?
            And from the iron trance of war
            with the  grave
And bring the [?] the excitement of peace?
            Unnerve me with the thrill of peace
The war has not yet ended.
Can you [?] the slaughter cease?
You, more beautiful than peace?
[*page break*]
And when The blood red vortices of error
Face into calm & life oh will I see you then
                                    you come then
Out of the darkness & the terror
You,

Then come the first 13 lines of part II of 'Ways'.

It was much easier, all alone.
The tall slim saplings were exhausted so
With tallness and with the slenderness they bowed
At the touch of wind or bird.

And the lightness of your hands
Bowed me also with their guerdon,
Love being gravel in the wound
When the silent lovers know
Swaying in the misty rain
The old oppression of the burden
Growing in them as they go,
Though trees are felled and grown again,
Far and farther each from each.

The draft continues:

And Will you come to me again
                              In some other
When this night drags somewhere  place
                              on the battle field

And will you find that other place
And will you make the distance yield
And will you let me kiss & kiss your face?
The day is kinder than the night
I love the day friendliness of light
        [send?] a quick
And boyish           enthusiasm of a boy
The ardours of the boy
                              resilience
Taking hardness [?] lightly,    with joy.
[*page break*]
                        rocky coasts
And yet I chose the grey rocks of the night
And wand bore the hardness of the rocks
Until the rock you touched became a stream
I know you kissed me in my sleep
And always, waking or in dream,
I know you bend above my dark blind head
    Pouring With           and
Raining all your quickness all your beauty
Waking
All that I had thought was dead.
        -----------------
'Wood Song' follows (see *Ha! Ha! Among the Trumpets*):

The pine trees cast their needles softly
Darling for your gipsy bed

And the tall blue saplings swaying
Whisper more than can be said.

Piteously the world is happening
Beyond this cool stockade of trees
Enduring passions penetrate
These quiet rides with agonies
That love can never consummate.

And we must go because we love
Beyond ourselves, beyond these trees
That sway above your golden head
Till wind and war and sky and dove
Become again the murmur of your breath
And your body the white shew-bread.
[*page break*]

The next is a draft of 'Beloved Beware', another of the Freda poems:

Love is not born complete
             dry
Love needs time to <u>grow</u>
     Its wings, born of water
     Like the dragon fly
<u>Like children or trees</u> -

2   Before you say let it be so
      Beloved

3   <u>Darling</u>, beware

Have 1   <u>Is there</u> room or time to grow?
we

4   Love is already there.
       ------------------------

When you look at me
Do I not answer
   As if you were dancing
<u>When you dance</u>
And I your dancer
      ----------------------

Behind the social smile
The millrace of the blood
<u>Hammers on my holding smile</u>
Beats against my smile
And am I answering your smile
Or the millrace of your blood?

---------------------
Think that in the head
The
And honeycombs are sweet
That that all the bees are dead
And under stress we change
What book of chemistry
Can tell what forms will gorw
From
Out of the corporeal mystery?
-----------------------
Love me not for what I am
Love me for myself
Only love me if you can
Give what no one else can claim
For both
Betw the woman & the man
Wither at the ouch of
Are utterly destroyed by shame.
-----------------------
If you love too much
By loving me, forswear
    music
The magic of the Now.
Beloved, beware
Love is already there.
-----------------------
[*page break*]

This represents the draft of a new poem, 'The Heart Compels':

The heart compels
I have good cause to fear
        pains [?]
The dark compulsion of the heart
        love brings
When life is too dear [?]
            comes so near.

[g]Yet I follow it devoutly
With every thought & every sense
Holding love as death is
Without recompense
Shorn of

**(The last four lines above are scored out.)**

Love is headstrong, moody,
Unrelenting, singular
Should you drive it off
It will haunt afar.

(I open my doors)
Living by an inner law
With all other laws at war.
[*page break*]

The heart compels
          in wonder
My ways into confusion
And love itself
Tears me asunder

Next, a draft of 'Peasant Song' (see *Ha! Ha! Among the Trumpets*):

         Always always the plough man goes
And    Only the Plough & stays
         The plough
         Oh carefully the seed is planted
         God grant that it thrive
              you
         And when I am dead
              Shall feel it    deep
         Keep it alive
                   know that within you the earth is alive.
         The earth is all alive.

         [?] in sleep [?] strives [?] & ?
         Bearing endless days,
         Giving, somehow, praise.
         [*page break*]
         Love has done with peace
         Love is at war
            [?]  the  [?]
         [?] against the frontiers
         Her harsh [?] engines
                 from
         Thunder afar.
         Then I [?] [?] the [?]

[?] All [?] in battle
                        air
On earth & sea & sky
This your mighty engine [?]
I care little, finding thee,
If I live or if I die.

The following is written round the top and sides of the pages:

Love always calls me
Again the heart compels
            all signs
And I must go, & gladly,
Into this new

Love shall rid you of [own?] –
Weariness
You shall love in weariness
As new

Love [?] [?] about a being
In the ache of weariness
You go:
Even in flight you stay
Power [?]

Love must hurt & maim [?]
Its beauty throws up terror & [?]
            sometimes breeds
Treads the green pastures
Leaving a desert shore

Next is a draft of 'Nothing about the Dead':

            The surface of the earth is scratched
            Over all the continents
                        burial
            With the gravestones of my friends.
But         I sit in the desert quietly
            And see their friendly lineaments
            Remembering their laughing faces
            And
            Till a quietness descends
            From the blindness of the sky

That    s all
Gathering the casual sounds –
The
Of restless lemurs in the trees,
Uncertain pipes in the dar
A peasant soldier's febrile flute,
The slink and snarl of desert hounds
The susurrance of insects
                    Cicadas

And
Into a [?] tremulous still &
                [?]        [?]
        Something pitiful and mute.
    I will not think of them for long
[page break]
A dream's length, a heart's
Dream & intuitions go.
Tomorrow in the desert & the guns
The heart will harden
        Heart hardens, sheds its song
                clings to the peaks [?]
        Love is unbelievable as snow
        And love    retreat to peaks of snow
        Elated, And all the cosmos runs
            While
        Like blood away, like blood away,
        Hard And
        [?] with terror & elation
        I shall have enormous hands
        My massive hands will tear
        That will tear against        the day
                    dryscratched
        and reach the [?]            lands
                    desiccated
        where my laughing comrades lie & wait
        (My silent)        enters
                    comes upon one suddenly
        Of my That no one goes to willingly
            For which you do not pay
        Ending your
            With sufferance or poverty
            And where you may,
                    you cannot
        Like blood away, like blood away

And what can love or friendship say
One way or the other way?

Two prose passages are included in the journal. The first contains the
showers episode and is preceded by an account of Lewis's laughing
and feeling 'exquisitely alone' and 'virginal' while he swims in a
river and includes a description of the Indian scene:

> There are many sadnesses, justified & inevitable & estab-
> lished: why should I make another? I make no sadnesses –
> and last night I was singing and there was my death quite
> clear & familiar at last after all the groping & revulsion and
> I sang of it in my tuneless man's voice Did she be close unto
> thee, Billy Boy, Billy Boy? Yes she lay close unto me as the
> bark is to the tree. And me Nancy tickled me fancy oh my
> darling Billy Boy: And the places on the map faded away
> from me pleasantly & the jungles of Burma came towards
> me & flowed round me familiarly & I could count the days
> that remained neatly, in a neat pile on a white cloth, & I know
> that this little gesture, this joy of my pen writing this word,
> is the good spending of one of those days.
>
> Though the world be wrong & commit men's
> blasphemies and deadly enemies against itself I will not add
> to those lecheries in the days that remain, nor hope less or
> love less, but more yea more & more love & ever love, & be
> less & less the nothing that does not exist & cannot breathe.
>
> I am glad & I am in love & I don't care.

<br>

>                         ineluctable
> Sadnesses manifold, (inevitable &) established
>                         everywhere in India.
> Grow as the rough grass, [?] with hunger
> I shall not add another, this is singing
> Counting my days upon my fingers
> Neat pile of days on a white napkin
> Now after all the groping & revulsion
> Come clean at last & I entertain my death
> With singing Did she lie close unto thee?
>                 Yes she lay close unto me
> As the bark is to the tree, my billy boy
> And my nancy tickled my fancy, Billyboy.
>
> The innumerable places on the map
> Fade from me pleasantly the jungles wind

                        coils
           Their mortal end about me dulcetly
           And this sweet joy of writing is the right spending
                              me      ninety
           Of one day that remains out of seventy.
           Tho' the world commit countless blasphemies
           I will not add dismay to its [?] treacheries
           But more love, more & more Yea
           Nor love less, but more & more love          this I
           And ever more love, growing less & less       bequeath
           The nothingness that exists not, cannot breathe  the stories
           This I write to you love, to whom.
                                       river
                     To you   aretheour songs
                           This I write to you love, to whom
                           the stories are the river('s)
                           You to whom we owe songs.

The second prose passage in the journal describes the sesamum field:

    Fields of golden sesamum, pollen trickling in untidy yellow
    streams down your green overalls & leaden boots, makes [?]
    of the earth in 50 yards of deep yellow flowers & you kneel-
    ing away among them listening to the order of a man you
    hate – listening coldly & obeying coldly & exactly because
    hatred takes away warmth. And later your heart is hot with
    an unforgivable sorrow kneeling over a man you love who
    has bled away in your hands, hiding swiftly his horrible
    wounds and gently slowly reluctantly his unresponsive face.

The journal ends with 'Indian Day' (see *Ha! Ha! Among the Trumpets*) and the draft of a new poem:

                                           breathe
            To whom nothingness is a thing that cannot
            Exist or breathe to whom time dulcetly
            Winds its sweet tragedies about
            Whom time's sweet --- jungles soft about
                                        dulcetly surround
            And stories are the songs of the rivers sing
                              at night
            Seeking the ocean's [?] turbulence
     Know           in your [?] on this      of madness
     On [?]   India. Torn by a century's wilderness

Many good men have entered, Now be brave
                                    be whole & modest,
                                    Without terror
As as a child be generous
            the [?]   that now contains
Bear as a child within you your huge error.
Endure what all must suffer
Without miracle, without saviour.


                              purgatory round
Be healed    The monsoon blows a small century
            About you yet be
            Your goodness & bewilderment Be modest
            Many good
            Good men know madness without terror
            Bear as a child within you this monstrous
                                    sweeping error.

**End**

# NOTES

## The principal texts cited are:

Alun Lewis: *Letters to my Wife*, ed. Gweno Lewis, Bridgend, 1989 (LW)
Alun Lewis: *Collected Poems*, ed. Cary Archard, Bridgend, 1994 (CP)
Alun Lewis: *A Cypress Walk*, ed. Freda Aykroyd, London, 2006 (CW)
Alun Lewis: *Collected Stories*, ed. Cary Archard, Bridgend, 1990 (CS)
John Pikoulis: *Alun Lewis A Life*, Bridgend, 1991 (AL)
Alun Lewis, *A Miscellany of his Writings*, ed. John Pikoulis, Bridgend 1982 (M)
'A Sheaf of Letters from Alun Lewis, 1941-1943', *Wales*, VIII, 28, February/March, 1948, Part I (W)


## Part One
Page 11: *The continuity between*…: London, p. 9
p. 12: *Teach us demolition*…: 'New World Order, *The Sandpiper*, December 6, 1940; *so many grains*…: unpublished letter to his friend, Mansel Davies; *tremendous trifles*:
unpublished letter to his parents; *imagine*…: Lewis's letters to his parents are, for the most part, unpublished; *I found myself*… letter to the author
p. 13: *I'm sitting*…: unpublished; *Alun in Blunderland*: LW, pp. 114/5; I couldn't possibly…: LW, p. 135; *Though he was sure*…: letter to the author
p. 14: *I'm as restless*…: LW, p. 109; *how much more*…: unpublished; Christopher Cheney, Lewis's tutor at Manchester University in 1935-7, was at this time attached to the General Staff in the War Office; *his history*…: 'The Young Historian: Some Letters from Alun Lewis', *The Anglo-Welsh Review*, 40, Winter 1969, pp. 3-21; 'Autumn 1939…: CP, p. 72
p. 15: 'From a Play': CP, p. 41; 'The Odyssey': CP, p. 80; 'On Embarkation', CP, p. 114
p. 16: *because I want*…: unpublished; *In a few moments: The Funny Bone*, 1956, London, 1958, p. 182

**Part Two**

p. 19: '"*Odi et Amo*"': CP p. 31; 'After Dunkirk': CP, p. 39

p. 20: *His life was*...: While working in Margam in 1947, Ron Berry met Owen, Lewis's platoon sergeant. He recalled: 'While Chalfont [Alun Gwynne Jones, later Lord Chalfont] reported Lewis died in a jeep accident, Owen said Lewis shot himself in a jungle latrine', *In the Frame*, Dai Smith, Cardigan, 2010, p. 237; A shouting...: LW, 330; *my long bamboo*...: CW, p. 166. In an unpublished journal, Lewis described Vivian Popham as 'red tubby, spectacled very confident and efficient, always creased with laughter, a great man for barmaids and carousals in a homely drunken way with all his cronies round him, a very good officer, a little too scornful, a little too confident. What he doesn't know he bloody well doesn't want to know. Which is a satisfactory working principle for a get-on or get-off man.'

p. 21:*He has a weak*...: CW, p. 155; *When I'm*...: CW, 194; *I did not*...: this and subsequent extracts are from Cresswell's letters to the author

p. 22: London, 2000, p. 21

p. 23: *there is not*...: letter to the author; *Another squaddie*...: interview with the author

p. 23: The sheet is in the Public Records Office

p. 24: 'Alun Lewis: The Way Back', Summer 1972, pp. 145-6; 'The Way Back': CP, p. 127

p. 25: *had some kind of*...:13 November, 1966, p. 26

p. 26: *Of course I am*...: letter to the author; no further reference to other citations from Gweno's letters are made in the notes; turned the burning...: *Alun Lewis and the making of the Caseg Broadsheets*, Brenda Chamberlain, London, 1970, pp. 5-6

p. 27: *nearest to complete*: ibid., p. 4; *I was delighted*...: LW, p. 391

p. 28: *poemagogic*: Anton Ehrenzweig, *The Hidden Order of Art*, London, 1967; *release from constraint*...: op. cit., p. 151; *When I think of it*...: CW, p. 80

p. 29: *Poetry Wales*...: Vol. 3, pp. 38-45; 'Attitude': LX, 3, Summer 1938, pp. 7-12; reprinted in CS, pp. 266-75; *intellectual perceptions*...: ibid., p. 270; *impotence to change*...: ibid., 272; *the flowers*...: ibid., p. 274; *Everything*...: ibid., p. 272; op.cit., pp. 41-2

p. 30: *Gweno thinks*: letter to the author; *I have read*...: unpublished commentary by the author

p. 31: op. cit., p. 27

p. 32: *I have read*...: no further reference to other citations from Freda's letters are made in the notes

p. 36: 'Post-Script: for Gweno', CP, p. 54; 'War Wedding': CP, p. 62; 'Midnight in India': CP, p. 162

p. 39: *Gweno, death*...: *In the Green Tree*, London, 1948, p. 39

p. 40: *like the atrophy*...: LW, p. 354; complete atrophy...: letter to Christopher Cheney, unpublished

p. 41: 'In Hospital: Poona (1): CP, p. 140; *we were walking*...: unpublished

p. 42: *you have often*...: LW, p. 241; *You saved me*...: LW, p. 275; ...*that little spiritual*...: LW, p. 247/8; *escape home*...: Lewis to Keidrych Rhys and Lynette Roberts. The published version of Lewis's letters to them, W, excludes this remark; 'Lines on a Young Girl': CP, p. 91

p. 43:*The vagueness*...: CP, p. 156

p. 44: 'Modern Reading': 'Some Letters of Alun Lewis', Summer, 1952; Roland Mathias: see his contribution to the *Poetry Wales* Alun Lewis number, op. cit., pp. 47-77

## Part Three

p. 47: *a tremendous, vivid*...: CW, p. 120; *more beautiful*...: CW, p. 29 (the poem does not appear in CP; the first five lines are printed in CW, p. 17

p. 48: *the steady expectation*...: CW, p. 81; *the greater part*...: CW, p. 110; *Life was too*...: 'The House', unpublished

p. 49: *the hostess*...: CW, p. 155; *God, what*...: CW,p. 89. (Only the first sentence of my quotation is printed; the rest was edited out of consideration for Gweno)

p. 50: *One day*...: *Modern Reading*, p. 16; *dappled moles*...: LW, p. 387; *rose moles*...: CW, p. 130; 'Duration': CS, p. 324; *If we were both*...: CW, p. 90; *last night*...: CW, p. 35; *Last night:* Freda's poems are privately printed in *Straws on the Fire of Love*, n.d.

p. 51: *that bitter day*...: CW, p. 155; *Only love me*...: CP, p. 200; *my whole being*...: CW, p. 83

p. 52: *she was always*...: CW, p. 120; *Unbearable ecstasy*...: CW, p. 21; *I've always*...: CW, pp. 83/4; 'Ways': CP, p. 135

p. 53: *the broken rhythm*...: CW, p. 66

        p. 54: 'Wood Song', CP., p. 151

p. 55: He tried to...: AL, p.181; *Alun stopped*...: CW, p.34

p. 56: I should be...: CW., p 148; *broken rhythm*...: CW, p. 66

p. 57: *the dark lane*...: CW, p. 104; 'The Wood': privately printed; 'The Exquisite Moment': cited in CW, p. 31

p. 58: *this morning*: CW, pp. 63/4; *examining ruthlessly*...: CW, p. 65

p. 59: '*I...write*...: CW, p. 67; 'After Dunkirk', CP, p. 39; *I've always wanted*... : CW, p. 83; *there's an exquisite*...: CW, pp. 98/9

p. 60: *There are situations*...: CW, p. 87; *uncanny understanding*...: CW, p. 81; *a spiritual Parnassus*...: CW, p. 124; *a spontaneous action*...: CW, p. 93; *all today*...: CW, 74, p. 105; *not a* bad *book*...: CW, p. 80; *I hadn't read it*...: CW, p. 93

p. 61: *Oh, Frieda*...: CW, p. 113; *Even in the*...: CW, p. 156; *Darling Frieda*... : CW, p 114

p. 62: *The trouble is*...: CW, pp. 120/121. The second paragraph of my quotation is omitted from CW; *You say something*...: CW, p. 128

p. 63: *swing into*...: CW, p. 81; *a kind of forest fire*...: CW, p. 163; 'The Transmigration of Love': not in CP but published in AL, p. 197 and CW, pp. 24/5; *When Frieda and I*...: unpublished; *I had been virginal*...: CW, p. 137; *holy, body*...: CW, p. 205; *and a nearness*...: CW, p. 212

p. 64: 'In Fear of My Love': privately printed; *I love your poems*...: these lines are omitted from CW; *there was no desperation*...: CW, p. 152

p. 65: *The problem is*...: pp. 157 – 162

p. 66: *I am just an instinct*...: CW, p. 114

p. 67: *When I had to stand...*: CW., p. 143

p. 68: *some brittle nowhere...*: CW, pp 146/7; *the real real...*: CW, pp. 116, 115; *Writing poetry...*: CW, p. 176; *The only things...*: CW, p. 104; *While he was prevented...*: op. cit., p. 20 p. 69: *We hanker after...*: CW, p. 83; *I've growingly...* : CW, pp. 98/9; *a calm independent love...*: CW, p. 99; *I had two...*: CW, p. 124

p. 71: *whatever it was...*: CW, pp. 145/6; *One way or another...*: CW, p. 148; *I know now...*: CW: p. 157; *no time left...*: CW, p. 153; *the veil to fall...*: CW, p. 144; *your letters were...*: CW, p. 167

p. 72: *Away from you...*: CW, p. 157; *I've been wandering...*: CW, pp. 186/7; *I've never been...*: CW, p. 174

p. 73: *I saw you...*: CW, pp. 198/9; *My body was thinking...*: CW, p. 170; *At other times...*: CW, pp. 179/80

p. 74: *I don't need...*: CW, p. 192; *I'm doing nothing...*: CW, p. 190; *I get this...* : CW, p. 195; *I want to mark...*: ibid.; *I'm getting fatalistic...*: CW, p. 200; *there are so many...*: CW., p. 201

p. 75: *Have I lost...*: CW, p. 205; *two great wonders:* ibid., *To be alone...*: ibid., *I couldn't look...*: CW, p. 212; 'Peasant Song' CP, p. 150; 'The Field': CW, p. 91

p. 76: *Frieda Mealie-frock...*: CW, p. 136

p. 77: *Why then this...*': unpublished letter to Dick Mills; 'A Fragment': CP, p. 161; 'To Rilke': CP, p. 124; 'Post-script: for Gweno', CP, p. 54

p. 78: '*In the nights...*': LW, p. 408; 'Midnight in India': LW, p. 408

p. 79: '*... I can't look...*': CW, p. 217; '*Frieda, I can't...*:': CW, p. 218

p. 80: '*You were afraid...*': CW, p. 182

## Part Four

p. 82: London 1966; '*I wish someone...*': *The Richard Burton Diaries*, ed. Chris Williams, New Haven and London, 2013, p. 581

p. 83: '*I have a little snap...*': unpublished letter

p. 84: 'a sifting': LW, p. 391; '*I'll take a header...*: unpublished letter; 'In the Green Tree': London; '*Gleanings from...*': edd. Gweno Lewis and Gwyn Jones, Cardiff, 1946, n.p..

p. 85: '*turning over...*': unpublished letter; '*The letters...*': LW, p. 6

p. 86: 'Alun Lewis My Son', privately published; '*whose life and quality...*': not included in CW; 'The Poet': CP, pp. 78/9

p. 89: 'From a Play': CP, p. 41; '*When I come home...*': *In the Green Tree,,* revised ed., ed. John Pikoulis, Cardigan 2006, p 57; The intelligence *corps*: Lewis had anticipated just such a situation in 'The Earth is a Syllable' a year before

p. 93: op. cit., p. 30; '*It was a painful..*': *The Christian Life and Unitarian Herald*, 10 May 1913, n.p..

p. 94: *Annie Besant...*: the pursuit of spiritual enlightenment through esoteric knowledge was popular among such writers; a journey I have...: Ian Hamilton, op. cit., p.7; a perpetual search...: LW p. 250; there are no landmarks: LW, p. 303; '*a Bible-black...*': *Poetry Wales*, op. cit., p. 29

p. 95: *... it isn't that she...*: CW, pp. 187/8; the trace-kicking...: LW p. 231;

*Thoughts on the Eve of a Great Battle*: M, pp. 124/5; 'Prelude and Fugue', CP, pp. 184/5
p. 96: *the little dashing...*: CW, p. 69; *The school-children...*: op. cit..; the distance between Gwladys and Tom may be suggested by a report in the Aberdare Leader in 1948 of a speech he made to a visiting party of young Danes in his capacity as Director of Education:

> I hope you will not mix us up with those foreign English. We have a wonderful language and 1,999,999 out of 2,000,000 Welshmen are poets. Their poetry is alliterative. Listen to a Welsh poet's description, in a line, of the Rhondda Valley. 'Cwm cil, fel cam ceiliog.' We are an older people then the English and in the centre of Aberdare we have erected a statue to the conductor, Caradog.

*The Biographical Index of W.W. Price Aberdar*, n.d., p. 272
p. 97: *... he lived in a place'*: 'The Case of Alun Lewis: A Divided Sensibility', *Llafur*, 1981, p. 26; *my Orphean uncle:* CW, p. 73; 'Bequest': CP, p. 191
p. 98: Sarah Jane Evans, interview with the author; *she told John Lehmann...: The Open Night*, London, 1952, p. 111; *Pleasant Place*: unpublished; *His relationship...*: letter to the author; *Mother seems...*: LW., p. 73
p. 99: *an unbalanced...*: LW, p. 96; mother's quiet support...: CW, p. 104
p. 100: 'The Housekeeper', CS, p. 98; 'The Miner's Son', unpublished
p. 101: *played and laughed...*: letter to John Lehmann, op. cit, p. 111; 'Private Jones', CS, p. 27
p. 102: 'On Embarkation': CP, p. 114; 'Ward "0" 3 b': CS, p. 207
p. 103: *Mother had to get...*: letter to the author; *At the door'*: 'Last Leaves of a Civilian's Journal', M, pp. 104/5; *Now you must...*: CW., p 111
p. 104: *There must be'*: CS, pp. 101/2; *'Obey without reasoning'...*: Alun Lewis, My Son
p. 105: *enough to pucker'*: unpublished letter; *I used to think'*: LW, p. 92; *'I didn't live...'*: unpublished letter; *'I got to loathe...'*: W, p. 413; *'the long novels...'*: CW, p. 67
p. 106: *'When I was...'*: M, p. 123; *'I suggested...'*: op. cit.; *'I'm no good...'*: CW, p. 67
p. 107: *'There was about Alun...'*: Dewi Lewis, letter to the author; *'One lazy eye...'*: letter to the author; *'Alun in the easy...'*: letter to John Petts
p. 108: *'full of advice...'*: LW, p. 69

## Part Five

p. 109: 'The Transmigration of Love': AL, p. 197, and CW, pp. 24-5, but not CP
p. 112: *... remembered how you...*: LW, p. 59; 'Destruction': CP, p. 90; *nervous strain...*: LW, p. 266
p. 113: *felt nothing...*: LW, p. 59; *I'm like life...*: LW, p. 75; *icy cold compression:* LW, p. 140; *so easily upset...*: LW, p. 138; *something falls...*: LW, p. 185; ...

*you are fundamental*...: part of this letter appears in LW, p 210 (see Appendix One); 'To Rilke': CP, p. 124; *'For IS is*...': LW, p. 354; *You were silent*...: LW, p. 374

p. 114: ...*you say I was*...: LW, p. 382; *abominably lonely*: LW, p. 364; *little highnecked colt*: LW, p. 323; *a fountain of joy*...: letter to Jean Gilbert, librarian at Pontingny Lewis met in 1937, unpublished; *Viking*: LW, p. 97

p. 115: 'Bequest', CP, p. 191; *The fashionable architect*...: letter to the author; *For the sake of poetic licence*...: letter to the author; *He had, after all*...: letter to the author

p. 116: '*The Aberdare Leader*': M, p. 83

p. 117: *Alun, my third son*...: op. cit.; *Take your chances*...: M, p. 107; *there's less chance*...: M, p. 111; *I left school*...: unpublished letter

p. 118: *I believe that*...: unpublished; *I've got few illusions*...: LW, p. 135; *gives us a personality*...: W, pp. 422/3; *When I pause*: LW, p. 122

p. 119: *As if this were*...': LW, p. 138; *I still have'*: LW, pp. 363/4; *icy cold compression*: LW, pp. 138/9; *'I am a slave*...': LW, p. 140

p. 120: *Even when you*...: LW, p. 374; 'War Wedding': CP, p. 62; *the violent half*: LW, p. 376

p. 121: 'The Children': CS, pp. 135/6; 'Duration', CS, pp. 321/7, 321/2 and 324/6; *She had come*...: CS, p. 136

p. 122: 'On Embarkation': CP, pp. 114/5

p. 96: 'Compassion': CP, p. 99; 'Encirclement;, CP, p. 105; 'The Soldier', CP, p. 105

p. 123: ... *it was lovely*...: LW, p. 161; ...*I had no idea*...: LW, p. 160; *the ghostly way*...: LW, p. 164; *by the station wall*: LW, p. 168

p. 124: *It's my own choice*...: letter to John Petts, unpublished; *this little Dachau*: LW, p. 198; see, too, his letter to Keidrych Rhys and Lynette Roberts, W, p. 421; *2/Lt A. Lewis*...: letter to Llewellyn Wyn Griffith, unpublished; as successfully... : unpublished; I find being...: op. cit., p. 28; *I can be*...: LW, p. 399; *one of the most*...: op. cit., p. 21; *our poet*: quoted in John Lehmann's 'The Open Night', London, 1952, p. 113

p. 125: *the complete village*...: letter to the author; *a sick animal*...: LW, p. 206; *only some attenuated*...: LW, p. 205; *not an officer*...: LW, p. 189; *I want to know*...: LW, p. 199; *And why do you say*...: LW, p. 210; Julian MacLaren-Ross: op.cit., p. 180; Jack Aistrop: letter to the author

p. 126: *I think Saturday*...: LW, pp. 231/2; 'Corfe Castle', CP, p. 98. This association of sex with outdoors continued in India. In 'Holi' (the Indian festival of Spring), drumskins sound as

> The youths and girls obey
> The wild God's uttermost intent,
> And sob, and turn away,
>
> And turn to the Indian forest
> And there they are as one –
> One with the dust and darkness
> When the god's last will is done. (CP, p. 132)

'Home Thoughts from Abroad' tells how 'the swart brown heather' bears 'no mark/ Of boy and girl and all they planned' (CP, p. 139). 'Pastorals' ends:

Oh in a slim spaced forest
In a gladed darkness deep
With long rough grasses touching
The night aware and animal
Behold the tawny-eyed
Wild elements conjoin
In the endlessly longed-for mutation
Of decay and generation. (CP, p. 202)

This is the tradition to which *'The Way Back'* belongs; *wished it to appear...*: CW, p. 199; 'On Embarkation': CP, pp. 114-7
p. 127: 'Destruction': CP, p. 90; *either the child...*: LW, pp. 251/3
p. 128: *little spiritual...*: LW, pp. 247/8; *like meeting an old friend...*: LW, p. 264; 'Goodbye': CP, p. 110
p. 129: 'Raiders' Dawn': CP, p. 22; 'Last Pages of a Long Journal': M, p. 120; *I'll teach you...*: LW p. 273; *I'm consumed...*: LW, p. 266
p. 130: *And yet I know...*: LW, p. 273; *about the non-arrival of...*: LW, p. 277; *the incomplete idea...*: LW, p. 275; 'Song': CP, p. 121; *dying to know*: LW, p. 289
p. 131: *Gweno hoped...*: unpublished; *long brave chain...*: LW, p. 274

## Part Six
p. 142: 'Maps': CW, pp. 16/7
p. 143: *I'm becoming...*op. cit; the latter is dated 3 October 1943
p. 144: *I don't know...*: LW, p. 387; *Make yourself separate...*: LW, p. 390; *Thank you...*: LW, p. 393
p. 145: *I want to be...*: CW, p. 73; *When I was...*: LW, p. 397; *I want to run...*: CW, p. 93; *I feel now...*: CW, p. 389; *I want to get...*: CW, p. 109; *deep freedom*, CW, p. 90; *this poem...*: CW, p. 99
p. 146: *One huge thing...*: CW, p. 106
p. 149: *fortitude and independence...*: op. cit., p. 39; *harder & shrewder...*: ibid..; *Well, Brenda...*: op. cit., p. 40
p. 151:*The Upanishads*: *The Principal Upanishads*, ed. S. Radhaknishnan, London 1953, p. 162; 'The Earth is a Syllable': CS, pp. 192,195
p. 152: *Frieda darling...*: CW, pp. 109, 118; *I've made my peace...*: LW, p. 396...': *If I grow healthier...*: excluded from CW
p. 153: *The knowing self...*: op. cit., p. 616; *one of those cyclical...*: LW, p. 400; *I wonder sometimes...*: LW, p. 398; 'They Came', CS , p. 166; 'Dusty Hermitage': CS, p. 157; *Poetry* (London): 1, 3, November 1940, pp. 84/5
p. 154: *What Edward Thomas*: to Dick Mills; *I know we are also...*': CW p. 169
p. 155: 'Peasant Song': CP, p. 150

## Part Seven

p. 158: *I've been aware…*: This passage is excluded from LW. (See Appendix One.)

p. 160: *And the long self-torture…*: LW, p. 424

p. 169: *Born and bred…*: M, p. 161; 'The Jungle': CP, p. 155

p. 170: *us will-o-the-wisps…*': LW, p. 365: *the long self-torture…*: LW, p. 424; *I wonder sometimes…*: LW, p. 398; *It's only one of those…*: LW, p. 400; *You should come…*: LW, p. 401; p. 171: *as if I'm to blame…*: LW, pp. 403/5; *the coarse swearing…*: LW, pp. 407, 409; *a universal pining…*: LW, p. 407; *I wish they'd leave…*: LW, p. 409; *You try so hard…*: LW, p. 410; *… it's a bad old world…*: LW, pp 411, 414

p. 172: *miserable volatile me*: LW, p. 417; *coldness and pride…*: LW, p. 418/9; *… everything is fluid…*': LW, p. 420

p. 173: *I'm as restless…*: M, p. 149; *this amazing country…*: M, p. 144; *I want to go East & East & East…*: M, p. 149; *God knows…*: op. cit., pp. 38/9

p. 174: unpublished

## Part Eight

p. 178: *'At Goppe Pass…*': *'History of The South Wales Borderers and The Monmouthshire Regiment'*, Part V, 1956, Pontypool, p. 21

p.180: 'All day it has rained…', CP, p. 23; '*Yesterday…*': unpublished

p. 181: *I'm not a pacifist…*: LW, p. 41; *I knew he was different…*: letter to the author; *military backwater*: letter to Andrew Davies, unpublished; *It's peculiar…* : unpublished

p. 182: *drop into the Army…*: unpublished; *But how coarse…*: unpublished; I have been garrisoned…: M, p. 118

p. 183: *…as war poet…*: M, p. 119

p. 185: *I sat on the floor…*: LW, p. 45

p. 186: unpublished; 'To Edward Thomas', CP, p. 29

p. 187: 'Up in the Wind', *The Annotated Collected Poems*, ed. Edna Longley, Tarset, 2008, p. 31; 'High up against…': London 1859, Harmondsworth, 1980, p. 62 (first published 1859); *a superb moment…*: op. cit., p. 24

p. 188: *As for fame…*: *Letters of T.E. Lawrence*, ed David Garnett, London 1938, p. 24

p. 189: *I'm gasping…*: CW, p. 164; *how different everything…*: CW, p. 72; 'Lance-Jack': CS, p. 63; James Angleton was one of the editors of *Furioso*, in New Haven, Conn.; he expressed his view in a letter to Lewis, unpublished; feverish mood, LW, p. 379; *In the Army…*, CS, p. 64; *But it is dangerous…*: CS, pp. 64/5

p. 190: *…you are natural…*: CW, p. 164

p. 191: *You guessed rightly…*: op. cit., p. 244; *The clearing again…*: CW, p. 153; *the lost rudiments…*: *The White Goddess*, amended and enlarged edition 1961, p. 21, p. 490

p. 192: *What is love…*: *Call Wind to Witness*, edited by Charles Hamblett, London 1942

p. 193: *The war comes uppermost*: CW, p. 109; *… the sun beating…*: Ian Hamilton, op. cit., pp. 46/7

p. 194: *the unknown place...*: LW, p. 301; *The sick have...*: CS, p. 205; 'In Hospital: Poona (1)': CP, p. 140; 'In Hospital: Poona (2)': CP, p. 141

p. 195: 'Burma Casualty', CP, p. 146

p. 196: '*As for the poems...*': unpublished; *Every time I look...*: LW, p. 394; 'The Mahratta Ghats', CP, p. 131; *to be anything positive...*: CW, p. 159; *last repository of worth...*: CW, p. 194

p. 197: '*The sun has sucked...*': 'In Hospital: Poona (2)', CP, p. 141; 'The Peasants': CP, p. 144; 'Prelude and Fugue': CP, p. 184; 'Peace', CP, p. 51

p. 198: *My head seemed...*: LW, p. 326; *your old husband...*: LW, p. 327; 'Water Music': CP, p. 13

p. 199: 'Lines on a Tudor Mansion': CP, p. 33; 'Ward "0" 3 b': CS, p. 212; *kind of drunken frenzy...*: unpublished part of a letter to Gweno, 9 September 1943

p. 200: 'The Orange Grove': CS, p. 213; *this mammoth jungular world...*: LW, 361; *the freedom, the new sights...*: letter to his parents, unpublished; *the infinite feeling...*: LW, p. 369; 'The Jungle', CP, p. 157; *... little George...*: LW, p. 272

p. 201: *as deep as childhood...*: LW, p. 379; *I'm in a mulish...*': unpublished; *Once Life...*: CS, p. 224

p. 202: *There is such a thing...*: LW p. 393; *I wonder whether...*: unpublished; *the conventional life...*: LW, p. 291; *miles & miles...*: CW, p. 105

p. 203: '*It really is...*': LW, p. 394; *I don't mind...*: CW, p. 100; *all the Indians booed...*: CW, p. 63; *loathed the whole gambit...*: LW p. 341; *I can't ever...*: In the Green Tree, revised ed, ed. John Pikoulis, Cardigan, 2006, p.28; *I can never be...*: ibid., *the sprawling gamble...*: LW, p. 389; *the deep brooding silences...*: LW, p. 391

## Part Nine

p. 206: 'The Jungle': CP, pp. 155-8; 'The Earth is a Syllable', CS, pp. 194/5; *a healer and an illuminator...*: *Quite Early One Morning*, London, 1954, p. 151 The broadcast took place on 5 January 1946

p. 209: *The war comes uppermost...*: CW, p. 109. The printed version differs from mine, which I took from the original; *Border Country*: London, 1962, p. 201

p. 210: 'The End of the Hunt': CS, p. 250; *And I...*: '*Love Letter*', *Call Wind to Witness*, op. cit.

## Part Ten

p. 214: *That other life...*: CW, p. 217

p. 215: *Love is one of the few things...*: CW., p. 121

p. 218: *We had been in position...*: op. cit.

p. 220: 'Song', CP, p. 121; 'The Suicide', CP, p. 192

p. 221: *always shone...*: letter to the author

p. 222: *something more definitely...*: *The Anglo-Welsh Review*, 40, Winter 1972, pp. 48-53; *... it's more fun...*: LW, p. 224; 'The Mountain over Aberdare', CP, p. 87; *never went to chapel...*, *Poetry Wales*, op. cit.

p. 223: *However much*...: 'Alun Lewis and the Vocation of Poetry', *The Anglo-Welsh Review*, 63, 1978, pp. 39/65; *a nice Indian*...: LW, p. 264; *found the old father*...: LW, p. 395/6

p. 225: *They spoke*...: op. cit., pp. 147/8; 'On the Welsh Mountains': CP, p. 178

p. 226: *a lion of sympathy*...: CW, p. 221; *funny, philosophical & patient*: letter to Dick Mills; Dick was born in heaven: CW, p. 82; *either amazingly brave*...: CW, p. 163

p. 227: *magical and infinitely*...: letter to the author; *I work either*...: This letter was omitted from CW

p. 228: *& I told Dick*...: CW, p. 218

p. 230: *a cocksparrow*: LW, p. 76; ... *since he went to college*...: CW, p. 187; *His work is dangerous*...: unpublished

p. 231: *the stillness and*...: LW, p. 13; ... *raw, hair strong*...: CS, pp. 227/8, 231

p. 233: *Glyn touched me deeply*...: LW, p. 411

p. 238: *for his view*...: *letter to the author; tremendous friends*...: the memoir is unpublished

p. 239: *Poor old Alun*....: unpublished letter; *hurt*...: CW, p. 88

p. 241: '*East and East and East*...': op. cit.

p. 243: *flesh of my flesh*: CW, p. 134; *Usually there were*...: LW, pp. 382/3

p. 244: ... *there are two*...: op. cit., p. 6; *continuity, almost identity*...: ibid., p. 8; *I think the war theme*...: unpublished

p. 245: the quarry, the pit...: op. cit., p. 3; We had outlawed...: *unpublished letter*; *They farm*...: unpublished letter

p. 246: *We'd have to choose*...: op. cit., p. 1; *entirely a friendly*...: unpublished letter; *a tattered, treasured*...: *Poetry Wales*, op. cit., p. 121; *By the way*...: op. cit.

p. 247: *Collected Poems*: Manchester

p. 249: *I knew nothing*...: *Diaries, Letters and Recollections*, ed. Patrick McGuiness, Manchester, 2008, p. 204; this reproduces only parts of Roberts's autobiography; *that upper-bourgois*...: unpublished letter to Glyn Jones; *used Keidrich Rhys*... : Glyn Jones, *Goodbye, What Were You?*, Llandysul, 1994, pp. 45-6; *large, eccentric and farouche*: 'Keidrych – A Memoir', *Planet*, 104, April-May 1994, pp. 20/6; *neurotic surreal husband*: CW, p. 98

p. 250: *the best sort of crank*: *The Collected Letters of Dylan Thomas*, ed. Paul Ferris, London 1985, p. 301; *a Welsh-speaking*...: op. cit.

p. 251: *a curious girl*...: op. cit., p. 418; *The Van Pool: Collected Poems*, ed. Charles Mundye, Bridgend, 2012

p. 252: *Lynette Roberts*...: LW, p. 111; *I was worried*...: unpublished letter; 'Letter to My Wife': *The Van Pool: Collected Poems*, p. 62

p. 254: *She's an exciting*...: LW, pp. 117, 153; *still together*: LW, p. 166; 'Third and Fourth': op. cit., p. 68; *As Keidrych wrote*...': LW, p. 196

p. 255: *A very worried*...: LW, p. 201; *always "fighting"*: LW, p. 316; *Keidrych*... *had such*...: LW, p. 224; 'Poem from Llanybri': *Collected Poems*, v.s., p. 3; *an offering of peace*...: *Diaries, Letters and Recollections*, p. 51; '*The Book of Taliesin*': London, 1983; 'Peace': CP, p. 51

p. 256: *dream of peace*: W, p. 421; *I remember too*...: unpublished letter to Glyn

Jones, 30<sup>th</sup> November 1978

p. 257: *...there was [a] young airman...*: *Diaries, Letters and Recollections*, p. 178; *K. has been discharged...*: LW, p. 357

## Part Eleven

p. 258: 'Alun Lewis and Edward Thomas', 23, 1981, pp. 25-44

p. 262: *I was without interest...*: M, p. 113; 'The Soubrettes', CP, p. 203; *It became ultimately...*: CW, p. 209; 'The Desperate', CP, p. 57

p. 263: 'Threnody for a Starry Night', CP, p. 43; 'Encirclement', CP, p. 105

p. 264: 'Compassion', CP, p. 99; 'War Wedding', CP, p. 65; 'Lance-Jack', CS, p. 63

p. 265: *the sex-hunger wretchedness...*': CW, p. 80; *I don't want...*: CW, p. 81; 'Southend at Dusk', CP, p. 180; 'The Island', CP, p. 152; 'By the Gateway of India: Bombay', CP., p. 126; *'the popsies...*': CS, p. 217

p. 266: *Like his father...*: op. cit.; 'Fever', CP, p. 55; 'The Rhondda', CP, p. 89

p. 267: 'Raiders' Dawn', CP, p. 22

p. 268: 'After Dunkirk', CP, p. 39; *Like the insipid...*: M, p. 120; 'Odi et Amo', CP, p. 31;

p. 269: *so feeling partly British...*': M. Wynn Thomas, in *Nations and Relations, Writing Across the British Isles*, ed. Tony Brown and Russell Stephens, Cardiff 2000, pp. 71-88

p. 270: 'The Soldier', CP, p. 24; see my 'The Two Voices in Alun Lewis's Poetry', *Welsh Writing in English*, I, 1995, pp. 40-51

p. 271: '*When I first began...*': letter to the author; 'Corfe Castle', CP, p. 98; the poem may have been influenced by Lynette Roberts's faux-naïve poems about Llanybri; *Three endless weeks...*: 'Burma Casualty', CP, p. 146

p. 272: 'The Mahratta Ghats': CP, p. 131; *the sun is always...*: LW, p. 320; 'Lady in Black', CP, p. 199: *Last night...*: 'In Hospital: Poona (1), CP, p. 140

p. 273: 'Burma Casualty', CP, p. 146

p. 274: 'Mahratta Ghats', CP, p. 131; *motion and mileage...*: 'The Journey', CP. p. 1

## Part Twelve

p. 281: *a writer as good...*: London, p. 9; *commitment to one's art...*: op. cit., p. 39

p. 282: '*Selected Poems*', London; *May I, Frieda?...*: CW, p. 216;

p. 283: *Alun Lewis, A Miscellany of his Writings*, Bridgend; 'It seemed to me... ': M, p. 134; '*Elegy...*': 75, p. 4

p. 285: *The Stones of the Field*, Carmarthen.

p. 287: *The Publishing Unwins*, London, 1972

p. 288: *He was going...*: CS, p. 19; *We've dug for...*: CS, p. 22; *responded with...* : letter to the author; *sulky engraving*: CW, p. 99; : *I feel it makes...*: unpublished correspondence; 'Post-script: For Gweno': CP, p. 54

p. 289: *still deep deep deep*: LW, p. 263; *There was always...*: letter to the author

p. 290: *About the novel...*: unpublished

p. 291: *He was, of course, in khaki…*: *In the Green Tree*, London, 1948, pp. 139/40. On the 25th March 1945, Dylan Thomas had told Jones: 'I've not seen any of Alun Lewis's Indian poems before, and could see, as you said, his death walking through them.' (op. cit., p. 549)

p. 293: *Neither I nor…*: letter to the author

p. 294: *I don't think…*: unpublished; indignation, grief…: unpublished

p. 295: 'The Lost Man' and 'The Boychick': AL, pp. 252-9

p. 296: *My garden girl…*: AL, p. 249; 'Bequest', CP, p. 191

p. 302: *an essay on the poets…*: *The New Welsh Review*, 44 1999, pp. 35-9

p. 305: *He recalled her efforts…*: AL, 1st edition, p. 197

p. 306: *I also got the impression…*: letter to the author

p. 307: *we climbed…*: LW, p. 8; *as we left…*: LW, p.9

p. 308: *When her youngest…*: LW, p.11; *When I lie down…*: LW, pp. 15/6

p. 310: *…there was something…*: LW, p. 18; *His deep-set…*: CW, p. 46; *It was obvious…*: LW, p. 19; *romantic rendezvous*: LW, p. 19

p. 311: *We must have…*: LW, p. 20; *now no trace…*: LW, p. 22; *It was reassuring…*: LW, p. 22

p. 312 : *I don't believe…*: LW, p. 23; *It was distressing…*: LW, p. 427

p. 313: 'An Exchange of Love Poems': 13, Vol IV, No 1, summer 1991

p. 315: *kept alive…*: CW, p. 205

p. 322: *Most books…*: CS, p. 7; *rather personal observations*: CS, p. 10; *I'm growing…*: W, p. 425; revised edition of *In the Green Tree*, Cardigan

p. 324: *The possibility…*: CW, pp. 53/4; *his last two letters…*: CW, p. 54/5

p. 325: *To me he wrote…*: CW, pp. 55/6; *uncanny understanding*: CW, p. 81; *There are situations*: CW, p. 87

p. 326: *the huge thing…*: CW, p. 106; *Otherwise I ache…*: CW, p. 118; *until long after…*: CW, pp. 115/6; *enchantment sealed my forehead*: CW, p. 161; *Tomorrow I shall see…*: CW, p. 158; *I know it was…*: CW, pp. 143/4

p. 327: *yellow-eyed proud…*: CW, p. 151; *I feel such a dolt…*: CW, pp. 145/6; *'from an old negative…*: CW, pp. 147

p. 328: *One way or another…*: CW, p. 148; *It's only now…*: CW, p. 147; *It seems …*: CW, pp. 151/2; *Absurd flap…*: CW, p. 171; *I went on then…*: CW, p. 170

p. 329: *I I I I I I I I I…*: CW, p. 168; *And to you…*': CW, p. 171; *You were afraid…* : CW, p. 170; *the lack of toughness…*: CW, p. 174

p. 330: *I've been wandering…*: CW, p. 186; *leadenness, the persistent oppression*: CW, pp. 178/9

p. 331: 'The Reunion': CS, pp. 226-233; *a sort of nervousness…*: *The Life and Letters of Edward Thomas*, London 1939, pp. 79/80

p. 332: *Should I start…*: CW, p. 215; 'A Fragment', CP, p. 161; *tedious fatigable me*: CW, p. 184; *…I am doing nothing…*: CW, p. 190; *I feel all the time…*: CW, p. 191

p. 333: *I'm far away…*: CW, p. 192; *I was very conscious…*: CW, p. 199; *I want to be less…*: CW, p. 216; *harrassed subaltern*: CW, p. 199; *I'll fight much better…*: CW, p. 212; *The first evening…*: CW, pp. 200/1

p. 334: *I want you to know…*: CW, p. 202; *I will come…*: CW, p. 214; *… what has happened…*: CW, p. 205; *oh with such trembling…*: CW, p. 215; *"If undelivered…*': CW, p. 219; *I've made everything…*: CW, p. 215; *The poems will be…*

: CW, p. 219
p. 335: *the impersonal, imperturbable*...: CW, pp. 220/2
p. 336: *in the only way*...: Ian Hamilton, op. cit., p. 44
p. 338: *Men move*...: *A Welsh Eye*, London, 1964, p. 91.

# Index

# Works by Alun Lewis

## Collected Poems, edited by Cary Archard

This volume contains the complete texts of Lewis' two published collections, *Raiders' Dawn* (1942) and *Ha! Ha! Among the Trumpets* which was published posthumously in 1945. The first brought him national recognition as an authentic poet of the war; the second, endorsed, by Robert Graves, sealed his reputation. The *Collected Poems* also includes 27 previously uncollected poems, and as a whole the volume confirms Lewis' standing a significant voice in British twentieth century British poetry. Some critics see him as the last of the great Romantic poets – a modern day Keats; others view him as a bridge between pre-war poets like Auden and Yeats and post-war poets like Hughes and Gunn.

Widely admired by poets from Larkin and Dylan Thomas to Gillian Clarke, Lewis created a body of work which has endured and which transcends the label to 'war poetry'; it is both complete in itself and full of the promise of greater things had he lived.

"A born poet… Lewis speaks words and they sing… the most assured poet of his generation." – *The Listener*

"Why should we read him now? Because his concerns are still our own. His sensuous poems are alive with insight, observation, paradox." – *Independent on Sunday*

## Collected Stories, edited by Cary Archard

Here are Lewis' war stories reprinted in their entirety for the first time. The popular and acclaimed 'Phoney War' stories of *The Last Inspection* (1942) are joined by those written in wartime India, including Lewis' masterpiece, 'The Orange Grove'.

The volume also collects stories published in student magazines and newspapers such as *The Guardian*, together with several previously unseen. *Collected Stories* shows Lewis' development from remarkable schoolboy writer to the mature and established author published in *Horizon* and *Lilliput*. The story was a form which Lewis embraced with growing enthusiasm as his time in the army, and in India, progressed and it seems inconceivable that he wouldn't have written more and even better work had he not died aged 28.

"Lewis was a true writer, and might well have been great." – *Financial Times*

"The ordeals are seized upon by Lewis with such intense sensitivity, you can feel him living again in the reclamation of that experience… What a talent was lost to the world." – *Sunday Times*

"His narratives excite the reader with their moments of illumination… wonderfully touching and memorable. These *Collected Stories* poignantly remind us what an authentic, inventive literary talent was lost." – *Independent on Sunday*

## Letters to my Wife, edited by Gweno Lewis

Letters to my Wife collected over 240 letters from Alun Lewis to his wife Gweno Ellis, beginning with his sudden enlistment in 1940 until his untimely death on active service in Burma in March 1944. They represent a unique, authentic account of army life, for officers and other ranks, in Britain and the East. Descriptions of the dreariness of long years of training are succeeded by an account of the journey to India via Brazil and South Africa, and by Lewis' response to the culture shock of India. There are also many insights into Lewis' character – his inclination to depression, his conflicted pacifism, his unwillingness (and perhaps innate unsuitability) to becoming an officer.

The letters also shed light on Lewis's development as a writer as he comments on his work and his growing reputation. And they are a record of his love for his war bride Gweno, whom he married in July 1941, before embarkation. Their experiences, no doubt representative of those of so many during the war, are described with charm and passion. In the whole it is clear to see why Lewis has been compared with Keats as one of the great letter writers of English literature.

"Passionate, tender, kindly, charming, interesting… leaves no doubt about the exceptional charm of the man, and none about the subtlety, intelligence and emotional force of the writer lost to us." – Andrew Motion, *The Observer*

"We are always aware, as in Keats's letters, of a man who is living his life, and making himself from what he makes of his experience. Keats would have said making his soul, and I do not think Lewis would have disagreed. … In time *Letters to my Wife* will surely come to be regarded as a classic." – Jeremy Hooker

"In historical and human terms this book rings true. There is nothing romantic in his outlook. He was a clear-eyed realist, and his letters make compelling reading." – Michael Duffy, TES

## Morlais

Written in the 1930s and now published for the first time, Morlais shows what an exciting talent Alun Lewis was and hints at what was lost by his death aged just 28.

Miner's son Morlais Jenkins is already destined to be educated out of his background when he is adopted by the local colliery owner and his wife on the death of their own son and Morlais' friend. His parents recognise the opportunity to make Morlais a better future but they must all pay a great price. Stifled by middle class life his adoptive mother encourages him to escape the conventions of class and be true to his artistic potential.

Full of vivid and authentic passages of daily life in a mining community, Morlais is an enthralling novel of the journey of a young boy becoming a young man in Depression Wales.

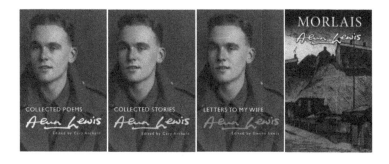